BIG DATA AND COMPETITION POLICY

BIG DATA AND COMPETITION POLICY

Maurice E. Stucke
Allen P. Grunes

OXFORD
UNIVERSITY PRESS

OXFORD

UNIVERSITY PRESS

Great Clarendon Street, Oxford, OX2 6DP,
United Kingdom

Oxford University Press is a department of the University of Oxford.
It furthers the University's objective of excellence in research, scholarship,
and education by publishing worldwide. Oxford is a registered trade mark of
Oxford University Press in the UK and in certain other countries

© Maurice Stucke & Allen Grunes 2016

The moral rights of the authors have been asserted

First Edition published in 2016

Impression: 2

Published in the United States of America by Oxford University Press
198 Madison Avenue, New York, NY 10016, United States of America

British Library Cataloguing in Publication Data
Data available

Library of Congress Control Number: 2016938161

ISBN 978–0–19–878813–3 (hbk.)
ISBN 978–0–19–878814–0 (pbk.)

Printed and bound by
CPI Group (UK) Ltd, Croydon, CR0 4YY

ACKNOWLEDGEMENTS

In his commencement address, the former president of Georgetown University, Rev Timothy Healy, would remark how the students reached graduation on the shoulders of many. So too this book was published with the help of many.

First, we want to thank our colleagues: Jonathan Kanter for inspiring the project and raising many good examples; Christian D'Cunha for reaching out to invite us to the European Data Protection Supervisor's workshop and conference; Gene Kimmelman and Barry Lynn for their many helpful suggestions on earlier drafts; Keith Waehrer for his considerable thoughts on how the competition agencies can take privacy degradation into account; Brian Bieron for taking the time to discuss Big Data (and providing helpful metaphors); Alec Burnside and Anne MacGregor for their ideas about the intersection of privacy and antitrust; and the anonymous reviewers for their helpful and thoughtful suggestions. Sibyl Marshall oversaw the editing of our book including the footnotes. We are very much indebted to Sibyl and Andrew Tucker for their tireless and selfless effort.

We would also like to recognize our advisory board of the Data Competition Institute for their terrific work in this field, which provided many insights: Ariel Ezrachi, Pamela Jones Harbour, Ioannis Lianos, Frank Pasquale, and Spencer Weber Waller. Not only have we benefitted from their scholarly contributions to this field, they were all very generous in discussing ideas and identifying relevant cases.

The ideas in this book also benefitted from the exchanges we had at numerous conferences. We would like to thank the organizers and participants of the Canadian Competition Bureau's *Workshop on Emerging Competition Issues: Keeping Pace in a Changing World*; the Institute for Corporate Counsel's conference, *Privacy, Big Data and the Intersection with Competition Law: New Issues of Importance to In House Counsel*; European Data Protection Supervisor & Academy of European Law's conference *Competition Rebooted: Enforcement and Personal Data in Digital Markets*; the American Bar Association Section of Antitrust Law and IBRAC's *Antitrust in the Americas* conference; the Federal Trade Commission's workshop *The 'Sharing' Economy: Issues Facing Platforms, Participants, and Regulators*; the American Marketing Association's *Marketing and Public Policy* conference; Uría Menéndez's roundtable, *Privacidad y Competencia en la Era del Big Data*; George Mason University's *Public Policy Briefing on Big Data, Privacy, and Antitrust*; and Concurrences Journal & Cadwalader, Wickersham & Taft's *Antitrust, Privacy & Big Data* conference.

This book also benefitted from a research grant we received for earlier work on the topic from the Media Democracy Fund; we are indebted to Helen Brunner's support and her efforts to promote a vibrant marketplace of ideas.

Maurice would like to thank the University of Tennessee, Doug Blaze, Carol Parker, and Greg Stein for supporting our research, including a sabbatical at the University of Oxford to undertake this research. Dame Lynne Brindley, the professors, and staff at Pembroke College were all gracious and hospitable; the discussion during lunch greatly contributed to this book.

Allen would also like to thank Henry Su for thoughtful conversation and companionship on a series of long walks at Great Falls.

Rachel Mullaly and Gemma Parsons at Oxford University Press were supportive in shepherding this book through the publication process.

Finally, we thank our families for all of their support—both before, during, and after the book.

CONTENTS

II THE COMPETITION AUTHORITIES' MIXED RECORD IN RECOGNIZING DATA'S IMPORTANCE AND THE IMPLICATIONS OF A FEW FIRMS' UNPARALLELED SYSTEM OF HARVESTING AND MONETIZING THEIR DATA TROVE

III WHY HAVEN'T MANY COMPETITION AUTHORITIES CONSIDERED THE IMPLICATIONS OF BIG DATA?

IV WHAT ARE THE RISKS IF COMPETITION AUTHORITIES IGNORE OR DOWNPLAY BIG DATA?

V ADVANCING A RESEARCH AGENDA FOR THE AGENCIES AND ACADEMICS

ABBREVIATIONS

ABA	American Bar Association
AHIP	America's Health Insurance Plans
AI	artificial intelligence
Am U L Rev	*American University Law Review*
API	application programming interface
ARPU	average revenue per user
BC L Rev	*Boston College Law Review*
BYU L Rev	*Brigham Young University Law Review*
CDO	collateralized debt obligation
CEO	chief executive officer
CFR	Code of Federal Regulations (United States)
CJEU	Court of Justice of the European Union
CMA	Competition & Markets Authority (United Kingdom)
Colum Hum Rts L Rev	*Columbia Human Rights Law Review*
CPU	central processing unit
DDPA	Driver's Privacy Protection Act (United States)
DOJ	Department of Justice (United States)
ECLR	*European Competition Law Review*
EDPS	European Data Protection Supervisor
EEA	European Economic Area
EPIC	Electronic Privacy Information Center (United States)
Eur J Fin	*European Journal of Finance*
FCC	Federal Communications Commission (United States)
Fordham J Corp & Fin L	*Fordham Journal of Corporate and Financial Law*
Fordham L Rev	*Fordham Law Review*
FSOC	Financial Stability Oversight Council
FTC	Federal Trade Commission (United States)
FUD	Fear, Uncertainty, and Doubt
GDP	gross domestic product
Geo LJ	*Georgetown Law Journal*
HHI	Herfindahl–Hirschman Index
HSR	Hart–Scott–Rodino Antitrust Improvements Act of 1976 (United States)
IBM	International Business Machines Corporation
ICN	International Competition Network
ICT	information and communication technologies
IM	instant messaging
IPO	initial public offering

J Am Med Ass'n	*Journal of American Medical Association*
J Competition L & Econ	*Journal of Competition Law and Economics*
J Indus Econ	*Journal of Industrial Economics*
J L & Econ	*Journal of Law and Economics*
J of Econ Persp	*Journal of Economic Perspectives*
J on Telecomm &	*Journal on Telecommunications &*
High Tech L	*High Technology Law*
Law & Pol'y Int'l Bus	*Law and Policy in International Business*
LIBOR	London Interbank Offered Rate
LIFO	Little In From Outside
LOFI	Little Out From Inside
Loyola U Chicago LJ	*Loyola University Chicago Law Journal*
M2M	machine to machine
MIT	Massachusetts Institute of Technology
NYU L Rev	*New York University Law Review*
OECD	Organisation for Economic Co-operation and Development
OEM	original equipment manufacturer
OFT	Office of Fair Trading (United Kingdom)
PCAST	President's Council of Advisors on Science and Technology (United States)
PNAS	*Proceedings of the National Academy of Sciences*
R&D	research and development
R&R	ratings and reviews
s / ss	section/s
SMEs	small and medium enterprises
SMU L Rev	*Southern Methodist University Law Review*
SSD	solid-state drive
SSNDQ	small, but significant, non-transitory decrease in quality
SSNIP	small, but significant, non-transitory increase in price
Stan Tech L Rev	*Stanford Technology Law Review*
Strategic Mgmt J	*Strategic Management Journal*
U Pa L Rev	*University of Pennsylvania Law Review*
UC Irvine L Rev	*University of California Irvine Law Review*
USC	United States Code
USDA	United States Department of Agriculture
WLM	Windows Live Messenger
Yale J L & Tech	*Yale Journal of Law and Technology*

TABLE OF CASES

US CASES

TABLE OF LEGISLATION

1

INTRODUCTION

Big Data and Big Analytics have become a big deal in today's economy.[1] They **1.01**
are converting ordinary household items, like thermostats, into smart technologies. They are helping San Francisco commuters find parking spaces. They are
enabling a host of free items on the Internet, ranging from search engines to
apps that better track our health. They are yielding revolutionary innovations,
such as driverless cars, scores of Internet-enabled devices, and better analytics
for manufacturing.

Big Data and Big Analytics raise many legal, moral, and ethical issues, such as **1.02**
cyber-security and the accountability of firms for their algorithms' actions. Our
focus is on Big Data's implications for competition policy. We are witnessing a competitive arms race for data (as opposed to more privacy)—the race to connect the
'data' bucket with the 'money' bucket by many tech firms and investors. Big Data is
playing a pivotal role in many companies' strategic decision-making. More companies are adopting data-driven business models and strategies to obtain and sustain a
competitive 'data-advantage' over rivals. Data-driven mergers are increasing, as are
the risks of abuses of dominant tech firms. Data-driven exclusionary practices and
mergers raise significant implications for privacy, consumer protection, and competition law. But one problem, as the European Data Protection Supervisor observed
in 2014, is that competition authorities, until recently, have not fully considered the
implications of Big Data.

Our aim is to explore how competition law can play an integral role in ensuring that **1.03**
we capture the benefits of a data-driven economy while mitigating its associated

---

[1] Organisation for Economic Co-operation and Development (OECD), *Data-Driven Innovation
for Growth and Well-being: Interim Synthesis Report*, October 2014, p 7, http://www.oecd.org/sti/
inno/data-driven-innovation-interim-synthesis.pdf (observing how '[d]eclining costs along the
data value chain ... have been a significant driver of the increasing generation and use of data, as well
as the accelerated migration of socioeconomic activities to the Internet thanks to the wide adoption
of e-services in an increasingly participative web. The resulting phenomenon—commonly referred
to as "big data"—signals the shift towards a data-driven economy, in which data enhance economic
competitiveness and drive innovation and equitable and sustainable development.').

1

risks. To be clear, we do not argue that Big Data is invariably bad. Big Data is neither inherently good, evil, nor neutral. Its social value depends on the industry and the purpose and effect of the data-driven strategy. Our focus is to assess the implications of a data-driven economy on competition policy and identify instances when privacy and competition concerns overlap. We will explore Big Data, its competitive implications, the competition authorities' approach to data-driven mergers and business strategies, and their current approach's strengths and weaknesses.

1.04 This issue is important. In 2015, the US Federal Trade Commission (FTC) mistakenly released portions of a report by its Bureau of Competition staff regarding the Google investigation.[2] (Although Alphabet Inc in 2015 has replaced Google Inc as the name of the publicly traded entity, we, for simplicity purposes, will refer to the company as Google.) The legal staff recommended prosecuting Google. The FTC instead opted to close its investigation after Google committed to change some of its data-driven business practices.[3] The FTC's action was controversial. Likewise, in 2015 when the European Commission's competition authority issued

---

[2] Federal Trade Commission Bureau of Competition, *Report re Google Inc*, 8 August 2012, pp 94, 96, 98, 100, and 102 ('FTC Staff Report'), http://graphics.wsj.com/google-ftc-report. A few caveats about this report, which the FTC released (mistakenly) under the Freedom of Information Act to the *Wall Street Journal*. First, only the Report's even pages were released, so the missing odd pages may have contained important qualifications. Second, other reports, including any prepared by Google, were not released. Third, although the Competition Staff recommended that the FTC file a complaint, the Commissioners elected not to. Google responded to the Report's disclosure:

> We understand that what was sent to the Wall Street Journal represents 50% of one document written by 50% of the FTC case teams. Ultimately both case teams (100%) concluded that no action was needed on search display and ranking. Speculation about consumer or competitor harm turned out to be entirely wrong. On the other issues raised, we quickly made changes as agreed with the FTC.

'The FTC Report on Google's Business Practices', *Wall Street Journal*, 24 March 2015, http://graphics.wsj.com/google-ftc-report/.
[3] Federal Trade Commission, 'Google Agrees to Change Its Business Practices to Resolve FTC Competition Concerns in the Markets for Devices Like Smart Phones, Games and Tablets, and in Online Search: Landmark Agreements Will Give Competitors Access to Standard-Essential Patents; Advertisers Will Get More Flexibility to Use Rival Search Engines', Press Release, 3 January 2013, https://www.ftc.gov/news-events/press-releases/2013/01/google-agrees-change-its-business-practices-resolve-ftc. After portions of the FTC Staff Report were disclosed and reports of meetings between White House and Google officials, the FTC Chair and two Commissioners responded, noting that the FTC conducted an 'exhaustive' investigation of Google's Internet search practices during 2011 and 2012:

> Based on a comprehensive review of the voluminous record and extensive internal analysis, of which the inadvertently disclosed memo is only a fraction, all five Commissioners (three Democrats and two Republicans) agreed that there was no legal basis for action with respect to the main focus of the investigation—search. As we stated when the investigation was closed, the Commission concluded that Google's search practices were not, 'on balance, demonstrably anticompetitive'.

Federal Trade Commission, *Statement of Chairwoman Edith Ramirez, and Commissioners Julie Brill and Maureen K. Ohlhausen Regarding the Google Investigation*, 25 March 2015, https://www.ftc.gov/news-events/press-releases/2015/03/statement-chairwoman-edith-ramirez-commissioners-julie-brill.

its statement of objections against Google,[4] some shouted protectionism (without knowing the facts and evidentiary record that supported the Commission's preliminary conclusion that Google degraded the quality of its search results by systematically favouring its own comparison shopping products in its general search results page).

What is clear is that the European Commission's statement of objections will not **1.05** end the matter. In 2015, the Commission stated that it was actively investigating other activities by Google, including 'whether Google has illegally hindered the development and market access of rival mobile applications or services by requiring or incentivising smartphone and tablet manufacturers to exclusively pre-install Google's own applications or services'.[5] In 2015, the FTC began investigating whether Google, in favouring its products on Android, violated the antitrust laws.[6] In 2016, Germany's Bundeskartellamt initiated proceedings against Facebook on suspicion of having abused its market power by infringing data protection rules. As Andreas Mundt, President of the Bundeskartellamt, stated:

> Dominant companies are subject to special obligations. These include the use of adequate terms of service as far as these are relevant to the market. For advertising-financed internet services such as Facebook, user data are hugely important. For this reason it is essential to also examine under the aspect of abuse of market power whether the consumers are sufficiently informed about the type and extent of data collected.[7]

Competition authorities will invariably investigate other companies, whose business models are built on Big Data.

As more companies undertake data-driven business strategies and mergers, compe- **1.06** tition officials and courts will likely confront the competitive implications of Big Data. They cannot ignore Big Data. The potential harm of data-driven mergers and abuses of dominant companies built on data, as we will show, is too significant to overlook or downplay. Some within the antitrust community are starting to appreciate the competitive benefits and risks of data-driven mergers and business strategies. Others, however, argue that competition law should have a limited role, if any,

---

[4] European Commission, 'Fact Sheet: Commission Sends Statement of Objections to Google on Comparison Shopping Service', 15 April 2015, http://europa.eu/rapid/press-release_MEMO-15-4781_en.htm.

[5] European Commission, 'Antitrust: Commission Opens Formal Investigation Against Google in Relation to Android Mobile Operating System', Press Release, 15 April 2015, http://europa.eu/rapid/press-release_MEMO-15-4782_en.htm.

[6] David McLaughlin, 'Google Said to Be Under US Antitrust Scrutiny Over Android', Bloomberg Business, 25 September 2015, http://www.bloomberg.com/news/articles/2015-09-25/google-said-to-be-under-u-s-antitrust-scrutiny-over-android-iezf41sg.

[7] Bundeskartellamt, 'Bundeskartellamt initiates proceeding against Facebook on suspicion of having abused its market power by infringing data protection rules', Press Release, 2 March 2016, http://www.bundeskartellamt.de/SharedDocs/Meldung/EN/Pressemitteilungen/2016/02_03_2016_Facebook.html.

in the era of Big Data. We disagree. One aim here is to move the debate beyond these ten myths.

A. Myth 1: Privacy Laws Serve Different Goals from Competition Law

1.07 Often, privacy concerns do not implicate competition concerns. A landlord, who secretly records a tenant's bedroom, violates the common law privacy tort, intrusion upon seclusion. The landlord's actions, however, do not violate competition law.

1.08 Likewise, some competition violations, like price-fixing cartels, generally do not raise privacy concerns. But data-driven business strategies, at times, will raise both privacy and antitrust concerns. As we will explore, data-driven mergers, like Facebook's acquisition of WhatsApp, have the potential to lessen non-price competition in terms of the array of privacy protections offered to consumers. Likewise, monopolies' data-driven exclusionary practices can hamper innovative alternatives that afford consumers greater privacy protection. Privacy competition—like other facets of non-price competition—already exists in certain industries, but some dominant companies do not face the competitive pressure to improve quality along this dimension.

1.09 As the European Competition Commissioner Margrethe Vestager observed,

> The more data you can collect, the more you know, the better product you can provide, but also the more powerful will you be towards others....It isn't solely a competition issue....It's very important for us to be able to say what is competition-related and what is an issue of privacy, ownership, data, [and] how you can be as secure on the net as you can be in the physical world.[8]

1.10 Thus one cannot quarantine privacy and competition concerns, unless one contorts antitrust's goals to a narrow economic objective that few others share.

B. Myth 2: The Tools that Competition Officials Currently Use Fully Address All the Big Data Issues

1.11 The reality, as we address, is that many of the current analytical economic tools do *not* address the Big Data issues. The competition authorities have better tools to assess price effects. But they have far cruder tools to assess a merger's effect on non-price competition, including product quality and the degradation of privacy

---

[8] *MLex Interview: Margrethe Vestager*, MLex Special Report, 22 January 2015 ('Vestager Interview'), http://mlexmarketinsight.com/wp-content/uploads/2015/01/MLex-Interview-Vestager-22-01-151.pdf.

protection. The agencies can currently challenge the egregious case, ie, where the evidence is compelling that the companies are competing along non-price dimensions, such as privacy protection, and the merger is intended to substantially lessen this competition. But often the analysis of quality is less straightforward.[9] This is problematic with the growth of multi-sided markets, where the products offered on one side are free. Quality, including privacy protection, will be an important aspect of non-price competition. When the competition agencies solely focus on the 'paid' advertising side of these multi-sided markets, and ignore the merger's impact on the 'free' side, both consumers and advertisers are harmed. We will see this in Chapter 15 with the merger wave of commercial radio stations in the US after the 1996 Telecommunications Act.

C. Myth 3: Market Forces Currently Solve Privacy Issues

The reality is that market forces are not solving privacy issues. Policymakers have **1.12** acknowledged that privacy's notice-and-consent model is broken and ineffective.

In competitive markets, consumers should reign supreme. Nearly all Americans **1.13** (93 per cent) in a 2015 report believed that being in control of who can get information about them is important.[10] But consumers do not reign supreme in many data-driven industries. Most are frustrated, feeling they have lost control over their personal data. Consumers are unaware of who has access to their personal information, what data is being used, how and when their data is being used, and the privacy implications of the data's use. 'While Americans' associations with the topic of privacy are varied', a 2014 survey by the Pew Research Center found, the majority 'feel that their privacy is being challenged along such core dimensions as the security of their personal information and their ability to retain confidentiality'.[11] In the survey, 91 per cent ' "agree" or "strongly agree" that consumers have lost control over how personal information is collected and used by companies'.[12] Likewise, 72 per cent of European Internet users 'still worry that they are being asked for too much personal data online'.[13]

---

[9] Ariel Ezrachi and Maurice E Stucke, 'The Curious Case of Competition and Quality', 3(2) *J of Antitrust Enforcement* (October 2015): pp 227–57, draft available at http://ssrn.com/abstract=2494656.

[10] Mary Madden and Lee Rainie, 'Americans' Attitudes About Privacy, Security and Surveillance', Pew Research Center, May 2015, http://www.pewinternet.org/files/2015/05/Privacy-and-Security-Attitudes-5.19.15_FINAL.pdf.

[11] Pew Research Center, 'Public Perceptions of Privacy and Security in the Post-Snowden Era', 12 November 2014, http://www.pewinternet.org/files/2014/11/PI_PublicPerceptionsof Privacy_111214.pdf.

[12] Ibid.

[13] European Commission, *Why We Need a Digital Single Market* (2015), https://ec.europa.eu/digital-agenda/sites/digital-agenda/files/digital_single_market_factsheet_final_20150504.pdf.

1.14 Even when companies allow individuals to see (and perhaps edit or delete) information about them, the companies still will collect data on them and target them with ads both online and offline.[14] The market does not always provide viable alternatives that protect our privacy. When alternatives emerge, many often do not do very well. As the economist Joseph Farrell has pointed out, consumer pessimism about online privacy may have contributed to the development of a 'dysfunctional equilibrium'.[15] Ordinarily, we would expect firms and consumers to have aligned incentives, and the market would supply the privacy protection consumers want. In a dysfunctional equilibrium, however, the market underprovides privacy protection because consumers do not believe that they have control over privacy or that companies really will protect their privacy. A small firm cannot simply decide to break out of the equilibrium on its own by adopting more privacy-protective policies and clearer disclosures. Since consumer demand will not shift by much, the smaller firm will simply sacrifice revenues.

1.15 Other reasons for the lack of privacy competition that we explore are the market's high entry barriers due to several data-driven network effects and exclusionary behaviour by dominant firms. Moreover, some companies present themselves as privacy enhancing when they play a dual role. One Massachusetts Institute of Technology (MIT) article noted how there were few options for those wishing to avoid being followed around on the web.[16]

1.16 Consequently, one cannot simply believe that market forces will always protect consumers.

D. Myth 4: Data-Driven Online Industries Are Not Subject to Network Effects

1.17 Some data-driven industries are subject to network effects. Network effects, as we discuss, are not always bad for consumers. Think of telephones, the

---

[14] Amanda Hess, 'Google Users Can Now Download Their Full Search Histories—and Delete Their Archive', *Independent Online* (UK), 7 May 2015, 2015 WLNR 13461451 ('And though Google is now inviting users to delete their search histories in a couple of clicks, it is very unclear what that means: the company's privacy policy still reserves the right to record your search results, tie them to your IP address or Google account, then target ads on Google properties and beyond.').

[15] Joseph Farrell, 'Can Privacy Be Just Another Good?', 10 *J on Telecomm & High Tech L* (2012): pp 251, 256–9.

[16] Tom Simonite, 'A Popular Ad Blocker Also Helps the Ad Industry: Millions of People Use the Tool Ghostery to Block Online Tracking Technology—Some May Not Realize That it Feeds Data to the Ad Industry', *MIT Technology Review*, 17 June 2013, http://www.technologyreview.com/news/516156/a-popular-ad-blocker-also-helps-the-ad-industry/.

benefit of which increases as others use them. But network effects, at times, enable big firms to become bigger until they dominate the industry. Data-driven industries, as Chapters 11–14 explore, can be subject to several network effects:

- Traditional network effects, including social networks such as Facebook;
- Network effects involving the scale of data;
- Network effects involving the scope of data; and
- Network effects where the scale and scope of data on one side of the market affect the other side of the market (such as advertising).

E. Myth 5: Data-Driven Online Markets Have Low Entry Barriers

Entry barriers for data-driven online industries are neither invariably low nor high. Each industry can differ. Entry barriers, once low, can increase due to network effects. One risk is that the economics of Big Data, as the OECD recently observed, 'favours market concentration and dominance'.[17] Data-driven markets 'can lead to a "winner takes all" result where concentration is a likely outcome of market success'.[18]   **1.18**

Moreover, the fact that venture funds are investing in online start-ups does not mean entry barriers are necessarily low. Industries with high entry barriers can still have entrants. The US Court of Appeals for the Eleventh Circuit, for example, was unprepared to say that a competitor's 'entry and growth' necessarily foreclosed a finding that the defendant possessed monopoly power, especially given defendant's 'overwhelming market share (90%), the large capital outlays required to enter the domestic fittings market, and [defendant's] undeniable continued power over…prices'.[19] Moreover, one has to examine in which particular markets the venture funds are investing. Few would likely fund a start-up in the search market, given Google's market share. In 2010 Microsoft tried, and spent over '\$4.5 billion into developing its algorithms and building the physical capacity necessary to operate Bing'.[20] We will explore the uphill battle Microsoft faced.   **1.19**

---

[17] OECD, *Data-Driven Innovation*, above note 1, p 7.
[18] Ibid.
[19] *McWane v Federal Trade Commission*, 783 F3d 814, 832 (US Ct of Apps (11th Cir), 2015).
[20] FTC Staff Report, above note 2, p 76.

F. Myth 6: Data Has Little, If Any, Competitive Significance, Since Data is Ubiquitous, Low Cost, and Widely Available

1.20 Beware of those who say this. Some companies take the position that data are like facts and argue that all data should be open. Mapping companies, for example, might believe that the data needed to develop a map should be accessible to others. Other companies, however, treat their mapping data as proprietary and will not share.

1.21 As we explore, data can be critical for a company's growth and success. In one of the mergers we analyse, Google's acquisition of Waze, it was Waze's inability to achieve sufficient scale of data that hindered its competitive significance in mapping services in the United Kingdom.[21] Thus, companies currently spend considerable money and effort to acquire and analyse personal data and to maintain a data-related competitive advantage. If any company propagates this myth, ask it if it would be willing to license its consumer data to its competitors, and if so, at what price.

G. Myth 7: Data Has Little, If Any, Competitive Significance, as Dominant Firms Cannot Exclude Smaller Companies' Access to Key Data or Use Data to Gain a Competitive Advantage

1.22 As Chapter 18 discusses, unlike Microsoft in the 1990s, today's dominant firms can use the velocity of data to discern trends well before others. In monitoring search queries, Google, for example, can predict flu outbreaks well before the government health agencies can. Some dominant platforms through similar nowcasting (such as watching for trends in their proprietary data of consumer behaviour while browsing the web and offline) can now monitor emerging business models in real time. In assessing these trends, dominant firms can quickly identify (and squelch) nascent competitive threats. The dominant firms can acquire these still small firms before they become significant competitive threats or use other means to blunt their growth.

1.23 Thus, in today's world, the dominant firms that have a significant data-advantage over rivals may enjoy a unique radar system that can track the flight path of competitive threats shortly after they take off from distant fields. The monopoly can

---

[21] Office of Fair Trading, Completed Acquisition by Motorola Mobility (Google, Inc) of Waze Mobile Ltd, ME/6167/13, 17 December 2013.

intercept or shoot down the threats long before they become visible to regulators and others.

H. Myth 8: Competition Officials Should Not Concern Themselves with Data-Driven Industries because Competition Always Comes from Surprising Sources

In the long run, monopolists, like the rest of us, die. But consumers should not **1.24** suffer the harm from anticompetitive mergers and monopolistic abuses, because eventually a disruptive innovator will emerge.

As Chapters 15, 16, and 18 discuss, the harm from anticompetitive data-driven **1.25** mergers and abuses by dominant firms can be significant. The harm not only involves higher advertising rates. The abuses of powerful tech firms can cause greater harm in the loss of choice, innovation, privacy, individual autonomy and freedom, and citizens' trust in a market economy. The issue of 'data justice' is gaining traction especially as an inequality issue, as companies use data to exploit society's more vulnerable members, thus furthering the income divide.[22] The harm, the OECD recognized, can strike 'the core values of democratic market economies and the well-being of all citizens'.[23]

I. Myth 9: Competition Officials Should Not Concern Themselves with Data-Driven Industries Because Consumers Generally Benefit from Free Goods and Services

Consumers do not invariably benefit when services are 'free', because these services **1.26** are not actually free. Consumers pay with their personal data and privacy. Because of the lack of transparency, consumers often do not know how much they actually pay for these services. In fact, economist Carl Shapiro, in a 2015 workshop, criticized the notion that because something is 'free', it must be good for consumers. Prices can be positive, zero, or negative (where consumers are subsidized).[24]

In a January 2015 interview, Commissioner Vestager discussed the linkages among **1.27** data, privacy, and competition: 'Very few people realize that, if you tick the box, your information can be exchanged with others....Actually, you are paying a price,

---

[22] *See generally* http://datajustice.org.
[23] OECD, *Data-Driven Innovation*, above note 1, p 7.
[24] Daniel Donegan, 'Summary of Committee Program on Antitrust and Zero Price Products', *The Price Point, Newsletter of the ABA Antitrust Pricing Conduct Committee*, Winter 2015, p 16.

an extra price for the product that you are purchasing. You give away something that was valuable. I think that point is underestimated as a factor as to how competition works'.[25] Vestager made a similar point during her confirmation hearings before the European Parliament, where she described data as 'the new currency of the Internet'.[26]

J. Myth 10: Consumers Who Use these Free Goods and Services Do Not Have Any Reasonable Expectation of Privacy

1.28 Granted some people share a lot of personal details online. But generally we can infer consumers' privacy preferences from their choices when

- consumers are *fully informed* about their choice's benefits and costs (including privacy risks), and
- the marketplace offers a *competitive array* of options that match actual privacy preferences.

As we discuss, that often is not the case today.

1.29 The issues we explore are timely. Until early 2015, the European and US competition authorities, which were supposed to screen mergers to prevent those likely to be anticompetitive, largely did not consider the implications of a data-driven economy on competition policy. There are some exceptions, as we discuss. But that is rapidly changing, with the Europeans taking the lead. The European Commission in 2015 launched an antitrust competition inquiry into the e-commerce sector in the EU. The inquiry, according to the Commission press release, 'will allow the Commission to identify possible competition concerns affecting European e-commerce markets'.[27] A final report of the sector inquiry is expected in 2017. Also in 2015, the European Commission adopted its 'Digital Single Market Strategy', which is built on three pillars: '(1) better access for consumers and businesses to digital goods and services across Europe; (2) creating the right conditions and a level playing field for digital networks and innovative services to flourish; (3) maximising the growth potential of the digital economy'.[28]

---

[25] Vestager Interview, above note 8.
[26] James Kanter, 'Antitrust Nominee in Europe Promises Scrutiny of Big Tech Companies', *New York Times*, 3 October 2014.
[27] European Commission, 'Antitrust: Commission Launches e-commerce Sector Inquiry', Press Release, 6 May 2015, http://europa.eu/rapid/press-release_IP-15-4921_en.htm.
[28] European Commission, 'A Digital Single Market for Europe: Commission Sets Out 16 Initiatives to Make It Happen', Press Release, 6 May 2015, http://europa.eu/rapid/press-release_IP-15-4919_en.htm.

The implications of Big Data on competition policy will likely be part of the mix. **1.30** The Commission, for example, will 'comprehensively analyse the role of online platforms (search engines, social media, app stores, etc.) in the market', and examine 'the non-transparency of search results and of pricing policies, how they use the information they acquire, relationships between platforms and suppliers and the promotion of their own services to the disadvantage of competitors—to the extent these are not already covered by competition law'.[29]

Other competition officials, however, are more closed-minded. Some believe that **1.31** privacy has little, if anything, to do with competition policy. Others believe that they have the right tools, know the proper questions, and simply must wait for the right case to present itself. This worldview, to put it bluntly, is misguided. Our purpose here is to show why the competition authorities' current toolkit for analysing many data-driven mergers and business strategies is outdated. The competition agencies, through 2015, have played a minor role in protecting consumers from the anticompetitive risks of a data-driven economy. Nor, as we discuss, can competition agencies simply push the issue to another agency. Privacy officials, with their behavioural remedies, cannot pick up the slack. Competition policy plays a key role in ensuring that citizens get the benefits of a data-driven economy, and in minimizing its risks.

Our book is divided into five parts. Part I outlines the four 'V's—volume, velocity, **1.32** variety, and value—of Big Data, and their competitive significance. We also examine why market forces have not provided consumers with better mechanisms to protect their privacy interests. Part II looks at how the competition authorities assess data-driven mergers and the issues they identified (and missed). Part III explains some of the challenges that Big Data currently present to the conventional antitrust wisdom. Given these challenges, some argue for a limited role, if any, for competition policy in data-driven markets. Part IV identifies several risks if competition authorities ignore or downplay data-driven mergers and the abuses by dominant tech firms. As the current analytical tools are at best average, and at worst useless, in assessing certain data-driven strategies, Part V advances a research agenda for the competition agencies and scholars to better understand the implications of a data-driven economy.

---

[29] Ibid.

Part I

THE GROWING DATA-DRIVEN ECONOMY

2

DEFINING BIG DATA

Before discussing the implications of a data-driven economy on competition policy, **2.01**
we should first define 'Big Data'. Big Data has various definitions, many of which
are broad and inclusive.[1] Although data is varied, this book focuses on personal
data, which is generally defined as 'any information relating to an identified or identifiable individual (data subject)'.[2] The Organisation for Economic Co-operation
and Development (OECD) provided the following list of personal data:

- User-generated content, including blogs and commentary, photos and videos, etc.
- Activity or behavioural data, including what people search for and look at on the
  Internet, what people buy online, how much and how they pay, etc.
- Social data, including contacts and friends on social networking sites.
- Locational data, including residential addresses, GPS, and geo-location (eg from
  cellular mobile phones), IP address, etc.
- Demographic data, including age, gender, race, income, sexual preferences, pol-
  itical affiliation, etc.
- Identifying data of an official nature, including name, financial information and
  account numbers, health information, national health or social security numbers, police records, etc.[3]

Although the term 'Internet of Things' has multiple definitions, what these definitions **2.02**
share is their 'focus on how computers, sensors, and objects interact with one another

---

[1] The President's Council of Advisors on Science and Technology in its report to the US President
noted the different definitions of Big Data, including those by business consultants ('high-volume, high-
velocity and high-variety information assets that demand cost-effective, innovative forms of information
processing for enhanced insight and decision making'); computer scientists ('a term describing the storage and analysis of large and/or complex data sets using a series of techniques including, but not limited
to, NoSQL, MapReduce, and machine learning'); and privacy experts ('data about one or a group of
individuals, or that might be analyzed to make inferences about individuals'). Executive Office of the
President, President's Council of Advisors on Science and Technology, *Report to the President, Big Data
and Privacy: A Technological Perspective*, May 2014, p 2 ('PCAST Report'), https://www.whitehouse.
gov/sites/default/files/microsites/ostp/PCAST/pcast_big_data_and_privacy_-_may_2014.pdf.
[2] OECD, *Exploring the Economics of Personal Data: A Survey of Methodologies for Measuring
Monetary Value*, OECD Digital Economy Paper No 220 (2013), p 7, http://dx.doi.org/10.1787/
5k486qtxldmq-en.
[3] Ibid, p 8.

and process data'.[4] As our focus is on personal data, the Internet of Things here involves devices sold to, or used by, individuals, rather than devices designed for internal businesses purposes, such as tracking inventory, electricity use, machine performance, etc.[5]

2.03   Big Data has commonly been characterized by four 'V's: the *volume* of data; the *velocity* at which data is collected, used, and disseminated; the *variety* of information aggregated; and finally the *value* of the data.[6] Each 'V' has increased significantly over the past decade.

A. Volume of Data

2.04   The volume of data collected has increased significantly,[7] and will likely continue to grow.[8] The firm Cisco seeks to forecast the growth of global data centre and cloud-based IP traffic. It predicts that the annual global data centre IP traffic will reach 8.6 zettabytes[9] by the end of 2018, up from 3.1 zettabytes in 2013.[10]

---

[4] Federal Trade Commission, *Internet of Things, Privacy & Security in a Connected World*, January 2015, p 5, https://www.ftc.gov/system/files/documents/reports/federal-trade-commission-staff-report-november-2013-workshop-entitled-internet-things-privacy/150127iotrpt.pdf.

[5] Ibid, p 5.

[6] OECD, *Data-Driven Innovation for Growth and Well-Being: Interim Synthesis Report*, October 2014, http://www.oecd.org/sti/inno/data-driven-innovation-interim-synthesis.pdf; The Executive Office of the President, *Big Data: Seizing Opportunities, Preserving Values*, May 2014, p 2 ('White House Big Data Report'), https://www.whitehouse.gov/sites/default/files/docs/big_data_privacy_report_may_1_2014.pdf (noting that most definitions 'reflect the growing technological ability to capture, aggregate, and process an ever-greater volume, velocity, and variety of data').

[7] White House Big Data Report, above note 6, p 2; Jeffrey Mervis, 'Agencies Rally to Tackle Big Data', 336(6077) *Science* (2012): p 22, https://www.sciencemag.org/content/336/6077/22.full; John Gantz and David Reinsel, *Extracting Value from Chaos*, IDC IVIEW, June 2011 (noting that in 2011, 'the amount of information created and replicated will surpass 1.8 zettabytes (1.8 trillion gigabytes)—growing by a factor of 9 in just five years'), https://www.emc.com/collateral/analyst-reports/idc-extracting-value-from-chaos-ar.pdf.

[8] McKinsey Global Institute, *Big Data: The Next Frontier for Innovation, Competition, and Productivity*, June 2011, p 2 ('McKinsey Report'), http://www.mckinsey.com/insights/business_technology/big_data_the_next_frontier_for_innovation (noting in 2011 that its 'research suggests that we are on the cusp of a tremendous wave of innovation, productivity, and growth, as well as new modes of competition and value capture—all driven by big data as consumers, companies, and economic sectors exploit its potential'); OECD, *Supporting Investment in Knowledge Capital, Growth and Innovation*, 10 October 2013, p 320, http://www.oecd-ilibrary.org/industry-and-services/supporting-investment-in-knowledge-capital-growth-and-innovation_9789264193307-en ('With the increasing deployment and interconnection of (real-world) sensors through mobile and fixed networks (ie sensor networks), more and more offline activities are also digitally recorded, resulting in an additional tidal wave of data'.); OECD, *Data-Driven Innovation*, above note 6, p 11 (noting one 2012 estimate that the amount of data traffic generated by mobile telephones will almost double every year reaching almost 11 exabytes (billions of gigabytes) by 2016).

[9] One zettabyte equals 1,099,511,627,776 gigabytes. CSG Network Memory and Storage Converter, http://www.csgnetwork.com/memconv.html.

[10] 'Cisco Global Cloud Index: Forecast and Methodology, 2013–2018' (2014), http://www.cisco.com/c/en/us/solutions/collateral/service-provider/global-cloud-index-gci/Cloud_Index_White_Paper.pdf.

To put 8.6 zettabytes in perspective, if every person in the world (7,211,239,210 **2.05** in 2014[11]) were to store some of the 8.6 zettabytes data on an iPhone 6 (say the largest with 128 gigabytes storage), that would require over ten iPhones per person (10.24420843 to be exact) or 73,873,437,491 iPhones in total. As the OECD noted:

> The digitisation of nearly all media and the increasing migration of social and economic activities to the Internet (through e-services such as social networks, e-commerce, e-health and e-government) are generating petabytes (millions of gigabytes) of data every second.[12]

One reason for the increase in data collection is the decrease in cost to col- **2.06** lect, store,[13] process,[14] and analyse data.[15] Moreover, with the rise of broadband access, smartphones, e-commerce, and social networks, consumers are actively and passively divulging more personal information.[16] Big Data here not only

---

[11] World Population Statistics, World Population 2014, 11 February 2014, http://www.worldpopulationstatistics.com/world-population-2014/.

[12] OECD, *Data-Driven Innovation*, above note 6, p 8; McKinsey Report, above note 8, p 3 (noting one estimate 'that enterprises globally stored more than 7 exabytes of new data on disk drives in 2010, while consumers stored more than 6 exabytes of new data on devices such as PCs and notebooks' and that '[o]ne exabyte of data is the equivalent of more than 4,000 times the information stored in the US Library of Congress').

[13] OECD, *Data-Driven Innovation*, above note 6, p 9 (noting that 'the average cost per gigabyte of consumer hard disk drives...dropped from USD 56 in 1998 to USD 0.05 in 2012, an average decline of almost 40% a year' and '[w]ith new generation storage technologies such as solid-state drives (SSDs), the decline in costs per gigabyte is even faster'); McKinsey Report, above note 8, p 2 (noting that the 'ability to store, aggregate, and combine data and then use the results to perform deep analyses has become ever more accessible as trends such as Moore's Law in computing, its equivalent in digital storage, and cloud computing continue to lower costs and other technology barriers' and that for 'less than $600, an individual can purchase a disk drive with the capacity to store all of the world's music').

[14] OECD, *Data-Driven Innovation*, above note 6, p 10 (noting how data processing tools 'have become increasingly powerful, sophisticated, ubiquitous and inexpensive, making data easily searchable, linkable and traceable, not only by governments and large corporations but also by many others').

[15] White House Big Data Report, above note 6, p 2 (noting in 2014 that 'technological advances have driven down the cost of creating, capturing, managing, and storing information to one-sixth of what it was in 2005').

[16] McKinsey Report, above note 8, p 2 (noting that in '2010, more than 4 billion people, or 60 percent of the world's population, were using mobile phones, and about 12 percent of those people had smartphones, whose penetration is growing at more than 20 percent a year', that '[m]ore than 30 million networked sensor nodes are now present in the transportation, automotive, industrial, utilities, and retail sectors', and that '[t]he number of these sensors is increasing at a rate of more than 30 percent a year'); OECD, *Data-Driven Innovation*, above note 6, p 8 ('The remarkable expansion of data is largely driven by the confluence of important technological developments, notably the increasing ubiquity of broadband access and the proliferation of smart devices and smart ICT [information and communication technologies] applications such as smart meters, smart grids and smart transport based on sensor networks and machine-to-machine (M2M) communication.').

refers to its absolute volume, but the volume relative to a comprehensive dataset on that topic.[17]

2.07 Social networking is one example. In 2014, the OECD noted that there were 'over 900 million active [Facebook] participants around the world' who 'generate on average more than 1500 status updates every second'.[18] By 2014, Facebook connected over 1.3 billion people around the world.[19] In September 2014, Facebook averaged 864 million *daily active* users, 703 million mobile daily active users, 1.35 billion monthly active users, 1.12 billion mobile monthly active users, with approximately 82.2 per cent of its daily active users outside the US and Canada.[20] To put this in perspective, the average number of active Facebook users in September 2014 was 12 times larger than the number of viewers for the most-watched US television event (namely Super Bowl XLVII between the Seattle Seahawks and Denver Broncos, which averaged 111.5 million viewers).[21]

2.08 But as the Executive Office of the US President recently observed, 'the volume of information that people create themselves—the full range of communications from voice calls, emails and texts to uploaded pictures, video, and music—pales in comparison to the amount of digital information created about them each day'.[22]

2.09 The Apple Watch and its likely rivals will collect even more data on our everyday activities and health. With the Internet of Things, sensors, microphones, and cameras will sweep in significantly more data about us, whether in our homes, cars, schools, at work, or during free time.[23] Cisco predicts an Internet of Everything,

---

[17] Viktor Mayer-Schönberger and Kenneth Cukier, *Big Data: A Revolution That Will Transform How We Live, Work, and Think* (London: John Murray, 2013), p 29.

[18] OECD, *Data-Driven Innovation*, above note 6, p 8.

[19] *Facebook/WhatsApp* (Case Comp/M.7217), Commission Decision C(2014) 7239, 3 October 2014, para 45.

[20] Facebook, Company Info, http://newsroom.fb.com/company-info/.

[21] Maury Brown, 'Super Bowl Most-Watched US TV Event of All-Time with 111.5 Million Viewers', *Forbes*, 3 February 2014, http://www.forbes.com/sites/maurybrown/2014/02/03/super-bowl-most-watched-tv-event-of-all-time-with-111-5-million-viewers/.

[22] White House Big Data Report, above note 6, p 2.

[23] European Data Protection Supervisor, 'Privacy and Competitiveness in the Age of Big Data: The Interplay Between Data Protection, Competition Law, and Consumer Protection in the Digital Economy', Preliminary Opinion, 26 March 2014 ('EDPS Preliminary Opinion'), p 35, https://secure.edps.europa.eu/EDPSWEB/webdav/shared/Documents/Consultation/Opinions/2014/14-03-26_competitition_law_big_data_EN.pdf; PCAST Report, above note 1 ('To some, it seems farfetched that the typical home will foreseeably acquire cameras and microphones in every room, but that appears to be a likely trend. What can your cell phone (already equipped with front and back cameras) hear or see when it is on the nightstand next to your bed? Tablets, laptops, and many desktop computers have cameras and microphones.'); OECD, *Supporting Investment*, above note 8, p 322 ('More than 30 million interconnected sensors are now deployed worldwide, in areas such as security, health care, the environment, transport systems or energy control systems, and their numbers are growing by around 30% a year.'); OECD, *Data-Driven Innovation*, above note 6, p 8 ('With the increasing deployment and interconnection of (real-world) sensors through mobile and fixed networks (i.e. sensor networks), more and more offline activities are also digitally recorded, resulting in an additional tidal wave of data.').

whereby 'people will be able to connect to the Internet in innumerable ways', such as swallowing 'a pill that senses and reports the health of their digestive tract to a doctor over a secure Internet connection' and 'sensors placed on the skin or sewn into clothing will provide information about a person's vital signs'.[24]

One's data trail begins before one's birth, with retailers, like Target, using **2.10** Big Data and Big Analytics to identify and target pregnant shoppers with coupons,[25] and increases until one's death. With the Internet of Things, smartphones, and facial recognition technology, more data will likely be collected on our children and grandchildren than collectively on all of our ancestors over the past few centuries.

B. Velocity of Data

The velocity at which data are generated, accessed, processed, and analysed **2.11** has also increased,[26] and for some applications is now approaching real-time.[27] Consequently, there is a 'growing potential for big data analytics to have an immediate effect on a person's surrounding environment or decisions being made about his or her life'.[28] We see this with automated stock trading and other machine learning, where autonomous systems, through algorithms, can 'learn from data of previous situations and to autonomously make decisions based on the analysis of these data'.[29]

One example of the velocity of data is 'nowcasting', which Google's Chief Economist **2.12** defines as ' "contemporaneous forecasting"—basically an ability to predict what is happening as it occurs'.[30] Companies mine their data 'to make real-time "nowcasts"

---

[24] Dave Evans, 'The Internet of Everything: How More Relevant and Valuable Connections Will Change the World' (2012), https://www.cisco.com/web/about/ac79/docs/innov/IoE.pdf.

[25] Charles Duhigg, 'How Companies Learn Your Secrets', *NY Times*, 16 February 2012, http://www.nytimes.com/2012/02/19/magazine/shopping-habits.html.

[26] McKinsey Report, above note 8, p 98 ('More and more sensors are being embedded in physical devices—from assembly-line equipment to automobiles to mobile phones—that measure processes, the use of end products, and human behavior. Individual consumers, too, are creating and sharing a tremendous amount of data through blogging, status updates, and posting photos and videos. Much of these data can now be collected in real or near real time.').

[27] White House Big Data Report, above note 6, p 5.

[28] Ibid (giving as examples of high-velocity data 'click-stream data that records users' online activities as they interact with web pages, GPS data from mobile devices that tracks location in real time, and social media that is shared broadly').

[29] OECD, *Data-Driven Innovation*, above note 6, p 4.

[30] Auction.com, 'Auction.com Launches Real Estate's First Nowcast—Leverages Industry, Transactional and Google Search Data to Provide Accurate Real-Time Market Intelligence', Press Release, 30 October 2014, http://www.auction.com/lp/company-information/press-releases/auction-com-launches-real-estates-first-nowcast-leverages-industry-transactional-and-google-search-data-to-provide-accurate-real-time-market-intelligence/.

ranging from purchases of autos to flu epidemics to employment/unemployment trends in order to improve the quality of policy and business decisions'.[31]

2.13 One example of nowcasting involves flu rates.[32] As *ScienceDaily* reported in 2014,

> Official reports of influenza infection rates are produced with a delay of at least one week. Yet researchers from Google and the Centers for Disease Control and Prevention (CDC) reported that data on searches for influenza related terms could be used to provide a real time estimate of the number of people with flu infections, with almost no delay.[33]

Nowcasting at times is inaccurate. Media reports of the flu, for example, can trigger in some cities a flu scare. People search flu-related terms, without there being a high incidence of flu in that city.[34] But researchers are now seeking to avoid such errors in using Google Trends data with 'adaptive nowcasting' models.[35]

2.14 Another example is real estate. Google in 2014 invested $50 million in Auction.com, the largest US online real estate auction company. Auction.com will use Google's 'big-data capabilities to try to predict U.S. home sales and other trends ahead of rivals'.[36] Thus we can see how nowcasting can confer a competitive advantage to those that can first access the data.

2.15 The velocity in processing data will likely increase in other fields that Google, Apple, and other tech firms are pioneering, such as driverless cars and monitoring

---

[31] OECD, *Data-Driven Innovation*, above note 6, p 9.

[32] Kenneth Cukier and Viktor Mayer-Schönberger, 'The Rise of Big Data: How It's Changing the Way We Think About the World', 92 *Foreign Affairs* (2013): pp 28, 33 (noting how Google's massive dataset of searches, while imperfect, provided strong correlations in near-real-time of outbreaks of seasonal flu).

[33] University of Warwick, 'Adaptive "Nowcasting" Key to Accurate Flu Data Trends Using Google Search Terms', *ScienceDaily*, 30 October 2014, www.sciencedaily.com/releases/2014/10/141030114853.htm ('Warwick, Adaptive Nowcasting').

[34] OECD, *Data-Driven Innovation*, above note 6, p 34 (noting how Google Flu Trends, 'which is based on Google Insights for Search and provides statistics on the regional and time-based popularity of specific keywords that correlate with flu infections' in January 2013, 'drastically overestimated flu infection rates in the United States', which experts estimated 'was due to "widespread media coverage of [that] year's severe US flu season" which triggered an additional wave of flu-related searches but by flu unaffected people').

[35] Warwick, Adaptive Nowcasting, above note 33 (noting that adaptive model 'monitors the relationship between Google search data and recent CDC measurements and integrates this information into its estimates of current flu levels').

[36] John Gittelsohn, 'Google Data to Help Auction.com Predict Homebuying Trends', Bloomberg Business, 30 October 2014, http://www.bloomberg.com/news/2014-10-30/google-data-to-help-auction-com-predict-homebuying-trends.html; Auction.com, 'Auction.com Launches Real Estate's First Nowcast', above note 30 (noting how this was 'the real estate industry's first Nowcast, a new housing report that combines industry data, proprietary company transactional data and publicly available Google Trends data to predict market trends as they are occurring—weeks before the findings of other benchmark studies are released'). The press release quotes Google's economist that, '[b]y layering industry-specific transactional data and subject-matter expertise over that search data, organizations such as Auction.com are able to create powerful predictive models for accurately forecasting buying behavior in the present and for the coming months.'

health metrics. The velocity of data acknowledges its time-value. Depending on its purpose, the older the data the less valuable it is. Current geo-location data, for example, may be very important for the commuter (or her driverless car) in assessing which roads are less congested. Historic traffic data is of less value for this purpose.

C. Variety of Data

Data's value increases not only with its volume and the velocity in processing it, but **2.16** also with the variety of information collected on an individual. Let us consider the breadth of data that the UK retailer Tesco collects about its shoppers. Tesco first gathers personal information from the application form for its loyalty programme, Clubcard, 'such as address, age, gender, the number of members in a household and their ages, dietary habits'.[37] Tesco next collects the shopper's purchase history, including purchases and 'visit history, both to stores and online'.[38] Tesco computes several summary attributes, which 'include share of wallet information, information on frequency and duration of visits. Also, information on customer preferences and tastes, as determined by some clever cluster analysis based on purchase history of specific fast-moving products'.[39] Then Tesco mines other databases to further develop its shopper profile, including 'credit reports, loan applications, magazine subscription lists, Office for National Statistics, and the Land Registry'.[40] Why the variety of data? As its former CEO noted, '[w]e could treat customers as individuals. And we could learn what they were interested in, what their behaviours were, and we could tailor and target all of their marketing so that it was relevant to that individual consumer.'[41]

As our Tesco example illustrates, data's value can increase through data fusion, **2.17** which 'occurs when data from different sources are brought into contact and new facts emerge'.[42] Through data fusion, companies can identify and improve their

---

[37] Krish Swarmy, 'Analyzing Tesco—The Analytics Behind a Top-Notch Loyalty Program', *Big Data Analytics*, 21 August 2011, http://stat-exchange.blogspot.com/2011/08/analyzing-tesco-analytics-behind-top.html.

[38] Ibid.

[39] Ibid.

[40] Ibid.

[41] Brad Howarth, 'How Tesco's loyalty card transformed customer data tracking', *CMO*, 21 May 2015, http://www.cmo.com.au/article/575497/how-tesco-loyalty-card-transformed-customer-data-tracking/.

[42] PCAST Report, above note 1, p x; OECD, *Data-Driven Innovation*, above note 6, p 12 (observing that '[i]n some cases, big data is defined by the capacity to analyse a variety of mostly unstructured data sets from sources as diverse as web logs, social media, mobile communications, sensors and financial transactions. This requires the capability to link data sets; this can be essential as information is highly context-dependent and may not be of value out of the right context. It also requires the capability to extract information from unstructured data, i.e. data that lack a predefined (explicit or implicit) model.').

profiles of individuals, better track their activities, preferences, and vulnerabilities, and better target them with behavioural advertising.[43] The White House reported in 2014:

> The fusion of many different kinds of data, processed in real time, has the power to deliver exactly the right message, product, or service to consumers before they even ask. Small bits of data can be brought together to create a clear picture of a person to predict preferences or behaviors. These detailed personal profiles and personalized experiences are effective in the consumer marketplace and can deliver products and offers to precise segments of the population—like a professional accountant with a passion for knitting, or a home chef with a penchant for horror films.[44]

2.18   Other retailers, including the high-end retailer Whole Foods Market Inc and discounter Wal-Mart Stores Inc, are also merging their disparate datasets to better understand customers' behaviour.[45] Wal-Mart is integrating shopping data from online and store transactions to create a fuller view of customer behaviour and better compete against Amazon, which originally sold books as a way to gather personal data on affluent, educated shoppers.[46]

D. Value of Data

2.19   The volume and variety of data being collected and the velocity in processing the data have increased because of data's value.[47] Big Data in effect is tied to Big Analytics, from which data's value is derived.[48] Data analytics, under one definition, 'are the technical means to extract insights and the empowering tools to better

---

[43] PCAST Report, above note 1, p x. Behavioural advertising is the 'collection of data from a particular computer or device regarding Web viewing behaviors over time and across non-affiliated Web sites for the purpose of using such data to predict user preferences or interests to deliver advertising to that computer or device based on the preferences or interests inferred from such Web viewing behaviors.' Digital Advertising Alliance, 'Self-Regulatory Principles for Online Behavioral Advertising Implementation Guide: Frequently Asked Questions', October 2010, http://www. aboutads.info/resource/download/OBA Self-Reg Implementation Guide - Frequently Asked Questions.pdf.

[44] White House Big Data Report, above note 6, p 7.

[45] Steven Norton, 'Big Companies Rein in Data Sprawl: Whole Foods, GE and Others Merge Disparate Data Sets to Cut Costs, Learn About Customers', *Wall Street Journal*, 21 October 2015, http://www.wsj.com/articles/big-companies-rein-in-data-sprawl-1445482009.

[46] George Packer, 'Cheap Words: Amazon is good for customers. But is it good for books?', *The New Yorker*, 17–24 February 2014, http://www.newyorker.com/magazine/2014/02/17/cheap-words.

[47] OECD, *Data-Driven Innovation*, above note 6, p 12 (noting how value, the fourth 'V', relates 'to the increasing socioeconomic value to be obtained from the use of big data' which 'ultimately motivates the accumulation, processing and use of data').

[48] Ibid, p 11 (noting that 'what is behind variety and velocity is primarily data analytics; that is the capacity to process and analyse unstructured diverse data in (close to) real-time'); *Publicis/Omnicom* (Case Comp M.7023), Commission Decision C(2014) 89 final, 9 January 2014, para 617 ('"big data" analytics...relates to the process of examining large amounts of data of a variety of types ("big data") to uncover patterns, correlations and other useful information').

understand, influence or control the data objects of these insights (e.g. natural phenomena, social systems, individuals)'.[49]

Big Data and Big Analytics have a mutual reinforcing relationship. Big Data would **2.20** have less value if companies couldn't rapidly analyse the data and act quickly upon it. Machine-learning, in turn, relies on accessing large data sets. As the European Data Protection Supervisor observed, '[d]eep learning computers teach themselves tasks by crunching large data sets using (among other things) neural networks that appear to emulate the brain.'[50] The algorithms' capacity to learn will increase with the more relevant data they process. Take for example, the Rubicon Project, 'a leading technology company automating the buying and selling of advertising'.[51] The company discussed the interplay among Big Data, machine learning, and data-driven network effects as a competitive strength:

> As we process more volume on our automated platform, we accumulate more data, such as pricing, geographic and preference information, data on how best to optimize yield for sellers and more. This additional data helps make our machine-learning algorithms more intelligent and this leads to more effective matching between buyers and sellers. As a result, more buyers and sellers are attracted to our platform, from which we get more data, which further reinforces the network effect and thereby increases market liquidity, which benefits both buyers and sellers.[52]

Here we see how Big Data's value derives from the other three 'V's. The volume of **2.21** data can enable firms to uncover correlations from large, unstructured datasets, which can outperform findings from smaller, but cleaner datasets.[53] Some argue that in some industries simple algorithms with lots of data will eventually outperform sophisticated algorithms with little data.[54] Big Data's value also comes from the variety of data and data fusion, such as a life insurance company learning of the insured's hobbies (including any risk-seeking ones).[55] Finally value comes from velocity, namely being the first to collect, analyse, and use the data. With real-time

---

[49] OECD, *Data-Driven Innovation*, above note 6, p 4.

[50] European Data Protection Supervisor, 'Towards a New Digital Ethics: Data, Dignity and Technology', Opinion 4/2015, 11 September 2015.

[51] The Rubicon Project, 'Who We Are' (2016), http://rubiconproject.com/whoweare/.

[52] The Rubicon Project, Amendment No 3 to Form S-1 Registration Statement, 30 April 2014.

[53] Cukier and Mayer-Schönberger, above note 32, pp 30–1 (discussing how Google's translations from a larger, less orderly dataset outperformed IBM's translations from a smaller, but cleaner dataset); *Publicis/Omnicom*, above note 48, para 617.

[54] Cukier and Mayer-Schönberger, above note 32, 36–9; Alon Halevy, Peter Norvig, and Fernando Pereira, 'The Unreasonable Effectiveness of Data', *IEEE Intelligent Systems*, March–April 2009, p 9, http://static.googleusercontent.com/media/research.google.com/en//pubs/archive/35179.pdf (observing that 'invariably, simple models and a lot of data trump more elaborate models based on less data . . . observations have been made in every other application of machine learning to Web data: simple n-gram models or linear classifiers based on millions of specific features perform better than elaborate models that try to discover general rules. In many cases there appears to be a threshold of sufficient data.').

[55] OECD, *Data-Driven Innovation*, above note 6, p 31 ('As the volume and variety of available data sets increases, so does the ability to derive further information from these data in particular

monitoring and self-learning computer algorithms that automatically update their inferences and predictions, companies can out-manoeuvre rivals in being the first to decipher material changes in the market.[56]

2.22 As the value from Big Data increases and the costs to collect and analyse data decrease, companies, researchers, and governments will 'data-ify' even more everyday activities to harness greater value. We are entering the age of datafication, where we take 'all aspects of life and turning them into data'.[57] As the Federal Trade Commission Chair observed:

> Thanks to smartphones and smart meters, wearable fitness devices, social media, connected cars, and retail loyalty cards, each of us is generating data at an unprecedented rate. In fact, in 2013 it was reported that an astonishing 90 per cent of the world's data was generated in the two preceding years. Today, the output of data is doubling every two years.[58]

One example is geo-location data. Companies and governments are increasingly tracking our movements through our smartphones, tablets, or smartwatches. Why? As McKinsey and Company identified, our personal location data can serve multiple purposes, such as telling us of nearby historical sites, shopping venues, restaurants, and traffic conditions. On a macro level, our location data can help with urban planning.[59] Not surprisingly, our geo-location data is valuable. Combined with the various other data about us, advertisers will know who we are, where we are going, why we are going there, how we will get there, and when we are travelling. Based on our consumer profile, advertisers can target us with places to eat, stores and attractions to visit, and things to buy. McKinsey estimated in 2011 that the major applications of personal location data would in ten years' time 'have the potential to create value of $100 billion or more for service providers alone'.[60]

---

when they are linked. In particular, personal information can be "inferred" from several pieces of seemingly anonymous or non-personal data.').

[56] Ibid, pp 30–1 ('The speed at which data are collected, processed and analysed is often also highlighted as one of the key benefits of data analytics today. The collection and analysis of data in (near to) real-time has empowered organisations to base decisions on "close-to-market" evidence. For businesses, this means reduction of time-to-market, and benefits due to first- or early-mover advantages.').

[57] Cukier and Mayer-Schönberger, above note 32, p 35.

[58] Edith Ramirez, Opening Remarks, FTC Workshop, *Big Data: A Tool for Inclusion or Exclusion?*, 15 September 2014, https://www.ftc.gov/system/files/documents/public_statements/582421/140915bigdataworkshop.pdf.

[59] McKinsey Report, above note 8, p 88 ('Location-based applications and services for individuals is a category that includes smart routing, automotive telematics, and mobile-phone based location services. The second category is the organizational use of individual personal location data that includes geo-targeted advertising, electronic toll collection, insurance pricing, and emergency response. Third is the macro-level use of aggregate location data that includes urban planning and retail business intelligence.') and p 90 ('Geo-targeted mobile advertising is one of the most common ways organizations can create value from the use of personal location data.').

[60] McKinsey Report, above note 8, p 93.

With such large datasets, data analytics need not determine causation, instead relying **2.23** on correlation,[61] such as knowing that consumers who buy X are likelier to purchase Y, and thus cross-promoting both products (or stocking them together). Relying on correlation has its risks, as when the causal relationship is clearly spurious.[62] An individual may not be a credit risk; but if she shops at certain stores, lives in certain neighbourhoods, or her social network consists of a certain group, she may be perceived as a credit risk.[63]

Big Data's value benefits, at times, both firms and consumers. Data can lower firms' costs **2.24** in identifying consumers and learning of their needs.[64] Firms can use data in providing 'smart' products that increase energy efficiency and overall welfare. Data on energy and consumption patterns can yield 'smart-grid' technologies to reduce or better manage electricity consumption, such as water heaters that collect data of consumers' hot water use to predict consumption, and heat accordingly.[65] Geo-location data can help reduce traffic congestion,[66] save commuters time, increase their well-being,[67] and reduce pollution.[68] Governments can use data to determine where to allocate scarce resources, such as identifying sluggish sectors of online commerce to see whether incumbents have anticompetitively blocked entry or thwarted innovation.[69] Companies may also use customer data for non-revenue purposes such as to fulfil their regulatory obligations.[70]

---

[61] OECD, *Data-Driven Innovation*, above note 6, p 32 ('Decision makers do not necessarily need to understand the phenomenon, before they act on it. In other words: first comes the analytical fact, then the action, and last, if at all, the understanding. For example, a company such as Wal-Mart Stores may change the product placement in its stores based on correlations without the need to know why the change will have a positive impact on its revenue').

[62] Ibid, p 33 (noting how 'big data analysis reveals that the United States murder rate was well correlated with the market share of Internet Explorer from 2006 to 2011'.).

[63] Tracy Alloway, 'Credit Where Credit's Due', *Financial Times* (UK), 5 February 2014, p 9.

[64] OECD, *Exploring the Economics of Personal Data*, above note 2, p 12 (noting on how data-driven business models can 'focus on understanding individual consumers better in order to provide tailored products and services, to reduce consumer search and transaction costs and to increase the efficiency of suppliers and providers, be they private or public sector entities').

[65] OECD, *Data-Driven Innovation*, above note 6, p 5.

[66] Ibid ('The transport sector's increasing ability to track the location of mobile devices has enabled both the monitoring of traffic to save time and reduce congestion as well as the provision of new location-based services.').

[67] Daniel Kahneman and Alan B Krueger, 'Developments in the Measurement of Subjective Well-Being', 20(1) *J of Econ Persp* (2006): pp 3, 8.

[68] OECD, *Data-Driven Innovation*, above note 6, p 16 (noting how geo-location data 'can lead to significant time savings and reduced congestion, notably in cities', and that global pool of personal geo-location data, which is estimated to growing by 20% a year since 2009, could by 2020 provide USD 500 billion in value worldwide in the form of time and fuel savings, or 380 megatonnes (million tonnes) of CO2 emissions saved).

[69] David Currie, Chairman, Competition and Markets Authority, 'EU Consumers in the Digital Era', Speech given at European Consumer Summit, Brussels, 1 April 2014, https://www.gov.uk/government/speeches/eu-consumers-in-the-digital-era; *see also* Cukier and Mayer-Schönberger, above note 32, p 35 (discussing how New York City uses datasets to better identify illegally-subdivided buildings, which pose greater fire risks).

[70] UK Competition and Markets Authority, *The Commercial Use of Consumer Data: Report on the CMA's Call for Information*, June 2015, para 2.91 (noting that 'not all consumer data collection is

2.25 Thus the exploitation of data can benefit citizens in many ways, including:

> [e]nhancing research and development (data-driven R&D); [d]eveloping new prod-
> ucts (goods and services) by using data either as a product (data products) or as a
> major component of a product (data-intensive products); [o]ptimising production
> or delivery processes (data-driven processes); [i]mproving marketing by providing
> targeted advertisements and personalised recommendations (data-driven market-
> ing); [d]eveloping new organisational and management approaches or significantly
> improving existing practices (data-driven organisation).[71]

2.26 As we explore, the four 'V's of data can also be quite valuable to advertisers to better
match their advertisements to consumers who may be interested in their products,[72]
to buy advertising in real-time auctions, and to measure the effectiveness of their
promotions and advertising.[73] The four 'V's of data can solve several problems advertisers face with 'traditional' media. In the offline world, advertisers had limited,
and sometimes faulty, information about how many people actually saw or heard
an advertisement.[74] The advertisers paid to reach people who had no interest in the
products being advertised.[75] Even among those potential buyers who were interested, it was difficult to figure out whether the advertisement or campaign influ-
enced the consumer's subsequent purchase decision.[76] Before loyalty cards, retailers

---

about generating revenue' and that some firms may 'need to collect and analyse data to meet regulatory obligations,' eg, checking financial transactions to spot suspicious activity), https://www.gov.
uk/government/uploads/system/uploads/attachment_data/file/435817/The_commercial_use_
of_consumer_data.pdf.

[71] OECD, 'Exploring Data-Driven Innovation as a New Source of Growth: Mapping the Policy
Issues Raised by "Big Data"', OECD Digital Economy Papers, No 222, 18 June 2013, p 4, http://
dx.doi.org/10.1787/5k47zw3fcp43-en.

[72] David S Evans, 'The Online Advertising Industry: Economics, Evolution, and Privacy',
23(3) *J of Econ Persp* (2009): pp 37, 42–3; Howard Beales, 'The Value of Behavioral Targeting',
Network Advertising Initiative, 24 March 2010, pp 6–17, http://www.networkadvertising.org/
pdfs/Beales_NAI_Study.pdf (discussing the results of a study analysing data on behaviourally targeted advertising).

[73] Avi Goldfarb and Catherine Tucker, 'Online Advertising', 81 *Advances in Computers* (2011):
pp 289, 292–4.

[74] Philip M Napoli, *Audience Evolution: New Technologies and the Transformation of
Media Audiences* (New York: Columbia University Press, 2010), pp 32–3 (discussing 'information vacuums regarding the nature of the interaction between content and audience' that
abounded in early models of audience understanding); cf ibid, pp 41–2 ('increased accessibility, usability, and affordability of large quantities of data has been one of the biggest changes
affecting the media landscape....[T]he processes of media buying and planning are becoming increasingly specialized as a result of...the increasing flow of complex audience data'
(citation omitted)).

[75] Cf Philip M Napoli, *Audience Economics: Media Institutions and the Audience Marketplace*
(New York: Columbia University Press, 2003), pp 29–31 (discussing 'the exchange of goods...
based upon...educated guesses about the size and composition' of the advertisement's audience and
the uncertainty that inheres in the process).

[76] Napoli, *Audience Evolution*, above note 74, p 32 (stating that in early motion picture markets
major companies 'ha[d] not the slightest idea what happen[ed] to [their] pictures, and...[had] no
way of finding out why [their] picture didn't do well with certain audiences').

and consumer goods manufacturers could track what items were sold, but had less data on the purchasers. Retailers could experiment with product placements (such as better shelf-space or an end-cap). With store loyalty cards, retailers and manufacturers obtained more data and better insights on customers, including what other items they bought and the frequency of purchases at that retail outlet.[77]

By collecting and analysing even more data about users, online advertisers take **2.27** a big step towards determining whether their ads influence purchases, and how to better influence purchases.[78] Advertisers can learn more about their consumer base: what else they did, if they used the products, what they told their friends about the product on their social network page. In identifying traits about their customers and the conditions that prompt them to purchase, advertisers can target others consumers who are interested in their product at the critical purchasing decision, thereby reducing 'waste'. Advertisers can obtain better information about the reach, frequency, and effectiveness of their advertising from initial exposure all the way to 'conversion' (that is a sale).[79] Firms can compare results of different advertisements or campaigns and quickly adjust. They can build audiences in an era of increasing fragmentation. They can enlist their customers to endorse their products on social networks. Retailers and advertisers can track how customers arrived onto the website, the reviews and other products they looked at, how long they dwelled on a page, what else they considered, whether others within their social network endorsed the product, and to what extent others in that community looked at the product.[80]

---

[77] Dunnhumby, 'Capabilities: Transforming Customer Data Into Customer Delight', http://www.dunnhumby.com/capabilities; Leo Mirani, 'Why an Obscure British Data-Mining Company Is Worth $3 Billion', *Quartz*, 12 January 2015, http://qz.com/323944/why-an-obscure-british-data-mining-company-is-worth-3-billion/.

[78] As the OECD discussed,

> Behavioural targeting is effective for advertisers because it produces more 'hits'. Surveying nine of the top 15 advertising networks, Beales [] found that behaviourally-targeted advertising accounted for around 18% of total advertising revenue during 2009 (USD 595 million), cost 2.68 times as much as run-of-network advertising and was more than twice as effective at converting users who click on the advertisements into buyers—a 6.8% conversion versus the 2.8% conversion from run-of-network advertisements. It also provides product and service information that is likely to be of interest to the particular consumer, thus reducing search and transaction costs.

OECD, *Exploring the Economics of Personal Data*, above note 2, p 14, citing Howard Beales, 'The Value of Behavioral Targeting', Network Advertising Initiative (2010), http://www.networkadvertising.org/pdfs/Beales_NAI_Study.pdf.

[79] *See, eg*, Rex Briggs and Greg Stuart, *What Sticks: Why Most Advertising Fails and How to Guarantee Yours Succeeds* (Chicago: Kaplan Trade Publishing, 2006), p 11 (discussing media measurements for online advertising); Goldfarb and Tucker, above note 73, pp 294–8 (discussing ad targeting).

[80] OECD, *Data-Driven Innovation*, above note 6, p 15 ('A firm could only collect scanner data from the checkout for customers using loyalty cards to infer what broader range of products might interest that customer. With click-stream data, firms now possess much more information. For example, firms now have information about the website that directed the user to the firm, whether the user used a search engine, what search terms were used to reach the firm's website. This allows

Taken together, these developments represent a true innovation in advertising. The dramatic growth of online advertising and the corresponding declines suffered by much of traditional media are evidence of this fact.

2.28 Data's value can also be asymmetrical: companies, for example, can use data to better exploit citizens, such as targeting those most vulnerable to a particular sales tactic or engaging in discrimination in pricing, services, and opportunities to those consumers with fewer outside options.[81] Indeed, consumers may be unaware that data is being collected on them, its use, or its value.[82]

2.29 To illustrate how Big Data is quantitatively and qualitatively different from the data collected before, we will look in the next chapter at smartphones. In particular, we will examine a surprising unanimous decision by the US Supreme Court on whether the government could search a suspect's smartphone without a warrant. Although the Fourth Amendment constitutional issues may seem far afield from competition policy, the case raises interesting privacy issues.

---

businesses to allocate their marketing budget more effectively and to target websites that reach their most valuable customers. Furthermore, firms can find out exactly what the user looks at on a web page. This enables them to improve users' online experience based on empirical evidence and statistical methods such as A/B testing rather than simply web developers' experience and subjective impressions.').

[81] *See, generally,* Ariel Ezrachi and Maurice E Stucke, *Virtual Competition: The Promise and Perils of the Algorithm-Driven Economy* (Cambridge, MA: Harvard University Press, forthcoming 2016); White House Big Data Report, above note 6, pp 7, 45.

[82] White House Big Data Report, above note 6, p 34 (noting how users 'emit lots of "digital exhaust", or trace data, that leaves behind more fragmentary bits of information, such as the geographical coordinates of a cell phone transmission or an IP address in a server log' and with the 'advent of more powerful analytics, which can discern quite a bit from even small and disconnected pieces of data, raises the possibility that data gathered and held by third parties can be amalgamated and analyzed in ways that reveal even more information about individuals').

3

SMARTPHONES AS AN EXAMPLE OF HOW BIG DATA AND PRIVACY INTERSECT

Smartphone subscriptions have accelerated. Reaching the first billion of smartphone subscriptions (in 2012) took over five years; reaching the second billion took less than two years.[1] Ericsson predicts smartphone subscriptions, between 2015 and 2020, will more than double to 26 billion connected devices.[2] Ninety per cent of the world's population over six years old will have a mobile phone by 2020.[3]   **3.01**

People are spending more time on their smartphones. Between 2013 and 2015, Americans' overall digital media usage grew 49 per cent.[4] In this period, their average time on mobile apps increased by 90 per cent, their average time browsing the web increased by 53 per cent, and even their average time on desktop computers increased by 16 per cent.[5] Both Google's and Apple's mobile platforms have grown as well, with 1.6 million apps available in July 2015 in the Google Play store and 1.5 millions apps available in June 2015 in Apple's App Store.[6]   **3.02**

With more people spending more time on their smartphones they are using (and producing) more data. Mobile data traffic was 55 per cent higher in the first quarter of 2015 than in the first quarter of 2014.[7] Indeed, AT&T   **3.03**

---

[1] Ericsson, *Mobility Report: On the Pulse of the Networked Society*, June 2015, p 7, http://www.ericsson.com/res/docs/2015/ericsson-mobility-report-june-2015.pdf.

[2] Ibid, p 3.

[3] Ibid, p 6.

[4] comScore, *The 2015 US Mobile App Report*, 22 September 2015, p 5, https://www.comscore.com/Insights/Presentations-and-Whitepapers/2015/The-2015-US-Mobile-App-Report.

[5] Ibid.

[6] Statistica, 'Number of Available Applications in the Google Play Store from December 2009 to February 2015', http://www.statista.com/statistics/266210/number-of-available-applications-in-the-google-play-store/; Statistica, 'Number of Available Apps in the Apple App Store from July 2008 to June 2015', http://www.statista.com/statistics/263795/number-of-available-apps-in-the-apple-app-store/.

[7] Ericsson, above note 1, p 3.

sought to justify its acquisition of T-Mobile in large part by the growth in mobile data usage:

> This transaction quickly provides the spectrum and network efficiencies necessary for AT&T to address impending spectrum exhaust in key markets driven by the exponential growth in mobile broadband traffic on its network. AT&T's mobile data traffic grew 8,000 percent over the past four years and by 2015 it is expected to be eight to 10 times what it was in 2010. Put another way, all of the mobile traffic volume AT&T carried during 2010 is estimated to be carried in just the first six to seven weeks of 2015. Because AT&T has led the U.S. in smartphones, tablets and e-readers—and as a result, mobile broadband—it requires additional spectrum before new spectrum will become available. In the long term, the entire industry will need additional spectrum to address the explosive growth in demand for mobile broadband.[8]

3.04   Smartphones nicely illustrate the intersection of Big Data and privacy. What are the privacy implications when more people spend more time on their smartphones browsing the web, watching videos, texting, emailing, or using apps that reflect their interests, political, religious, or social views, or connecting with others on Facebook or other social networks? Do people have a reasonable expectation of privacy in the data their smartphones collect? If so, is that expectation of privacy objectively reasonable?

A. Why the Odds Favoured the Government in *Riley*

3.05   A 2014 US Supreme Court case, *Riley v California*, addresses these privacy issues in the context of the government's warrantless search.[9] The Fourth Amendment to the US Constitution prohibits unreasonable searches and seizures, and requires the government first to obtain a warrant, supported by probable cause. Several expanding exceptions exist for warrantless searches and seizures. The issue in *Riley* was whether the police may, without a warrant, search 'digital information on a cell phone seized from an individual who has been arrested'.[10]

3.06   The odds favoured the United States and state of California, who argued for a warrantless search. Relying on its precedent, the Supreme Court could have easily agreed.

3.07   First, warrantless searches and seizures occur more frequently under the Court's exceptions than searches and seizures pursuant to a warrant. Thus, the term 'exception,' the Court recognizes, is a misnomer.[11]

---

[8] AT&T, 'AT&T to Acquire T-Mobile USA from Deutsche Telekom', Press Release, 20 March 2011, http://www.att.com/gen/press-room?pid=19358&cdvn=news&newsarticleid=31703.

[9] *Riley v California*, 134 S Ct 2473 (2014).

[10] Ibid, p 2480.

[11] Ibid, p 2482.

Second, one of the Court's significant exceptions for requiring a warrant is when the police lawfully arrest a person. As part of a search incident to arrest, the police can conduct a warrantless search of any physical object on the accused (such as his wallet's contents). If the accused had both a wallet and a smartphone, then, arguably, the police could search the contents of both.   **3.08**

Third, a year earlier, the Court, in upholding the warrantless collection of a DNA sample from persons arrested, but not convicted, of a felony, emphasized how an individual's legitimate privacy expectations are necessarily diminished when the individual is taken into police custody.[12]   **3.09**

Fourth, a lot of information on a smartphone is shared with third parties, so the accused—under another line of Supreme Court cases—would have no reasonable expectation of privacy.[13]   **3.10**

Fifth, in a 2011 decision, the Court deliberately avoided the issue of whether a constitutional privacy interest exists in avoiding disclosure of personal matters.[14] Two Justices in that case expressly rejected any right to informational privacy under the Fourteenth or Fifth Amendment of the US Constitution.[15]   **3.11**

Finally, the facts in *Riley* were damning. The information on Riley's smartphone implicated him with an attempted murder by a violent street gang, the 'Bloods'.   **3.12**

Thus, this case should have been an easy win for the Obama administration and state police departments who argued that the police do not need a warrant to search the digital information on a smartphone seized from those lawfully arrested.   **3.13**

B. The Surprising Unanimous Decision

So is searching your smartphone the same as searching your wallet or purse? Shocking many observers, the Supreme Court unanimously[16] responded no. The   **3.14**

---

[12] *Maryland v King*, 133 S Ct 1958 (2013).

[13] *United States v Miller*, 425 US 435, 443, 96 S Ct 1619, 1624 (1976) (government, consistent with the Fourth Amendment, can obtain 'information revealed to a third-party and conveyed by him to government authorities, even if the information is revealed on the assumption that it will be used only for a limited purpose and the confidence placed in the third-party will not be betrayed'); The Executive Office of the President, *Big Data: Seizing Opportunities, Preserving Values*, May 2014, pp 32–3, https://www.whitehouse.gov/sites/default/files/docs/big_data_privacy_report_may_1_2014.pdf.

[14] *National Aeronautics and Space Administration v Nelson*, 562 US 134, 131 S Ct 746 (2011).

[15] Ibid, p 159 (Justice Scalia, with whom Justice Thomas joins, concurring in the judgment).

[16] Justice Alito filed a separate opinion where he concurred in part and concurred with the result. He agreed that 'because of the role that these devices have come to play in contemporary life, searching their contents implicates very sensitive privacy interests that this Court is poorly positioned to understand and evaluate.' *Riley*, above note 9, p 2497.

Court declined to extend its precedent to smartphones, or even simpler cell phones, in part because the data they contain quantitatively and qualitatively differ from other physical objects.[17] Smartphones' 'immense storage capacity' had for the Court several significant consequences for privacy.

3.15 First was the *variety* of data typically stored on one's phone, which 'collects in one place many distinct types of information—an address, a note, a prescription, a bank statement, a video—that reveal much more in combination than any isolated record'.[18]

3.16 Second was the *volume* of data on any one facet of a person's life:

> [A] cell phone's capacity allows even just one type of information to convey far more than previously possible. The sum of an individual's private life can be reconstructed through a thousand photographs labelled with dates, locations, and descriptions; the same cannot be said of a photograph or two of loved ones tucked into a wallet.[19]

The volume and variety of data also provided a historical timeline:

> [T]he data on a phone can date back to the purchase of the phone, or even earlier. A person might carry in his pocket a slip of paper reminding him to call Mr. Jones; he would not carry a record of all his communications with Mr. Jones for the past several months, as would routinely be kept on a phone.[20]

3.17 Third was 'an element of pervasiveness that characterizes cell phones but not physical records. Prior to the digital age, people did not typically carry a cache of sensitive personal information with them as they went about their day. Now it is the person who is not carrying a cell phone, with all that it contains, who is the exception.'[21]

3.18 The data captured on a smartphone, the Court found, were also qualitatively different from physical records:

> An Internet search and browsing history, for example, can be found on an Internet-enabled phone and could reveal an individual's private interests or concerns—perhaps a search for certain symptoms of disease, coupled with frequent visits to WebMD. Data on a cell phone can also reveal where a person has been. Historic location information is a standard feature on many smart phones and can reconstruct someone's specific movements down to the minute, not only around town but also within a particular building.[22]

---

[17] Ibid, p 2489.

[18] Ibid.

[19] Ibid.

[20] Ibid.

[21] Ibid, p 2490.

[22] Ibid; *see also* OECD, *Supporting Investment in Knowledge Capital, Growth and Innovation*, October 2013, p 321, http://www.keepeek.com/Digital-Asset-Management/oecd/industry-and-services/supporting-investment-in-knowledge-capital-growth-and-innovation_9789264193307-en ('Mobile telephones have become a leading data collection device, combining geo-location data and Internet connectivity to support a broad range of new services and applications related to traffic, the environment or health care.'); OECD, *Data-Driven Innovation for Growth and*

The volume and variety of data on one's phone are amplified with the mobile ap- **3.19** plication software or 'apps'. The Court noted that '[t]he average smart phone user has installed 33 apps, which together can form a revealing montage of the user's life'.[23] The apps

> ...offer a range of tools for managing detailed information about all aspects of a person's life. There are apps for Democratic Party news and Republican Party news; apps for alcohol, drug, and gambling addictions; apps for sharing prayer requests; apps for tracking pregnancy symptoms; apps for planning your budget; apps for every conceivable hobby or pastime; apps for improving your romantic life. There are popular apps for buying or selling just about anything, and the records of such transactions may be accessible on the phone indefinitely.[24]

The Supreme Court historically elevated the privacy expectations in one's home. **3.20** For example, the Court held that convicting someone for privately possessing ob- scene materials in one's home violated the person's First Amendment rights.[25] But, in *Riley*, the Court observed how a smartphone, which fits in one's back pocket, passively and actively collects more personal data than typically found in one's home: 'A phone not only contains in digital form many sensitive records previously found in the home; it also contains a broad array of private information never found in a home in any form—unless the phone is.'[26]

C. Reflections

To be clear, *Riley* involved the Fourth Amendment to the US Constitution. The **3.21** Court never addressed our specific competition issues. Nor does the Court's ruling limit private companies from collecting and using personal data from our smart- phones. But what was remarkable for our purposes was the Court's foresight of the privacy implications as smartphones become the key platforms for collecting and analysing personal data. The Court recognized that the sharing of data on

---

Well-Being: Interim Synthesis Report, October 2014, p 36, http://www.oecd.org/sti/inno/data-driven-innovation-interim-synthesis.pdf ('Mobile broadband in particular is essential as mobile devices are now becoming the leading means for data collection and dissemination. These multi-purpose mobile devices generated more than 1.5 exabytes (billions of gigabytes) of data every month in 2013 worldwide.').

[23] *Riley*, above note 9, p 2490.
[24] Ibid.
[25] *Stanley v Georgia*, 394 US 557, 565, 89 S Ct 1243, 1248 (1969) ('Whatever may be the justifi- cations for other statutes regulating obscenity, we do not think they reach into the privacy of one's own home. If the First Amendment means anything, it means that a State has no business telling a man, sitting alone in his own house, what books he may read or what films he may watch.'). It is unclear whether the constitutional principle underlying the holding in *Stanley* is the privacy of one's home or intellectual privacy. Ibid, p 565 ('Our whole constitutional heritage rebels at the thought of giving government the power to control men's minds.').
[26] *Riley*, above note 9, p 2491.

smartphones with third parties did not undercut an individual's reasonable expectation of privacy in the data. Many apps, for example, permit developers to use the private information for commercial ends. Smartphones are becoming the key platform for targeted advertising.[27] Nonetheless, the fact that citizens share private information with third-party app and operating system developers and smartphone providers did not undercut one's reasonable expectation of privacy under the Fourth Amendment. Likewise, the fact that some of the data was stored on remote servers rather than on the smartphone itself did not undercut the expectation of privacy.[28]

3.22   In contrast to its earlier decisions,[29] the Court did not leave citizens with a Hobson's choice: do you want a smartphone (and forfeit any expectation of privacy for information divulged to others) or do you want a judicially protected expectation of privacy (which requires you to withhold the data including through the use of smartphones).[30] The Court recognized that cell phones 'are now such a pervasive and insistent part of daily life'.[31] It 'is no exaggeration', the Court said, 'that many of

---

[27] OECD, *Supporting Investment*, above note 22, p 321 (in 2011, almost 6 billion mobile subscriptions worldwide of which roughly 13% (780 million) were smartphones capable of collecting and transmitting geo-location data and that these 'mobile telephones generated approximately 600 petabytes (millions of gigabytes) of data every month in 2011'); OECD, *Exploring the Economics of Personal Data: A Survey of Methodologies for Measuring Monetary Value*, OECD Digital Economy Papers, No 220, 2 April 2013, p 14, http://dx.doi.org/10.1787/5k486qtxldmq-en.

[28] *Riley*, above note 9, p 2491 ('Cell phone users often may not know whether particular information is stored on the device or in the cloud, and it generally makes little difference.').

[29] *See, eg, Whalen v Roe*, 429 US 589, 97 S Ct 869 (1977) (patient either had to forego prescribed needed medication or have the medical information disclosed to a state agency); *Nelson*, above note 14, p 139 (to continue conducting the pure scientific research they did for decades at Jet Propulsion Laboratory, which the government owned and California Institute of Technology operated, contract employees had to subject themselves to a background check and disclose personal information or find a new job).

[30] Google, for example, relied on the *Miller* doctrine to argue that even non-Gmail users have no expectation of privacy in not having their emails scanned when communicating with Gmail users. Google recognized that the non-Gmail plaintiffs were not bound to Google's contractual terms, but 'they nonetheless impliedly consent to Google's practices by virtue of the fact that all users of email must necessarily expect that their emails will be subject to automated processing', which presumably includes scanning for behavioural advertising. *In re Google Inc Gmail Litigation*, Case No 5:13-MD-02430-LHK (US Dist Ct (ND Cal), 13 June 2013), Google's Motion to Dismiss Complaint, Memorandum of Points & Authorities, p 19, http://www.consumerwatchdog.org/resources/googlemotion061313.pdf. Moreover, Google argued that the fact that some continued to email Gmail users—despite knowing of Google's automated scanning (as confirmed in their complaints)—showed 'that Google's automated scanning was completely immaterial to these Plaintiffs' decisions to communicate with Gmail users and suggests that they were aware of Google's automated scanning all along'. Ibid, p 20. The Court rejected Google's argument that all Gmail users had consented to the alleged interceptions based on Google's Terms of Service and Privacy Policy, which 'did not provide sufficient disclosures to conclude that Gmail users had consented to the alleged interceptions'. The Court also rejected Google's contention 'that all email users, regardless of whether they had viewed any disclosures, had impliedly consented to the alleged interceptions, because all email users, including non-Gmail users, understand that such interceptions are part of how emails are transmitted'. *In re Google Inc Gmail Litigation*, 2014 WL 1102660 *9 (US Dist Ct (ND Cal), 18 March 2014).

[31] *Riley*, above note 9, p 2484.

the more than 90% of American adults who own a cell phone keep on their person a digital record of nearly every aspect of their lives—from the mundane to the intimate'.[32] Nowhere in *Riley* did the Court suggest that individuals should willingly sacrifice their expectations of privacy in order to benefit from their phones' many technological benefits: 'With all they contain and all they may reveal, they hold for many Americans the privacies of life.'[33]

Riley shows how Big Data and privacy interests intersect. The volume and variety of data on a smartphone invariably raise multiple privacy interests, including associational privacy (in our choices of the persons, groups, or causes with which we wish to associate), physical privacy (in not having our movements tracked), informational privacy (in choosing with whom we wish to disclose our personal information), decisional privacy (in not having the government intrude in our personal decisions), and intellectual privacy (namely, the freedom to explore topics and issues without governmental monitoring). The Court implicitly recognized that personal information in the age of Big Data will invariably be shared with others. That by itself does not forfeit our privacy interests. **3.23**

Riley also resurrects the importance of our control over our information. Yes, Apple may track my smartphone's location (to enable me quickly to locate it). But this should not mean the government can search without a warrant my iPhone for this data. With the rise of the Internet of Things and Big Data, there will be few facts, if any, that will not, at one time or another, be divulged to another. Thus an important aspect of privacy will be our right to control to whom and for what purpose the data is divulged. **3.24**

Finally, the Court recognized the distinction between scattered disclosure of bits of information to the public and the electronic compilation of data. A few taps on one's phone reveal information that 30 years ago would have been far too costly or time-consuming to obtain. The police could never track your movements as efficiently as your smartphone can. Freed from the cost of buying and developing film, we take far more pictures that reveal our preferences and behaviour. And the very fact that smartphones collect and store so much data (including things that we may not ever use, such as our movements or search history) and that there are over a million apps, many of which are free or for a nominal fee, reflects what we give up in exchange (our personal data) is valuable. The next chapter addresses the rise of data-driven business models and the strategic implications of Big Data. It examines why companies invest so heavily to develop apps to access our data, and spend money to maintain, index, and analyse the increasing volume of data. **3.25**

---

[32] Ibid, p 2490.
[33] Ibid, pp 2494–5 (internal quotation omitted).

4

THE COMPETITIVE SIGNIFICANCE
OF BIG DATA

4.01 Big Data and the rise of data-driven business models have been for several years a hot topic in the business literature. Several years ago, a *McKinsey Quarterly* article asked, 'Are you ready for the era of "big data"?'[1] A *Harvard Business Review* article discussed how Big Data has the potential to transform traditional businesses: it 'may offer them even greater opportunities for competitive advantage (online businesses have always known that they were competing on how well they understood their data)'.[2] This chapter highlights six themes from the business literature regarding the strategic implications of Big Data. It then responds to two claims that downplay Big Data's competitive significance: first, the claim, without empirical support, that data is ubiquitous, low cost, and widely available, and second, that data is non-rivalrous, and therefore collecting a particular piece of data does not prevent others from collecting the same data by similar or other means. This claim, we discuss, conflates two distinct concepts: it conflates data's functionality with its value and it conflates non-rival, non-subtractable goods with non-excludable goods. To illustrate data's competitive significance, we review one lawsuit over the Twitter 'Firehose'.

A. Six Themes from the Business Literature Regarding the Strategic Implications of Big Data

4.02 One theme, from the business surveys, is that Big Data 'is now mainstream, and even the most cautious firms have adopted a Big Data strategy of some form'.[3] Only

---

[1] Brad Brown et al, 'Are You Ready for the Era of "Big Data"?', *McKinsey Quarterly*, October 2011, http://www.mckinsey.com/insights/strategy/are_you_ready_for_the_era_of_big_data.

[2] Andrew McAfee and Erik Brynjolfsson, 'Big Data: The Management Revolution', *Harvard Business Review*, October 2012, p 62, https://hbr.org/2012/10/big-data-the-management-revolution/ar/1.

[3] NewVantage Partners LLC, 'Big Data Executive Survey 2016: An Update on the Adoption of Big Data in the Fortune 1000: Executive Summary' (2016), p 2, http://newvantage.com/

5.4 per cent of firms, in one 2016 survey, reported that they did not have any Big Data initiatives planned or underway.[4] Big Data is on many senior executives' minds. One survey of two marketers from B2B and B2C organizations in the UK and Europe found that 83 per cent of marketers have decided already to invest in Big Data, 'because of the granular and detailed understanding it gives them about their consumers'.[5]

Second, companies are increasingly adopting business models that rely on personal **4.03** data as a key input.[6] Data-driven business models, for example, often involve multi-sided platforms. Companies offer consumers free services with the aim of acquiring valuable personal data to assist advertisers to better target them with behavioural ads. As several European Commission officials observed,

> In the digital economy, large sets of data (so-called 'big data') are becoming increasingly valuable as they reveal patterns of information that enable companies to understand user behaviour and preferences and improve (or target) their products and services accordingly. This makes the availability of 'big data' a significant competitive advantage for companies active in, for instance, targeted online advertising, online search, social networking services and software products.[7]

---

wp-content/uploads/2016/01/Big-Data-Executive-Survey-2016-Findings-FINAL.pdf (survey of 44 firms listed among the Fortune 1000).

[4] Ibid, p 5.

[5] Amy Gravelle, 'Can Big Data Turn Today's Marketers Into Tomorrow's Data-Empowered CEOs?', *Marketing Magazine*, 24 February 2014, http://www.marketingmagazine.co.uk/article/1282025/big-data-turn-todays-marketers-tomorrows-data-empowered-ceos; dnx, 'When Will Marketing Be Promoted to the Boardroom? The Reality of Big Data's Promise' conducted by Circle Research, 21 March 2014, reprinted as 'eMarketer Roundup: Using Big Data to Power Marketing Performance eMarketer', April 2014, http://www.quantita.pe/documentos/eMarketer_Roundup_Using_Big_Data_to_Power_Marketing_Performance.pdf (survey of marketing professionals in Europe in January 2014 about the ways marketing departments use big data, 30% identified 'Store multichannel information' (eg, sales, website, mobile, social media data, etc.), 29% said to segment customers (discover new micromarkets), 29% said to determine marketing strategy, 23% said to analyse buying behaviour patterns, 23% said to justify marketing strategy, 21% said to develop personalized communications or individual customers, 15% said to predict future trends, 13% said to develop personalized offers for individual customers, 12% said to respond to customer requests and/or complaints in real time (eg, on social media), 8% said to collaborate with other organizations (eg, share data), 4% said to set price points, 2% said to sell lists of data to generate revenue, Other—4%, and None of these—2%).

[6] OECD, *Data-Driven Innovation for Growth and Well-Being: Interim Synthesis Report*, October 2014, p 11, http://www.oecd.org/sti/inno/data-driven-innovation-interim-synthesis.pdf (noting one estimate that 'big data technology and services' will grow from USD 3 billion in 2010 to USD 17 billion in 2015, which represents a compound annual growth rate of almost 40%) and p 18 ('while in 2012 58% of businesses indicated that they were deploying or planning "big data" projects, in 2013 it was already 64% of businesses'); OECD, *Exploring the Economics of Personal Data: A Survey of Methodologies for Measuring Monetary Value*, OECD Digital Economy Papers, No 220 (2013), p 7, http://dx.doi.org/10.1787/5k486qtxldmq-en (noting in 2013 how such models are 'increasingly common'); Lisa Kimmel and Janis Kestenbaum, 'What's Up with WhatsApp?: A Transatlantic View on Privacy and Merger Enforcement in Digital Markets', 29(1) *Antitrust* (Fall 2014): pp 48–55.

[7] Eleonora Ocello, Cristina Sjödin, and Anatoly Suboĉs, 'What's Up with Merger Control in the Digital Sector? Lessons from the Facebook/WhatsApp EU Merger Case', 1 *Competition Merger Brief* (February 2015): p 6.

4.04 Facebook, for example, makes its money by advertisement revenue.[8] It collects information and processes content 'shared by its users'.[9] It provides some information to marketers who can target Facebook users with ad campaigns.[10] Marketers can 'specify the types of users they want to reach based on information that users choose to share'.[11] As the European Data Protection Supervisor found, '[t]hrough the supply of payment-free services, these companies compete for the attention and loyalty of individuals whose use of those services will generate personal data with a high commercial value.'[12]

4.05 These data-driven business models can be procompetitive, yielding innovations that benefit both consumers and the company. Collecting and analysing data can provide the company with insights on how to use resources more efficiently and to outmanoeuvre dominant incumbents.[13] The European Commission noted in 2015 that 'the use of big data by the top 100 EU manufacturers could lead to savings worth €425 billion', and that, 'by 2020, big data analytics could boost EU economic growth by an additional 1.9%, equalling a GDP increase of €206 billion'.[14]

4.06 Third, companies, with data-driven business models, are increasingly undertaking strategies to obtain and sustain a competitive advantage. Companies strive to acquire a 'big data-advantage'[15] over rivals. Big Data, one 2014 survey found, is playing 'a pivotal role in the strategic decision-making of an organization: 69% of marketers from the sample were 'already using it to shape their overall operational and commercial approach' and 90% 'felt that failing to put it at the heart of a business strategy will lead to competitive disadvantages'.[16]

4.07 Data will increasingly drive many companies' operations—everything from hiring employees to evaluating their performance. As Google noted,

> Data is central to everything we do—even when we choose a paint color for a conference room wall or plan a lunch menu. Laszlo Bock, SVP of People Operations,

---

[8] *In re Hulu Privacy Litigation*, 86 F Supp 3d 1090, 1093 (US Dist Ct (ND Cal), 2015).

[9] Ibid.

[10] Ibid.

[11] Ibid.

[12] Preliminary Opinion of the European Data Protection Supervisor, *Privacy and Competitiveness in the Age of Big Data: The Interplay Between Data Protection, Competition Law, and Consumer Protection in the Digital Economy*, 26 March 2014, p 10, https://secure.edps.europa.eu/EDPSWEB/webdav/shared/Documents/Consultation/Opinions/2014/14-03-26_competitition_law_big_data_EN.pdf.

[13] OECD, *Data-Driven Innovation*, above note 6, p 16.

[14] European Commission, *Why We Need A Digital Single Market*, Fact Sheet, http://ec.europa.eu/priorities/digital-single-market/docs/dsm-factsheet_en.pdf.

[15] McKinsey Global Institute, *Big Data: The Next Frontier for Innovation, Competition, and Productivity*, June 2011, p 6 ('McKinsey Report'), http://www.mckinsey.com/insights/business_technology/big_data_the_next_frontier_for_innovation.

[16] Gravelle, above note 5; *see also* NewVantage Partners, above note 3, p 4 (survey finding that 'the ability to develop greater insights into their business and customers (37.0%) as the single biggest driver of Big Data investment...closely followed by advantages gained from speed faster time to answer, faster time to decision, and faster speed to market (29.7%)').

and David Radcliffe, VP of Real Estate and Workplace Services, explain our data-centric approach to creating work environments that help Googlers live longer, healthier and more productive lives.[17]

Google, for example, studies the effect that certain greetings to new employees have on their productivity nine months later.[18] Google even uses data to lay out the workplace in ways that promote even casual collisions among engineers or creative people to foster innovation.[19]

The management consulting firm McKinsey and Company observed that '[t]he **4.08** use of big data is becoming a key way for leading companies to outperform their peers' and in one example, estimated that a retailer embracing Big Data 'has the potential to increase its operating margin by more than 60 percent.'[20] McKinsey found from its survey that firms were securing significant returns from their Big Data investments:

> The average initial increase in profits from big data investments was 6 percent for the companies [McKinsey] studied. That increased to 9 percent for investments spanning five years, since the companies that made them presumably benefited from the greater diffusion of data analytics over that period. Looked at from another vantage point, big data investments amounted to 0.6 percent of corporate revenues and returned a multiple of 1.4 times that level of investment, increasing to 2.0 times over five years. That's not only in the range of the 1.1 to 1.9 multiples observed in the computer-investment cycle of the '80s but also exceeds the multiples others have identified for R&D and marketing expenditures.[21]

Likewise, one Massachusetts Institute of Technology (MIT)-led study showed that the more companies characterized themselves as data-driven, the better they performed on objective measures of financial and operational results: '[C]ompanies in the top third of their industry in the use of data-driven decision making were, on average, 5% more productive and 6% more profitable than their competitors.'[22]

---

[17] Google, 'Google Careers: The Proof is in the Perks', http://www.google.com/about/careers/lifeatgoogle/proof-in-the-perks.html.
[18] 'Inside Google Workplaces, From Perks to Nap Pods', CBS News, 22 January 2013, http://www.cbsnews.com/news/inside-google-workplaces-from-perks-to-nap-pods/ (quoting Google executive, 'When an employee starts on their first day, we have data that says, if the manager shows up and says, "Hi nice to meet you, you're on my team, we're gonna be working together", and does a few other things, those people end up 15 per cent more productive in nine months.')
[19] Google, 'The Proof is in the Perks', above note 17.
[20] McKinsey Report, above note 15, p 6.
[21] Jacques Bughin, 'Big Data: Getting A Better Read On Performance', *McKinsey Quarterly*, February 2016, p 2 (random sample of 714 companies).
[22] *See* McAfee and Brynjolfsson, above note 2, pp 60, 64.

4.09 Thus the acquisition and use of Big Data, McKinsey notes, 'will become a key basis of competition for existing companies, and will create new competitors who are able to attract employees that have the critical skills for a Big Data world'.[23] And as McKinsey predicted, '[i]n a big data world, a competitor that fails to sufficiently develop its capabilities will be left behind'.[24]

4.10 Fourth, given that data's value depends on its volume, variety, and how quickly the data is collected and analysed, companies will increasingly focus on opportunities to acquire a data-advantage through mergers.[25] According to one estimate, Big-Data related mergers doubled between 2008 and 2013—from 55 to 134.[26] Chapter 7 explores several data-driven mergers, such as Google/Waze.

4.11 Fifth, as data-driven mergers increase, one might expect—as in the TomTom/Tele Atlas merger[27] and Microsoft/Yahoo! joint venture—the merging parties to raise data-driven efficiencies.[28]

4.12 Sixth, businesses—to obtain or maintain their competitive advantage—will have strong incentives to limit their competitors' access to these datasets, prevent others from sharing the datasets, and will likely be adverse to data-portability policies that threaten their data-related competitive advantage.[29] Companies will battle over who gets the valuable consumer data. For example, the *Financial*

---

[23] McKinsey Report, above note 15, p 13; *see also* ibid, p 23 ('Companies including Tesco, Amazon, Wal-Mart, Harrah's, Progressive Insurance, and Capital One, and Smart, a wireless player in the Philippines, have already wielded the use of big data as a competitive weapon—as have entire economies.'); Ocello et al, above note 7 (noting how 'data can be relevant in competition law cases as an "asset" ie a competitive advantage enjoyed by the merged entity post-transaction').

[24] McKinsey Report, above note 15, p 6; *see also* ibid, p 111 ('The use of big data will become a key basis of competition across sectors, so it is imperative that organizational leaders begin to incorporate big data into their business plans.').

[25] OECD, *Data-Driven Innovation*, above note 6, pp 11–13; Chris Ciaccia, 2013 Tech Predictions: A Ciaccia Look Back, TheStreet.com, 4 December 2013 (noting a 'slew of data-driven mergers' in 2013 and predicting that there 'are plenty more to come in 2014 and beyond, as companies continue to make sense of what the data actually means').

[26] European Data Protection Supervisor, 'Report of Workshop on Privacy, Consumers, Competition and Big Data', 11 July 2014, p 1 ('EDPS Workshop Report'), https://secure.edps. europa.eu/EDPSWEB/webdav/site/mySite/shared/Documents/Consultation/Big%20data/14-07-11_EDPS_Report_Workshop_Big_data_EN.pdf.

[27] *TomTom/Tele Atlas* (Case Comp/M.4854), Commission Decision C(2008) 1859 [2008] OJ C 237/53, pp 53–4, paras 245–50.

[28] US Department of Justice, 'Statement of the Department of Justice Antitrust Division on its Decision to Close Its Investigation of the Internet Search and Paid Search Advertising Agreement Between Microsoft Corporation and Yahoo! Inc', Press Release, 18 February 2010, http://www. justice.gov/opa/pr/statement-department-justice-antitrust-division-its-decision-close-its-investigation-internet; *Microsoft/Yahoo! Search Business* (Case Comp/M.5727), Commission Decision C(2010) 1077 [2010] OJ C 020/08.

[29] OECD, *Data-Driven Innovation*, above note 6, pp 6 and 42 ('Given these significant costs, creators and controllers of data do not necessarily have the incentives to share their data.'); McKinsey Report, above note 15, p 12.

Times in 2011 pulled its iPad and iPhone apps from Apple's App Store.[30] The battle was over who would control the subscription data. Apple wanted to own the valuable data about *Financial Times* subscribers. As *Reuters* reported, 'to reduce its dependence on Apple and develop apps more quickly for rival tablet computers, the FT in June launched a Web-based version of its mobile app, the first of its kind by a major publisher'.[31] Because 'the collection and analysis of consumer data is key to developing an accurate understanding of how to recruit and retain customers', the UK competition authority found in its 2015 fact-finding project, '[i]n some sectors it can be a key competitive asset in targeting offers.'[32] Chapter 18 explores several anticompetitive strategies to prevent rivals from accessing data, such as through exclusivity provisions with third-party providers or foreclosing rivals' opportunities to procure similar data by making it harder for consumers to switch to other apps, technologies, or platforms. Firms, especially dominant ones, will be tempted to break the law or liberally interpret the law to acquire and analyse data from individuals, and to prevent others including individuals, to access this data.

Thus, data, the OECD observed, can be a key competitive input: 'Big data now **4.13** represents a core economic asset that can create significant competitive advantage for firms and drive innovation and growth.'[33] Indeed, in bankruptcies, a company's data on its customers and their shopping habits can be valuable. When Toysmart. com proposed selling its customer data in its 2000 bankruptcy auction, for example, the personal data reportedly was the online toy store's most valuable asset.[34] The Federal Trade Commission (FTC) blocked the sale of the personal data except if sold to a qualifying buyer in the same family commerce market, who adheres to Toysmart.com's privacy policy, and agrees to seek the customer's affirmative consent

---

[30] 'Financial Times Pulls Its Apps From Apple Store', Reuters, 31 August 2011, http://www. reuters.com/article/2011/08/31/us-apple-ft-idUSTRE77U1O020110831.

[31] Ibid.

[32] UK Competition and Markets Authority, *The Commercial Use of Consumer Data: Report on the CMA's Call for Information*, CMA 38, June 2015, para 2.88, https://www.gov.uk/government/uploads/system/uploads/attachment_data/file/435817/The_commercial_use_of_consumer_data. pdf.

[33] OECD, *Supporting Investment in Knowledge Capital, Growth and Innovation*, 10 October 2013, p 319, http://www.oecd-ilibrary.org/industry-and-services/supporting-investment-in-knowledge-capital-growth-and-innovation_9789264193307-en; *see also* OECD, *Data-Driven Innovation*, above note 6, p 10 (observing how business models reveal that 'Internet firms share one major commonality besides relying on the Internet as the backbone of their business operation, namely the use of large streams of data that is now commonly referred to as "big data" '); OECD, *Exploring the Economics of Personal Data*, above note 6, p 4 (observing in 2013 how '[f]irms are now able to attain significant market valuations by employing business models predicated on the successful use of personal data within the existing legal and regulatory frameworks').

[34] Joshua Brustein, 'RadioShack's Bankruptcy Could Give Your Customer Data to the Highest Bidder', Bloomberg Business, 24 March 2015, http://www.bloomberg.com/news/articles/2015-03-24/radioshack-s-bankruptcy-could-give-your-customer-data-to-the-highest-bidder.

before changing its privacy policy for data gathered under the Toysmart.com policy.[35] The issue also arose in RadioShack's bankruptcy, with the FTC cautioning RadioShack about selling the personal data of its 117 million customers:

> We understand that RadioShack's customer information constitutes a potentially valuable asset. We are concerned, however, that a sale or transfer of the personal information of RadioShack's customers would contravene RadioShack's express promise not to sell or rent such information and could constitute a deceptive or unfair practice under Section 5 of the FTC Act.[36]

Consequently, the competition authorities must understand both the competitive benefits and risks of these data-driven strategies.

B. Responding to Claims of Big Data's Insignificance for Competition Policy

4.14   To downplay the competitive significance of Big Data, some claim, without empirical support, that data 'is ubiquitous, low cost, and widely available'.[37] If this were true, then one would not expect companies to incur costs—much less offer 'free' products such as social networks, search engines, browsers, maps, and email. Rather than incur additional costs to procure data, companies simply would harvest the publicly available data. This is not the case.

4.15   Facebook, for example, offers, and incurs the cost for, social networking services to secure users' data and provide a platform to target them with behavioural advertising.[38] Facebook, the European Commission noted, does not sell its user data or offer data analytics services to advertisers or other third parties as standalone products separate from the advertising space itself.[39] Google limits access to its map data and the data it collects from its map users. That data is not cheap or easy to acquire. In 2015, Uber, for example, reportedly offered Nokia several billion dollars to acquire its mapping business, called 'Here'. As one analyst commenting on the offer said, '[i]t's extraordinarily difficult to get this type of

---

[35] *FTC v Toysmart.Com, LLC*, Civil Action No 00-11341-RGS (D Mass, 21 July 2000), Stipulated Consent Agreement and Final Order, https://www.ftc.gov/sites/default/files/documents/cases/toysmartconsent.htm.

[36] Letter from Jessica L Rich, Office of the Director, Bureau of Consumer Protection, Federal Trade Commission to Elise Frejka, Esq, 16 May 2015, https://www.ftc.gov/system/files/documents/public_statements/643291/150518radioshackletter.pdf; *see also* Brustein, above note 34.

[37] Darren S Tucker and Hill B Wellford, 'Big Mistakes Regarding Big Data', *Antitrust Source*, December 2014, p 7, http://www.americanbar.org/content/dam/aba/publishing/antitrust_source/dec14_tucker_12_16f.authcheckdam.pdf.

[38] *Facebook/WhatsApp* (Case Comp/M.7217), Commission Decision C(2014) 7239 final, 3 October 2014, para 70.

[39] Ibid.

mapping data....Other than Google, Here is one of the few companies that can offer this data right now'.[40]

There is also a difference between the price to obtain data and the data's value to the firm.[41] For example, suppose you agree to divulge your email address and some other information to get 20 minutes of Internet service at the airport. We can infer several things. First, the value of the personal data likely exceeds the Internet service provider's cost in providing 20 minutes of Internet service (otherwise why provide the service?). Second, the Internet service provider could not obtain the same data as quickly from other sources at a lower cost (otherwise why request the data?). Third, consumers may be unwilling to sell this data to others at the same price. The value the customer places on this information depends on the context, including her trust in the Internet service provider, her need for Internet service at the airport, and her other options. **4.16**

Thus, as the OECD found, 'the market price for a record sold to one customer does not reflect the full monetary value of the underlying data but rather provides an indication of the market clearing price that individual customers pay for a copy of the data'.[42] A piece of data by itself may be cheaply acquired, but when coupled with the company's other personal data, its value can increase significantly.[43] Moreover datasets are often 'dirty' with mistakes and errors. Firms can create value by 'cleansing' large datasets so that they can be analysed and the findings deployed. The value does not come solely from the data. As we will see in Chapters 11–14 on data-driven network effects, Big Data's value also comes from Big Analytics, including algorithms that learn by trial-and-error. Thus repeated interactions with customers provide not only data but the opportunity to learn from consumer responses. **4.17**

As the OECD observed, data's value is not absolute, but relative to how much other data the company has, and the intended use of the data: **4.18**

> The monetary, economic and social value of personal data is likely to be governed by non-linear, increasing returns to scale. The value of an individual record, alone,

---

[40] Mark Scott and Mike Isaac, 'Uber May Drop Google Maps, Buy Nokia's Here Mapping Business', *Financial Review*, 8 May 2015, http://www.afr.com/technology/apps/uber-may-drop-google-maps-buy-nokias-here-mapping-business-20150508-ggwvlt.

[41] OECD, *Data-Driven Innovation*, above note 6, p 26 (noting how data value and quality typically depend on the intended use: 'Data that is of good quality for certain applications can thus be of poor quality for other applications.').

[42] OECD, *Exploring the Economics of Personal Data*, above note 6, p 27.

[43] Ibid:

> The price at which data is exchanged in an open market relates only to a specific context. The monetary value of a phone number, in and of itself, may be relatively low as a standalone item. However, when that phone number is tied with an income level and a set of particular interests, the monetary value of the phone number would likely increase for some market participants. So prices observed in the market need to be considered in context.

may be very low but the value and usability of the record increases as the number of records to compare it with increases. These network effects have implications for policy because the value of the same record in a large database could be much more efficiently leveraged than the same record in a much smaller data set. This could have implications for competition and for other key policy items such as the portability of data.[44]

4.19   So policymakers cannot assume that data is inherently valuable or cheap. Data's value will depend on its context. Even a basic issue, namely how to objectively value data, remains unsettled. The current methodologies, the OECD found, all have shortcomings.[45] The market prices for some personal data vary, ranging in the US, for example, in 2013 between 50 cents for a street address to USD 35 for a military record.[46] Consequently, if, as the OECD concluded, 'no single, perfect measure of value of personal data' currently exists,[47] one cannot say that data is generally inexpensive.

4.20   Some argue that data is non-rivalrous, and therefore collecting a particular piece of data does not prevent others from collecting identical data by similar or other means.[48] This claim conflates two distinct concepts: it conflates data's functionality with its value and it conflates non-rival, non-subtractable goods with non-excludable goods.

4.21   Some data can be non-rivalrous, which means that 'the use of the data by one person does not diminish the stock of the good; the same record can be sold many times to many customers, and the same record can be used multiple times by the same customer'.[49] Electronic data can be easily copied; if publicly accessible, others could simultaneously use the same data.

4.22   But the fact that data can be easily copied does not mean that data retains its value. One example is your credit card number. A stolen credit card number is more valuable to the first thief than to later thieves, as by then the credit card company will likely be aware of the theft. The data persists but has little, if any, value. Likewise, the first few people would likely benefit financially in trading on insider information. The information's value diminishes as others learn of it, and as the stock's price adjusts.

4.23   Even if *all* personal data were non-rivalrous (ie, 'one person consuming them does not stop another person consuming them'), and the data's use by some

---

[44] Ibid, p 34; EDPS Workshop Report, above note 26, p 1 (noting how Internet companies 'could enjoy "economies of scope", network effects of 'more data attracting more users attracting more data, culminating in winner-takes-all markets and near monopolies which enjoy increasing returns of scale due to the absolute "permanence" of their digital assets').
[45] OECD, *Exploring the Economics of Personal Data*, above note 6, p 4.
[46] Ibid.
[47] Ibid, p 19.
[48] Tucker and Wellford, above note 37, p 3.
[49] OECD, *Exploring the Economics of Personal Data*, above note 6, p 25.

does not devalue it for others, it does not logically follow that *all* data is non-excludable (ie, 'if one person can consume them, it is impossible to stop another person consuming them').[50] If data were both non-rivalrous and non-excludable, then data, by definition, would be a public good, like public parks, public radio, and public sewer systems. Companies, like Facebook, would not invest in its social network if any rival could easily capture the underlying data. The problem with public goods is that, by definition, the 'combination of non-rivalry and non-excludability means that it can be hard to get people to pay to consume them, so they might not be provided at all if left to market forces'.[51] That is not the case with data-driven business models. Companies incur significant costs to collect and store data precisely because data is excludable. Indeed, being the first to access and process the data can yield a significant competitive advantage. As the OECD found,

> Computerised information (software, databases) that is readily available in markets is easily replicable. However, the data on customers and product sales that firms gather for marketing and new product development are protected as a valuable corporate secret. Exploiting these data also requires investments in new capabilities and organisational change and therefore takes time. The data will therefore not be replicable until the technology and skill needed to capture and analyse such data become generic.[52]

Some argue that the value is not from the data itself, but the algorithms that pro- **4.24**
cess the data. But if this were true, noted Lukas Biewald, co-founder and CEO of CrowdFlower, the big tech players IBM, Facebook, Google, and Microsoft wouldn't open-source some of their algorithms 'without worrying too much about giving away any secrets'.[53] As he noted, 'it's because the actual secret sauce isn't the algorithm, it's the data. Just think about Google. They can release TensorFlow without a worry that someone else will come along and create a better search engine because there are over a trillion searches on Google each year.'[54] The algorithms learn, Biewald observes, from the data humans create. The more data, the more opportunities to experiment, the more the algorithms can learn.

In some industries, the algorithms are proprietary, with firms spending money **4.25**
to refine them. But as we will see in Chapters 12 and 14, Big Data helps train

---

[50] 'Economics A–Z', *The Economist*, http://www.economist.com/economics-a-to-z/p#node-21529442.

[51] Ibid.

[52] OECD, *Supporting Investment*, above note 33, p 232.

[53] Daniel Gutierrez, *Human-in-the-Loop is the Future of Machine Learning*, insideBIGDATA, 11 January 2016, http://insidebigdata.com/2016/01/11/human-in-the-loop-is-the-future-of-machine-learning/.

[54] Ibid.

the proprietary algorithm to learn, such as recognizing a particular person's face, or identifying relevant information for a search query. For example, Facebook has access to a large database that others lack—namely a photograph library of 4.4 million labelled faces. Its proprietary algorithm, DeepFace, through trial-and-error, can significantly outperform rival algorithms with smaller datasets.[55] Likewise, as we will see, Google's search engine algorithms, through a greater volume of search queries, have an advantage over the smaller search engines' algorithms, such as Bing's.

4.26 Thus, data's competitive significance (and value) arise in part from the ability of firms to exclude others from access and analysing it as quickly. Google's competitors, for example, cannot immediately scan the contents of emails sent between Gmail users, and thereby quickly update user profiles and target them with behavioural advertisements;[56] nor would competitors have instantaneous access to the search inquiries on Google. Rival mapping companies cannot immediately access and process the data that Waze collects from its users. Indeed, as we will see in Chapter 6, Waze turned to community-sourcing for its mapping data precisely because replicating Google's mapping data would have been too costly.

C. If Data is Non-Excludable, Why are Firms Seeking to Preclude Third Parties from Getting Access to Data?

4.27 The issue of exclusionary behaviour arose in an industry-proposed do-not-track standard.[57] The FTC asked industry participants to craft a new 'Do Not Track' policy for online data, similar to the 'Do Not Call' registry that helped reduce the nuisance of telemarketers telephoning individual homes. But what started as a group effort by technology companies and privacy experts to craft a new type of consumer protection quietly morphed into a committee where a few powerful Internet firms were deciding on the rules of the game. The World-Wide-Web

---

[55] John Bohannon, 'Unmasked: Facial recognition software could soon ID you in any photo', 347 *Science* (20 January 2015): pp 492, 493.

[56] Public Citizen, *Mission Creep-y: Google Is Quietly Becoming One of the Nation's Most Powerful Political Forces While Expanding Its Information-Collection Empire*, November 2014, p 17, https://www.citizen.org/documents/Google-Political-Spending-Mission-Creepy.pdf (noting how 'Gmail gave Google a new source of ad-based revenue. From the time Gmail was launched on April 1, 2004, it was tracking the content of e-mail messages in order to deliver relevant ads to its users.'); *In re Google Inc Gmail Litigation*, Case No 5:13-MD-02430-LHK (US Dist Ct (ND Cal) 13 June 2013), Google's Motion to Dismiss Complaint, Memorandum of Points & Authorities, p 3 (acknowledging that Google's automated systems scan email content to display advertisements targeted to email content and the 'revenues from these advertisements enable Google to provide the Gmail service for free to the public').

[57] Allen Grunes, 'Tracking Not Allowed (Unless You're Google)', *Politico*, 1 October 2015, http://www.politico.com/agenda/story/2015/10/tracking-not-allowed-unless-youre-google-000261.

Consortium, under the influence of dominant players, such as Google, Yahoo!, Facebook, and Comcast, proposed in July 2015 a 'Do Not Track' standard that distinguishes between first and third parties. Basically, when individuals are on the platform's own apps and websites, the platforms can continue to track them and collect data on them, but 'third parties' like the smaller apps cannot. So, when a user activates the 'Do Not Track' signal, if he or she enters a query into the Google search engine, signs onto Gmail, or uses Google Chrome or Android, he or she will still be allowing Google to gather information and use it to deliver targeted ads. The proposed 'Do Not Track' standard does not really prevent tracking. Instead, the proposed standard would mainly limit the ability of potential rivals to collect comparable data. The European governmental advisory group on privacy also expressed concern that the proposed specification was inadequate under the European legal framework.[58]

Consequently, one should be sceptical of claims that data are ubiquitous, low cost, **4.28** and widely available. If personal data were as freely available as sunshine, companies would not spend a considerable amount of money offering free services to acquire and analyse data to maintain a data-related competitive advantage. Firms would not pay significant amounts for consumer data in bankruptcy proceedings. Companies would not acquire firms primarily for the data. Nor would some companies take huge risks, including breaking the law, to get (and prevent others from accessing) consumer data.

D. The Twitter Firehose

To illustrate Big Data's competitive significance, let us consider the 2013 legal **4.29** dispute between PeopleBrowsr and Twitter.[59] Twitter, of course, enables users to post 'tweets' of 140 characters or less. Operating in a 'Twitter Big Data Analytics' market, PeopleBrowsr used 'data mining techniques to derive insights from the flow of information generated on Twitter'.[60] PeopleBrowsr paid Twitter over USD 1 million annually to access every tweet posted on Twitter, ie, the Twitter 'Firehose'.[61]

---

[58] Article 29 Data Protection Working Party, 'Comments in Response to W3C's Public Consultation on the W3C Last Call Working Draft, 14 July 2015, Tracking Compliance and Scope', 1 October 2015, https://lists.w3.org/Archives/Public/public-tracking-comments/2015Oct/att-0003/20151001_Ares_2015_4048580_W3C_compliance.pdf (noting that data controllers bound by the EU legal framework must require the individual's consent for collecting the information, and must 'regardless of whether they are a first party or a third party...require unambiguous consent for the processing of personal data including for the purposes of online behavioral advertising').

[59] *PeopleBrowsr, Inc v Twitter, Inc*, Case No C-12-6120 EMC, 2013 WL 843032, p *1 (US Dist Ct (ND Cal), 6 March 2013).

[60] Ibid.

[61] Ibid.

Specifically Twitter provided PeopleBrowsr 'an application programming interface ("API") that gave PeopleBrowsr a streaming data feed of all of the public Tweets posted daily by Twitter users'.[62] PeopleBrowsr analysed the tweets 'to sell information to its clients, such as insight regarding consumer reactions to products and services as well as identification of the Twitter users who have the most influence in certain locations or communities'.[63] PeopleBrowsr alleged that its product depended on accessing the tweets through the Twitter Firehose, and that it 'invested millions of dollars and years of work in building its business based on access to the Firehose in reliance on Twitter's representations that it would maintain an "open ecosystem" for the use of its data'.[64] So when Twitter sought to cut off PeopleBrowsr's direct access to the Twitter Firehose, PeopleBrowsr sued. Among its state law claims, PeopleBrowsr sued Twitter for violating California's Unfair Competition Law.[65] The litigants eventually settled, with Twitter allowing PeopleBrowsr to continue accessing the tweets until the end of 2013, and obtain the tweets thereafter through an authorized reseller.[66]

4.30　Whatever the merits of PeopleBrowsr's legal claims, the case reflects the value of quickly accessing on average over 340 million public tweets per day. First the data had value. PeopleBrowser after all paid over a million dollars annually for it. But the value was not the tweet itself, which is publicly available. The value came from the velocity in processing the volume and variety of tweets. PeopleBrowsr would not have paid Twitter a million dollars if it simply could have copied the data off Twitter's website. Moreover, the data was not valuable only to PeopleBrowsr. It was valuable to PeopleBrowsr's clients and competitors. Importantly here, Twitter disclaimed any notion that the Twitter Firehose was somehow a public good:

> PeopleBrowsr's complaint asks the Court to prevent Twitter from controlling its own ability to contract for access to its own Firehose. If ever allowed, claims like those asserted here would destroy the incentives of companies to innovate and compete, fearing that they will have to share their property with every free rider that comes along. For precisely this reason, PeopleBrowsr's claims also run contrary to the caselaw analyzing claims that effectively limit the ability of firms to develop and control the future of their own platforms.... Twitter must be permitted to develop

[62] *PeopleBrowsr, Inc v Twitter, Inc*, Case No C-12-6120 EMC, 2012 WL 7070542 (US Dist Ct (ND Cal), 27 December 2012), Defendant Twitter, Inc's Notice of Motion and Motion to Dismiss Plaintiffs' Complaint.

[63] *PeopleBrowsr*, above note 59, p *1.

[64] Ibid.

[65] Ibid. Twitter unsuccessfully sought to remove the case to federal court on the grounds that PeopleBrowsr's unfair competition law claims were based on section 2 of the Sherman Act, over which federal courts have exclusive jurisdiction. The federal district court remanded the case to state court, since a violation of the state unfair competition law does not necessarily require establishing a Sherman Act violation.

[66] Ryan Tate, 'Twitter Settles High-Profile Legal Fight Over Data Access', *Wired*, 25 April 2013, http://www.wired.com/2013/04/twitter-settles-with-peoplebrowsr/.

and control the future of its own platform relationships, or the growth and vitality of this aspect of Twitter's business is put directly at stake.[67]

Twitter noted that the amount of data potentially available to PeopleBrowsr and other data analysis firms was 'vast, including other data providers like Google, Facebook, and others'.[68] But to underscore the excludability of this data, Twitter noted that Peoplebrowsr was 'suing to protect its own monopoly', namely as the only outside firm with full access to the Twitter Firehose.[69]

Firms whose business models are built on securing a data-advantage understand **4.31** the need for the exclusivity of particular data streams (or accessing and exploiting the data more quickly than their rivals). Such actions ensure that independent data sources are not available to competitors through licensing, purchase, or collection. A reality check would be to ask the companies with data-driven business models if they would have any qualms if they were required to give their data to competitors for free. If data were indeed non-excludable and non-rivalrous, they should have no reason to complain, since this would increase overall social welfare.[70] Twitter certainly did not argue that its data was a public good. Nor would Peoplebrowsr agree that Twitter's denial of access to this data was without competitive significance.

E. The Elusive Metaphor for Big Data

Ultimately, we see that Big Data defies easy metaphors. Big Data has been sub- **4.32** ject to many metaphors; each has its shortcomings. Some argue, for example, that data cannot be analogized to oil, whose consumption by some prevents its use by others.[71] Sarah Watson observed that comparing data to a natural resource 'suggests that it has great value to be mined and refined but that it must be handled by experts and large-scale industrial processes'.[72] The industrial metaphors for Big Data, she observes, suggest only one subset of values: 'How we think about data—and more importantly what we do with it—will depend on the value systems that our conceptual metaphors capture and reify'.[73]

---

[67] *PeopleBrowsr*, Defendant's Motion to Dismiss, above note 62.
[68] Ibid.
[69] Ibid.
[70] OECD, *Data-Driven Innovation*, above note 6, p 25 ('Maximizing access to the non-rivalry good will in theory maximize social welfare as every additional private benefit comes at no additional cost.').
[71] Ibid, p 22 ('Although data is a factor of production, the use of data, in contrast to oil, does not affect in principle its potential to meet the demands of others as oil can be consumed.').
[72] Sara M Watson, 'Data is the New "_____"', *DIS Magazine*, http://dismagazine.com/discussion/73298/sara-m-watson-metaphors-of-big-data/.
[73] Ibid.

4.33 Industrial metaphors, whether oil or fuel, devalue the privacy concerns. If Big Data is not simply a commodity to be consumed, but as we discuss, a portrait of our daily activities, then any metaphor must capture all of its significant values. Perhaps Big Data is the aura of our daily activities and thoughts: it can be transformed into useable energy forms, but doing so may reveal (and at times disturb) the source's distinctive, personal thoughts and activities.

4.34 Thus Big Data has important competitive and privacy implications. Companies will compete for a data-advantage. But we cannot assume, as the next chapter discusses, that data-driven business strategies, left unchecked, will necessarily promote privacy. In a nutshell, the free market will not necessarily protect privacy.

5

WHY HAVEN'T MARKET FORCES ADDRESSED CONSUMERS' PRIVACY CONCERNS?

As the four 'V's of data accelerate, an even greater variety of valuable data will **5.01** be quickly collected and analysed to better understand, predict, and even manipulate what we watch and consume, with whom we socialize, and possibly for whom and for what we vote. This raises significant privacy and consumer protection concerns. But the rise of data-driven mergers and business strategies also raise significant competition policy issues that the authorities must address.[1] This chapter explores several explanations as to why market forces are not necessarily promoting services that afford great privacy protections. One possible explanation is that consumers—especially younger ones—are not concerned about privacy. But the survey data undercuts this claim. This chapter also discusses several problems in inferring consumers' privacy preferences from their choices. A second possible explanation is that competition, at times, can worsen, rather than improve, the privacy protections. But that still leaves markets where competitive market forces should be responsive to consumers' demand for better privacy protections, but are not. The fundamental problem in these markets is that consumers lack viable alternatives. Here we see the core concern of competition policy—namely the accumulation of market power—intersect with privacy concerns. The reason why market forces have not yielded the privacy protections that individuals desire is the absence of meaningful competition.

---

[1] Lisa Kimmel and Janis Kestenbaum, 'What's Up with WhatsApp?: A Transatlantic View on Privacy and Merger Enforcement in Digital Markets', 29(1) *Antitrust* (Fall 2014): p 53 (noting that 'new technologies and business models make data collection and analysis a nearly ubiquitous feature of everyday life', so that 'we can expect questions about the role of antitrust enforcement in protecting consumers from privacy risks that may be associated with digital market mergers will continue to surface in merger reviews on both sides of the Atlantic').

A. Market Forces Are Not Promoting Services that Afford Great Privacy Protections

5.02 Normally, we expect competition to pressure firms to deliver the benefits from data-driven strategies, while protecting consumers from the harms associated with monopolization and restraints of trade.[2] If some companies are less transparent over their data policies, then consumers could opt for competitors with clearer policies that more closely align with their privacy preferences. If some firms use consumers' data to exploit them, then competition should prompt other firms to inform consumers of such exploitation, offer them services to better protect them against exploitation, and provide an array of privacy-enhancing services and technologies that match consumer preferences.

5.03 That is clearly not the case today. As the European Data Protection Supervisor observed, '[d]espite the risks to the personal data of individuals using these services, the market for privacy-enhancing services remains comparatively weak'.[3] The privacy trade-offs are clearly a concern. As author Sue Halpern wrote:

> [A]s human behavior is tracked and merchandized on a massive scale, the Internet of Things creates the perfect conditions to bolster and expand the surveillance state. In the world of the Internet of Things, your car, your heating system, your refrigerator, your fitness apps, your credit card, your television set, your window shades, your scale, your medications, your camera, your heart rate monitor, your electric toothbrush, and your washing machine—to say nothing of your phone—generate a continuous stream of data that resides largely out of reach of the individual but not of those willing to pay for it or in other ways commandeer it.[4]

5.04 As the Internet of Things expands, it will be harder (and less realistic) for citizens to safeguard their privacy. With sensors connected to so many everyday devices, 'users will be unable to consult the privacy policy on the device itself, but would have to find paper documentation or more likely browse from another device to the

---

[2] European Commission, *Guidelines on the Assessment of Non-Horizontal Mergers under the Council Regulation on the Control of Concentrations Between Undertakings*, 18 October 2008, para 10, http://eur-lex.europa.eu/legal-content/EN/ALL/?uri=CELEX:52008XC1018%2803%29 ('Effective competition brings benefits to consumers, such as low prices, high quality products, a wide selection of goods and services, and innovation.').

[3] European Data Protection Supervisor (EDPS), 'Privacy and Competitiveness in the Age of Big Data: The Interplay Between Data Protection, Competition Law and Consumer Protection in the Digital Economy', Preliminary Opinion, March 2014, p 8 ('EDPS Preliminary Opinion'), https://secure.edps.europa.eu/EDPSWEB/webdav/shared/Documents/Consultation/Opinions/2014/14-03-26_competitition_law_big_data_EN.pdf.

[4] Sue Halpern, 'The Creepy New Wave of the Internet', *The New York Review of Books*, 20 November 2014, http://www.nybooks.com/articles/archives/2014/nov/20/creepy-new-wave-internet/.

relevant web sites'.[5] Moreover, because of the network effects we discuss in Part IV, users gravitate to the larger platforms. Today, you can choose an email provider that does not scan the content of your emails to target you with ads. But you cannot effectively prevent others from using advertising-supported email (such as Gmail). Thus the privacy risk remains whenever others share personal information by Gmail and other popular advertising-supported services. As we will see with network effects, when one's friends and family rely on advertising-supported platforms, it will be harder to turn to superior privacy alternatives.

The greater problem is that consumers are largely unaware of the information being **5.05** collected about them and how the data is being used.[6] For example, consumers typically do not directly interact with data brokers, who amass detailed profiles on them, and do not know how these consumer profiles are being used.[7] As the Federal Trade Commission (FTC) reported in 2014:

> Data brokers acquire a vast array of detailed and specific information about consumers; analyze it to make inferences about consumers, some of which may be considered sensitive; and share the information with clients in a range of industries. All of this activity takes place behind the scenes, without consumers' knowledge.[8]

One data broker, the FTC reported, had '3000 data segments for nearly every US consumer'.[9] Nor do consumers know who is tracking them across the web and how they are using this information. At best consumers catch an occasional glimpse, as when a display advertisement for a pair of shoes follows consumers around the web for weeks after a single click on an Amazon page.

---

[5] EDPS Preliminary Opinion, above note 3, p 35; Executive Office of the President, President's Council of Advisors on Science and Technology, *Report to the President, Big Data and Privacy: A Technological Perspective*, May 2014, p 15 ('PCAST Report'), https://www.whitehouse. gov/sites/default/files/microsites/ostp/PCAST/pcast_big_data_and_privacy_-_may_2014.pdf ('To some, it seems farfetched that the typical home will foreseeably acquire cameras and microphones in every room, but that appears to be a likely trend. What can your cell phone (already equipped with front and back cameras) hear or see when it is on the nightstand next to your bed? Tablets, laptops, and many desktop computers have cameras and microphones.'); OECD, *Supporting Investment in Knowledge Capital, Growth and Innovation*, 10 October 2013, p 322, http://www.oecd-ilibrary.org/industry-and-services/supporting-investment-in-knowledge-capital-growth-and-innovation_9789264193307-en ('More than 30 million interconnected sensors are now deployed worldwide, in areas such as security, health care, the environment, transport systems or energy control systems, and their numbers are growing by around 30% a year.'); OECD, *Data-Driven Innovation for Growth and Well-Being: Interim Synthesis Report*, October 2014, p 8, http://www.oecd.org/sti/inno/data-driven-innovation-interim-synthesis.pdf ('With the increasing deployment and interconnection of (real-world) sensors through mobile and fixed networks (i.e. sensor networks), more and more offline activities are also digitally recorded, resulting in an additional tidal wave of data.').

[6] *See* Chapter 21.

[7] FTC, *Data Brokers: A Call for Transparency and Accountability*, May 2014, p iv, https://www. ftc.gov/system/files/documents/reports/data-brokers-call-transparency-accountability-report-federal-trade-commission-may-2014/140527databrokerreport.pdf.

[8] Ibid, p vii.

[9] Ibid, p iv.

5.06 Companies whose advertising-supported business model is based on collecting and using personal data to target users with behavioural ads want to keep it that way. Unlike consumers, these companies are not interested in fostering technologies that promote privacy and block ads. It would be like asking a broadcaster or cable company to support a device that allows consumers to fast-forward through ads.

5.07 For companies whose business model is dependent upon tracking consumers and using the data to target them with behavioural ads, privacy technologies and legislation can represent a threat. They warn investors how additional privacy safeguards and ad blocking technologies would harm their business. For example, in its 2014 Annual Report, Google identifies various risks that could adversely affect its business, financial condition, results of operations, cash flows, and the trading price of its common and capital stock.[10] One risk is that '[n]ew technologies could block online ads, which would harm [its] business.'[11] As Google explains,

> Technologies have been developed that can block the display of our ads and that provide tools to users to opt out of our advertising products. Most of our revenues are derived from fees paid to us by advertisers in connection with the display of ads on web pages for our users. As a result, such technologies and tools could adversely affect our operating results.[12]

5.08 Facebook also identifies the threat of privacy innovations to its business model. Like Google, nearly all of Facebook's revenue is generated from advertising. For 2014, 2013, and 2012, advertising accounted for 92 per cent, 89 per cent, and 84 per cent of its revenue, respectively.[13] The risks Facebook identifies include 'the

---

[10] *See, eg,* Google Inc, Annual Report Pursuant to Section 13 or 15(D) of the Securities Exchange Act of 1934 for the fiscal year ended December 31, 2014, p 12, http://www.sec.gov/Archives/edgar/data/1288776/000128877615000008/goog2014123110-k.htm (discussing how '[p]rivacy concerns relating to [its] technology could damage [its] reputation and deter current and potential users from using [its] products and services').

[11] Ibid, p 16.

[12] Ibid; *see also* Bazaarvoice, Inc, Annual Report Pursuant to Section 13 or 15(D) of the Securities Exchange Act of 1934 for the fiscal year ended April 30, 2015, http://www.sec.gov/Archives/edgar/data/1330421/000119312515235103/d929871d10k.htm (noting that 'the U.S. government, including the White House, Congress, and the FTC are reviewing the need for greater regulation for the use, collection and disclosure of information concerning consumer behavior on the Internet, including regulation aimed at restricting certain targeted advertising practices,' how '[p]roposed legislation could, if enacted, impose additional requirements and/or prohibit the use, collection, storage and disclosure of information concerning consumer behavior on the Internet and restrict or otherwise prohibit the use of certain technologies that track individuals' activities on web pages or across the Internet', and how '[s]uch laws and regulations could restrict [its] ability to collect and use web browsing data and personal information, which may result in financial penalties, litigation, regulatory investigations, negative publicity, reduced growth opportunities and other significant liabilities').

[13] Facebook Inc, Form 10-K Annual Report, filed 29 January 2015, http://files.shareholder.com/downloads/AMDA-NJ5DZ/650609882x0xS1326801-15-6/1326801/filing.pdf.

degree to which users opt out of social ads or certain types of ad targeting; the degree to which users cease or reduce the number of times they click on our ads;...[and] the impact of new technologies that could block or obscure the display of our ads'.[14] Besides individuals deleting cookies or using 'ad blocking' software that prevents cookies from being stored on a user's computer, Coupons.com warns investors how *even the default privacy setting* can hurt its business:

> ...the Safari browser blocks third-party cookies by default, the developers of the Firefox browser have announced that a future version of the Firefox browser will also block third-party cookies by default, and other browsers may do so in the future. Unless such default settings in browsers were altered by Internet users to permit the placement of third-party cookies, we would be able to set fewer of our cookies in users' browsers, which could adversely affect our business.[15]

5.09 Besides privacy concerns, the data-driven economy also raises consumer protection concerns, including behavioural advertising, which 'relies on the sophisticated analysis of data about users—including their actions, choices, and revealed preferences—to make predictions about which advertisements might appeal to which consumers'.[16] With companies collecting detailed information on consumers' online and offline activities, often without consumers' knowledge and consent, the risk of abusive practices increases. Consumers can pay higher prices due to the erroneous information collected or inferred about them.[17] Moreover, data-driven behavioural advertising can yield behavioural exploitation, where the more vulnerable are discriminated against. They end up with fewer choices of goods or services, higher prices, and poorer quality, thereby increasing wealth inequality.

5.10 Nor has the political market provided consumers the privacy protections they request. Most US adults (including young adults) in one survey believed there

---

[14] Ibid, pp 10–11.

[15] Coupons.com Inc, Annual Report Pursuant to Section 13 or 15(D) of the Securities Exchange Act of 1934 for the fiscal year ended December 31, 2014, p 21, https://www.sec.gov/Archives/edgar/data/1115128/000156459015001837/coup-10k_20141231.htm.

[16] Pamela Jones Harbour and Tara Isa Koslov, 'Section 2 in a Web 2.0 World: An Expanded Vision of Relevant Product Markets', 76 *Antitrust LJ* (2010): p 780.

[17] The march towards near-perfect price discrimination in the online world is explored in Ariel Ezrachi and Maurice E Stucke, *Virtual Competition: The Promise and Perils of the Algorithm-Driven Economy* (Cambridge, MA: Harvard University Press, forthcoming 2016); *see also* PCAST Report, above note 5, p 8 ('Harm arising from false conclusions about individuals, based on personal profiles from big-data analytics. The power of big data, and therefore its benefit, is often correlational. In many cases the "harms" from statistical errors are small, for example the incorrect inference of a movie preference; or the suggestion that a health issue be discussed with a physician, following from analyses that may, on average, be beneficial, even when a particular instance turns out to be a false alarm. Even when predictions are statistically valid, moreover, they may be untrue about particular individuals—and mistaken conclusions may cause harm. Society may not be willing to excuse harms caused by the uncertainties inherent in statistically valid algorithms. These harms may unfairly burden particular classes of individuals, for example, racial minorities or the elderly.').

should be a law that gives people the right to know all the information websites know about them; and believed there should be a law that requires websites and advertising companies to delete all stored information about an individual.[18] Such broad legal protections do not exist. In another 2015 survey, 49 per cent of American adults who used the Internet believed incorrectly 'that by law a supermarket must obtain a person's permission before selling information about that person's food purchases to other companies'.[19] Indeed, eight surveys from 1999 until 2012 'have consistently shown that while Americans are quite aware that marketers are collecting data about them and are wary of that, they have little understanding about how that takes place or about the laws that govern those activities'.[20]

B. Why Hasn't the Market Responded to the Privacy Concerns of So Many Individuals?

5.11 The online markets have provided many products and services free of charge, but often at a heavy cost to our privacy. So why hasn't the market responded to our privacy concerns?

5.12 One possible explanation is that competition, at times, can worsen, rather than improve, the situation.[21] For example, competition becomes a race to the bottom, where companies profit more in shrouding, rather than clarifying, their privacy policies.[22] Ordinarily, the likelihood of timely and sufficient entry into the relevant market will alleviate concerns about these harmful competitive effects. But the behavioural economics literature describes how entry can increase, rather than reduce, behavioural exploitation.[23] That still leaves markets, however, where competitive

---

[18] Chris Jay Hoofnagle et al, 'How Different are Young Adults from Older Adults When it Comes to Information Privacy Attitudes and Policies?', 14 April 2010, http://ssrn.com/abstract=1589864.

[19] Joseph Turow, Michael Hennessy, and Nora Draper, 'The Tradeoff Fallacy: How Marketers Are Misrepresenting American Consumers and Opening Them Up to Exploitation', University of Pennsylvania Annenberg School of Communication, June 2015, p 4, https://www.asc.upenn.edu/news-events/publications/tradeoff-fallacy-how-marketers-are-misrepresenting-american-consumers-and).

[20] Ibid, p 7.

[21] Maurice E Stucke, 'Is Competition Always Good?', 1 *J of Antitrust Enforcement* (2013): p 162.

[22] EDPS Preliminary Opinion, above note 3, p 11 (noting that, as of 2014, 'relatively few companies in the digital economy have detected financial advantage in enhancing the privacy of their offerings').

[23] Maurice E Stucke, 'Behavioral Exploitation and its Implications on Competition and Consumer Protection Policies', in Swedish Competition Authority (ed), *The Pros and Cons of Consumer Protection* (Stockholm: Konkurrensverket Swedish Competition Authority 2012), pp 77–122.

market forces should be responsive to consumers' demand for better privacy protections, but are not.

C. Are Individuals Concerned About Privacy?

A second possible explanation is that consumers—especially younger ones—are **5.13** not concerned about privacy. No doubt some are less concerned about their privacy; but the evidence undermines any broad conclusion of our indifference to privacy.[24] One 2015 survey found that 70 per cent 'considered the privacy of their personal information to be more important to them now than it was five to ten years ago, with only 5% saying it was less so'.[25] A 2015 survey of 1,506 American adults found:

- 91 per cent disagreed (77 per cent of them strongly) that '[i]f companies give me a discount, it is a fair exchange for them to collect information about me without my knowing';[26]
- 71 per cent disagreed (53 per cent of them strongly) that '[i]t's fair for an online or physical store to monitor what I'm doing online when I'm there, in exchange for letting me use the store's wireless internet, or Wi-Fi, without charge';[27]
- 55 per cent disagreed (38 per cent of them strongly) that '[i]t's okay if a store where I shop uses information it has about me to create a picture of me that improves the services they provide for me.'[28]

The evidence suggests that, rather than trading off privacy for free or cheap goods **5.14** and services, many 'feel resigned to the inevitability of surveillance and the power of marketers to harvest their data'.[29] Contrary to the popular assumption that age affects views about privacy, younger consumers in another survey were as concerned about privacy as older consumers.[30] As the US President's Council of Advisors on Science and Technology recognized, '[m]uch of the public's concern is with the harm done by the use of personal data, both in isolation or in combination.'[31]

---

[24] UK Competition and Markets Authority, *The Commercial Use of Consumer Data: Report on the CMA's Call for Information*, June 2015, paras 20–1, 4.1–4.42 ('CMA Report'), https://www.gov.uk/government/uploads/system/uploads/attachment_data/file/435817/The_commercial_use_of_consumer_data.pdf (discussing surveys).

[25] Ibid, para 4.56.

[26] Turow et al, above note 19, p 3.

[27] Ibid, p 4.

[28] Ibid.

[29] Ibid; CMA Report, above note 24, para 4.66 ('feeling of a loss of control appears to be a core theme, perhaps helping to explain consumers' specific fears about how their data might be used').

[30] Hoofnagle et al, above note 18.

[31] PCAST Report, above note 5, p 5.

D. The Problem with the Revealed Preference Theory

5.15 One rejoinder is that consumers, if concerned about privacy, would behave differently and not divulge private information to third parties. This assumes that the consumers' 'true' privacy preferences are revealed through their online activity. We can generally infer consumers' privacy preferences from their choices only when consumers are fully informed about their choice's benefits and costs (including privacy risks), and the marketplace offers a competitive array of options that match actual privacy preferences.

5.16 Several problems exist with this assumption. One problem is that consumers often do not know what data is being collected, how it is being used, and for what purpose.[32] Chapter 21 discusses the ineffectiveness of the current notice-and-consent framework for privacy.

5.17 A second problem, as the recent economics literature documents, is that consumer decision-making can be affected by heuristics, biases, and situational factors; so consumers' choices do not necessarily reflect their actual preferences.[33]

5.18 One example is power of the default option. As the behavioural experiments reflect, the setting of the default often can determine the outcome—even when transaction costs are nominal. Default options have played an important role in participation and investments in retirement savings, contractual choices in health clubs, organ donations, car insurance plans, and participation in class actions.[34] So consumers, for various reasons—time constraints, inertia, lack of knowledge—may not 'opt out' of the commercial use of their personal data (even if a choice exists). Knowing the power of defaults, Congress amended the Driver's Privacy Protection Act of

---

[32] Alessandro Acquisti, Laura Brandimarte, and George Loewenstein, 'Privacy and human behavior in the age of information', 347 *Science* (30 January 2015): pp 509–14.

[33] Ibid.

[34] OECD, *Consumer Policy Toolkit* (2010), pp 46–7; Richard H Thaler and Cass R Sunstein, *Nudge: Improving Decisions About Health, Wealth, and Happiness* (New Haven, CT: Yale University Press, 2008), pp 78, 129–30; Stefano DellaVigna, 'Psychology and Economics: Evidence from the Field', 47 *J of Econ Literature* (2009): 322 n 11; Eric J Johnson, Steven Bellman, and Gerald L Lohse, 'Defaults, Framing and Privacy: Why Opting In–Opting Out', 13 *Marketing Letters* (2003): pp 5–15 (consent to receive email marketing); C Whan Park, Sung Youl Jun, and Deborah J Macinnis, 'Choosing What I Want Versus Rejecting What I Do Not Want: An Application of Decision Framing to Product Option Choice Decisions', 37 *J of Marketing Research* (2000): pp 187–202 (car option purchases); European Consumer Consultative Group, *Opinion on Private Damages Actions*, 2010, p 4, http://ec.europa.eu/consumers/empowerment/docs/ECCG_opinion_on_actions_for_damages_18112010.pdf (in European countries, where the default option was opt-in, so that consumers had to opt into the class, the rate of participation in class actions for consumer claims was less than 1%; whereas under opt-out regimes (where the default is that one is a class member unless one opts out), participation rates were typically very high (97% in the Netherlands and almost 100% in Portugal)).

1994 (DPPA), which limits the states' ability to sell or disclose personal information from their motor vehicle records.[35] Previously, to prevent disclosure of their personal information, individuals had to opt out. Congress amended the DPPA, so that residents now must opt in by expressly consenting to the state's disclosure of their private information for surveys, marketing, and solicitations. Under the amended DPPA,

> States may not imply consent from a driver's failure to take advantage of a state-afforded opportunity to block disclosure, but must rather obtain a driver's affirmative consent to disclose the driver's personal information for use in surveys, marketing, solicitations, and other restricted purposes.[36]

Companies, whose business model is built on amassing personal data to better target consumers with behavioural ads, have every incentive to require consumers to opt-out.[37] Consequently consumers' behaviour at times may reflect the privacy default (opt-out versus opt-in) rather than their privacy preference.

Besides the default option, firms can manipulate consumers' behaviour by giving **5.19** them the illusion of control.[38] The firm might overcome consumers' reluctance to share information by telling consumers that they can delete any tracking cookies on their servers or any personal information, knowing that most will likely forget to do so regularly.

A third problem, as the survey data found, is that 'large percentages of Americans **5.20** often don't have the basic knowledge to make informed cost-benefit choices about ways marketers use their information'.[39] To make an informative trade-off, consumers would have to know the value of their data, the value of the services they are receiving, and the costs in divulging the information. Such information is not widely available.[40] Indeed, the company that harvests the data offers consumers an immediate benefit (a free service or product, or discount by using its loyalty card), while downplaying any harm. The loss of privacy is often not mentioned, is not immediate, and less tangible than the immediate benefit.[41] In one study, individuals used a search engine to purchase batteries and sex toys. When the search engine provided only the merchants' websites and a comparison of prices, most people did not pay attention to the manufacturers' privacy policies. They chose the merchants with

---

[35] 18 USC s 2721 (2012).
[36] *Reno v Condon*, 528 US 144–5, 120 S Ct 669 (2000).
[37] Acquisti et al, above note 32, pp 512–13.
[38] Ibid, p 513.
[39] Turow et al, above note 19, p 3.
[40] CMA Report, above note 24, para 4.39 (finding that '[s]ome consumers identify a "value exchange" from sharing data, but most feel they lack information on how they benefit and perceive firms benefit more than they do. Furthermore, many consumers appear unhappy with how well firms explain why they collect data and consider that more could be done to improve transparency.').
[41] Acquisti et al, above note 32, p 509.

the lowest price. But when the search engine provided salient, easily accessible information about the differences in privacy policies, most people opted for merchants that charged a higher price (5 per cent) but offered greater privacy protection.[42]

5.21 A fourth problem is that personal valuations of privacy and data, as the OECD found, are complex and context dependent:

> First, people tend to differ with respect to their individual valuation of personal data (i.e., the amount of money sufficient for them to give away personal data) and their individual valuation of privacy (i.e., the amount of money they are ready to spend to protect their personal data from disclosure). Second, empirical studies point out that both the valuation of privacy and the valuation of personal data are extremely sensitive to contextual effects.[43]

5.22 One example of context is whether some aspects of privacy are a fundamental right, which, unlike a property right, consumers cannot bargain away (especially in markets with unequal bargaining power).[44] Even if privacy were a property right, the valuation of privacy can differ depending on the reference point: citizens may demand more money to give up a pre-existing privacy right than they would be willing to pay for such a right.[45] Moreover, one's valuation of personal data (the amount one is willing to receive to disclose the data) is not necessarily the same as one's valuation of privacy. People may be more or less willing to disclose data depending on the context, including to whom the data is revealed, and how much the person trusts that institution.[46] Consequently, just as the Court in *Riley* did not assume

---

[42] Ibid, p 510.

[43] OECD, *Exploring the Economics of Personal Data: A Survey of Methodologies for Measuring Monetary Value*, OECD Digital Economy Papers, No 220 (2013), p 5, http://dx.doi.org/10.1787/5k486qtxldmq-en.

[44] *See* Marc Rotenberg, 'Fair Information Practices and the Architecture of Privacy (What Larry Doesn't Get)', *Stan Tech L Rev* [2001]: pp 1, 32, http://journals.law.stanford.edu/sites/default/files/stanford-technology-law-review/online/rotenberg-fair-info-practices.pdf ('Subtly, but powerfully and profoundly, the substitution of "notice and choice" for "notice and consent" transferred the protection of privacy from the legal realm, and from an emphasis on the articulation of rights and responsibilities, to the marketplace, where consumers would now be forced to pay for what the law could otherwise provide.').

[45] For example, one study found that duck hunters would pay, on average, USD 247 to obtain the privilege of keeping a particular wetland undeveloped, but if they already had the right to block development, they would demand an average of USD 1,044 to give it up. *O Centro Espírita Beneficiente União Do Vegetal v Ashcroft*, 389 F3d 1016 (US Ct of Apps (10th Cir), 2004) (citing Judd Hammack and Gardner M Brown, Jr, *Waterfowl and Wetlands: Toward Bioeconomic Analysis* (Baltimore, MD: Johns Hopkins, 1974), p 26), affirmed and remanded *Gonzales v O Centro Espírita Beneficente União do Vegetal*, 546 US 418, 126 S Ct 1211 (2006); *see also* Acquisti et al, above note 32, p 510; OECD, *Economics of Personal Data*, above note 43, p 30 (noting one study where 'the fraction of consumers who will reject an offer to obtain money in exchange for reduced privacy is larger than the fraction of consumers who will accept an economically equivalent offer to pay money in exchange for protection of privacy').

[46] OECD, *Economics of Personal Data*, above note 43, pp 30, 32 ('the price at which people are willing to sell their own personal data depends on how they perceive the data will be used and how much they trust the entity receiving the data'); CMA Report, above note 24, box 2.16 (noting one study where 'UK consumers assigned different values to their personal data depending on the type

that people sacrificed their privacy expectations when using smartphones, so too one cannot conclude that individuals who use advertising-supported email, search the web, or download apps do not value privacy.

Even if the above four problems were resolved—ie, consumers know what data **5.23** is being collected, how it is being used, and for what purpose; are unaffected by biases and heuristics; and have the basic knowledge to make informed cost–benefit choices about the ways marketers use their information and their choices cannot be manipulated by the context—a fifth problem with the revealed-preferences argument is that consumers never had an opportunity to choose among a competitive array of options that match their actual privacy preferences. Imagine an apparatchik arguing that consumers do not desire an independent press, because so many read the state-controlled newspaper. That argument would be true only if consumers had a meaningful choice and opted for the state-run newspaper. In the online world we see consumer resignation. While 84 per cent of consumers want to have control over what marketers can learn about them, 65 per cent have come to accept that they have little control over what marketers can learn about them online.[47]

E. The Lack of Viable Privacy-Protecting Alternatives

Our privacy needs are not being met. The fundamental problem in many online **5.24** markets is that we lack viable alternatives. Here we see the core concern of competition policy—namely the accumulation of market power—intersect with privacy concerns. The reason why market forces have not yielded the privacy protections that we desire is the *absence* of meaningful competition.

Google, its Executive Chairman admitted in a 2010 interview, gathered a lot of **5.25** data to enable it to deliver better-targeted ads. Eric Schmidt stated that competition prevented Google from abusing people's privacy:

> All of our testing indicates that the vast majority of people are perfectly happy with our policy. And this message is the message that nobody wants to hear so let me say it again: the reality is we make decisions based on what the average user tells us and we do check. And the reason that you should trust us is that if we were to violate that trust people would move immediately to someone else. We're very non-sticky so we have a very high interest in maintaining the trust of those users.[48]

---

of data and level of familiarity with the organisation collecting it' and how the survey respondents 'on average valued their full name and date of birth at £12.14 if sharing with a familiar organisation, but £15.02 if an unfamiliar organisation' and 'valued their location at £13.99 for a familiar organisation but £17.66 for an unfamiliar one').

[47] Turow et al, above note 19, p 14.

[48] Shane Richmond, 'Google's Eric Schmidt: You can Trust Us with Your Data', *The Telegraph*, 1 July 2010, http://www.telegraph.co.uk/technology/google/7864223/Googles-Eric-Schmidt-You-can-trust-us-with-your-data.html.

Schmidt's argument is appealing. Google, after all, does not charge people for using its search engine, email, browser, and other products.

5.26 The problem is that Google, as reflected below, appears to have violated its privacy policy and different jurisdictions' privacy laws multiple times without losing its dominance. Google in 2011 agreed to settle FTC charges that it used deceptive tactics and violated its own privacy promises to consumers when it launched its social network, Google Buzz.[49] The FTC for the first time in its history required a company to implement a comprehensive privacy policy to protect the privacy of consumers' information, and called for regular, independent privacy audits for 20 years.[50]

5.27 A year later, the FTC alleged that Google again breached its privacy commitments. Google paid a record USD 22.5 million civil penalty to settle the FTC charges that 'it misrepresented to users of Apple Inc.'s Safari Internet browser that it would not place tracking "cookies" or serve targeted ads to those users, violating an earlier privacy settlement between the company and the FTC'.[51] Google also settled with the state attorneys general of 37 states and the District of Columbia for USD 17 million.[52]

5.28 In 2012, the EU Data Protection Authorities investigated whether Google's new privacy policy complied with the European Data Protection legislation. Its investigation found, among other things, that Google provided 'insufficient information to its users (including passive users), especially on the purposes and the categories of data being processed'.[53] Google users could not determine which categories of data Google used and for what purpose. Second, Google under its new privacy policy, could 'combine almost any data from any services for any purposes'.[54] The EU warned Google that it could not empower itself 'to collect vast amounts of personal data about internet users', without demonstrating 'that this collection was proportionate to the purposes for which they are processed'.[55] Moreover, 'Google did not

---

[49] FTC, 'FTC Charges Deceptive Privacy Practices in Google's Rollout of Its Buzz Social Network: Google Agrees to Implement Comprehensive Privacy Program to Protect Consumer Data', Press Release, 30 March 2011, http://www.ftc.gov/news-events/press-releases/2011/03/ftc-charges-deceptive-privacy-practices-googles-rollout-its-buzz.

[50] Ibid.

[51] FTC, 'Google Will Pay $22.5 Million to Settle FTC Charges it Misrepresented Privacy Assurances to Users of Apple's Safari Internet Browser', Press Release, 9 August 2012, http://www.ftc.gov/news-events/press-releases/2012/08/google-will-pay-225-million-settle-ftc-charges-it-misrepresented.

[52] Office of the Attorney General State of Mississippi, Press Release, 'Attorney General Announces $17 Million Multistate Settlement With Google Over Tracking of Consumers', 19 November 2013, http://www.ago.state.ms.us/releases/attorney-general-announces-17-million-multistate-settlement-with-google-over-tracking-of-consumers/.

[53] Letter from the Article 29 Data Protection Working Party to Larry Page, 16 October 2012, http://www.cnil.fr/fileadmin/documents/en/20121016-letter_google-article_29-FINAL.pdf.

[54] Ibid.

[55] Ibid.

set any limits to the combination of data nor provide clear and comprehensive tools allowing its users to control it. Combining personal data on such a large scale creates high risks to the privacy of users.'[56] The EU officials asked Google to change its privacy policy so that it complied with European privacy laws. Allegations followed that Google failed to adequately revise its privacy policies—prompting further fines, including EUR 900,000 (USD 1.23 million), the maximum amount permitted under Spain's data protection law,[57] and EUR 150,000, the maximum amount permitted under France's privacy statute.[58]

Besides obtaining data for its mapping technology, Google's Street View cars, one **5.29** consumer group noted, secretly collected 'huge amounts of personal information from millions of unencrypted wireless networks, including e-mails, medical and financial records, passwords and more'.[59] That landed Google in more trouble. In 2013, Google paid the state attorneys general USD 7 million, as part of its settlement for illegally collecting between 2008 and 2010 residents' personal information, such as email and text messages, passwords, and web histories while collecting mapping data from its Street View cars.[60] Like the earlier FTC action, Google, as part of this settlement, promised to 'engage in a comprehensive employee education program about the privacy or confidentiality of user data'.[61] Italy (EUR 1 million/USD 1.37 million),[62] France (EUR 100,000), and Germany (EUR 145,000)[63] also fined Google for privacy violations involving its Street View service.

---

[56] Ibid.

[57] Jacob Siegal, 'Google Slapped with $1.2 Million Fine for Breaking Privacy Laws', *BGR*, 19 December 2013, http://bgr.com/2013/12/19/google-privacy-law-violations/.

[58] Specifically, Google was fined for (i) not sufficiently informing its users of the conditions in which their personal data were processed, nor of the purposes of this processing, (ii) not complying with its obligation to obtain user consent prior to the storage of cookies on their terminals, (iii) failing to define how long it would retain the consumer data, and (iv) combining, without any basis under French law, all the data it collected about its users across all of its services. CNIL, 'The CNIL's Sanctions Committee Issues a 150 000 € Monetary Penalty to Google Inc', 8 January 2014, http://www.cnil.fr/english/news-and-events/news/article/the-cnils-sanctions-committee-issues-a-150-000-EUR-monetary-penalty-to-google-inc/.

[59] Public Citizen, *Mission Creep-y: Google Is Quietly Becoming One of the Nation's Most Powerful Political Forces While Expanding Its Information-Collection Empire*, November 2014, p 35, https://www.citizen.org/documents/Google-Political-Spending-Mission-Creepy.pdf.

[60] Casey Newton, 'Google Reaches $7 Million Settlement with States over Street View Case', CNET, 12 March 2013, http://www.cnet.com/news/google-reaches-7-million-settlement-with-states-over-street-view-case/.

[61] Connecticut Office of the Attorney General, 'Attorney General Announces $7 Million Multistate Settlement with Google Over Street View Collection of WiFi Data', Press Release, 12 March 2013, http://www.ct.gov/ag/cwp/view.asp?Q=520518&A=2341.

[62] Stephanie Bodoni, 'Google Pays Penalty for Street View Cars Roaming Italy', Bloomberg Business, 4 April 2014, http://www.bloomberg.com/news/articles/2014-04-04/google-pays-penalty-for-street-view-cars-roaming-italy (fining Google 'after the local regulator found its Street View cars drove incognito across the country, violating the privacy of citizens caught on camera without their knowledge').

[63] Ibid.

5.30 In 2014, Google settled with the FTC for unfairly billing consumers millions of dollars for in-app charges incurred by children without their parents' consent.[64] Moreover, there are other instances where Google reportedly collected personal data without the person's knowledge.[65]

5.31 So if Google, as one consumer group stated, 'has at times committed major violations of the public's trust',[66] why hasn't Google significantly lost its market power? Why hasn't the public punished Google for breaching its privacy policies and privacy violations? Either the public is not disturbed by Google's behaviour or consumers do not have meaningful alternatives. The former is less likely. A 2014 survey of over 2,500 Americans found that they were more concerned about a company like Google gaining access to their personal data, than the US National Security Agency or their boss, parents, or spouse.[67] An earlier pre-Edward Snowden 2012 survey found that on any given day, more than half of American adults using the Internet used a search engine, Google was their overwhelming choice, and that while satisfied with the search results, most disapproved of their personal information being collected for search results or for targeted advertising.[68]

5.32 Few can begrudge Google's success. But in an open letter to Google, the CEO of publisher Axel Springer SE explained Springer's and other companies' fear of Google.[69] With Google controlling the largest search engine (Google),[70] the largest video

---

[64] FTC, 'FTC Approves Final Order in Case About Google Billing for Kids' In-App Charges Without Parental Consent', Press Release, 5 December 2014, http://www.ftc.gov/news-events/press-releases/2014/12/ftc-approves-final-order-case-about-google-billing-kids-app ('When Google first introduced in-app charges to the Google Play store in 2011, the FTC's complaint alleged, Google billed for such charges without any password requirement or other method to obtain account holder authorization. The complaint also alleged that even after requiring a password to incur in-app charges, the company failed to tell parents that entering the password would then open a 30-minute window during which children could make unlimited charges without authorization.').

[65] Public Citizen, *Mission Creep-y*, above note 59, p 33 (noting how Google 'in March 2014 acknowledged scanning and indexing the contents of e-mails belonging to the 30 million student users of its "Apps for Education" suite'); *see also* Scott Cleland, 'Google's Privacy Rap Sheet', 14 June 2014, http://googleopoly.net/wp-content/uploads/2014/06/Googles-Privacy-Rap-Sheet-June-14.pdf.

[66] Public Citizen, *Mission Creep-y*, above note 59, p 4.

[67] Troy Mathew, 'What's Worse than Your Mom Seeing Your Web History? The NSA, Google', Survata Blog, 27 October 2014, https://www.survata.com/blog/whats-worse-than-your-mom-seeing-your-web-history-the-nsa-google/.

[68] Kristen Purcell, Joanna Brenner, and Lee Rainie, *Search Engine Use 2012*, Pew Research Center, 9 March 2012, http://www.pewinternet.org/2012/03/09/search-engine-use-2012/ (68% were 'NOT OKAY with targeted advertising because I don't like having my online behavior tracked and analyzed'); CMA Report, above note 24, para 4.53 ('relatively high proportions of consumers rate their search history and location as extremely sensitive').

[69] Mathias Döpfner, 'An Open Letter to Eric Schmidt: Why We Fear Google', *Frankfurter Allgemeine*, 17 April 2014, http://www.faz.net/aktuell/feuilleton/debatten/mathias-doepfner-s-open-letter-to-eric-schmidt-12900860.html.

[70] comScore, 'comScore Releases March 2014 U.S. Search Engine Rankings', Press Release, 15 April 2014, http://www.comscore.com/Insights/Press-Releases/2014/4/comScore-Releases-March-

platform (YouTube),[71] one of the biggest browsers (Chrome), the most widely used email provider (Gmail), and the biggest operating system for mobile devices (Android), his concern, along with others, is their dependence on Google: 'In this case, the statement "if you don't like Google, you can remove yourself from their listings and go elsewhere" is about as realistic as recommending to an opponent of nuclear power that he just stop using electricity', Mathias Döpfner wrote, 'He simply cannot do this in real life—unless he wants to join the Amish.'[72]

It is not just Google. The UK competition authority heard from a number of respondents representing both business and consumer perspectives that 'the balance of power over the collection and use of data had moved from consumers towards businesses': **5.33**

> We were told by one large business that big data collectors collect information consumers are not aware of, do things with it that they were not asked about, and don't allow them to opt out or exercise choices about it. We were also told by a business consultancy that, as a result of increasing digitisation, there has been a shift from a primary focus on volunteered information (such as consumers completing forms) to 'passive' data collection. Another response from an industry body referred to the 'information asymmetry' in favour of suppliers and against consumers. Reasons given for this alleged shift in power included technological changes, business practices and lack of effective enforcement of the current regime.[73]

Data-driven industries, including ones where the products are offered for free, may be susceptible to market (and at times monopoly) power. Thus one fundamental concern is that while governments promote the use of Big Data, they 'will also need to protect citizens against unhealthy market dominance' as '[c]ompanies such as Google, Amazon, and Facebook—as well as lesser-known "data-brokers", such as Acxiom and Experian—are amassing vast amounts of information on everyone and everything'.[74] **5.34**

Consequently, one explanation for market forces not providing the privacy protections that individuals desire is competition-related, namely key industries are **5.35**

2014-U.S.-Search-Engine-Rankings (Google Sites leading the US explicit core search market with 67.5% market share).

[71] comScore, 'comScore Releases March 2014 US Online Video Rankings', 18 April 2014, http://www.comscore.com/Insights/Press-Releases/2014/4/comScore-Releases-March-2014-US-Online-Video-Rankings (Google Sites, 'driven primarily by video viewing at YouTube.com, ranked as the top online video content property in March with 155.6 million unique viewers' followed by Facebook (88.4 million viewers), AOL, Inc (69.4 million), Yahoo Sites (55.7 million), and NDN (50.9 million). 'Nearly 46.6 billion video content views occurred during the month, with Google Sites generating the highest number at 11.1 billion, followed by Facebook with 4.6 billion and AOL, Inc with 1.3 billion. Google Sites had the highest average engagement among the top ten properties.').

[72] Döpfner, above note 69.

[73] CMA Report, above note 24, para 5.51.

[74] Kenneth Neil Cukier and Viktor Mayer-Schönberger, 'The Rise of Big Data', *Foreign Affairs* (May–June 2013): pp 36, 37, https://www.foreignaffairs.com/articles/2013-04-03/rise-big-data.

dominated by a few companies with data-driven business models that have little, if any, incentive to promote personal privacy, and face little, if any, competitive pressure to change their views. They can breach the public trust over privacy issues, without fearing retaliation. Consumers simply lack viable competitive alternatives. Data-driven firms in some markets may wield sufficient economic power to act to a considerable extent independent of their customers' preferences.

5.36 Mainstream economics would suggest that if firms were not supplying the level of privacy consumers wanted there would be new entry or repositioning by competitors lured by the prospect of growth. But, as economist Joseph Farrell has pointed out, if consumers have learned that 'there is no privacy; get over it' and thus expect a less protective policy independent of what policy a firm actually were to choose, a firm would be unable to benefit from making privacy-protective promises. The result can be like a self-fulfilling prophecy. Existing companies have little incentive to offer more protection, because it is costly, and new competitors trying to compete on the basis of more privacy protection will not see the shift in demand that would occur in a well-functioning market. The result, Prof Farrell identifies, is a 'dysfunctional equilibrium.'[75]

5.37 It is axiomatic that market forces, if left unchecked, do not always beget competition; instead, market forces can beget mergers, consolidation, and concentration— especially in winner-take-all markets. Dominant firms can abuse their power. They can undertake anticompetitive data-driven strategies to attain or maintain their monopoly.

5.38 To prevent such market failures, over 100 countries now have competition laws. One important check on market power is merger law. To halt the '"rising tide" of concentration in American business', the US Congress decided 'to clamp down with vigor on mergers'.[76] Congress's premise was that mergers tend to accelerate concentration in an industry. The next chapter looks at the recent track record of EU and US competition authorities in assessing data-driven mergers.

---

[75] Joseph Farrell, 'Can Privacy Be Just Another Good?', 10 *J on Telecomm & High Tech L* (2012): pp 258–9; *see also* CMA Report, above note 24, para 17 ('An absence of competition over privacy may indicate data markets failing to deliver what consumers want. This may occur where the implicit price of data used by firms is unclear, and where consumers are unable or unwilling to drive competition and incentivise firms to improve the degree to which consumers' privacy is protected.') and para 4.41 ('if consumers are limited in their ability to make informed decisions and to challenge firms over the use of their data, this may mean that firms have limited incentives to compete over the protection they afford to consumer data').

[76] *United States v Pabst Brewing Co*, 384 US 552, 86 S Ct 1669 (1966), quoting *United States v Von's Grocery Co*, 384 US 276, 86 S Ct 1482 (1966).

PART II

THE COMPETITION AUTHORITIES'
MIXED RECORD IN RECOGNIZING
DATA'S IMPORTANCE AND
THE IMPLICATIONS OF A FEW
FIRMS' UNPARALLELED SYSTEM
OF HARVESTING AND MONETIZING
THEIR DATA TROVE

6

THE US'S AND EU'S MIXED RECORD
IN ASSESSING DATA-DRIVEN MERGERS

The Google/DoubleClick merger sparked a debate over data-driven mergers and **6.01** privacy in the US. Rather than rehash the merits of the Federal Trade Commission's (FTC) 2007 decision to close its investigation, this chapter examines several recent data-driven mergers to see whether, and to what extent, the competition agencies' analysis has improved. The record is mixed. In the US and EU, privacy experts have seen very little progress from the agencies. In 2014, the FTC closed its investigation of Alliance Data Systems' acquisition of Conversant, sparking the following response from two consumer groups:

> The failure of the [FTC] to address key consumer protection issues with this acquisition underscores the need for a greater commitment by the FTC to tackle the competition and privacy issues of today's data-driven digital marketing era. We specifically urge the commission to launch a formal review of 'Big Data' consolidation. The level of commercial data gathering on Americans is unprecedented, growing daily without respite, and is ending up in the hands of fewer companies.[1]

The good news is that a closer examination of several recent investigations reveals **6.02** how some agencies—notably the European Commission and US Department of Justice—are at least starting to engage with the issue of Big Data. The bad news, as we shall see, is that they are still missing key issues.

A. The European Commission's 2008 Decision Not to Challenge the TomTom/Tele Atlas Merger

If you have ever driven a car with GPS, you have relied on navigation and mapping **6.03** data. One trailblazer in this area is TomTom which, in 2003, pioneered the market for Portable Navigation Devices, selling over 77 million devices in 35 countries

---

[1] Letter from Jeff Chester, Executive Director, Center for Digital Democracy and Edward Mierzwinski Director, US PIRG Education Fund, to Chairwoman Edith Ramirez, Federal Trade Commission, 5 November 2014.

over the next decade.[2] As its 2014 Annual Report states, 'TomTom empowers movement.'[3] In 2014, 800 million people around the world relied daily on TomTom's products.[4]

6.04 Not surprisingly, Big Data was an issue when in 2007 TomTom sought to acquire Tele Atlas, one of two main suppliers, both in Europe and North America, of 'navigable digital map databases'.[5] The vertical merger enabled the leading manufacturer of portable navigation devices and navigation software to obtain a key input, namely navigable digital map data.

6.05 One issue for the European Commission was whether the relevant product market was 'navigable digital map databases' or more broadly map databases. If the latter, then the merger was less likely to raise concerns. The Commission found that the volume, velocity, and variety of the data required for a navigable digital map database differed from ordinary map databases. The navigation devices that TomTom and its primary competitors sold required navigable digital map databases that are 'sufficiently detailed, accurate and updated' and that 'contain the necessary attributes and add-on layers', such as 'road type, road class, traffic flow information (one-way, two-way, lane separation) and turn restrictions'.[6] Thus the European Commission defined a narrower product market, namely

> ...a compilation of digital data which typically includes (i) geographic information which contains the position and shape of each feature on a map (such as roads, railways, rivers and indications of land use), (ii) attributes which contain additional information associated with features on the map (such as street names, addresses, driving directions, turn restrictions and speed limits) and (iii) display information. Suppliers keep map data in a relational database which is not in itself a digital map. The relational database is used by customers to generate digital maps and provide services based on map information. The map data included in the databases is derived from a multitude of sources such as aerial photographs, satellite images, official government map databases and other government sources as well as from field data generated by field forces using customised vehicles.[7]

By settling on a narrow product market, the Commission recognized that data was what differentiated digital maps from maps more broadly.

6.06 Another issue was whether Google or Microsoft could quickly enter the navigable digital map database market and become significant competitors. TomTom argued

---

[2] TomTom, Annual Report 2014, p 7, http://annualreport2014.tomtom.com/overview/key-facts-and-figures.

[3] Ibid.

[4] Ibid.

[5] *TomTom/Tele Atlas* (Case Comp/M.4854), Commission Decision C(2008) 1859 [2008] OJ C 237/12, pp 53–4, para 3.

[6] Ibid, p 22 n 12.

[7] Ibid, p 5 (internal footnote omitted).

yes. Google and Microsoft were customers of Tele Atlas and NAVTEQ; both provided map services over the Internet. Thus, both tech companies, argued TomTom, 'could use their technical knowledge and financial capabilities to upgrade their map databases to navigable quality by using feedback from their user communities'.[8] TomTom also claimed entry barriers had decreased, for among other things, 'improved aerial photography, improved quality of satellite images and the possibility to use feedback from end-user communities'.[9]

The Commission disagreed. The entry barriers for this data market were very **6.07** high: while it may be 'possible to produce a basic digital map database for many territories relatively quickly and at limited cost by compiling data from various public sources, producing a navigable digital map database is costly and very resource-intensive'.[10] Tele Atlas and its competitor NAVTEQ manually compiled data of each road's features by driving their own vehicles along each road.[11] These 'field surveys', the Commission found, were 'crucial for the accuracy as well as for the completeness of the databases because they are used both to verify data accumulated from other sources and to record additional data not available by other means'.[12] TomTom, the OECD similarly found, collected a lot of data (5 billion data points) each day.[13] Accordingly, obtaining and processing this data, even for Google and Microsoft, would be costly and time-consuming.

TomTom raised another interesting argument: an entrant could avoid the cost of **6.08** driving along every road to collect the necessary mapping data, and instead could rely on its subscribers to supply this information as they drove along the roads. (Later in this chapter, in the Google/Waze merger, we will examine this model.) The Commission again disagreed that entry barriers had decreased due to a positive feedback loop from subscribers. It identified four reasons why a 'Wikipedia-like' collaborative approach using end-user feedback was unlikely to create a navigable digital map database:

> First, developing an IT-tool making it easy for end-users to edit map data would be very complicated due to the very long list of inputs for navigable data (editing

---

8 Ibid, p 23.
9 Ibid, p 24.
10 Ibid, p 7.
11 Ibid ('operating field forces using a fleet of vehicles that drive along each road in the database').
12 Ibid.
13 Organisation for Economic Co-operation and Development (OECD), *Data-Driven Innovation for Growth and Well-Being: Interim Synthesis Report*, October 2014, p 20, http://www.oecd.org/sti/inno/data-driven-innovation-interim-synthesis.pdf ('These applications are very data-intensive. For example, TomTom, a leader in navigation hardware and software, had in its databases in 2012 more than 5000 trillion data points from its navigation devices and other sources, describing time, location, direction and speed of individual anonymised users, and it adds 5 billion data points every day. Overall, estimations by MGI (2011) suggest that the global pool of personal geolocation data was at least 1 petabyte in 2009, and growing by about 20% a year.').

a digital map database is much more complicated than editing a text document like Wikipedia).

Second, while users may have an incentive to edit an existing high-quality product they are already using, they have few incentives to help create a new product or increase the quality of a poor product that is functioning badly.

Third, the veracity of all edits must be checked by the mapping company, something which is very resource consuming.

Fourth, updating a digital map database using customer feedback is unlikely to succeed simply because of information asymmetries.[14]

6.09   The Commission's second reason raises a chicken-or-egg problem that we will see in markets with significant data-driven network effects. To attract users, one needs a quality product; but to get a quality product one needs a minimum number of users (and their data). Moreover, we will examine in Chapter 18 how dominant firms can use anticompetitive tactics to prevent smaller companies from gaining scale to improve quality to attract additional users.

6.10   The Commission concluded that it was 'still indispensable to employ field forces in customised vehicles which record and update very large volumes of road data in order to produce high-quality navigable digital map databases'.[15] Creating such navigable digital map databases of a quality comparable to the merging party would require 'substantial up-front investments',[16] be 'resource-intensive and expensive',[17] and be time-consuming.[18]

6.11   Ultimately, the Commission did not block the merger. The Commission found that the merged entity would likely have the *ability* to exercise market power. TomTom, post-merger, *could* increase prices, degrade quality, or delay access for some portable navigation device manufacturers and navigation software providers competing with TomTom.[19] But TomTom, the Commission concluded, lacked the economic incentive to do so. Basically, TomTom would not recover downstream its loss in profits upstream if it simply stopped selling map data to rivals.[20] Nor was a partial input foreclosure strategy likely to be profitable, where the merged entity would increase prices or degrade the quality of its maps data to its downstream rivals. Basically

---

[14]   *TomTom/Tele Atlas*, above note 5, p 25.

[15]   Ibid, p 26.

[16]   Ibid.

[17]   Ibid, p 27.

[18]   Ibid, p 28 (noting that it 'is beyond dispute that the creation of a navigable digital map database of a quality comparable to those created by Tele Atlas and NAVTEQ is a time-consuming exercise. To build a database covering the EEA, vast volumes of data have to be collected from various sources and field survey teams have to drive down every road in the EEA and record all features on the way.').

[19]   Ibid, p 45.

[20]   Ibid, p 48.

the likely profits gained downstream from foreclosing rivals would not offset the loss of profits upstream.[21]

Apparently, the Commission predicted correctly. As the *Guardian* reported, **6.12**

> the stock market did not like TomTom's purchase, which was funded by debt and a new share issue. Its shares plunged from their high of €64.80. At the start of 2009, the company wrote off more than €1bn on the Tele Atlas purchase. Shares hit an all-time low of €2.84.[22]

Its revenues and profits have declined significantly between 2010 and 2014.[23] Perhaps what motivated TomTom's purchase of Tele Atlas was not dreams of market power, but the fear that 'Google and smartphones would change the world of mapping, away from high-priced profitable devices to lower-priced services'.[24] Google did change the competitive landscape. TomTom's shares took a hit when Google added free turn-by-turn navigation to its Google Maps app on its Android 2.0 system. TomTom now supplies Apple with mapping data, and the race is on to supply self-driving vehicles and location-based technologies.

Notable for us is that the Commission recognized data's significant competitive **6.13** implications. Tele Atlas competed to obtain a data-advantage over rivals (or at least not being at a data-disadvantage), and the volume, variety, and velocity of mapping data had significant value. Moreover, quickly accessing and processing this volume and variety of data represented a key entry barrier.

We can also see from TomTom/Tele Atlas how the upfront investment in navi- **6.14** gable mapping data brings the requisite quality level that appeals to end-users, who in turn are likelier to provide feedback to TomTom to quickly improve the maps' accuracy, which attracts more users. In 2014, TomTom reported several sources for its mapping data: first, from government authorities; second, from its own field surveys and mobile mapping vans; and third, from the scale of its users, which encompasses 'hundreds of millions of users, who share map feedback with us as changes in the real world are detected'.[25] TomTom received over 200,000 consumer reports monthly. With the growing Internet of Things, TomTom is

---

[21] Ibid, pp 49–50.

[22] Charles Arthur, 'Navigating Decline: What Happened to TomTom?: Corinne Vigreux, Who Co-Founded the Company, Talks About the Rise of Google Maps, the Future of Satellite Mapping and Self-Driving Vehicles', *The Guardian*, 21 July 2015, http://www.theguardian.com/business/2015/jul/21/navigating-decline-what-happened-to-tomtom-satnav.

[23] Hoovers, 'Financials Information for TomTom NV', http://www.hoovers.com/company-information/cs/revenue-financial.TomTom_NV.c3827770341aeb07.html.

[24] Arthur, above note 22.

[25] TomTom, 2014 Annual Report, above note 2, p 10.

exploring new sensor data from the cars themselves[26]—which would amplify the four 'V's of data.

B. Facebook/WhatsApp

6.15 Texting and social networks, as any parent of teenagers knows, are huge. The average US teenager in 2015 sent and received 30 texts per day.[27] Texting is also popular with adults: 97 per cent of smartphone owners surveyed in the US 'used text messaging at least once' during the 2014 week-long study period 'making it the most widely-used basic feature or app'.[28]

6.16 Likewise, social platforms have grown in popularity. Facebook, one 2015 study found, was 'the most popular and frequently used social media platform' among 13 to 17-year-old American teenagers, with 71 per cent of all teens using the site.[29] Both Facebook and many texting apps are free—broadening their appeal among younger users. The currency in these markets is data.

6.17 Not surprisingly both privacy and Big Data issues arose in 2014 when Facebook announced its largest acquisition to date, buying the popular messaging app, WhatsApp, for USD 19 billion in cash and stock. When the deal was announced, Mark Zuckerberg, Facebook's co-founder and CEO, said, 'WhatsApp is on a path to connect 1 billion people. The services that reach that milestone are all incredibly valuable.'[30]

6.18 Both Facebook and WhatsApp offer popular texting applications for smartphones.[31] Facebook has the texting app 'Facebook Messenger' and the photo and video-sharing platform 'Instagram'. Consumers use these apps to communicate by text, photo, voice, and video messages. By 2014, 300 million of Facebook's 1.3 billion social network users worldwide were using the Facebook Messenger app.[32]

---

[26] Ibid, p 10.

[27] Amanda Lenhart, *Teens, Social Media & Technology Overview 2015*, Pew Research Center, 9 April 2015, http://www.pewinternet.org/files/2015/04/PI_TeensandTech_Update2015_0409151.pdf.

[28] Aaron Smith, 'US Smartphone Use in 2015', Pew Research Center: Internet, Science & Tech, 1 April 2015, http://www.pewinternet.org/2015/04/01/us-smartphone-use-in-2015/#smartphones.

[29] Lenhart, above note 27.

[30] Seth Fiegerman, 'Facebook to Buy WhatsApp for $16 Billion', Mashable, 19 February 2014, http://mashable.com/2014/02/19/facebook-whatsapp/.

[31] European Commission, 'Mergers: Commission Approves Acquisition of WhatsApp by Facebook', Press Release, 3 October 2014, http://europa.eu/rapid/press-release_IP-14-1088_en.htm; *Facebook/WhatsApp* (Case Comp/M.7217), Commission Decision C(2014) 7239 final, 3 October 2014, paras 2–3.

[32] European Commission, 'Mergers', above note 31.

Here, privacy was an important facet of non-price competition. Unlike Facebook, **6.19** WhatsApp did not sell advertising space or collect a lot of personal data on its mobile app users. WhatsApp charged users a nominal fee, and promised not to 'collect names, emails, addresses or other contact information from its users' mobile address book or contact lists' other than mobile phone numbers.[33] In contrast, Facebook's texting apps are free. Facebook harvests its users' data to target them with advertisements. Consumer groups have criticized Facebook's privacy policy:

> Facebook messaging is notorious for its extensive data collection practices. When Facebook revamped its messaging system in November 2010, it automatically opted in all Facebook users and initially disabled users' ability to delete individual messages. Without user consent, the new messaging system also pulled data from Facebook's social graph to prioritize messages from certain users. Currently, even when users delete a message, it continues to be stored on Facebook's servers. At the end of 2013, Slate reported that even when a user chooses not to send a message, Facebook still tracks what the user wrote.[34]

So pre-merger consumers could choose between two popular texting apps with **6.20** different price/privacy trade-offs. Neither the FTC nor European Commission, however, challenged the merger. Unlike the European Commission, the FTC never publicly commented on the merger's antitrust implications. The Director of the FTC's Bureau of Consumer Protection, however, did warn Facebook about using data on the WhatsApp users. In her letter to the merging parties, she wanted to 'make clear that, regardless of the acquisition, WhatsApp must continue to honor [its privacy] promises to consumers'.[35] If Facebook, post-merger, wanted to use data collected by WhatsApp in any way 'that is materially inconsistent with the promises WhatsApp made' when the data was collected, then Facebook first must obtain the individuals' affirmative consent.[36] She also reminded Facebook not to misrepresent the extent to which it maintains, or plans to maintain, the privacy or security of WhatsApp user data.[37]

Although the FTC has highlighted the Facebook/WhatsApp transaction as an ex- **6.21** ample of coordination between the agency's competition and consumer protection bureaus, this merger reveals the scope and limitations of the competition agencies' analytical tools. In the TomTom/Tele Atlas merger, the product was data, which

---

[33] Electronic Privacy Information Center, In Re WhatsApp, https://epic.org/privacy/internet/ftc/whatsapp/ (quoting WhatsApp's privacy policy from 2012).

[34] Ibid.

[35] Letter from Jessica Rich, Director, Bureau of Consumer Protection to Erin Egan, Chief Privacy Officer, Facebook, Inc and Anne Hoge, General Counsel, WhatsApp Inc, 10 April 2014 ('Rich Letter'), https://www.ftc.gov/system/files/documents/public_statements/297701/140410facebookwhatappltr.pdf.

[36] Ibid, p 3.

[37] Ibid.

was traded in the market. Thus, the European Commission could inquire whether, if the price of navigable digital mapping data increased by a small, but significant, non-transitory amount, purchasers would likely switch to other databases. Here, in contrast, the data was not traded on the market. Moreover, Facebook offered both its social networking platform and texting service for free to collect data on its users for behavioural advertising.

6.22 What is interesting here is that competition occurs on several levels: on one level, companies compete to attract consumers to spend time on their platforms and, for those with advertising-driven models, the personal data; on a second level, companies compete over the means to collect the personal data, which in this case is texting apps. On a third level, they compete on the 'paid' advertising side of the multi-sided platform. Thus the Facebook/WhatsApp merger could potentially harm several different groups: advertisers, with higher rates; users of text apps (with less quality, innovation, and privacy protection for their data); and lastly competitors who are foreclosed from achieving scale.

6.23 As Chapter 15 explores, competition authorities at times consider only the merger's impact on the advertising side of multi-sided platforms, ignoring its impact on the free side. The European Commission, to its credit, considered this data-driven merger's impact on both sides of the platform, and considered the accumulation of user data as a theory of competitive harm.

6.24 The European Commission first identified how Facebook offered its social networking platform and texting services for free, in order to amass a significant amount of personal data: 'Facebook collects data regarding the users of its social networking platforms and analyses them in order to serve advertisements on behalf of advertisers, which are "targeted" at each particular user of its social networking platforms.'[38] Because WhatsApp, before the merger, unlike Facebook, did not collect valuable data on its users for advertising purposes, the transaction, the Commission found, did 'not increase the amount of data potentially available to Facebook for advertising purposes'.[39]

6.25 That, of course, could change post-merger. So the Commission considered two theories of harm, whereby Facebook could strengthen its position in online advertising by: '(i) introducing advertising on WhatsApp, and/or (ii) using WhatsApp

---

[38] European Commission, 'Mergers', above note 31.

[39] *Facebook/WhatsApp*, above note 31, para 166 (noting that WhatsApp 'did not collect data about its users concerning age, verified name, gender, social group, activities, consuming habits or other characteristics that are valuable for advertising purposes', did 'not store messages once they are delivered', and had no record of the content of that message once delivered).

as a potential source of user data for the purpose of improving the targeting of Facebook's advertising activities outside WhatsApp.'[40]

6.26 Under the Commission's first theory of harm, Facebook 'could introduce targeted advertising on WhatsApp by analysing user data collected from WhatsApp's users (and/or from Facebook users who are also WhatsApp users)', which would 'have the effect of reinforcing Facebook's position in the online advertising market or sub-segments thereof'.[41] The public version of the Commission's decision redacted commercially sensitive information, so we do not see all the facts upon which the Commission relied. It appears from what was published that Facebook could introduce ads on WhatsApp, but, given certain post-merger strategies, Facebook lacked the incentive. (The details of Facebook's plans were also redacted.)[42] Basically, although Facebook could put ads on WhatsApp, it would not want to.

6.27 But even if Facebook did introduce ads on the formerly ad-free WhatsApp, the Commission found that there 'will continue to be a sufficient number of other actual and potential competitors who are equally well placed as Facebook to offer targeted advertising'.[43] Under its first theory, the Commission's primary concern was the advertiser, not consumers.

6.28 The Commission's second theory of harm considered the implications of a data-driven economy on competition policy. The Commission inquired whether Facebook would use WhatsApp users' data to better target them elsewhere on Facebook's platform.[44]

6.29 Here too Facebook reportedly had 'no current plans to modify WhatsApp's collection and use of user data'.[45] Some market participants, however, believed otherwise. The merger would give Facebook access to more data on hundreds of millions of WhatsApp users. The increase in data under Facebook's control would 'materially strengthen' Facebook's position in providing online advertising services, and in particular behavioural advertising.[46] Other market

---

[40] Ibid, para 167.

[41] Ibid, para 168.

[42] Ibid, paras 173–5.

[43] Ibid, para 179.

[44] Ibid, para 180 ('post-Transaction, the merged entity could start collecting data from WhatsApp users with a view to improving the accuracy of the targeted ads served on Facebook's social networking platform to WhatsApp users that are also Facebook users').

[45] Ibid, para 182.

[46] Ibid, para 184 ('certain respondents suggested that post-Transaction Facebook would integrate its social networking platform and consumer communications app with WhatsApp and described a number of alternative forms that such integration could take. According to these respondents, such integration would allow Facebook to have access to additional data from WhatsApp users to be monetised through advertising.').

participants disagreed, predicting that if Facebook began collecting data from WhatsApp users (eg, age, gender, country, message content), then 'some users' would 'switch to different consumer communications apps that they perceive as less intrusive'.[47]

6.30 In the end, the Commission never predicted whether Facebook would or would not collect data from WhatsApp users. Even if Facebook were to collect and use data from WhatsApp users, the transaction 'would only raise competition concerns,' the Commission stated 'if the concentration of data within Facebook's control were to allow it to strengthen its position in advertising'.[48]

6.31 Looking at the advertising side, the Commission concluded that it would not as there 'are currently a significant number of market participants that collect data alongside Facebook', namely Google, 'which accounts for a significant portion of the Internet user data', and 'companies such as Apple, Amazon, eBay, Microsoft, AOL, Yahoo!, Twitter, IAC, LinkedIn, Adobe and Yelp, among others'.[49]

6.32 The Commission also estimated the share of data collection across the web (Figure 6.1):[50]

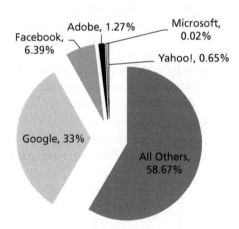

Figure 6.1 Share of Data Collection Across the Web

---

[47] Ibid, para 186.
[48] Ibid, para 187.
[49] Ibid, para 188.
[50] *Source*: ibid.

The Commission gave the following caveats: the data originated from an external market intelligence company 'for purposes unrelated to the assessment of the Transaction'; the data are presented 'for purely illustrative purposes' and 'without prejudice to any possible market definition as regards the provision of data'.[51] Thus the Commission concluded that, 'regardless of whether the merged entity will start using WhatsApp user data to improve targeted advertising on Facebook's social network, there will continue to be a large amount of Internet user data that are valuable for advertising purposes and that are not within Facebook's exclusive control'.[52]

On the consumer side, the Commission concluded that the merger was unlikely **6.33** to lessen competition for texting apps. The Commission recognized that one important, non-price parameter of competition was 'privacy and security, the importance of which varies from user to user but which are becoming increasingly valued, as shown by the introduction of consumer communications apps specifically addressing privacy and security issues'.[53] But the Commission cited the differences in Facebook's and WhatsApp's privacy protections as evidence of their not being close competitors.[54] The Commission, in its closing statement, repeated that Facebook Messenger and WhatsApp were 'not close competitors and that consumers would continue to have a wide choice of alternative consumer communications apps after the transaction'.[55] The Commission also found no significant costs prevented consumers from switching between different communications apps. Moreover, the Commission found that, 'while network effects exist in the market for consumer communications apps', they were 'unlikely to shield the merged entity from competition from new and existing consumer communications apps'.[56]

This decision represents the vanguard of the current analysis of data-driven merg- **6.34** ers in multi-sided markets, where the product or service is free. Nonetheless, the analysis is limited.

First, although the estimated market share of data collected across the web is inter- **6.35** esting, data is not fungible. It is unclear whether the data from Adobe, Microsoft, or others have the same value to Facebook for advertising purposes as data from WhatsApp. Competition officials cannot simply estimate an overall data market and assess the merging companies' share of this market. As the OECD observed, '[a]ssessing the market value and market concentration through the economic value of the personal data will also not be very helpful in most cases as data has no intrinsic value, and its value depends on the context of its use.'[57]

---

[51] Ibid, para 188 n 107.
[52] Ibid, para 189.
[53] Ibid, para 87.
[54] Ibid, paras 102, 107.
[55] European Commission, 'Mergers', above note 31.
[56] *Facebook/WhatsApp*, above note 31, para 135.
[57] Ibid, para 87.

6.36 Second, the Commission concluded that, 'even if Facebook were to collect and use data from WhatsApp for advertising purposes, the transaction would not raise competition concerns because large amounts of valuable user data would remain available to competitors beyond Facebook's exclusive control'.[58] Other competitors may control valuable data. But the search data that is valuable to Google may not be as valuable to Facebook. Likewise, other companies will not necessarily have the kind of data that Facebook would control post-merger that provides it a competitive advantage and perhaps market power. Even if other companies could acquire the same type of user data, they may be unable to access, analyse, and capitalize on the data as quickly as Facebook could. Here, velocity can be key. Suppose Facebook can analyse in real-time what people are texting and use this information to target them with ads across its social platform. So, if I text my friend on catching up for lunch, Facebook can use this data instantly to advertise potential restaurants. Moreover, with the variety of data from my social network (including places my friends and I have written about or reviewed), Facebook can tailor the ads narrowly to my tastes. Rivals may have other valuable data about individuals, but nonetheless be at a competitive disadvantage without the texting data that advertisers covet.

6.37 Third, data is not a public good. The Commission concluded that the combination of the merging parties' data 'would not provide them with a unique, non-replicable advantage, because competitors would be able to obtain large amounts of data or data analytics services in other ways, for instance, from data brokers or data analytics services providers, or by collecting and analysing data themselves'.[59] Returning to Big Data's four 'V's, we can agree that currently there exists a large *volume* and *variety* of Internet user data that is *valuable* for advertising purposes. We can also assume that not all of this data is within Facebook's exclusive control. This does not mean that such data is freely available to other market participants and potential entrants. Facebook, as the Commission noted, neither sold the user data it collected nor provided data analytics services to advertisers or other third parties as a stand-alone product separate from the advertising space itself.[60] So the competition authority needs to consider not only how much data the merged entity has relative to the outside world, but how much data the merged entity has relative to what is readily available elsewhere. If only a few companies control the type of data necessary to compete effectively, and each firm does not license the data to others, then the merger may soften competition.

---

[58] Eleonora Ocello, Cristina Sjödin, and Anatoly Suboĉs, 'What's Up with Merger Control in the Digital Sector? Lessons from the Facebook/WhatsApp EU Merger Case', 1 *Competition Merger Brief* (February 2015): p 6.

[59] Ibid, p 6.

[60] *Facebook/WhatsApp*, above note 31, para 70.

Fourth, while recognizing that Facebook may start collecting and using data from **6.38**
WhatsApp users, the Commission had a crimped view about Facebook controlling
so much data:

> For the purposes of this decision, the Commission has analysed potential data con-
> centration only to the extent that it is likely to strengthen Facebook's position in
> the online advertising market or in any sub-segments thereof. Any privacy-related
> concerns flowing from the increased concentration of data within the control of
> Facebook as a result of the Transaction do not fall within the scope of the EU com-
> petition law rules but within the scope of the EU data protection rules.[61]

This misses an important issue, namely, would consumers be harmed if Facebook
were to start collecting and using data from WhatsApp users? The European
Commission officials, however, justified their reasoning as consistent with the following statement by the Court of Justice of the European Union (CJEU) in *Asnef-*
Equifax: 'any possible issues relating to the sensitivity of personal data are not, as
such, a matter for competition law, they may be resolved on the basis of the relevant
provisions governing data protection.'[62] As the antitrust lawyer Alec Burnside commented, the CJEU never provided any analysis for this cryptic statement.[63]

The Commission simply erred in stating that the concerns of one firm controlling so **6.39**
much data were strictly a privacy issue, not a competition issue. It erred in considering the issue of data concentration only on one side of a multi-sided platform, namely
its potential impact on the advertising market. That considers only half the picture.
Data concentration can affect multiple sides of a multi-sided market. For example,
data concentration can raise entry barriers for those introducing a new texting app,
search engine, social network, or whatever product or service collecting data. The
Commission also erred in assuming that any privacy-related concerns flowing from
the increased concentration of data were beyond the scope of competition law. Indeed,
in 2015, the three Commission officials who cited the *Asnef-Equifax* case elaborated
how the degradation in privacy protections could violate the competition laws:

> a website that, post-merger, would start requiring more personal data from users or
> supplying such data to third parties as a condition for delivering its 'free' product
> could be seen as either increasing its price or as degrading the quality of its product.
> In certain circumstances, this behaviour could arguably amount to an infringement
> of competition law (irrespective of whether or not it also constitutes an infringement
> of data protection rules).[64]

---

[61] Ibid, para 164.

[62] Ocello et al, above note 58, p 7, quoting Case C-238/05 *Asnef-Equifax v Asociación de Usuarios*
de Servicios Bancarios (Ausbanc) [2006] ECR I-11125.

[63] Alec J Burnside, 'Setting the Scene', Paper presented at Antitrust, Privacy & Big Data: A Conference
Organized in Partnership with Concurrences, 3 February 2015, p 3, http://www.cadwalader.com/
uploads/books/02988a47b5380206e491de648f24924b.pdf. *See also* Alec J Burnside, 'No Such Thing as
a Free Search: Antitrust and the Pursuit of Privacy Goals', CPI Antitrust Chronicle, May 2015.

[64] Ocello et al, above note 58, p 6.

6.40 A fifth problem with the *Facebook/WhatsApp* decision involves the Commission's assumption of consumers readily detecting quality degradation. In addressing the likelihood of consumer lock-in, the Commission assumed that consumers could readily detect the exercise of market power post-merger and switch to rivals. As three officials commented, 'consumers switch almost instantaneously if an app fails to fulfil their needs.'[65] This may be true post-merger when the app's price significantly increases, the app stops working, or its performance declines significantly. Here, in contrast, the merger could have substantially lessened the degree of privacy protections afforded to the data. The Commission never explored whether competition along this important parameter would likely diminish post-merger, whether consumers would readily detect the degradation of privacy protection, and if so, whether a sufficient number of consumers would switch to other texting apps that afforded greater privacy protections. We will explore this further in Chapter 17.

6.41 Sixth, as we shall see in Chapters 11–14, the Commission failed to consider how the merger increases entry barriers, given several data-driven network effects. The Commission considered only the traditional direct network effects, which while important, are only part of the picture.

6.42 Finally, it is hard to fathom under the Commission's analysis why Facebook acquired WhatsApp. Under neoclassical economic theory, companies merge for efficiencies and/or market power. Here, Facebook ultimately paid a lot of money—USD 21.8 billion (USD 4 billion of which in cash)—to acquire a company that in 2013 earned only USD 10.21 million in revenues (mainly from subscribers in a few countries), suffered a net loss of USD 138.146 million, and given its pre-existing privacy policy, did not amass a lot of user data.

6.43 For the Commission, the 'purchase price is not a parameter for determining the likely effects of a transaction on competition'.[66] But one wonders why Facebook paid so much for a company losing so much money. Certainly not for any prospective efficiencies. Facebook promised to run WhatsApp as a separate company, and significant technical hurdles prevented the integration of WhatsApp and Facebook.[67] Thus, it is doubtful that merger-specific efficiencies were driving this merger.[68] If efficiencies were not driving the merger, then, absent folly and hubris on Facebook's part, the data-driven merger must somehow have provided a sustainable competitive advantage. But the Commission predicted that it would not.

6.44 It does not add up. If the market, despite the high market shares, had, as the Commission depicted, low entry barriers, little likelihood of market power from

---

[65] Ibid, p 5.
[66] Ibid, p 1.
[67] *Facebook/WhatsApp*, above note 31, paras 138–9, 160.
[68] Indeed, the word 'efficiency' does not appear in the Commission's decision.

network effects, and a small, if any, data-advantage, one is puzzled why Facebook spent so much on what would seem so little.

One does not expect the competition authority to chase down every anticompetitive **6.45** theory. But Facebook dominates the social networking industry, and the merger involved the two most popular texting apps. The Commission never analysed whether the acquisition was a defensive mechanism aimed to deprive its remaining competitors of the scale necessary to compete effectively. Would the addition of WhatsApp amplify the data-driven network effects we will see in Chapters 11–13 (making it harder for another firm to displace Facebook)? Facebook would continue scooping up data with its popular texting service, Facebook Messenger, while WhatsApp represented a moat to prevent inroads from rival, privacy-focused texting apps. Other theories suggest that the merger would enable Facebook to increase (or at least defend) its market power, through data. The theories' overarching themes are about attention and user data:

> WhatsApp has proven it can capture the former, and while Facebook says it has very little of the latter from WhatsApp, that can change, and messaging can become a rich data source for Facebook's core advertising business. Perhaps that sounds scary, but it's not much different from how Gmail works now.[69]

Meanwhile, under Facebook's control, WhatsApp's reputation for privacy has di- **6.46** minished. In 2015, WhatsApp received terrible privacy marks (even worse than its owner Facebook's marks). The Electronic Frontier Foundation told WhatsApp that it would be included in the consumer group's annual privacy report, and 'yet it barely budged on its privacy practices'.[70] The consumer group criticized WhatsApp for not publicly requiring a warrant before giving content to law enforcement, not publishing a transparency report or a law enforcement guide, not informing users about government data demands, not providing advance notice to users about government data demands, and not publishing information about its data retention policies, including retention of IP addresses and deleted content.[71] Moreover, in 2015, two security failures of WhatsApp were reported: hackers without a WhatsApp account could monitor the activities of WhatsApp users even if they turned on the privacy settings, and a security flaw enabled others to see users' profile photos even if they set it to 'Contacts-only'.[72]

---

[69] Jared Newman, 'Facebook's WhatsApp Acquisition Explained', *Time*, 20 February 2014, http://time.com/8806/facebooks-whatsapp-acquisition-explained/.

[70] Andy Greenberg, 'Rating Tech Giants on Privacy: Google Slips, WhatsApp Fails', *Wired*, 18 June 2015, http://www.wired.com/2015/06/rating-tech-giants-privacy-google-slips-whatsapp-fails/.

[71] Electronic Frontier Foundation, *Who Has Your Back? Fifth Annual Report on Online Service Providers' Privacy and Transparency Practices Regarding Government Access to User Data*, 17 June 2015, https://www.eff.org/files/2015/06/18/who_has_your_back_2015_protecting_your_data_from_government_requests_20150618.pdf.

[72] Tech2 News, 'WhatsApp Security Flaw Allows Anyone to Track You Regardless of Your Privacy Settings', 13 February 2015, http://tech.firstpost.com/news-analysis/whatsapp-security-flaw-allows-anyone-to-track-you-regardless-of-your-privacy-settings-254265.html.

6.47   The European Commission opined that, notwithstanding the industry's network effects, consumers could easily switch to other texting apps. If that were true, one would expect the privacy-sensitive WhatsApp users to switch after these privacy shortcomings were revealed. But Facebook's dominance in texting has increased, not weakened. When the deal was announced, WhatsApp had 450 million users worldwide.[73] By the time the Commission announced its decision, WhatsApp had 600 million users.[74] By late 2015, WhatsApp had over 900 million active monthly users, more than the second-place Facebook Messenger (which had around 700 million active monthly users).[75] According to Facebook's CEO, 'numerous ways of monetizing the app will present themselves once it clocks 1 billion users'.[76] That occurred in early 2016,[77] along with Facebook reporting that it was exploring new business models for WhatsApp to 'allow organizations to communicate with individuals with the user's consent'.[78]

6.48   The consumer interest group Electronic Privacy Information Center noted how it 'pointed to the very clear consumer harm that would result from Facebook's acquisition of WhatsApp', how 'it was clear that the practical consequence of the merger would be to reduce the privacy protections for consumers and expose individuals to enhanced tracking and profiling', and how the 'failure of the Federal Trade Commission to take this [issue] into account during merger review is one of the main reasons consumer privacy in the United States has diminished significantly over the last 15 years'.[79]

C. FTC's 'Early Termination' of Its Review of the Alliance Data Systems Corp/Conversant Merger

6.49   In 2014, the FTC quickly reviewed the merger between Alliance Data Systems Corporation, 'a leading global provider of data-driven marketing and loyalty solutions' and Conversant, Inc, 'a leading digital marketing company'.[80] The USD 2.3 billion merger review was so quick that it never reached the Second Request stage, where the

---

[73]   Ocello et al, above note 58, p 1.

[74]   Ibid.

[75]   'How Popular is WhatsApp?', http://www.whatsappfor.org/facts/popular-whatsapp-world/.

[76]   'WhatsApp Has 900 Million Users, Closer Than Ever to a Real Business Model', NeuroGadget, 28 September 2015, http://neurogadget.com/2015/09/28/whatsapp-has-900-million-users-closer-than-ever-to-a-real-business-model/16373.

[77]   Deepa Seetharaman, 'WhatsApp Joins the Billion Users Club', *Wall Street Journal*, 1 February 2016, http://blogs.wsj.com/digits/2016/02/01/whatsapp-joins-the-billion-users-club/.

[78]   Natalia Drozdiak, 'WhatsApp to Drop Subscription Fee', *Wall Street Journal*, 18 January 2016.

[79]   Comments of the Electronic Privacy Information Center (EPIC) to the Federal Trade Commission, In re: Remedy Study, 'Assessment of the FTC's Prior Actions on Merger Review and Consumer Privacy', FTC File No P143100, 17 March 2015, https://epic.org/privacy/internet/ftc/Merger-Remedy-3-17.pdf.

[80]   Conversant Media, 'Alliance Data to Acquire Ad Tech Leader Conversant for Approximately $2.3 Billion', Press Release, 11 September 2014 ('Conversant Press Release'), http://www.conversantmedia.com/press-release/alliance-data-acquire-ad-tech-leader-conversant-approximately-23-billion.

agency formally requests more information and documents. Instead, the FTC granted early termination, a measure typically reserved for mergers that on their face do not present competitive concerns. This prompted the following rebuke by two consumer groups:

> We are deeply concerned that the commission failed to examine sufficiently the consequences to competition—and to privacy—of the consolidation of two powerful sets of consumer data. This merger reflects the continuing consolidation of the consumer data marketplace, an issue that the FTC must address. The Alliance/ Conversant deal also raises serious privacy concerns, including with its intended goal of further unleashing powerful tracking technologies that follow individuals across all of their devices and applications. Both companies play leading roles providing data for financial services targeting, and Conversant is at the forefront of online lead-generation practices. The commission's approval of this transaction without appropriate safeguards directly undermines its role as the country's chief privacy regulator. The FTC cannot, on the one hand, express concern about the discriminatory and privacy implications of 'Big Data' and the invisible role of data-brokers, but at the same time silently consent to expanded commercial surveillance of the American people.[81]

6.50 The merging companies built their business models on Big Data. They collected a lot of data on individuals' behaviour both online and offline. The enormous volume and variety of data helped them identify 'individual needs, preferences and motivations'.[82]

6.51 They then analysed the data to target us with 'personalized messages...aimed at engendering loyalty and driving sales'.[83] Conversant states that '[v]irtually every aspect of these ads are [sic] personalized to perfectly reflect the unique needs, interests and motivations of each individual'.[84]

6.52 They next delivered targeted messages, broadly 'ranging from direct mail, point of sale, email, mobile, social and targeted display'.[85] Conversant offered the following example of how it uses your personal data to track and target you:

> [Conversant] might generate new memberships for a health club by facilitating the placement of offers on websites relating to fitness or athletics. It would then manage both sides of the process including the tracking of effectiveness of the ads and settlement. Going forward, the CJ product offering [CJ serves as an intermediary between 'publishers' (ie, websites or mobile applications) and 'advertisers' (eg, retail, travel and financial services companies)] is evolving not only to link the advertiser

---

[81] Letter from Jeff Chester, Executive Director, Center for Digital Democracy and Edward Mierzwinski, Director, U.S. PIRG Education Fund, to Chairwoman Edith Ramirez, Federal Trade Commission, 5 November 2014 ('Chester Letter'), http://images.politico.com/global/2014/11/04/ftcletter110514.pdf.

[82] Conversant Media, Our Approach, http://www.conversantmedia.co.uk/our-approach ('The Conversant Personalization Platform leverages profiles assembled from vast amounts of diverse marketing information including proprietary brand data along with Conversant-exclusive behavioral, demographic, purchase and ad interaction data.').

[83] Conversant Press Release, above note 80.

[84] Conversant Media, Our Approach, above note 82.

[85] Conversant Press Release, above note 80.

to appropriate publisher sites, but also to use enormous amounts of data to link the advertiser to specific individuals, wherever they browse. The use of data to drive the 'personalization' desired by the advertising community is in complete alignment with Alliance Data's overall model of data-driven targeted marketing.[86]

6.53 Their business strategy is built on tracking us across our desktops, tablets, and mobile devices, using our data to target us day and night, online and offline with personalized ads, and assessing how effectively they exploited the personal data, using the marketing campaign's return on investment.[87]

6.54 The companies acquired data in part through cookies.[88] But this merger, the two consumer interest groups noted, would help Alliance/Conversant collect personal data beyond cookies:

> [T]his transaction illustrates the dramatic and unfettered growth of so-called 'cookie-less' cross-screen/device-tracking. Facebook, Google, Conversant, and others have developed data tracking technologies and techniques to supplement and supplant their 'cookie'-based tracking. The goal is to use a single identifier to track and target individuals regardless of what device they use, such as mobile phones. For example, Experian now offers an 'OmniView Identity-Linkage Engine' that provides a persistent 'single customer view by establishing identification keys for consumers at an individual, household, and address level that serve as a common denominator between all data sources'.[89]

6.55 The volume, velocity, and variety of data provided, according to the merging parties, significant value in identifying 'a brand's ideal target from more than 263 million verified, anonymous profiles with more than 200 individual attributes' and then leveraging 'vast amounts of exclusive browsing, shopping, interaction, and purchase data that powers superior audience modeling, targeting accuracy and campaign optimization'.[90] Thus, this merger accelerated the four 'V's of Big Data; the issue was whether the concentration of data in one company raised any competitive concerns. The FTC never said.

6.56 Under conventional antitrust analysis, the competition agency focuses on the buyers of the merging parties' products and services (except in the case of monopsony, where the focus is on the sellers to the merged entity). Here, under the conventional analysis, the competition agency would inquire whether the

---

[86] Ibid.

[87] Ibid (discussing how it uses first-party transactional data and its own proprietary data sources, linked to a persistent, anonymous Common ID which can recognize and target individuals across devices (desktop, tablet, mobile)).

[88] Conversant, Inc, Annual Report Pursuant to Section 13 or 15(d) of the Securities Exchange Act of 1934 for the Year Ended December 31, 2013, filed 3 March 2014, p 14 ('Conversant 2013 Annual Report'), http://files.shareholder.com/downloads/AMDA-2MDMHL/3704485697x0xS1080034-14-14/1080034/filing.pdf ('Websites typically place small files of non-personalized (or "anonymous") information, commonly known as cookies, on an Internet user's hard drive. Cookies generally collect information about users on a non-personalized basis to enable websites to provide users with a more customized experience. Cookie information is passed to the website through an Internet user's browser software.').

[89] Chester Letter, above note 81.

[90] Conversant 2013 Annual Report, above note 88, p 8.

merger would harm advertisers, namely would they have to pay higher prices for Alliance/Conversant's services post-merger. This was unlikely. Alliance and Conversant's strategic rationale for the merger was to create 'a truly unique end-to-end marketing services company that will empower clients to more effectively market to their customers across all channels'.[91] Moreover, the advertisers were large, consumer-based industries with sufficient clout to prevent Alliance/Conversant from raising prices.

The FTC could have pursued another conventional theory of harm, namely whether **6.57** the merger increased entry barriers. Interestingly, the merging companies touted how their merger increased not only the volume and variety of data[92] but also provided the company with needed scale.[93] As Chapters 12–13 discuss, the increasing returns to scale and scope from data can constitute a network effect, which enable some firms to dominate the market. A dominant data-collector could hurt both advertisers and consumers. It is unclear, however, whether the increase in Alliance/Conversant's scale, here, would lead to greater market power.

The problem is that the conventional antitrust analysis focuses on the output of **6.58** behavioural advertising and welfare of advertisers who use our personal data to target us. The concern is that the merger enables Alliance/Conversant to charge higher prices, which may also reduce the output of behavioural ads and perhaps prevent some firms from tracking us.

We, the consumers, are not part of this equation. If the merger helps advertisers, in **6.59** enabling Alliance/Conversant to better track and target us, that under the conventional antitrust theory ends the inquiry. The merger, however, could lead to even more intrusive tracking of our behaviour, which in turn reduces our welfare. The competition authority's response is typically, 'That isn't our concern.' If the behavioural tracking and advertising are legal, then the FTC does not opine whether more or less of that conduct is socially desirable. That inquiry is left to the legislative branch.

One US court struggled with a similar issue when the FTC challenged a tobacco **6.60** merger. The judge noted how the FTC's action—namely to prevent the tobacco companies from raising price—appeared 'anomalous' when juxtaposed to other government efforts to reduce Americans' consumption of tobacco.[94] Other government agencies sought to discourage consumption by 'increasing the prices of tobacco products through taxes, regulating tobacco advertising,

---

[91] Conversant Press Release, above note 80.

[92] Ibid.

[93] Ibid (noting how the 'combination of the two companies provides scale in the rapidly growing display, mobile, video, and social digital channels').

[94] *FTC v Swedish Match*, 131 F Supp 2d 151, 153–4 n 1 (US Dist Ct (D DC), 2000).

and decreasing the amount of shelf space devoted to tobacco products at stores'. Here the FTC was vigorously opposing a chewing tobacco merger because it could lead to higher prices. As the court remarked, the FTC's effort 'appears to be incoherent with [the government's] other efforts respecting tobacco'. The court ultimately enjoined the merger, siding with the FTC: if the acquisition were permitted then consumption of loose leaf tobacco would not decline. Rather, consumers simply would pay more or switch to other tobacco products. Thus, there was, the court found, 'ultimately no public health benefit to permitting the acquisition'.

6.61 One could argue that smokeless tobacco is like Alliance/Conversant's tracking and profiling of our behaviour. It is not up to the FTC to judge whether society would be better off with more or less privacy intrusions; that inquiry is left to others. The competition authority simply asks whether the merger may substantially lessen competition among the data brokers.

6.62 But a rejoinder is that the privacy concerns involving Big Data differ from smokeless tobacco. When tobacco producers merge, many consumers (addicted to nicotine) would still demand tobacco; they just pay higher prices. The issue then is who should get the money—the tobacco company or government (through higher taxes). Here, in contrast, a merger of data-gatherers could increase advertising rates and, if demand is more elastic than tobacco, reduce the output of behavioural tracking and behavioural ads.

6.63 So, unlike tobacco, we have a trade-off: the merger can benefit advertisers (by lowering the price of behavioural ads or enabling the merged firm to better track us) while harming individuals who do not like being tracked. Alternatively, the merger could harm advertisers (by raising the price of behavioural ads or cost of tracking) while increasing individuals' welfare (if less tracking occurs). The merger could also reduce our welfare (if the advertisers' demand is inelastic and we end up paying for the higher advertising costs). Competition authorities do not know how to reconcile these trade-offs. Going forward, they cannot avoid this trade-off with data-driven mergers involving multi-sided platforms.

6.64 The merger may also hit our pocketbooks. This data-driven merger significantly increases the variety and volume of personal data that Alliance/Conversant possesses to better target us with personalized messages across multiple channels, and thereby increase its clients' sales. The merger, in concentrating so much sensitive data in one company's hands, would likely enable Alliance/Conversant's clients to optimize prices through price discrimination. Basically, Alliance/Conversant could devise better ways to identify consumers who can be charged more. Even though consumers do not interact with the merging parties, the merger could reduce their welfare. Thus the FTC should have considered whether the merger may foster price discrimination (particularly against more vulnerable members of the community) and reduce individuals' privacy. If so, the merger reduces consumer welfare and constitutes an unreasonable restraint of trade.

D. Google/Nest Labs and Google/Dropcam

6.65 Why would Google spend USD 3.2 *billion* in cash to buy a manufacturer of thermostats and carbon monoxide detectors? Why would it spend USD 555 million for a home monitoring camera, which, with its advertised 130° field of view, can 'capture an entire room without ever having to pan or zoom'?[95] And do those acquisitions raise any competition concerns? The answer is not obvious.

6.66 In February 2014, the FTC again granted early termination to Google's acquisition of Nest Labs, Inc, which makes Nest Learning Thermostat, and Nest Protect, a smart carbon monoxide detector.[96] In June 2014, Google acquired Dropcam, a home monitoring camera.

6.67 It is highly unlikely that Google suddenly became interested in thermostats and security cameras. Rather, these were likely data-driven mergers. The concern here is that Google 'could use data collected from people's homes to better target its advertising'.[97] According to one report,

> Nest's thermostat, for instance, doesn't just turn itself on and off when you tell it. Over time, as the Nest Learning Thermostat uses its sensors to train itself according to your comings and goings, the entire network of Nests in homes across the country becomes smarter.
>
> The paramount value of the devices, in a sense, lies not in the hardware itself but the interconnectedness of that hardware. As the devices talk to each other, by building an aggregate picture of human behavior, they anticipate what we want before even we know.
>
> …
>
> Now imagine that infrastructure not just connected, but connected by Google. With its product and design expertise, Nest provides Google an ideal platform for stretching the power of its own intelligent machines beyond the web and into the internet of things.
>
> …

---

[95] Nest, Meet Nest Cam, https://www.dropcam.com/dropcam-pro.

[96] FTC, 'Google Inc; Nest Labs, Inc', Early Termination Notice 20140457, 4 February 2014, http://www.ftc.gov/enforcement/premerger-notification-program/early-termination-notices/20140457.

[97] John Ribeiro, 'Google's Acquisition of Nest Gets US FTC Clearance', *PC World*, 5 February 2014, http://www.pcworld.com/article/2095040/googles-acquisition-of-nest-gets-us-ftc-clearance.html.

This may sound creepy, but much like using Google for search, it could become the price of admission for participation in the internet of things. Every choice we make using connected devices leaves a trace. And no one is better than Google at figuring out how to turn those traces into dollars.[98]

6.68 In acquiring Nest and Dropcam, Google can acquire even more potentially sensitive data about what occurs in purchasers' homes.[99] Google sees these in-home smart technologies as the next frontier. As Google disclosed to the US Securities and Exchange Commission,

We expect the definition of 'mobile' to continue to evolve as more and more 'smart' devices gain traction in the market. For example, a few years from now, we and other companies could be serving ads and other content on refrigerators, car dashboards, thermostats, glasses, and watches, to name just a few possibilities.[100]

6.69 Thus the Internet of Things, such as 'smart' thermostats, serves as a means to better track us, extract more data about us, better profile us for personalized ads, induce us to consume more, and possibly charge those with fewer outside options higher prices. The smart technology can also become an advertising platform to target us with these ads. We see in the Google/Nest Labs merger how the distinction between our online and offline activities fades (especially with home security cameras). We may not worry about the data from our thermostats per se. But the thermostats will interact increasingly with other smart technology; the data collected from the televisions, thermostats, security cameras, smartphones, computers, cars, and appliances will capture many personal details used to profile us and target us with personalized ads. We shift from the world of outsized Times Square billboards to a world where at every turn a targeted ad greets us from our own belongings. To complement 'smart' security cameras and thermostats will likely come 'smart' door locks and door bells that identify and greet homeowners, perhaps with advertisement in the form of information, such as possible purchases for an upcoming trip booked online. Google expects 'that users will be using [its] services and viewing [its] ads on an increasingly wide diversity of devices in the future, and thus [its] advertising systems are becoming increasingly device-agnostic'.[101] In this multi-device future, advertisers can write one ad campaign, which the super-platforms, like Google or Apple, would

---

[98] Marcus Wohlsen, 'What Google Really Gets Out of Buying Nest for $3.2 Billion', *Wired*, 14 January 2014, http://www.wired.com/2014/01/googles-3-billion-nest-buy-finally-make-internet-things-real-us/.

[99] Steve Lohr, 'Google's Nest to Acquire Dropcam for $555 Million', *New York Times* Bits blog, 20 June 2014, http://bits.blogs.nytimes.com/2014/06/20/googles-nest-to-acquire-dropcam-for-555-million/ (reporting how 'the Nest and Dropcam products, in different ways, are high-tech sensors that monitor the activity of people in homes, which is potentially sensitive data').

[100] Google Inc, Letter to Securities and Exchange Commission, 20 December 2013, http://www.sec.gov/Archives/edgar/data/1288776/000128877613000074/filename1.htm.

[101] Ibid.

'serve dynamically to the right user at the right time on whatever device makes the most sense'.[102]

Moreover, the data from these smart technologies will interest governments. As **6.70** James Clapper, the US Director of National Intelligence, testified to the US Senate, '[i]n the future, intelligence services might use the [internet of things] for identification, surveillance, monitoring, location tracking, and targeting for recruitment, or to gain access to networks or user credentials.'[103]

These mergers share two issues with the Facebook/WhatsApp merger: what are **6.71** the competitive implications of personal data? How should the competition agencies treat the merging parties' pledge not to commingle data? Like WhatsApp, Nest Labs reported its intent to protect its customer data from its parent company, Google.[104] While this is reassuring, is this akin to a company promising to run its divisions separately and not raise prices? Typically, the competition authority rejects such pricing pledges. Moreover, if the company breaches its privacy pledge, it is unclear what recourse, if any, the competition agency has. Typically, such breaches are left to the privacy official, whose penalties generally have been weaker. So if compliance were left to privacy officials, would that deter companies from breaching their data-protection promises?

As Nest Labs reported in mid-2015 on its website, its 'privacy statement may change **6.72** from time to time', and the company would 'provide notice of any changes on the website or by contacting you'.[105] As of mid-2015, Nest Labs's website identified six previous policy statements. Moreover, the *Wall Street Journal* reported how Google would 'connect some of its apps to Nest, allowing Google to know when Nest users are at home or not'.[106] Nest Lab's co-founder remarked, 'We're not telling Google anything that it doesn't already know.'[107] One reason is that the 'popular Google

---

[102] Ibid.

[103] Spencer Ackerman and Sam Thielman, 'US Intelligence Chief: We Might Use the Internet of Things to Spy on You', *The Guardian*, 10 February 2016, http://www.theguardian.com/technology/2016/feb/09/internet-of-things-smart-home-devices-government-surveillance-james-clapper.

[104] Nest Labs, Inside Nest blog, 'The Nest Family Is Growing', 20 June 2014, https://nest.com/blog/2014/06/20/the-nest-family-is-growing/ ('Dropcam will come under Nest's privacy policy, which explains that data won't be shared with anyone (including Google) without a customer's permission. Nest has a paid-for business model and ads are not part of our strategy. In acquiring Dropcam, we'll apply that same policy to Dropcam too.').

[105] Nest Labs, Inc, 'Privacy Statement for Nest Products and Services', Nest, Policy active as of 17 June 2015, https://nest.com/legal/privacy-statement/. Previous privacy policies are at https://nest.com/legal/privacy-statement/archive/. The former Dropcam Terms of Service/Privacy Policy are available at https://www.dropcam.com/tos/dropcam.

[106] Rolfe Winkler and Alistair Barr, 'Nest to Share User Information with Google for the First Time', *Wall Street Journal* Digits blog, 24 June 2014, http://blogs.wsj.com/digits/2014/06/24/nest-to-share-user-information-with-google-for-first-time/.

[107] Ibid.

Maps app can already determine where users live and work based on where they carry their phones'.[108]

6.73 While Nest's statements are meant to assure us, a company's public commitment to safeguard privacy may not mean much, especially when many consumers cannot easily detect the degradation in privacy protection. In 2012, Lorrie Faith Cranor and Aleecia McDonald calculated that 'if internet users read every privacy policy they encountered online they would spend 25 days a year engaged in this activity'.[109] Few have the time to read the often opaque privacy statements. Even fewer would continually monitor changes to a company's privacy statement. Even if they did, the privacy policies can become hazier on how the data will be used. Thus, unlike a price increase, which may be more salient to consumers and competition authorities, the merging parties may find it easier to exercise market power by degrading their privacy protections post-merger. They can provide notice in a lengthy 'terms and conditions' for a software update, which many just simply accept without reading. So mergers can lead to small but significant reductions in quality in terms of privacy protections, without any significant risk of antitrust scrutiny.

6.74 Google and other smart appliance companies are now partnering with insurance companies, whereby the insurer offers a discount if you install Google's (or another company's) smart technology.[110] One insurance company spokeswoman told the *Chicago Tribune*, '[w]e believe customers seeking to monitor their homes with devices like Nest Protect demonstrate responsible behavior [including helping to mitigate such incidents as fires]. As a result, we offer these customers discounts on their home insurance policy.'[111] Many insurers in 2015 said they did not collect the personal data, or if they did, the data did not influence their decisions about policy cancellations, renewals, or claims. Nonetheless, one privacy lawyer observed, 'It's just a small series of steps from the collection of data to analysis to behavior modification to outright control. The question is, where on that continuum will consumers draw a line and say thus far and no further?'[112]

---

[108] Ibid.

[109] Joseph Turow, Michael Hennessy, and Nora Draper, *The Tradeoff Fallacy: How Marketers Are Misrepresenting American Consumers and Opening Them Up to Exploitation*, A Report from the Annenberg School for Communication, University of Pennsylvania, June 2015, p 8.

[110] Becky Yerak, 'Home Insurers Gaining an Entry: Policyholders Offered Discounts for Installing Watchful Devices, Privacy Concerns Arise', *Chicago Tribune*, 16 October 2015, p C1, http://www.chicagotribune.com/business/ct-insurers-home-monitoring-1016-biz-20151015-story.html.

[111] Ibid.

[112] Ibid.

E. Google/Waze

In a 2013 interview, Waze CEO Noam Bardin described the competitive battle **6.75** against Google: 'What search is for the Web, maps are for mobile.'[113] The search mechanism on smartphones, he said, was the map. To find restaurants, for example, you may look at Yelp reviews. But you may start your search on Yelp with a map of restaurants in a specific neighbourhood; alternatively, you may start with the users' reviews and end with the map location of your dining choice, with directions thereto. Very few companies hold this mapping data, and Google was outdistancing its rivals on maps, as it did with search. Waze, its CEO felt, posed the only real competition to Google maps. (Waze used to benchmark its map quality to Google's until Google terminated Waze's access to its APIs, or application programming interface, which is a set of programming instructions and standards for accessing the program and requesting services from that program.[114])

The stakes are large, as geo-location and mapping data are key for advertisers. Using **6.76** users' geo-location data, Google and Waze can track where people are and influence where they will go by providing them information on nearby advertisers (such as promoting a nearby Taco Bell). The first step is to target users by their location. The next step is to combine all the data on the user (tastes, search history, etc) to target him with behavioural ads. But as Waze's CEO recognized, the big question that Waze struggled with daily was whether third-party apps (like his company's) had room in the future on mobile eco-systems controlled by the super-platforms, Apple and Google. Independent app developers both are friends with, and enemies of, the super-platforms that control the mobile operating system, like Android and Apple's iOS. They are friends in that the super-platform wants to attract app developers and users to its operating system. They are enemies in that the super-platform may want users to use its own competing mapping app. So Waze's CEO raised in his interview a fundamental question in mobile: when the independent app has this 'frenemy' relationship, is there enough space for the independent app developer to achieve scale and what is the end-game? The favourable outcome is either being acquired or reaching sufficient scale to compete head-on against the super-platform that controls the mobile operating system.

[113] Liz Gannes, 'Maps Are for Mobile What Search Is for the Web, Says Waze CEO Noam Bardin (Video)', All Things Digital, 26 April 2013 ('Bardin Interview'), http://allthingsd.com/20130426/maps-are-for-mobile-what-search-is-for-the-web-says-waze-ceo-noam-bardin/.

[114] Ibid. David Orenstein, 'Application Programming Interface', *Computerworld*, 10 January 2000, http://www.computerworld.com/article/2593623/app-development/application-programming-interface.html.

6.77 To compete, Waze offered a 'dynamic mapping product that enables drivers to build and use live maps, real-time traffic updates and turn-by-turn navigation'.[115] For Waze's maps, the data's velocity or 'freshness' was key.[116] Waze's competitive advantage over Google, its CEO felt, was real-time data. Google supposedly spent 'billions' annually on updating mapping data. Apple, with its reliance on TomTom, was disadvantaged, as even TomTom could not compete against Google's resources. Waze, in contrast, relied on crowd-sourcing to keep its maps up to date, as well as provide real-time navigation. Thus Waze's biggest weapon against Google was its 44 million users, who both actively and passively contributed to its maps. Google 'uses money, we use people'.[117]

6.78 Depending how you see it, money or people won in 2013 when Google bought Waze for USD 1.3 billion. Here too a consumer group voiced concern over the merger's impact on data and privacy:

> Google already dominates the online mapping business with Google Maps. The Internet giant was able to muscle its way to dominance by unfairly favoring its own service ahead of such competitors as Mapquest in its online search results. Now with the proposed Waze acquisition the Internet giant would remove the most viable competitor to Google Maps in the mobile space. Moreover, it will allow Google access to even more data about online activity in a way that will increase its dominant position on the Internet.[118]

6.79 Neither the FTC nor the UK's Office of Fair Trading (OFT) challenged the merger.[119] The FTC, unlike the OFT, did not issue a closing statement, so we do not know its reasoning. So we will focus on the OFT's explanation for closing its investigation.

6.80 Since both the Waze and Google Maps apps were (and still are) offered for free, the OFT considered the merger's effect on non-price competition, namely innovation and quality.[120] The relevant product market, for the OFT's analysis, was

---

[115] UK Office of Fair Trading, Completed Acquisition by Motorola Mobility Holding (Google, Inc.) of Waze Mobile Limited, ME/6167/13 (17 December 2013), para 3 ('OFT, Google/Waze'), http://webarchive.nationalarchives.gov.uk/20140402142426/http:/www.oft.gov.uk/shared_oft/mergers_ea02/2013/motorola.pdf.

[116] Ibid, para 17 ('the up-to-dateness or "freshness" of the map is considered important by users, both in terms of the accuracy of the directions and also the real-time information regarding incidents on the route such as traffic congestion and alternative routing').

[117] Bardin Interview, above note 113.

[118] Consumer Watchdog, Letter to Antitrust Division, US Department of Justice, 12 June 2013, http://www.consumerwatchdog.org/resources/cltrdojwaze061213.pdf.

[119] Sara Forden and David McLaughlin, 'Google Said to Avoid U.S. Antitrust Challenge Over Waze', Bloomberg Business, 1 October 2013, http://www.bloomberg.com/news/2013-10-01/google-said-to-avoid-u-s-antitrust-challenge-over-waze.html; OFT, Google/Waze, above note 115.

[120] OFT, Google/Waze, above note 115, para 27 ('OFT considers the extent to which current and future rivalry between the two firms may be removed, with the effect being to reduce the incentives on the parties to invest in further development of their mapping product, to innovate, and to reduce the quality of service offered to users.').

'turn-by-turn navigation applications for mobile devices (including smartphones and tablets)'.[121] The OFT examined 'the possibility that the merger may result in the loss of a growing and innovative competitor in the form of Waze which provided a constraint on Google and might provide an increasingly strong constraint going forward in the supply of turn-by-turn navigation applications for mobile devices'.[122]

Two companies dominated the UK market: Apple Maps, which based on its UK **6.81** sales of smartphones, accounted somewhere up to 30 per cent of the supply of turn-by-turn applications on mobile devices and Google Maps, with over 50 per cent.[123]

Ultimately, the OFT did not challenge the merger because the evidence did not **6.82** indicate that Waze acted as a strong competitive constraint on Google Maps in the UK.[124] The evidence was not determinative of 'Waze becoming a significant competitor in the UK or that it would be a disruptive force in the market'.[125] Waze simply had an insufficient number of UK users to significantly constrain Google and Apple Maps.[126]

Waze, to be an effective competitor, needed two things: first, quality and timely **6.83** map data and, second, a large user base.[127] Interestingly, it was Waze's inability to achieve sufficient scale to benefit from the data-driven network effects that hindered its competitive significance. (We will explore these network effects in Chapter 12.)

Here we see the chicken-or-egg dilemma. The more users who supply Waze with **6.84** traffic and road data, the better Waze's application becomes, the more likely Waze attracts additional users. But to attract users, Waze needed an appealing product, namely up-to-date and accurate UK road and traffic conditions. But to get the data necessary to effectively compete against Google's mapping technology, Waze needed more users. But to get more users, it needed the appealing product.

The OFT's decision raises several issues. One is over entry barriers. On the one **6.85** hand, the OFT noted that Waze had a relatively small presence in the UK; it was unable to reach the scale necessary to represent a significant competitive threat. On the other hand, the OFT suggested that Waze's inability to scale up was unlikely

---

[121] Ibid, para 13.
[122] Ibid, para 26.
[123] Ibid, para 30.
[124] Ibid.
[125] Ibid, para 52.
[126] Ibid, paras 65, 74 (finding 'Apple Maps represents a close competitor and a strong constraint on Google Maps reflecting the level of competition observed in the smartphone market,' that 'the remaining application providers such as TomTom or Navfree currently represent some competitive constraint on Google', and that 'other products and services that offer some form of map-based or navigational service... are likely to provide some, albeit limited, competitive constraint on Google Maps').
[127] Ibid, para 55.

to represent an entry barrier for other start-ups or existing competitors. It is hard to see how any competitor not pre-installed on a mobile phone could quickly scale up—especially when competing against Apple and Google. The OFT, for example, noted that Microsoft would likely be at a competitive disadvantage in offering turn-by-turn navigation applications for mobile smartphones and tablets. Seemingly of all the potential entrants, Microsoft had several advantages: Microsoft is a familiar name for operating systems generally; it was developing at the time an operating system for smartphones and tablets, on which it could pre-install Bing Maps, and tie to its search engine, Bing. And Microsoft has money. So if Microsoft could not make a successful go at it, how easy would it be for any independent app developer *not* pre-installed on a smartphone, *not* automatically collecting trace data, and *not* integrated with other important functions (such as search and social networks) to challenge Google and Apple?

6.86 Second, the OFT never addressed competition in the secondary market and lock-in effects. OFT made much of Apple as a significant competitive constraint for Google post-merger. But Apple was a constraint at the point of purchase of a smartphone. While Apple iPhone users could download Google maps, users of Google's Android system could not download Apple Maps on their smartphones. Apple Maps was (and as of mid 2016 is) only available on Apple iPhones.[128] To switch to Apple Maps, Android users would have to switch phones, which would likely mean getting out of their existing phone contract and incurring the expense of a new iPhone. Android smartphone users dissatisfied with Google Maps could, however, download Waze or another app. So Waze was a more viable option for Android smartphone users than Apple Maps, and it was unclear how Apple represented a strong direct competitive constraint on Google for existing Android users.

6.87 Third, the OFT assumed that for the merger to be anticompetitive, Waze either had to be a significant competitor or would likely become a disruptive force in the market. The OFT's inquiry of whether the acquisition would substantially lessen competition makes sense in competitive markets where no firm dominates. But it does not make sense where one company controls over half the market, and where data-driven network effects can help the strong become even stronger. Under the OFT's logic, a monopolist could acquire the few nascent competitive threats, so long as these competitors have not reached scale and become disruptive forces in the marketplace. As a basic principle, should a monopoly be allowed to acquire smaller competitors? Since competition law prohibits mergers that tend to create monopolies, it follows that competition law also prohibits mergers that help maintain monopolies. Rather than ask whether Waze currently is a significant competitor, the

---

[128] Ibid, para 60.

competition authority instead should ask whether the merger is reasonably capable of helping the monopoly maintain its dominant position.

Take for example Aluminum Company of America's acquisition of a smaller **6.88** competitor, Rome Cable Corporation.[129] The acquisition, the US Supreme Court noted, gave the dominant firm Alcoa only 1.3 per cent additional control of the aluminium conductor line market.[130] While an aggressive competitor, Rome, given its tiny market share, was unlikely a significant competitor or a disruptive force in the market.[131] It is unlikely that the Department of Justice (DOJ) in the *Alcoa* case could prove why and how prices would increase as a result of the merger, or the magnitude of the price increase. If the agencies or courts required proof of the merger's actual and specific anticompetitive effects post-merger, then already dominant firms could acquire smaller rivals, notwithstanding the competition laws. This standard, besides being unrealistic, contravenes the legislative intent. In the Alcoa/Rome Cable merger, the Supreme Court did not ramble through the wilds of economic theory. Instead, the Court turned to the Clayton Act and its legislative history: the legislative history of the 1950 Celler–Kefauver Amendments to the Clayton Act showed that 'the objective was to prevent accretions of power which "are individually so minute as to make it difficult to use the Sherman Act test against them"'.[132] The Court was clearly concerned about the trend towards concentration. It noted how '[i]t would seem that the situation in the aluminum industry may be oligopolistic'.[133] The Court was concerned about the 'likelihood that parallel policies of mutual advantage, not competition, will emerge' in this industry.[134] This trend towards oligopoly, observed the Court, 'may well be thwarted by the presence of small but significant competitors'.[135]

The fourth issue, which the OFT never discussed, is whether the merger would **6.89** eliminate a potentially significant competitive threat. Granted this is a trickier issue than assessing the risk of eliminating an already significant competitor. But in data-driven mergers in markets characterized with network effects, one or two firms may already dominate the market; all that is left are small firms, which, as Waze's CEO

---

[129] *United States v Aluminum Co of America*, 377 US 271, 272–3, 84 S Ct 1283, 1285–6 (1964) ('*Alcoa*').

[130] Ibid, pp 273–4 (finding that Rome and Alcoa in the year before the merger produced respectively 0.3% and 32.5% of total industry production of bare aluminium conductor, 4.7% and 11.6% of insulated aluminium conductor, and 1.3% and 27.8% of the broader aluminium conductor line); *see also* ibid, p 280 ('The acquisition of Rome added, it is said, only 1.3% to Alcoa's control of the aluminum conductor market.').

[131] Moreover, the evidentiary record showed that Rome 'was an aggressive competitor'. Ibid, p 281.

[132] Ibid, p 280 (citations omitted).

[133] Ibid.

[134] Ibid.

[135] Ibid.

stated, may eventually reach scale and become significant threats, are acquired, are squeezed out, or otherwise fail.

6.90   Thus the OFT should have considered how the merger could enable the acquirer to attain or maintain its dominant position in the relevant market (here turn-by-turn navigation applications for smartphones and tablets) or in another market. One way the merger could help Google maintain its dominance in maps is by increasing entry barriers. Would pre-installing Waze on Android smartphones increase entry barriers for other apps relying on sourcing for their mapping data? In effect, does Waze become the moat to protect Google Maps? A new entrant would first have to contend with Google's free mapping app, which is the default option on Android phones; moreover, if it sought to crowd-source its traffic data, it would also have to contend with Waze, the 'world's largest community-based traffic and navigation app' which is now part of Google's platform (and has access to Google data and mapping technology). As the TomTom/Tele Atlas decision reflects, acquiring a mapping database can be quite expensive. Waze sought to improve its mapping data through crowd-sourcing. But to attract users, one needs a sufficiently reliable navigation mapping system, which requires data from enough users. Offering the service for free is by itself insufficient to reach scale. As we shall see in Chapter 14, having the navigation app pre-installed on the smartphone and integrated with the phone's other services and apps can provide a key competitive advantage. Indeed, one explanation for Apple Maps rebounding after its rocky start (given its quality issues) was its being the default option on iPhones.[136]

6.91   A fifth issue, which the OFT never discussed, is the competitive implications of the merged entity collecting and sharing data. This raises the issues we addressed in the Facebook/WhatsApp merger. Google, like Facebook, already collects a lot of data from its other applications. One issue is whether the additional geo-location and user data from Waze, as a 'social network' app, increases Google's power in location-based advertising. Does the Waze data increase (or help maintain) Google's market power for other services (such as search, social networking, etc)?

6.92   A sixth issue is whether Google could leverage its increased market power from its mapping data to other markets. A Google employee, in a 2010 internal email, identified geo-location data as 'extremely valuable' to Google's future business.[137] With Waze, Google obtains even more real-time geo-location data from individuals

[136] Charles Arthur, 'How Apple Maps Won on UK iPhones Over Google Maps—Despite Waze: Data Supplied by ComScore Sheds Further Light on the Effectiveness for Apple of Muscling Google Off the iPhone's Maps', *The Guardian*, 26 November 2013, http://www.theguardian.com/technology/2013/nov/26/apple-maps-europe-google (finding from comScore's data that iPhone users use the default Apple Maps far more than Google's iPhone apps).

[137] Amir Efrati, 'Google Calls Location Data "Valuable"', *Wall Street Journal*, 1 May 2011, http://www.wsj.com/articles/SB10001424052748703703304576297450030517830.

using the app on their Android and Apple smartphones. Google collects the location and route information 'to create a detailed location history of all of the journeys you have made while using the Application'.[138] If you use Waze, Google can use your geo-location data, your search query data, and other information it receives about you for advertising purposes, namely 'advertisements about sites, shops and other places and attractions in your close vicinity, or that we believe, based on your search query history, you may find interesting'.[139] The outcome is not necessarily anticompetitive: the inflowing data from Waze, for example, could be used to improve (and increase scale) for other Google applications. But, as we will see in Chapter 12, it can also reinforce a positive feedback loop where the strong get even stronger.

F. The DOJ's 2014 Win against Bazaarvoice/PowerReviews

At times significant antitrust developments come from unlikely sources. That is true **6.93** with Big Data, where one important legal development came from a merger few of us have likely heard of, involving a product that many of us use. Unlike some of the preceding billion-dollar deals in this chapter, this merger was so small that the companies never had to report it to the competition authorities.

The merger involved 'Ratings and Reviews platforms', which as the US court found, **6.94** 'combine software and services to enable manufacturers and retailers, among other companies, to collect, organize, and display consumer-generated product reviews and ratings online'.[140] You probably read (or perhaps even wrote) an online review for something you bought—perhaps a dishwasher or flannel sheets. An online ratings and reviews platform, the court found, is 'a valuable asset for retailers and manufacturers to feature on their websites because it tends to increase sales, decrease product returns, improve a website's ranking by Internet search engines, and provide valuable information regarding consumer sentiment'.[141]

The United States successfully challenged the already consummated merger be- **6.95** tween the two leading providers of these online ratings and reviews platforms.[142] The case, from a litigation perspective, appeared straightforward. Bazaarvoice and PowerReviews repeatedly acknowledged in their business records how the other was its only significant commercial competitor.[143] The DOJ uncovered a lot of

---

[138] Waze, Privacy Policy, https://www.waze.com/legal/privacy/.
[139] Ibid.
[140] *United States v Bazaarvoice*, Case No 3:13-cv-00133-WHO, 2014 WL 203966, p *2 (US Dist Ct (ND Cal), 8 January 2014), slip op, p 4, http://business.cch.com/ald/USBazaarvoice182014.pdf.
[141] Ibid, slip op, p 6.
[142] Ibid, slip op, p 4.
[143] Ibid, slip op, p 6.

incriminating evidence of how Bazaarvoice's and PowerReviews' executives expected the transaction to have anticompetitive effects. The incriminating evidence, the court found, was 'overwhelming'.[144]

6.96 Because the business records were very good for the DOJ and very bad for Bazaarvoice, the DOJ could have taken the easy path—namely, rely on the damaging documents that laid out Bazaarvoice's anticompetitive plans. Granted, the DOJ had some obstacles. One was the lack of complaining customers. None of Bazaarvoice's 104 customers whose depositions were part of the record complained that the merger had actually hurt them.[145] Nonetheless, the DOJ likely would have won on the incriminating documents and Bazaarvoice's controlling over 50 per cent of the relevant market.

6.97 What is interesting is that the DOJ pressed on to what we believe is the next 'network effects' involving the intersection of Big Data and competition policy.

6.98 First, the parties and court recognized the four 'V's of Big Data. The acquisition increased Bazaarvoice's reach to 1.8 billion monthly visitors and their consumer data. Bazaarvoice, as a result of the acquisition, had 'access to a large amount of data'.[146] The value of this data was tied to its variety and the velocity with which it could be accessed and processed. As the court found, the Ratings and Reviews (R&R) platforms included 'analytics software' that the manufacturers and retailers used to analyse the information collected from ratings and reviews.

> With these tools, manufacturers and retailers can track and analyze real-time consumer sentiment. Manufacturers and retailers can use this information to identify product design defects, make product design decisions, or identify consumers for targeted marketing efforts. R&R provides valuable data about consumer preferences and behavior, which retailers and manufacturers can use to make inventory purchasing or product design decisions.[147]

6.99 Second, data-driven industries, the DOJ argued and the court found, can have significant network effects, which increase switching costs and entry barriers:

> Bazaarvoice's network allows R&R content to be shared, or syndicated, for example, between brand manufacturers and their retailers. As more manufacturers sign up for Bazaarvoice's R&R platform, the Bazaarvoice network becomes more valuable

---

[144] Ibid, slip op, p 6 ('Exhibit after exhibit manifest that Bazaarvoice and PowerReviews viewed themselves as operating in a "duopoly" and that removing PowerReviews—an established company offering R&R at cheaper price points with a significant customer base as measured by the Internet Retailer 500 ("IR500"), a well-recognized list of the leading 500 internet retailers—would eliminate Bazaarvoice's only meaningful commercial competitor.').

[145] Ibid, slip op, p 8 (reasoning why relying on customer testimony about the merger's effects would be a mistake given the customers' difficulties 'to discern what is actually happening in the market').

[146] Ibid, slip op, p 118.

[147] Ibid, slip op, p 13.

to retailers because it allows them to gain access to a greater volume of R&R by publishing 'syndicated' R&R content received from manufacturers' websites. Similarly, as more retailers purchase Bazaarvoice's R&R platform, the Bazaarvoice network becomes more valuable for manufacturers because it allows them to syndicate content to a greater number of retail outlets. The feedback between the manufacturers and retailers creates a network effect that is a significant competitive advantage for Bazaarvoice.[148]

The network effects conferred a 'significant and durable competitive advantage for Bazaarvoice'.[149] The company's internal documents described how this data-driven network effect stifles smaller competitors. For example, before the merger, Bazaarvoice's Chief Revenue Officer wrote to the CEO: 'We've seen the network effect already in our renewals—customers that are using syndication generally can't leave us, and that's a great thing'.[150] The network effects would only increase after the merger, a PowerReviews Board member noted, and 'will be nearly impossible for someone to break'.[151] Bazaarvoice used these network effects as a selling point for financing. It prepared a document for an investor roadshow before its initial public offering (IPO) in which it explained the 'powerful network economies at play by linking retailers and brands/manufacturers'.[152] Bazaarvoice identified its 'ability to leverage the data' from its customer base as 'a key barrier [to] entry'.[153] The company claimed that 'any company entering the market would have to start from the beginning by securing all of the retail clients', which would be difficult because most of the larger retailers were already using the Bazaarvoice platform.[154] It boasted to potential investors that 'the power of [Bazaarvoice's] network effect and significant advantage on a global scale is starting to crowd out competition ...'.[155] As the court found, the 'acquisition of PowerReviews will extend the reach of Bazaarvoice's network and deprive its remaining competitors of the scale that is necessary to compete effectively'.[156] These documents reflect the importance of data-driven network effects and scale, which can serve as a 'protective moat' for dominant firms.[157] The data-driven network effects can prevent competitive inroads and scare off potential entrants.

6.100

To rebut the government's evidence of high entry barriers, Bazaarvoice identified Amazon and Google as potential rapid entrants. Bazaarvoice estimated that Amazon's internal ratings and review solution accounted for 28 per cent of the

6.101

---

[148] Ibid, slip op, p 24 (internal citations omitted).
[149] Ibid, slip op, p 94.
[150] Ibid, slip op, p 95.
[151] Ibid, slip op, p 94.
[152] Ibid, slip op, p 95.
[153] Ibid.
[154] Ibid.
[155] Ibid (internal citations omitted).
[156] Ibid, slip op, p 96.
[157] Ibid (internal citations omitted).

Ratings and Reviews platform market.[158] But the court recognized that, '[a]s a matter of economic reality, companies do not simply enter any market they can— they will only do so if it is within their strategy to do so and they have the requisite ability to do so'.[159] Otherwise, in every data-driven merger, a company could defend its merger because some bigger company on the data food chain could enter. This, the court found, 'would give eCommerce companies carte blanche to violate the antitrust laws with impunity with the excuse that Google, Amazon, Facebook, or any other successful technology company stands ready to restore competition to any highly concentrated market'.[160]

6.102 Bazaarvoice also raised Big Data as a defence, namely that it purchased PowerReviews to 'compete more effectively in advertising and "big data", which is in a much broader market than [Ratings & Reviews platforms]'.[161] Bazaarvoice ultimately wanted to expand beyond online ratings to compete against Google and Amazon in the broader e-commerce space.[162] But the court found that a company cannot justify an anticompetitive acquisition in a smaller market, on the grounds that the acquisition will provide the company with 'breathing space' as it prepares to compete in a broader market against entrenched firms like Google and Amazon.

6.103 After the DOJ's legal victory, Bazaarvoice agreed in 2014 to divest all assets of the PowerReviews business, to another company, Viewpoints, LLC.[163] After its relaunch in July 2014, PowerReviews, according to its website, 'has experienced explosive customer growth, signing more than 100 new enterprise customers, including some of world's leading brands such as Avery, Crocs, The North Face, Tempur Sealy, Vans, Whirlpool and World Kitchen'.[164] So it appears that the DOJ's intervention restored competition. It will be interesting to see how the legal findings inform other data-driven mergers.

G. Synopsis of Merger Cases

6.104 The six recent data-driven mergers highlight the enforcers' hits and misses in understanding the implications of Big Data. Among the hits, the conventional antitrust analysis can handle mergers, like TomTom/Tele Atlas, where one or both

---

[158] Ibid, slip op, p 8.
[159] Ibid, slip op, p 133.
[160] Ibid.
[161] Ibid, slip op, p 7.
[162] Ibid, slip op, p 21.
[163] Bazaarvoice, Inc, 'Bazaarvoice Reaches Settlement with DOJ in Antitrust Litigation', Press Release, 24 April 2014, http://investors.bazaarvoice.com/releasedetail.cfm?ReleaseID=842502.
[164] PowerReviews, 'PowerReviews Celebrates 10th Anniversary, Accelerates Momentum with More Than 100 Customer Wins', 17 June 2015, http://www.powerreviews.com/blog/powerreviews-celebrates-10th-anniversary-accelerates-momentum-with-more-than-100-customer-wins/.

companies primarily sell data (or data analysis) to third parties.[165] The competition authorities recognize the importance of quality competition when the product or service is offered for free.[166] They recognize how privacy considerations can fall within the ambit of non-price quality competition.[167] They also reject claims that they lack jurisdiction over free products, which some have argued (unsuccessfully) do not represent economic activity.[168] Some agencies have also picked up how data-driven network effects can increase entry barriers.

Among the misses, based on their public statements, the competition agencies, as of **6.105** 2015, have not fully considered the implications of a data-driven economy on competition policy. Neither the EU nor US have challenged a merger based solely on its lessening non-price competition.[169] Nor have they publicly discussed the competitive implications of data-driven mergers, like Google/Nest Labs, where data, not the products, are key. The competition authorities missed (or did not publicly acknowledge) key issues, such as whether and how individuals can be harmed after the company acquires a significant variety and volume of personal data that it can analyse in real-time.

The competition agencies' framework for analysing data-driven mergers in multi- **6.106** sided markets, where one side is free, remains underdeveloped.[170] As the European Data Protection Supervisor observed in 2014:

> A full market analysis for any of the 'free' digital services has yet to be carried out. In the [European] Commission's analysis of the Google/DoubleClick merger, only

---

[165] This includes cases where data analytics is part of the services. One such case involved an advertising merger, where both firms used their marketing data analytics capabilities in-house to target and optimize their creative advertising campaigns and advertising buying. Neither party controlled the primary sources of data; post-merger it still needed to use its clients' databases, and purchase data from various first-party data sources. *Publicis/Omnicom* (Case Comp/M.7023), Commission Decision C(2014) 89 final, 9 January 2014; *see also* Lisa Kimmel and Janis Kestenbaum, 'What's Up with WhatsApp?: A Transatlantic View on Privacy and Merger Enforcement in Digital Markets', 29(1) *Antitrust* (Fall 2014): p 52 (discussing the Nielsen Holdings NV/Arbitron Inc merger, which the FTC believed was likely to harm competition in 'the market for national syndicated cross-platform audience measurement services (capable of tracking viewers across television and Internet platforms)' given that 'Nielsen and Arbitron were the only two companies that maintained the broad audience measurement panels necessary to compete in the downstream cross-platform market').

[166] *Microsoft/Skype* (Case Comp/M.6281), Commission Decision C(2011)7279, 7 October 2011, para 81 (noting that '[s]ince consumer communications services are mainly provided for free, consumers pay more attention to other features' and '[q]uality is therefore a significant parameter of competition'); *Microsoft/Yahoo! Search Business* (Case Comp/M.5727), Commission Decision C(2010) 1077, 18 February 2010.

[167] Kimmel and Kestenbaum, above note 165, p 53 (acknowledging that non-price competition 'could be an important theory for evaluating competitive harm in digital markets where non-price dimensions of competition, like innovation and privacy, may play a more important role in marketplace dynamics').

[168] OFT, Google/Waze, above note 115, paras 7–8.

[169] Kimmel and Kestenbaum, above note 165, p 53.

[170] Mark R Patterson, 'Non-Network Barriers to Network Neutrality', 78 *Fordham L Rev* (2010): pp 2843, 2870 (discussing quality degradation by search engines and how antitrust lacks a well-developed analytical approach to dealing with informational issues).

paid-for services, that is, direct sale of online advertising space, intermediary services in online advertising and provision of display ad serving technology, were identified as relevant. Since that case was closed, the evolution of the digital economy has been marked by an explosion of data collection. An equivalent, relevant market analysis today would examine new business models and assess the value of personal information as an intangible asset. It could be expected to reveal the need for undertakings to collect huge amounts of data to be able to monetise the service provided, mainly through advertising, and at the same time to compete with other paid-for service providers.[171]

6.107 Two FTC attorney-advisors acknowledged in 2014 that 'many of the mergers that the agencies have analysed involving markets for data have not involved the same consumer-facing data at issue in the Google/DoubleClick and Facebook/WhatsApp transactions'.[172] But they suggested that 'the antitrust principles are the same' for data-driven mergers and other conventional mergers.[173]

6.108 As Part III explores, the overall principles may be similar, but data-driven mergers and business strategies raise unique challenges for which the competition authorities are currently ill equipped.

---

[171] European Data Protection Supervisor, *Privacy and Competitiveness in the Age of Big Data: The Interplay Between Data Protection, Competition Law and Consumer Protection in the Digital Economy*, Preliminary Opinion, March 2014, p 27, https://secure.edps.europa.eu/EDPSWEB/webdav/ shared/Documents/Consultation/Opinions/2014/14-03-26_competitition_law_big_data_ EN.pdf; *see also* European Data Protection Supervisor, *Report of Workshop on Privacy, Consumers, Competition and Big Data*, 11 July 2014, p 2, https://secure.edps.europa.eu/EDPSWEB/webdav/ site/mySite/shared/Documents/Consultation/Big data/14-07-11_EDPS_Report_Workshop_ Big_data_EN.pdf.

[172] Kimmel and Kestenbaum, above note 165, p 55 n 63.

[173] Ibid.

PART III

WHY HAVEN'T MANY COMPETITION AUTHORITIES CONSIDERED THE IMPLICATIONS OF BIG DATA?

The EU and US Horizontal Merger Guidelines share a common analytical framework in defining relevant markets, measuring market concentration, their theories of unilateral and coordinated anticompetitive effects, assessing the entry barriers, and the available defences. Their analytical tools typically have broad applicability—from assessing mergers involving homogeneous commodities, such as cement, to innovative, dynamic industries. But the next several chapters examine how data-driven mergers, such as Google/Nest Labs, can differ from other, more conventional mergers in several important ways. Given these differences, the competition agencies may not fully consider the implications of Big Data in their merger analysis. **III.01**

One key reason why the agencies have not fully considered the implications of Big Data in their merger analysis is that the agencies' merger review has migrated towards assessing what is measurable—namely short-term pricing effects, primarily under their unilateral effects theory, and short-term productive efficiencies. As Chapter 7 explores, this price-centric approach fails in data-driven markets, where products or services are often offered for free, many consumers are accustomed to not paying for the products or services, and the potential harms, while significant, are harder to quantify. Such was the case of Facebook/WhatsApp, where Facebook Messenger and several other texting apps were free of charge. The competition authorities traditionally assess mergers through the lens of price competition. They have far cruder tools to assess a merger's impact on non-price considerations, such as quality generally and privacy protections in particular. **III.02**

III.03 Another reason why the competition agencies have not fully considered the implications of Big Data is that data-driven mergers can defy the agencies' conventions that work well for other mergers. Chapter 8 explores three conventions: the categorization of mergers, the belief that similar products/services compete more fiercely than dissimilar products/services, and the focus on the services' or products' substitutability. Data-driven mergers often defy the competition authorities' existing way to categorize mergers as horizontal, vertical, or conglomerate. Google, for example, did not compete against Nest Labs over thermostats. Nor was Google a key buyer or supplier to Nest. Nor was Google a perceived potential entrant in the thermostat market. Data-driven mergers can differ from traditional mergers in that key data at times are neither sold nor bought. The acquirer buys the target not for its product per se (thermostats) but the data the smart thermostats collect. Traditional merger analysis considers the substitutability of goods, whereas data-driven mergers often involve the variety (non-substitutability) of data. The key here is the third 'V'—variety—of Big Data, where market power can be gained by acquiring non-substitutable data.

III.04 A third reason why the competition agencies have not fully considered the implications of Big Data, as Chapter 9 discusses, is the difficulty at times in incorporating the intangible, non-economic injury from invasions of privacy interests into their competition analysis. Some data-driven mergers may raise concerns about degrading individuals' privacy interests, even where the individuals do not deal with the companies, such as the Alliance Data Systems Corp/Conversant merger.

7

AGENCIES FOCUS ON WHAT IS MEASURABLE (PRICE), WHICH IS NOT ALWAYS IMPORTANT (FREE GOODS)

When receiving his Nobel Prize in 1974, the economist Friedrich August von Hayek **7.01** compared economics with the physical sciences. In the physical sciences, what is measureable is generally important. But that cannot be assumed of economics:

> Unlike the position that exists in the physical sciences, in economics and other disciplines that deal with essentially complex phenomena, the aspects of the events to be accounted for about which we can get quantitative data are necessarily limited and may not include the important ones. While in the physical sciences it is generally assumed, probably with good reason, that any important factor which determines the observed events will itself be directly observable and measurable, in the study of such complex phenomena as the market, which depend on the actions of many individuals, all the circumstances which will determine the outcome of a process ... will hardly ever be fully known or measurable. And while in the physical sciences the investigator will be able to measure what, on the basis of a prima facie theory, he thinks important, in the social sciences often that is treated as important which happens to be accessible to measurement. This is sometimes carried to the point where it is demanded that our theories must be formulated in such terms that they refer only to measurable magnitudes.[1]

Over the past 35 years, the agencies' merger review has migrated towards assess- **7.02** ing what is measurable—namely short-term pricing effects, primarily under their unilateral effects theory, and short-term productive efficiencies. This price-centric approach, however, fails in data-driven markets where products or services are often offered for free, many consumers are accustomed to not paying for the products or services, and the potential harms, while significant, are harder to quantify.

This chapter, using the United States as an example, examines how price effects have **7.03** predominated antitrust analysis. The competition agencies have never disclaimed

---

[1] Friedrich August von Hayek, *Prize Lecture: The Pretence of Knowledge*, 11 December 1974, Nobelprize.org, http://www.nobelprize.org/nobel_prizes/economic-sciences/laureates/1974/hayek-lecture.html.

the importance of non-price competition. Indeed, the consensus is that the merger's or restraint's effect on dynamic efficiencies, including innovation, are often more important than the effect on short-term prices.[2] Nonetheless, as Hayek warned, economic factors that were easier to measure (such as the merger's likely short-term impact on price, output, or productive efficiency in narrowly defined markets) became disproportionately important. Factors that were harder to assess or measure (like the merger's impact on innovation, systemic risk, and the risks that the increasing concentration of power pose to democracy and individual autonomy) were often ignored or discounted.

A. The Push Towards Price-Centric Antitrust

7.04   As the United States remarked in 2009, '[a] central question for competition policy is how competition affects prices.'[3] Nothing in the competition laws limits the agencies to consider only a restraint's impact on price. In their merger guidelines, the US and EU competition authorities acknowledge the importance of non-price parameters of competition, such as quality and innovation. They recognize how an increase in market power 'can also be manifested in non-price terms and conditions that adversely affect customers, including reduced product quality, reduced product variety, reduced service, or diminished innovation'.[4] The competition authorities specifically recognize the importance of quality competition.[5] In assessing whether

---

[2] Organisation for Economic Co-operation and Development (OECD), *Policy Roundtables: Dynamic Efficiencies in Merger Analysis*, 15 May 2008, p 10, http://www.oecd.org/ competition/mergers/40623561.pdf ('[I]nnovation is responsible for most of the increase in material standards of living that has taken place since the industrial revolution. It seems likely that dynamic efficiencies have a considerably greater potential to benefit consumers than static efficiencies have.').

[3] OECD, *Policy Roundtables: Two-Sided Markets*, 17 December 2009, p 151, http://www.oecd. org/daf/competition/44445730.pdf.

[4] US Department of Justice (DOJ) and Federal Trade Commission (FTC), *Horizontal Merger Guidelines*, 19 August 2010, s 1 ('US Horizontal Merger Guidelines'), http://www.justice.gov/ atr/horizontal-merger-guidelines-08192010; European Commission, *Guidelines on the Assessment of Horizontal Mergers under the Council Regulation on the Control of Concentrations Between Undertakings* [2004] OJ C 31/03, para 8 ('EC Horizontal Merger Guidelines'), http://eur-lex. europa.eu/legal-content/EN/TXT/?uri=celex:52004XC0205%2802%29 (likewise recognizing the importance of quality, noting that '[e]ffective competition brings benefits to consumers, such as low prices, high quality products, a wide selection of goods and services, and innovation', and how firms can exercise market power by, among other things, 'reducing the choice or quality of goods and services'); *see also* DOJ, *Antitrust Enforcement and the Consumer* (1996), s 1, http:// www.justice.gov/sites/default/files/atr/legacy/2015/03/06/antitrust-enfor-consumer.pdf ('Free and open competition benefits consumers by ensuring lower prices and new and better products.'); FTC, *Competition Counts: How Consumers Win When Businesses Compete*, March 2007, https:// www.ftc.gov/system/files/attachments/competition-counts/pdf-0116_competition-counts.pdf ('Competition in America is about price, selection, and service. It benefits consumers by keeping prices low and the quality and choice of goods and services high.').

[5] *United States v Bazaarvoice, Inc*, Case No 3:13-cv-00133-WHO (US Dist Ct (ND Cal), 31 October 2013), Plaintiff's Post-Trial Proposed Findings of Fact, paras 198–216 (discussing how

a merger may substantially lessen quality or other parameters of non-price competition, the competition agencies, according to their guidelines, will 'employ an approach analogous to that used to evaluate price competition'.[6]

Nonetheless, the antitrust analysis gravitates to whether the merger will likely give   **7.05**
the parties the power to raise the product's or service's price above competitive levels. Price has become the common denominator in merger review. In defining the relevant market and assessing entry conditions, the competition officials generally inquire what would happen if the products' or services' price increased a small but significant non-transitory amount, on the magnitude of 5 per cent. The so-called Small, but Significant, Non-transitory Increase in Price (SSNIP) test is used to assess how customers would react, and whether the exercise of market power would prompt sufficient entry to timely defeat the price increase. The agencies' theories of anticompetitive harm are often focused on the likely impact on prices. Granted, the competition authorities will occasionally analyse whether the merger, besides raising price, may also reduce quality.[7] But competition authorities rarely analyse a merger's effect solely—or even primarily—on non-price parameters of competition.

So why is price king? Price has always played an important role in competition   **7.06**
policy. But with the Chicago School's rise in the late 1970s, some US economists and lawyers found it fashionable to dismiss competition law's other economic, political, social, and moral concerns over trends towards concentration and concentrated economic power.[8] Instead, the competition agencies and courts used concentration only as a screen. The agencies would challenge only those few mergers that, under the prevailing neoclassical economic thinking, would demonstrably lead to higher prices post-merger in narrowly defined markets. Although section 7

---

transaction will reduce innovation and product variety); *United States v AT&T, Inc*, Case No 1:11-cv-01560-ESH (US Dist Ct (D DC), 30 September 2011), Second Amended Complaint, para 3 (alleging that unless the acquisition is enjoined, 'customers of mobile wireless telecommunications services likely will face higher prices, less product variety and innovation, and poorer quality services due to reduced incentives to invest than would exist absent the merger').

   [6] US Horizontal Merger Guidelines, above note 4, s 1.

   [7] OECD, *Policy Roundtables: The Role and Measurement of Quality in Competition Analysis*, 28 October 2013, p 83 ('OECD Quality Report'), http://www.oecd.org/competition/Quality-in-competition-analysis-2013.pdf.

   [8] Richard A Posner, *Antitrust Law: An Economic Perspective* (Chicago, IL: University of Chicago Press, 1976) (efficiency is the only goal of antitrust law); Robert H Bork, *The Antitrust Paradox: A Policy at War with Itself* (New York: Free Press, 1978) (only goal of antitrust is to increase total welfare, which he calls consumer welfare); Richard A Posner, 'The Chicago School of Antitrust Analysis', 127 *U Pa L Rev* (1979): p 931. For recent criticisms of that view, *see* Harry First and Spencer Weber Waller, 'Antitrust's Democracy Deficit', 81 *Fordham L Rev* (2013): pp 2572–4; Barak Orbach, 'How Antitrust Lost Its Goal', 81 *Fordham L Rev* (2013): p 2253; Ariel Ezrachi, 'Sponge', University of Oxford Centre for Competition Law and Policy Working Paper CCLP (L) 42, Oxford Legal Studies Research Paper No 16/2015, 1 March 2015, http://ssrn.com/abstract=2572028.

of the Clayton Act is designed to arrest concentration in the economy, whatever its cause, in its incipiency, the agencies began quantifying a particular merger's likely impact on prices. The US Department of Justice (DOJ) also alleged in its complaints how the merger *will* (rather than may) lessen price competition in narrowly defined markets.[9]

7.07 One explanation is that the US courts, in accepting the Chicago School's ideologies, demanded more evidence from antitrust plaintiffs to overcome their belief in self-correcting markets. The lower courts continue to cite the US Supreme Court 1963 decision, *Philadelphia National Bank*, which outlined a presumption of anti-competitive harm where the merged entity controls 'an undue percentage share of the relevant market', and the merger significantly increases concentration.[10] But they began pressing the competition agencies to explain how, and the extent to which, the prices for one or both of the merging firms' products or services would increase post-merger. As one US antitrust official observed:

> Judges are more accustomed to making decisions based on facts about what happened; in mergers, they are called on to predict what might happen in the future—something which I think a court is reluctant to do, especially when faced with a merger that may involve many products, only a small portion of which may be anticompetitive, and in the face of local businessmen and women addressing all the advantages of the merger, including claims of efficiencies.
>
> More and more when we go to court, the judges seem to be asking for concreteness; the anecdotal evidence seems less important to them than surveys, which seem systematic, but may be flawed. If the issue is product market, the courts seem to want to know exactly how many customers would be willing to switch. And if it's competitive effects, they want to know how big an effect will result. More and more, in order to persuade a court that a merger is going to be harmful, we feel the need to do the best we can to quantify. So, in our investigations and case preparations we are asking both our economists and the parties what effects from the merger can be quantified and how we can best do it.[11]

---

[9] Maurice E Stucke, 'Should Competition Policy Promote Happiness?', 81 *Fordham L Rev* (2013): p 2608 (citing cases).

[10] *United States v Philadelphia National Bank*, 374 US 321, 363, 83 S Ct 1715, 1741 (1963); *see, eg, Federal Trade Commission v Sysco Corp*, Case No 1:15-CV-00256 (APM), 2015 WL 3958568, p *9 (US Dist Ct (D DC), 26 June 2015). The merging parties can rebut the presumption with proof that the market-share statistics provide an inaccurate account of the merger's probable competitive effects. *Federal Trade Commission v Heinz*, 246 F3d 715 (US Ct of Apps (DC Cir), 2001). If defendants rebut the presumption, the burden of 'producing additional evidence of anticompetitive effect shifts to the government, and merges with the ultimate burden of persuasion, which remains with the government at all times'. *United States v Baker Hughes Inc*, 908 F2d 981, 983 (US Ct of Apps (DC Cir), 1990).

[11] Constance K Robinson, Director of Operations, DOJ, Antitrust Division, 'Quantifying Unilateral Effects in Investigations and Cases', Speech given at the George Mason Law Review Symposium, *Antitrust in the Information Revolution: New Economic Approaches for Analyzing Antitrust Issues*, Arlington VA, 11 October 1996, http://www.justice.gov/atr/public/speeches/1005.htm.

One federal district court, for example, completely misconstrued the Clayton Act's **7.08** incipiency standard. The court stated that 'a strong presumption of anticompetitive effects based on market concentration is especially problematic in a differentiated products unilateral effects context'.[12] How the court found this in light of the Clayton Act's legislative history or Supreme Court case law is a mystery. To make matters worse, the judge next stated that '[w]ithout the benefit of presumptions, the burden remains upon plaintiffs to come forward with evidence of actual anticompetitive effects'.[13] This is squarely inconsistent with the Clayton Act's incipiency standard. Not surprisingly, the DOJ lost that merger challenge.[14]

Even the agencies' victories came when they showed that higher prices were likely. **7.09** Faced with more demanding courts, the agencies now calculate diversion ratios, the estimated consumer demand at post-merger prices, and the profit margins of the merging parties' competing products.[15] The concern is that absent this proof, the agency risks prohibiting mergers that would yield significant cost savings to society's benefit. Requiring such certainty and actuality of injury to competition, however, is contrary to both the Clayton Act's plain language, which requires the

---

[12] *United States v Oracle Corp*, 331 F Supp 2d 1122 (US Dist Ct (ND Cal), 2004).

[13] Ibid, p 1165.

[14] The court was probably correct, as a matter of economic theory, that concentration does not matter in unilateral effects cases involving differentiated products, where the focus is not on concentration at the firm level but on the closeness of substitution of individual products. That does not justify disregarding the legal standard. If it did, the converse would also need to be true: in a unilateral effects case, the government need not plead and prove a product market. Scott A Sher and Andrea Agathoklis Murino, 'Unilateral Effects in Technology Markets: Oracle, H&R Block, and What It All Means', 26(3) *Antitrust* (Summer 2012): pp 46, 47 (noting 'the tension' between US judicial precedent—which is rooted in market definition and high market shares—and the unilateral effects analysis increasingly taken by the U.S. competition agencies—which focuses far less on market definition and much more on competitive effects); Joshua H Soven, 'Afterword: Does Antitrust Need More Schools?', 78 *Antitrust LJ* (2012): pp 273, 275 (noting how the FTC in several unilateral effects cases, said it may be sufficient to rely entirely on direct effects evidence and not define a market or use market shares). But courts, interpreting the Clayton Act, have required such a showing. *United States v El du Pont de Nemours & Co*, 353 US 586, 593, 77 S Ct 872, 877 (1957) (determining the relevant market is a 'necessary predicate' to finding a Clayton Act violation because the threatened monopoly must be one which will substantially lessen competition 'within the area of effective competition'); *Brown Shoe Co v United States*, 370 US 294, 324, 335, 82 S Ct 1502 (1962) (defining relevant market is necessary predicate when challenging vertical and horizontal mergers).

[15] *See* DOJ and FTC, *Commentary on the Horizontal Merger Guidelines*, March 2006, p 27, http://www.justice.gov/sites/default/files/atr/legacy/2006/04/27/215247.pdf ('In all merger cases, the Agencies focus on the particular competitive relationship between the merging firms, and for mergers involving differentiated products, the "diversion ratios" between products combined by the merger are of particular importance.'); EC Horizontal Merger Guidelines, above note 4, para 29 ('When data are available, the degree of substitutability may be evaluated through customer preference surveys, analysis of purchasing patterns, estimation of the cross-price elasticities of the products involved, or diversion ratios.'); *see also* Rachel Brandenburger and Joseph Matelis, 'The 2010 U.S. Horizontal Merger Guidelines: A Historical and International Perspective', 25(3) *Antitrust* (Summer 2011), http://www.justice.gov/atr/public/articles/280478.htm; Carl Shapiro, 'The 2010 Horizontal Merger Guidelines: From Hedgehog to Fox in Forty Years', 77 *Antitrust LJ* (2010): p 701.

plaintiff to prove that the merger *may* substantially lessen competition or tend to create a monopoly, and its purpose to supplement the Sherman Act by reaching incipient restraints.[16]

7.10 Likewise, before adopting a decision, either in approving or prohibiting the merger, the European Commission 'must carry out complex economic assessments'.[17] The General Court in *Cisco* noted that the Commission enjoys, for that purpose, 'a certain margin of discretion of which the Court must take account'.[18] Even so, the European courts still 'must not only ascertain whether the evidence relied on is factually accurate, reliable and consistent but also whether that evidence contains all the information which must be taken into account in order to assess a complex situation and whether it is capable of substantiating the conclusions drawn from it.'[19] Not surprisingly, the Commission noted how, 'over the past two decades, [its] antitrust and merger policy...more effectively placed the emphasis on consumer welfare, notably through an increasingly refined economic analysis'.[20]

7.11 The EU and US agencies' merger review migrated towards assessing what was measurable—namely, short-term pricing effects, primarily under their unilateral effects theory.[21] Economics morphed from being a reality check on what the

---

[16] *Brown Shoe Co v United States*, 370 US 294, 323 n 39, 82 S Ct 1502 (1962) ('The concept of reasonable probability conveyed by these words is a necessary element in any statute which seeks to arrest restraints of trade in their incipiency and before they develop into full-fledged restraints violative of the Sherman Act. A requirement of certainty and actuality of injury to competition is incompatible with any effort to supplement the Sherman Act by reaching incipient restraints.') (quoting S Rep No 1775, 81st Cong, 2d Sess. 6, US Code Cong and Adm News 1950, p 4298); US Horizontal Merger Guidelines, above note 4, s 1 (referring to the congressional intent 'that merger enforcement should interdict competitive problems in their incipiency and that certainty about anticompetitive effect is seldom possible and not required for a merger to be illegal').

[17] Case T-79/12 *Cisco Systems and Messagenet v Commission*, ECLI:EU:T:2013:635, 11 December 2013, para 49.

[18] Ibid, para 49, citing Case T-119/02 *Royal Philips Electronics v Commission* [2003] ECR II-1433, para 77.

[19] *Cisco Systems and Messagenet*, above note 17, para 50.

[20] European Commission, *Report on Competition Policy 2010*, COM(2011) 328 final, 10 June 2011, p 5, http://ec.europa.eu/competition/publications/annual_report/2010/part1_en.pdf; *Cisco Systems and Messagenet*, above note 17, para 62 (when the Commission relies on 'a form of future conduct which it contends will be engaged in by a merged entity following a merger, it is required to establish, on the basis of convincing evidence and with a sufficient degree of probability, that the conduct will actually occur'); Case T-210/01 *General Electric v Commission* [2005] ECR II-5575, para 464.

[21] It is harder to quantify the likelihood of a merger fostering collusion and the resulting likely price increase. Thus the coordinated effects theory became another casualty in the agencies' drive to quantify. Charles A James, Assistant Attorney General, DOJ, Antitrust Division, 'Rediscovering Coordinated Effects', Speech given at American Bar Association Annual Meeting, Section of Antitrust Law, Washington DC, 13 August 2002, pp 7–8, http://www.justice.gov/atr/public/speeches/200124.pdf (noting that 'one interesting side-effect of the 1992 [Horizontal Merger] Guidelines has been the emergence of unilateral effects as the predominant theory of economic harm pursued in government merger investigations and challenges'); 'Interview with Deborah P. Majoras, Chairman, Federal Trade Commission', *Antitrust Source*, March 2005, http://www.americanbar.org/content/dam/aba/publishing/antitrust_source/mar05_fullsource323.authcheckdam.pdf

agencies were doing (ie is the case consistent with economic theory or are the lawyers getting it completely wrong?) to the sine qua non (what is the proof of economic harm and is it strong enough to show real effects?). If the agencies and courts rely on economics as the sine qua non, they will enjoin a small percentage of mergers where they are confident, under the prevailing neoclassical economic thinking, that the merger would demonstrably lead to higher post-merger prices.

B. What the Price-Centric Approach Misses

The competition authorities never disclaimed the importance of non-price competition.[22] Nonetheless those factors that were easier to measure (such as the merger's likely short-term impact on price, output, or productive efficiency) became disproportionately important. **7.12**

One example is innovation. A European competition official, looking at the static effects of anticompetitive mergers, observed that the 'most immediate short-term impact is normally a price increase for the products in question'.[23] But he added that the 'most harmful effects' from a merger 'are of a dynamic nature'.[24] Competition authorities from around the world want dynamic efficiency considerations to feature more frequently and prominently in their merger decisions. The problem, they recognize, is that they generally lack the analytical tools to measure how the merger likely impacts (either positively or negatively) dynamic efficiencies.[25] Even in a static analysis, determining whether a merger will likely yield productive efficiencies that negate any potential anticompetitive effects is quite difficult.[26] Assessing the **7.13**

('Following the adoption of the 1992 Horizontal Merger Guidelines, coordinated effects analysis languished as an active instrument of merger review and enforcement. Over the last decade, mergers were much more likely to be reviewed (or challenged) on the basis of unilateral effects concerns. More often than not, when a merger complaint included a coordinated effects allegation, it had the flavor, if not the reality, of being an afterthought.'); EC Horizontal Merger Guidelines, above note 4, para 4 (noting that unilateral effects theory 'has been the most common basis for finding that a concentration would result in a significant impediment to effective competition').

[22] OECD Quality Report, above note 7, p 22 (Background Note).

[23] Carles Esteva Mosso, 'EU Merger Control: The Big Picture', Speech given at European Commission Sixth Annual GCR Conference, Brussels, 12 November 2014, p 2, http://ec.europa.eu/competition/speeches/text/sp2014_06_en.pdf.

[24] Ibid.

[25] OECD, *Dynamic Efficiencies*, above note 2, p 10 ('real-world problem is that no one has figured out a robust way to do that yet, and rather than engage in speculation, courts have tended to avoid dynamic efficiency analysis in cases where it could have been relevant'); Eleonora Ocello, Cristina Sjödin, and Anatoly Suboĉs, 'What's Up with Merger Control in the Digital Sector? Lessons from the Facebook/WhatsApp EU Merger Case', 1 *Competition Merger Brief* (February 2015): p 3 n 15 (internal footnotes omitted) (agencies cannot use the traditional tools for market definition, such as the SSNIP test, 'to capture the changes in substitutability brought by technological developments that may occur in the next two to three years').

[26] OECD, 'Mergers and Dynamic Efficiencies', Policy Brief, September 2008, p 1 ('OECD Policy Brief'), http://www.oecd.org/dataoecd/55/48/41359037.pdf.

merger's likelihood in promoting or inhibiting innovation, and the magnitude of the potential benefit or harm are even more problematic.[27]

7.14 Given the difficulty in measuring dynamic efficiencies, competition officials do not fully account how mergers impact innovation.[28] When the merging parties, however, raise innovation (eg in high tech cases), the agencies tend to credit any showing by the parties that antitrust enforcement could harm their innovation. This increases the risk of false negatives: because agencies do not have good tools, anticompetitive deals in the name of innovation are likelier.

7.15 It is not just innovation. Other important factors that are hard to assess or measure (like the merger's impact on systemic risk) are also ignored or discounted.[29] The financial markets, when viewed as a complex adaptive system, can become more vulnerable as one bank increases in size and becomes too big and integral to fail. Assessing the merger's short-term static price effects (eg, whether the banks post-merger can raise rates for specific categories of borrowers) is often easier than assessing and quantifying the merger's long-term impact on the efficiency, resilience, competitiveness, and stability of the overall financial network.[30] But if the government ignores systemic risk, its merger analysis is incomplete and potentially flawed. This harm increases when the government, overconfident that its merger analysis identifies all the significant anticompetitive risks, goes beyond approving mega-mergers that are viewed as market extensions (despite the long-term risks

---

[27] OECD, *Dynamic Efficiencies*, above note 2, p 10 (noting the uncertainty inherent in innovative activity regarding its cost, timing, and the likelihood and extent of its commercial success, difficulties in measuring innovation itself, the problem of how to conceptually transform innovation into some measure of welfare, and informational asymmetry between the merging parties and the enforcement agencies).

[28] American Bar Association Section of Antitrust Law, *Mergers and Acquisitions: Understanding the Antitrust Issues* (4th edn, Chicago, IL: American Bar Association, 2015) pp 134–5 (noting that while the agencies have filed complaints alleging anticompetitive concentration in 'innovation markets… it is rare for a complaint to allege harm only in an innovation market, and no court has invalidated a transaction solely because it reduced competition in an innovation market').

[29] *See, eg,* Thomas J Horton, 'The Coming Extinction of Homo Economicus and the Eclipse of the Chicago School of Antitrust: Applying Evolutionary Biology to Structural and Behavioral Antitrust Analyses', 42 *Loyola U Chicago LJ* (2011): p 491; Jesse W Markham, Jr, 'Lessons for Competition Law from the Economic Crisis: The Prospect for Antitrust Responses to the Too-Big-to-Fail Phenomenon', 16 *Fordham J Corp & Fin L* (2011): p 313 (discussing how antitrust neither prevented nor redressed the recent systemic threats caused directly by companies too big and integral to the functioning of markets); Eleanor M Fox, 'The Politics of Law and Economics in Judicial Decision Making: Antitrust As A Window', 61 *NYU L Rev* (1986): p 583 ('Contemporary analysis routinely omits from the economic equation the soft data and the dynamic implications that would, if accounted for, favor the entrepreneur. In particular, the model omits the freedoms, the opportunities, the prospects for change, and the spur from the sense of having a fair chance that comes from an environment hospitable to those without power.' (footnotes omitted)).

[30] Sally J Goerner, Bernard Lietaer, and Robert E Ulanowicz, 'Quantifying Economic Sustainability: Implications for Free-Enterprise Theory, Policy and Practice', 69 *Ecological Economics* (2009): p 77; Howard A Shelanski, 'Enforcing Competition During an Economic Crisis', 77 *Antitrust LJ* (2010): pp 239–45.

these mergers may pose) and seeks to dismantle any restraints on future industry concentration.

C. The Elusiveness of Assessing a Merger's Effect on Quality Competition

The competition agencies, when they lack the tools to quantify how the merger is **7.16** likely to impact a key parameter of competition or aspect of an effective competitive process, may recognize the importance of that parameter of competition; but they generally do not challenge a merger for lessening competition primarily on this parameter. We see this dynamic with quality competition. At a 2013 OECD roundtable, the competition authorities agreed that quality was an important parameter of competition.[31] They all agreed that quality drives innovation and economic growth and that a decrease in quality can be just as harmful to consumers (if not more harmful, given health and safety concerns) as a price increase.[32] Thus maintaining and improving quality is an important objective for competition policy.

Assessing and measuring quality, however, are trickier. This may not be an issue if **7.17** quality is reflected in price. Consumers at times assess quality using price as a proxy, namely you get what you pay for.[33]

Rarely, if ever, do competition authorities assess a merger's impact primarily or **7.18** solely on quality. One challenge for the competition authorities is identifying the important components of quality. One metric is to divide quality components along vertical (where all consumers recognize that component as valuable) and horizontal (where consumers disagree over the component's desirability or value) dimensions.[34] But even for the vertical components, consumers may rank the components differently. A second challenge is in measuring the highly ranked vertical quality dimensions. With the advent of price comparison websites, price often provides a transparent and consistent benchmark. Quality comparisons are often complex and subjective.[35] At times, competition authorities can see how market participants 'define, measure, and assess quality in the ordinary course of business' or see whether the academic and popular economics 'reveal useful measures of quality'.[36]

---

[31] OECD Quality Report, above note 7, p 22.

[32] Ibid, p 5.

[33] For problems with this heuristic, see generally Ariel Ezrachi and Maurice E Stucke, 'The Curious Case of Competition and Quality', 3 *J of Antitrust Enforcement* (2015): pp 227–57.

[34] Ibid.

[35] OECD Quality Report, above note 7, p 78 (European Union) ('Making a precise definition of quality for a given product is a complex task in competition investigations given the many subjective features that may contribute to a perception of quality by customers, the multi-dimensional nature of quality, and the absence of measurable variables.').

[36] Ibid, p 121.

But for many products, quality attributes may be difficult to measure objectively. As the European Commission noted:

> [E]ven if some quality-related features are measurable, the overall perception of the products' quality is often based on a combination of several features. If one were to take cars as an example, the number of measurable variables at which customers may look when assessing the quality is immense and very complex, ranging from speed, acceleration, emissions, consumption to precise parameters of the individual components. The assessment of quality is thus often a complex and imprecise exercise in itself, and involves the balancing of evidence which is often of subjective nature such as different perception of customers.[37]

7.19 Thus, when well-accepted quantitative metrics of quality exist (eg in the health care industry), the agency will likelier assess a merger's impact on quality.[38] In many other industries that do not lend themselves to well-accepted quality metrics that can be analysed quantitatively and objectively, the agency will likely avoid assessing quality. The OECD found that few competition authorities 'have developed an effective means' by which to systematically identify the vertical dimensions of quality and objectively measure how a restraint would affect these quality dimensions.[39] Thus quality becomes an add-on: the competition authority alleges how the merger may increase price and lessen quality, and focuses on proving the former.

D. Why Quality Competition is Paramount in Many Data-Driven Multi-Sided Markets

7.20 Consumers every day use free products and services, such as Skyping, emailing, texting, Googling something, watching videos, and reading blogs, articles, and books online. Competition, if any, primarily takes place in several areas: first, on non-price parameters (such as quality, which includes privacy protections and innovation) on the 'free' side of the market; second, on the 'paid' side of the multi-sided market (such as advertising); and third, among firms to collect valuable data as a key input across different markets. Data-driven mergers in these multi-sided markets may substantially lessen competition in any of these segments, and along some parameters (such as quality, including privacy protection) but not others (such as price or innovation). When the product is free, quality, the European Commission found, will often be a significant parameter of competition.[40]

---

[37] Ibid, p 79.
[38] Ibid, p 124 (US noting 'the development of quantitative metrics for measuring different aspects of hospital quality (e.g., mortality, complications) is now a well-developed discipline').
[39] Ibid, p 5 (Executive Summary).
[40] *Microsoft/Yahoo! Search Business* (Case Comp/M.5727), Commission Decision C(2010) 1077 [2010] OJ C 020/08, para 101; *Microsoft/Skype* (Case Comp/M.6281), Commission Decision C(2011)7279, 7 October 2011, para 81.

For some online markets, some well-accepted components of quality can be an-   **7.21**
alysed quantitatively and objectively. One example might be a search engine intentionally degrading the search results to favour less relevant sponsored ads over
more relevant, organic search results.[41] However, when evaluating these multi-sided
platforms involving free goods and services, the competition authorities will often
struggle if quality is subjective, multi-dimensional, and difficult to quantify.

When the product's price is zero and the most important parameter of competi-   **7.22**
tion (quality) is subjective, multi-dimensional, and difficult to quantify, competition agencies have far cruder tools for defining the relevant market, assessing
entry, and predicting the likely competitive effects under a unilateral (or coordinated) effects theory.

Ordinarily, competition authorities begin their analysis by defining the relevant   **7.23**
market. To do so they inquire what would happen if the hypothetical monopolist
imposed a small, but significant, non-transitory increase in price—ordinarily in the
range of 5 to 10 per cent.[42] The European Commission, as its staff observed in the
Facebook/WhatsApp merger, cannot apply the SSNIP test to digital products or
services that are offered for free to users.[43] This is 'because 5 per cent of nothing is
nothing, and because the nature of the product may be such that the hypothetical
monopolist would still find it profit-maximizing to price at zero'.[44]

Because cross-elasticity of demand cannot be estimated by using price, the com-   **7.24**
petition authority would have to assess consumer demand by a decrease of some
non-price parameter of quality. The 2010 Horizontal Merger Guidelines, while an
improvement over the earlier guidelines, lack a detailed analytical framework for
how the agencies should assess these non-price parameters, such as innovation or
quality. Nor do the European Commission's Merger Guidelines provide a framework. The Commission uses the expression 'increased prices' as 'shorthand for these
various ways in which a merger may result in competitive harm'.[45]

Rather than ask about a SSNIP, one possible solution is for the agency to inquire   **7.25**
about a small, but significant, non-transitory decline in quality (SSNDQ). But
absent well-accepted quantifiable measures of quality, the SSNDQ test has been
to date unworkable. The EU delegate to the 2013 OECD roundtable expressed 'the
view that it would be rather challenging to replace the SSNIP test with an SSNDQ
test, insofar as the latter relies heavily on market data that is inherently difficult to

---

[41] *Microsoft/Yahoo! Search*, above note 40, paras 202–5.
[42] Ocello et al, above note 25, p 3.
[43] Ibid.
[44] David S Evans, 'The Antitrust Economics of Free', *Competition Policy International* (Spring 2011): p 22, http://ssrn.com/abstract=1813193.
[45] EC Horizontal Merger Guidelines, above note 4, para 8.

measure'.[46] Price often provides a transparent and consistent benchmark. But for many products and services, quality attributes can be complex, subjective, and hard to observe and measure.[47] One jurisdiction, in reviewing hospital mergers, used the SSNDQ test to define product market. But even the UK competition official 'emphasised that, while the UK competition agencies may conduct SSNIP tests (and, implicitly, SSNDQ tests where quality is a relevant competition consideration), the information obtained from these assessments is simply one factor to be taken into account within a broader consideration of the functioning of competition within a sector'.[48] Thus outside industries with well-accepted metrics of quality (such as health care), competition authorities infrequently identify a specific dimension of quality and then assess the consumers' likely response to an SSNDQ in that dimension of quality.

7.26 Even if the competition authority could conduct the SSNDQ test, the quality component would have to be measurable, objective, well accepted, and transparent.

7.27 The European Commission's decision in *Intel* is illustrative. The Commission noted the challenge and subjectivity involved in assessing the quality-adjusted price of high tech products.[49] Moreover the Commission acknowledged the lack of a single parameter that defines product quality, particularly when the product in question is complex such as a computer's central processing unit (CPU).[50] Consumers also had difficulty assessing quality for computers. The Commission cited a market survey, that showed that 'price is by far the most important factor when choosing a computer at retail level', and how 'quality and therefore also CPU awareness play[ed] a secondary role, in particular because consumers tend to lack the respective technical knowledge to develop a preference for Intel or AMD CPUs'.[51]

E. Challenges in Conducting an SSNDQ on Privacy

7.28 For many data-driven mergers involving free products, the agency might attempt to assess what a small, but significant, non-transitory decrease in quality would entail. Privacy protection would be part of this assessment. The European Commission in *Facebook/WhatsApp* recognized that privacy protection over one's personal data can

---

[46] OECD Quality Report, above note 7, p 164; *see also* ibid, p 9 (noting that SSNDQ test 'in practice...is unworkable' given 'the inherent difficulties of measuring quality alongside the existing complications of the applying the SSNIP test itself within real market situations').

[47] Ibid, pp 121, 124 (US), 60 (Canada).

[48] Ibid, p 163.

[49] *Intel Corporation* (Case Comp/37.990), Commission Decision D(2009) 3726 final [2009] OJ C 227/07, para 909.

[50] Ibid, para 1691.

[51] Ibid, para 1609 n 1919.

be an important parameter of non-price competition.[52] Other competition officials also recognize that privacy protection can be viewed as part of quality.[53] As the European Commission officials observed, the degree to which companies protect the consumers' privacy interests is a parameter of quality competition:

> In two-sided markets, where products are offered to users for free and monetised through targeted advertising, personal data can be viewed as the currency paid by the user in return for receiving the 'free' product, or as a dimension of product quality.[54]

7.29 Suppose the competition authority wanted to apply the SSNDQ test: what then would a *small* but *significant* non-transitory decrease in privacy protection look like?

7.30 One possibility may be found in the *Qihoo 360 v Tencent* litigation in China. Qihoo 360 and Tencent both offer free products to consumers to build their user bases. The large Internet companies derive revenue from the sale of online advertising as well as the sale of additional services to consumers. The dispute arose when Qihoo introduced antivirus software that allowed users to control the number of ads that Tencent's instant messaging (IM) software displayed. Tencent responded by making its IM software incompatible with all Qihoo software, with users being forced to choose between having Tencent's IM software or Qihoo's antivirus software on their computers.

7.31 The case is noteworthy because the Chinese Supreme People's Court considered the multi-sided nature of Internet markets, and accepted that the SSNDQ test, rather than the more commonly used SSNIP test, would have been more appropriate given the product's lack of price.[55] In that litigation, economic evidence was submitted including various quality parameters that could be evaluated by the SSNDQ test.[56]

7.32 As we will see in Chapter 17, recent economic work also suggests that it may be possible to model a decrease in quality (including privacy) in a way that is familiar to economists.

---

[52] *Facebook/WhatsApp* (Case Comp/M.7217), Commission Decision C(2014) 7239 final, 3 October 2014, para 87; Ocello et al, above note 25, p 5 (noting 'privacy, as a non-price parameter of competition in the market').

[53] *See, eg,* Deborah Feinstein, 'Big Data in a Competition Environment', 5 *Competition Policy International Antitrust Chronicle* (May 2015): p 2.

[54] Ocello et al, above note 25, p 6.

[55] David S Evans and Melissa Yanhua Zhang, '*Qihoo 360 v Tencent*: First Antitrust Decision by the Supreme Court', *Competition Policy International* (2014), https://www.competitionpolicyinternational.com/assets/Uploads/AsiaOctober214.pdf; Charles River Associates, '*Qihoo v Tencent*: Economic Analysis of the First Chinese Supreme Court Decision Under the Anti-Monopoly Law', *CRA Insights: China Highlights*, February 2015, http://www.crai.com/sites/default/files/publications/China-Highlights-Qihoo-360-v-Tencent-0215_0.pdf.

[56] American Bar Association (ABA), 'The Price Point', Winter 2015, http://www.americanbar.org/content/dam/aba/publications/antitrust_law/at320000_newsletter_2015winter.authcheckdam.pdf.

7.33 But one potential issue is that the SSNDQ cross-elasticity test assumes that consumers could easily detect the quality degradation, which would prompt the decision to switch to rival products or services.[57] That is not always the case. In assessing the Microsoft/Skype acquisition, the European Commission did consider quality in examining whether Microsoft 'could, post-transaction, differentiate Skype's user experience according to the platforms or the [operating system] by degrading the interoperability of Skype with competing [operating systems] and platforms in order to favour user experience on its own [operating system] or platform and consequently increase its market power in these markets'.[58] The Commission found that, while Microsoft could degrade the interoperability of Skype, it likely would not:

> If Microsoft were to degrade Skype's user experience on competing (and growing) OS [operating system], such as Android, iOS, Mac OS and other platforms it would give its main competitors an advantage with the risk that over time the consumer appeal of Skype's brand would be lost. In this case, Microsoft would have lost a significant part of its initial investment for the acquisition of Skype. This is particularly true with regard to mobile [operating system] platforms where Microsoft's market position is much weaker than it is in PC [operating systems].

> Neither Skype nor WLM [Microsoft's communication services offered under the brands 'Windows Live Messenger'] are 'must-have' products in the consumer communications services markets. There are many alternatives to Skype, and consumers increasingly use non-Windows platforms for online communications...Hence, any attempt to withhold Skype from, or degrade the Skype's user experience on non-Windows platforms would hurt Skype, and therefore Microsoft. It would not harm the competing [operating system] platforms. For instance, Google is pre-installing Google Talk on Android and Apple is pre-installing Facetime on iOS.[59]

7.34 One cannot fault the Commission's analysis on quality, but one can see its limitations. The Commission first assumed that consumers could readily detect any degradation in Skype's quality, which includes not only the degradation in online communications and interoperability, but other important parameters of quality. But it is altogether unclear whether consumers can readily detect small incremental quality degradations. Many consumers, for example, did not detect the quality degradation of everyday household products such as tomato sauce and meat.[60]

7.35 But it would be even harder for consumers to detect a small, but significant, degradation in privacy protection. As we saw in the Facebook/WhatsApp merger, many users do not spend several weeks reading all the privacy policies of the online products and services that they use. Few customers have the inclination to read the dense

---

[57] *See, eg, Microsoft/Skype*, above note 40, paras 144–69.

[58] Ibid, para 135.

[59] Ibid, paras 147–8.

[60] Ezrachi and Stucke, above note 33.

privacy policies, especially on their smartphones, as they generally have no power to negotiate something better. Even if they did read the privacy statement, it still would be hard for consumers to detect—from the legalese in the company's privacy notices—a small, but significant, degradation in the privacy protections afforded to their data.

Second, the European Commission assumes that consumers could readily assess **7.36** the quality parameters of rival products, and shift to alternatives that offers superior quality. Although some markets offer clear alternatives in privacy protections, other markets, especially those with data-driven network effects, do not.

Third, consumers may not switch even in the face of welfare-reducing privacy **7.37** degradation. As the European Commission itself recognized, consumers may experience status quo bias, whereby they stick with the default option even when a superior alternative exists.[61] This may be especially the case when the products are free and readily assessing quality distinctions is difficult. Search engines, for example, estimate the value of being the default choice on a browser, and pay the browser for this right.[62] Google, for example, is the default engine on Apple's Safari Internet browser. Google reportedly paid Apple USD 82 million in 2009, and USD 1 billion in 2013 and 2014 for this partnership.[63] Likewise, after the Internet browser Firefox made Yahoo! the default search engine, Yahoo!'s share grew from 8.6 per cent in November 2014 to 10.9 per cent of the US search market in January 2015, its highest share in the previous five years.[64] It appears that this growth was attributable to Firefox. When Firefox users were separated out from Yahoo!'s overall share, Yahoo!'s remaining share was reportedly 'flat or down slightly vs last month'.[65] Here, many Firefox users were using Google, and after Firefox changed the default, Google sought to persuade Firefox users to switch back to Google. But, according to reports, many Firefox users stuck with the new default engine Yahoo![66]

---

[61] *Facebook/WhatsApp*, above note 52, paras 111, 124 (discussing status quo bias). For the importance of default options generally, *see* Chapter 5, para 5.17.

[62] Greg Sterling, 'As Apple-Google Deal Expires, Who Will Win the Safari Default Search Business?', Search Engine Land, 5 February 2015, http://searchengineland.com/apple-google-deal-expires-will-win-safari-default-search-business-214277.

[63] *See* para 18.41.

[64] Greg Sterling, 'Firefox Deal Continues to Boost Yahoo as US Search Share Grows Again in January', Search Engine Land, 2 February 2015, http://searchengineland.com/firefox-deal-continues-boost-yahoo-us-search-share-grows-january-213998.

[65] Ibid.

[66] Ibid (StatCounter CEO Aodhan Cullen posted: 'Some analysts expected Yahoo to fall in January as a result of Firefox users switching back to Google. In fact Yahoo has increased US search share by half a percentage point.'); Gregg Keizer, 'Yahoo Loses Some US Share Gained from Firefox Deal', *Computerworld*, 17 April 2015, http://www.computerworld.com/article/2911108/yahoo-loses-some-us-share-gained-from-firefox-deal.html (noting that after a January 2015 peak of 13%, Yahoo!'s search share dropped in February to 12.8%, and in March to 12.7%).

7.38 So why does Google pay Apple USD 1 billion annually to be the default search browser on all Apple devices running iOS, when it could simply tell Apple users that Google is just one (or two clicks) away? If Google offered superior search results, why did many Firefox users simply stay with the new default search engine? Defaults matter.

7.39 Status quo bias also arose in the Commission's case involving Microsoft's Windows Media Player.[67] Although consumers could download other media players from the Internet, many did not, a function not attributable necessarily to the superiority of Microsoft's media player but to status quo bias.[68] As the Commission recently recognized, pre-installing software on a large number of smartphones may make it less likely that consumers will switch to alternatives, even when they are superior quality.[69] Likewise the OFT discussed in its *Google/Waze* decision how integrating the pre-installed application with other functions on the platform may further reduce the likelihood of consumers switching.[70]

7.40 Thus, another confounding variable in data-driven industries is a company's ability to use status quo bias to degrade quality, including less visible aspects such as privacy protections, on its free product. Even where consumers can perceive quality differences when confronted with side-by-side comparisons in blind tests, it is not altogether clear that consumers will act upon these quality differences in real life. If many consumers would stick with the default 'free' app on their smartphone, then those apps pre-installed on a large base of smartphones, tablets, or personal computers (such as email, search engine, etc) would have more latitude in shading quality, especially on harder to measure aspects, such as privacy protection. Thus in today's environment, companies can shroud a small, but significant, degradation in quality (ie privacy protection).

F. Using SSNIP for Free Services

7.41 Given the difficulties in applying the SSNDQ test, competition agencies at times try other tacks. Returning to their price metric, they, for example, inquire how consumers would respond, post-merger, if charged a small, but significant, amount for the formerly free service.[71] Such was the case in the Microsoft/Skype deal,

---

[67] *Microsoft (Tying)* (Case Comp C-3/39.530) [2009] OJ C 242/04; Maurice E Stucke, 'Behavioral Antitrust and Monopolization', 8 *J Competition L & Econ* (2012): p 545.

[68] *Microsoft (Tying)*, above note.

[69] *Facebook/WhatsApp*, above note 52, paras 111, 124 (discussing status quo bias).

[70] UK Office of Fair Trading, *Completed Acquisition by Motorola Mobility Holding (Google, Inc) of Waze Mobile Limited*, ME/6167/13, 11 November 2013, paras 57–61, http://webarchive. nationalarchives.gov.uk/20140402142426/http://www.oft.gov.uk/shared_oft/mergers_ea02/2013/motorola.pdf.

[71] *Microsoft/Skype*, above note 40, paras 75–6 (finding that '[c]onsumer communications services are mostly offered for free' and that the 'parties have provided an internal document of Skype

where the European Commission observed that Skype was offered for free and 'if prices were charged for this service, the large majority of consumers would switch to alternative providers…as for instance Google, Facebook, Viber, ooVoo or Fring'.[72] A company can exercise market power by charging for a formerly free product. Thus estimating how many consumers would cease using the formerly free service is an appropriate consideration.

But consumers' high price-sensitivity is not determinative.[73] One fallacy is to assume **7.42** the converse: if the producer cannot raise price post-merger (because of switching), then the producer lacks market power and the merger will not harm consumers. As the US recognizes, 'non-price effects may coexist with price effects, or can arise in their absence'.[74] The 2010 Horizontal Merger Guidelines provide an example where the loss of variety, without an increase in price, can reduce consumers' welfare.[75] Price is only one parameter of competition, and not a very important one in multi-sided markets, where sellers can dominate the market for free goods and services. Google, for example, does not charge consumers for many of its services (such as search, browser, email, videos, and maps). But Google, the competition authorities recognize, has significant market power.[76]

Nor is it true that because the items are offered for free, the market is competitive. At **7.43** times, the competitive price can be negative (whereby the company pays consumers to use the service or for the full value of their personal data). Thus companies can exercise market power by eliminating payments to consumers and offering the product for free. (Just imagine your reaction if your employer said you could work 'for free' over the weekend.)

---

revealing that [>75] % of the users of its Skype Manager product, which are mainly private customers, would cease to use the product if Skype started charging for its use').

[72] Ibid, paras 156–7.

[73] Ibid, para 77 ('The Commission takes the view that this demonstrates high price sensitivity. Success of providers of consumer communications services depends very much on whether they are free of charge. If a provider starts charging for a service which was used for a long time free of charge and there exist alternative services offered for free, it can be expected that consumers would immediately switch to these competing services.').

[74] US Horizontal Merger Guidelines, above note 4, s 1.

[75] Ibid, s 6.4, example 21:

Firm A sells a high-end product at a premium price. Firm B sells a mid-range product at a lower price, serving customers who are more price sensitive. Several other firms have low-end products. Firms A and B together have a large share of the relevant market. Firm A proposes to acquire Firm B and discontinue Firm B's product. Firm A expects to retain most of Firm B's customers. Firm A may not find it profitable to raise the price of its high-end product after the merger, because doing so would reduce its ability to retain Firm B's more price-sensitive customers. The Agencies may conclude that the withdrawal of Firm B's product results from a loss of competition and materially harms customers.

[76] European Commission, 'Commission Seeks Feedback on Commitments Offered by Google to Address Competition Concerns—Questions and Answers', Memo, 25 April 2013, http://europa.eu/rapid/press-release_MEMO-13-383_en.htm.

7.44   Even if 'free' is the competitive price, the company can exert market power along non-price dimensions, such as reducing privacy protections. Finally, the merger— in yielding a key source of valuable personal data—may help the company maintain its dominant position in other markets, without adversely affecting price or short-term quality in the affected market.

G. How a Price-Centric Analysis Can Yield the Wrong Conclusion

7.45   Even when the products have a price, we can see how antitrust's price-centric model can be ill suited for many data-driven mergers. Let us reconsider the Facebook/WhatsApp merger. Both companies competed in offering different privacy protections for the use of their texting apps. Facebook offered its texting app for free, but harvested its users' data to target them with behavioural ads. Unlike Facebook, WhatsApp did not sell advertising space or collect a lot of personal data on users of its mobile app. Instead, WhatsApp charged a small subscription fee to some subscribers for its texting app.[77] Suppose Facebook, post-merger, 'would start requiring more personal data from users or supplying such data to third parties as a condition for delivering its "free" product'. [78] The European Commission recognized that could be seen as either increasing its price or as degrading the quality of its product.[79]

7.46   But let us assume that WhatsApp's privacy protections were valuable to many of its users. Suppose Facebook planned to reduce the privacy protections that WhatsApp had provided, but it would now offer the app for free. (To be clear, Facebook never raised this defence.) The US competition authorities recognize that this loss of variety can violate the Clayton Act.[80]

7.47   The risk, however, is if the agency views the merger largely through a price lens. Declining prices post-merger are often viewed as procompetitive (except for monopsonies). Except they are not when many consumers prefer the quality (namely the enhanced privacy protection) over the dollar per year savings.

---

[77] WhatsApp, *Frequently Asked Questions: What Are WhatsApp's Subscription Fees?*, http://www.whatsapp.com/faq/en/general/23014681 (after a free one-year trial period, US users have the option of extending their subscription for USD 0.99 per year).

[78] Ocello et al, above note 25, p 6.

[79] Ibid.

[80] US Horizontal Merger Guidelines, above note 4, s 6.4. ('If the merged firm would withdraw a product that a significant number of customers strongly prefer to those products that would remain available, this can constitute a harm to customers over and above any effects on the price or quality of any given product. If there is evidence of such an effect, the Agencies may inquire whether the reduction in variety is largely due to a loss of competitive incentives attributable to the merger.')

We may see this in other data-driven mergers, like Google/Nest Labs. The candi- **7.48**
date theory of harm is not whether the price for thermostats and surveillance cameras would likely increase post-merger. Instead Google, in switching Nest Labs to a
data-driven, advertising-dependent revenue model, may lower the price of its smart
thermostats to attract more users, thereby collecting more personal data to target
them with behavioural ads and to broaden its advertising platform. Moreover, the
acquirer may offer other perks for customers to share more data with them. (Nest
Labs, for example, stores its users' personal information on its cloud servers for as
long as they remain Nest customers.[81]) As the cost of storing data declines, Google
and other smart technology manufacturers might permanently save the consumers
data (including surveillance camera footage, along with emails, texts, geo-location
data, and search inquiries). This could be viewed as a benefit (your videos are forever
archived and retrievable; no need to worry about storage limits for your email account) or a privacy concern (having one company control so much data about your
personal life).

Here again under a price-centric model, consumers are better off. Previously, **7.49**
they paid USD 240 for Nest Learning Thermostat. Post-merger they pay only
USD 200. Their consumer surplus increased by USD 40, but not necessarily their
welfare, especially if there are no viable alternatives that offer greater privacy
protections.

Although the competition agencies recognize that the loss of variety could violate **7.50**
the law, they rarely bring these cases without evidence of higher prices. Thus the
agency, relying on its price-centric antitrust tools, might easily miss the key issue
driving the merger: the competitive significance of Google acquiring this data from
many consumers' homes to their already large dataset.

H. Reflections

As we saw in the TomTom/Tele Atlas merger, the competition officials' price- **7.51**
centric analytical tools can assess data-driven mergers where the datasets are
bought and sold. They can assess how buyers would respond to a SSNIP for accessing that data.

---

[81] *See Privacy Statement for Nest Products and Services*, Nest, 17 June 2015, https://nest.com/
legal/privacy-statement/. Google in mid-2015 offered 'Cloud Recording' as an optional service
for its surveillance cameras. Users could save 'up to 30 days of footage...to review after it's happened' and can 'share and save clips of...recorded footage'. Google offered users 50% off for each
additional camera they subscribe to the same cloud recording plan. Dropcam, 'What is Cloud
Recording And How Does it Work?', 16 January 2014, http://support.dropcam.com/entries/
38283613-What-is-Dropcam-Cloud-Recording-and-how-does-it-work-.

7.52 As we saw in the Bazaarvoice/PowerReviews merger, the competition agencies can challenge the egregious case where the companies' internal documents clearly reveal the merger's anticompetitive purpose and effect.

7.53 But they otherwise struggle with data-driven mergers where assessing the harm is harder to quantify (such as the merger's impact on quality, privacy protection, or innovation) even when these non-price considerations are paramount. They are more comfortable, with their current toolkit, in assessing what is more readily quantifiable (namely short-term price effects and efficiencies).

7.54 Nor have they addressed how the acquisition of data could help a dominant firm maintain its market power; nor have they considered the greater social, political, and ethical concerns when a few companies amass a significant amount of our personal data. Although competition policy—especially its bias against monopolies—historically involved the concerns of freedom and autonomy, today the loss of economic liberty is recognized only to the extent it adversely affects competition in a tangible measurable way, such as higher prices under the agencies' unilateral effects theory.

7.55 Consequently, antitrust's price-centric tools work well when data is bought and sold, but are ill suited for many data-driven strategies where the product or service is free, and the cost is privacy. With the acceleration of the four 'V's of data and data-driven business models, mergers, and business strategies, the agencies' price-centric antitrust analysis will be of little help to assess these mergers' and restraints' effects on individuals.

8

DATA-DRIVEN MERGERS OFTEN FALL OUTSIDE COMPETITION POLICY'S CONVENTIONAL CATEGORIES

Another reason why the competition agencies have not fully considered the impli- **8.01**
cations of Big Data is that data-driven mergers can defy the agencies' conventions
that work well for other mergers. This chapter explores three conventions: the
categorization of mergers, the belief that similar products/services compete more
fiercely than dissimilar products/services, and the focus on the services' or products' substitutability.

A. Categorization of Mergers

Competition agencies categorize mergers as horizontal, vertical, and/or con- **8.02**
glomerate.[1] The competition agencies review and challenge horizontal mergers
(ie between companies that directly compete) more often than vertical mergers (where the merging parties operate at different levels of the supply chain,
with one party supplying a key input or being a key customer).[2] Rarely do they
challenge conglomerate mergers.[3] Regardless of the category, the ultimate

---

[1] European Commission, *Guidelines on the Assessment of Non-Horizontal Mergers Under the
Council Regulation on the Control of Concentrations Between Undertakings* [2008] OJ C 265/07, para 3
('EC Non-Horizontal Merger Guidelines'), http://eur-lex.europa.eu/LexUriServ/LexUriServ.do?
uri=OJ:C:2008:265:0006:0025:en:PDF ('Two broad types of non-horizontal mergers can be dis-
tinguished: vertical mergers and conglomerate mergers.').
[2] Ibid, para 11 ('Non-horizontal mergers are generally less likely to significantly impede effective
competition than horizontal mergers.').
[3] Ibid, para 92 (acknowledging 'that conglomerate mergers in the majority of circumstances will not
lead to any competition problems,' but 'in certain specific cases there may be harm to competition');
Deborah Platt Majoris, 'Merger Enforcement at the Antitrust Division', Speech given at KPMG/Chicago
School of Business Mergers and Acquisitions Forum, Chicago, 27 September 2002, http://www.justice.
gov/atr/speech/merger-enforcement-antitrust-division-0 ('[A]ntitrust should rarely, if ever, interfere with
any conglomerate merger. Under only the rarest conditions will a conglomerate merger, unlike a horizontal or vertical merger, likely give the merged firm the ability and incentive to raise price and restrict output.
Conversely, conglomerate mergers have the potential as a class to generate significant efficiencies.').

assessment is the same, namely whether the merger may substantially lessen competition or tend to create a monopoly (or monopsony). But the analytical framework differs depending on whether it is a horizontal, vertical, or conglomerate merger.

8.03   As we have seen, data-driven mergers can be horizontal. Facebook and WhatsApp offered competing texting apps. Google and Waze directly competed with turn-by-turn navigation applications for smartphones and tablets. Data-driven mergers can be vertical, as when TomTom, the leading manufacturer of portable navigation devices and navigation software, acquired Tele Atlas, a key supplier of navigable digital map data. At times, a merger can be both horizontal and vertical (such as when a company supplies and competes with the acquired company).

8.04   But data-driven mergers often defy the agencies' three general categories. We saw this with Google's acquisition of Nest Labs. The merger was not horizontal. Google never sold smart thermostats, carbon monoxide detectors, and surveillance cameras. Nor were Google and Nest Labs in a vertical relationship; neither company supplied the other's industry with a key input or was a key customer. Nor was this a conglomerate merger in the antitrust sense. Neither company was 'active in closely related markets (e.g., mergers involving suppliers of complementary products or of products which belong to a range of products that is generally purchased by the same set of customers for the same end use)'.[4]

8.05   When a merger like Google/Nest Labs falls outside the horizontal, vertical, or conglomerate categories, the agency lacks an existing guideline (or analytical framework) to assess the merger. It will likely close the investigation (if it even opened one). But that does not mean that these mergers are harmless. Several European Commission officials in 2015 identified a potential theory of harm:

> In the digital economy, large sets of data (so-called 'big data') are becoming increasingly valuable as they reveal patterns of information that enable companies to understand user behaviour and preferences and improve (or target) their products and services accordingly. This makes the availability of 'big data' a significant competitive advantage for companies active in, for instance, targeted online advertising, online search, social networking services and software products. From a competition law perspective, a possible theory of harm is that combining the merging parties' datasets could provide them with a competitive advantage, by helping them to improve the merged entity's product or service post-merger in a way that competitors are unable to match.[5]

---

[4] EC Non-Horizontal Merger Guidelines, above note 1, para 91.
[5] Eleonora Ocello, Cristina Sjödin, and Anatoly SuboČs, 'What's Up with Merger Control in the Digital Sector? Lessons from the Facebook/WhatsApp EU Merger Case', 1 *Competition Merger Brief* (February 2015): p 6.

A related candidate theory of harm is whether the merger increases the company's **8.06** market power in any market (such as search, online advertising, etc) by tipping the market to the merging party. As we shall see in Chapters 11–13, some industries, like the search engine market, have several data-driven network effects, where the scale and scope of data play a critical role. Although the merger could benefit consumers, it might also insulate the platform from competitive pressure by inhibiting smaller competitors' growth and increasing entry barriers.

So even though some data-driven mergers, like Google/Nest Labs, fall outside **8.07** antitrust's conventional categories, the mergers could still harm competition and consumers. The competition agencies cannot ignore these outliers. But they currently lack an analytical framework for identifying which outlying merger deserves closer scrutiny.

B. Belief that Similar Products/Services Compete More Fiercely than Dissimilar Products/Services

Outside of offences treated per se illegal (such as price-fixing), antitrust plain- **8.08** tiffs ordinarily must define a relevant market, where the goods (or services) are interchangeable with one another, but not with products (or services) outside the market. The conventional antitrust analysis is that similar products compete more closely against one another than dissimilar products. As the European Commission states:

> A relevant product market comprises all those products and/or services which are regarded as interchangeable or substitutable by the consumer, by reason of the products' characteristics, their prices and their intended use. A relevant product market may in some cases be composed of a number of individual products and/or services which present largely identical physical or technical characteristics and are interchangeable.[6]

Likewise, the US agencies note in industries with differentiated products, 'some prod- **8.09** ucts can be very close substitutes and compete strongly with each other, while other products are more distant substitutes and compete less strongly. For example, one high-end product may compete much more directly with another high-end product than with any low-end product.'[7] For many household goods this makes sense.

---

[6] European Commission, 'Form CO Relating to the Notification of a Concentration Pursuant to Regulation (EC) No 139/2004', at *EU Competition Law: Rules Applicable to Merger Control, Situation as at 1 April 2010*, p 59 ('Form CO'), http://ec.europa.eu/competition/mergers/legislation/merger_compilation.pdf.
[7] US Department of Justice (DOJ) and Federal Trade Commission (FTC), *Horizontal Merger Guidelines*, 19 August 2010, s 6.1 ('US Horizontal Merger Guidelines'), http://www.justice.gov/atr/public/guidelines/hmg-2010.html.

8.10 One illustrative merger while we were at the US Department of Justice (DOJ) involved white bread.[8] Although there was a high cross-elasticity of demand between the merging parties' white bread, there was little substitution to other types of bread. Here, we see high functional interchangeability, as arguably white bread is roughly equivalent to wheat bread for the uses to which they are put, namely sandwiches. But purchasers (or their children) did not treat wheat or multi-grain bread as substitutes for white bread. White bread, the DOJ discussed,

> differs significantly in product attributes from other types of bread, such as variety bread (e.g., wheat, rye or French) and freshly baked in-store breads, in taste, texture, uses, perceived nutritional value, keeping qualities, and appeal to various groups of consumers. These differing attributes give rise to distinct consumer preferences for each type of bread.[9]

Finding that a small but significant increase in the price of white pan bread by all producers would not be rendered unprofitable by consumers substituting to other breads, the DOJ defined the product market as white pan bread.

8.11 Standard product market definition looks at competition at the firm level; products may be further differentiated within a relevant market when some products are closer substitutes than others.[10] One example is baby wipes. The DOJ alleged baby wipes as the relevant product market, but private label was not an effective constraint.[11] Here, product market definition—either as premium baby wipes brands or baby wipes generally—is less critical, as the merging parties' brands were each other's most significant competitive constraint. At times, the competition authority simply defines the product market more narrowly, such as super-premium ice cream.[12] Regardless, our overall point is that antitrust tends to focus on substitutability whether defining the product market or ascertaining unilateral effects within that market.

8.12 Substitutability played a key role in the Facebook/WhatsApp merger. The European Commission, according to several officials, recognized 'how privacy could be

---

[8] *United States v Interstate Bakeries Corp & Continental Baking Co*, Civil Action No 95C 4194, 1995 WL 803599 (US Dist Ct (ND Ill), 1995).

[9] Ibid, Competitive Impact Statement, 21 July 1995, http://www.justice.gov/atr/case-document/competitive-impact-statement-132.

[10] European Commission, *Guidelines on the Assessment of Horizontal Mergers Under the Council Regulation on Control of Concentrations Between Undertakings* [2004] OJ C 31/03, para 28 ('EC Horizontal Merger Guidelines'), http://eur-lex.europa.eu/legal-content/EN/TXT/?uri=celex:520 04XC0205%2802%29.

[11] *United States v Kimberly-Clark Corp & Scott Paper Co*, Case No 3:95 CV 3055-P (US Dist Ct (ND Tex), 1995), Complaint, paras 36–7, http://www.justice.gov/atr/case-document/complaint-141.

[12] FTC, 'FTC to Challenge Nestle, Dreyer's Merger: Agency Will Allege $2.8 Billion Ice Cream Deal Violates Antitrust Laws', Press Release, 4 March 2003, https://www.ftc.gov/news-events/press-releases/2003/03/ftc-challenge-nestle-dreyers-merger.

regarded as a non-price parameter of competition which may be degraded by the merged entity post-merger'.[13] The Commission also recognized that the degradation in privacy protection could infringe EU competition law (whether or not it also infringes the data protection rules).[14] But this theory of harm is relevant only 'where privacy is an important factor in the decision to purchase a product or service, i.e. a key parameter of competition'.[15]

This analysis would seem to make sense. It is consistent with how the agencies **8.13** usually look at competition, which is to ask questions about substitutability. But the requirement that privacy be an 'important' factor in the decision to purchase or a 'key' parameter of competition would be too narrow, if construed to capture only mergers between two privacy-protective services, while ignoring mergers where one product is privacy-protective and the other is not (even though the merger would likely result in harm). Under the Commission's reasoning, because Facebook Messenger and WhatsApp had different privacy protections, this, among other things, suggested that they were not close competitors.[16] In reality, however, this analysis has flaws.

It does not follow that texting apps with substantially similar privacy policies com- **8.14** pete more fiercely than ones with dissimilar privacy policies. For one thing, the most meaningful competitive distinction between the firms may be their privacy policies. If a customer is choosing between texting apps, she is not likely to say, 'Oh Facebook has crummy privacy protections. Let me look at other apps that also have inferior privacy protections.' Firms offer an array of privacy choices, but the fact that they offer privacy protection at all suggests that they realize that consumers value privacy. From an economic standpoint, privacy is a dimension on which they are competing, whether they offer a lot of protection for the data or a little.[17]

In choosing a texting app, the primary consideration, given the network effects, **8.15** is whether their friends, family, and acquaintances use the app. WhatsApp and Facebook are the leading texting apps. The Commission noted how consumer communications apps featured a significant degree of 'multi-homing', that is, users who installed, and use, on the same handset several consumer communications apps.[18] In particular, WhatsApp and Facebook Messenger were the two main consumer communications apps simultaneously used by the majority of the users in

---

[13] Ocello et al, above note 5, p 6.
[14] Ibid.
[15] Ibid.
[16] *Facebook/WhatsApp* (Case Comp/M.7217), Commission Decision C(2014) 7239 final, 3 October 2014, paras 102, 107.
[17] Keith Waehrer, 'Online Services and the Analysis of Competitive Merger Effects in Privacy Protections and Other Quality Dimensions', Working Paper, 12 January 2016, http://waehrer.net/ Merger%20effects%20in%20privacy%20protections.pdf.
[18] *Facebook/WhatsApp*, above note 16, para 105.

the EU. The interesting dynamic is that a very high percentage of WhatsApp users were already using Facebook's social network. Facebook members could easily use Facebook Messenger. Facebook Messenger is integrated in the company's social network. Moreover, the texting apps offered similar functionalities.[19] Nonetheless, many Facebook social network subscribers opted for a texting app that afforded them significantly greater privacy protection than Facebook Messenger.[20]

8.16 So the difference in privacy protections, rather than suggest that the texting apps were complements, could easily reflect a critical competitive difference. Users who want to join a social network join the largest one, Facebook, because that is where their friends, family, and acquaintances likely are. But for texting apps, they had a choice between two equally sized competitors but with different privacy protections. Facebook Messenger and WhatsApp texting apps were not complements, in the sense that an increase in demand in one app increases the demand of the other (such as peanut-butter and jelly). Instead, Facebook sought users who spend more time on its texting app Messenger than WhatsApp. WhatsApp, to induce Facebook social network users to switch from Messenger, offered greater privacy protections.

8.17 Three Commission officials in their post-merger analysis of Facebook/WhatsApp offered a slightly different explanation:

> ...the Commission regarded privacy as one of many parameters of competition between consumer communications apps, the others being price, reliability of the service, functionalities offered, size of the underlying network, trendiness, etc. While the Commission recognised that an increasing number of users value privacy and security (as shown by the growing popularity of apps that offer increased security of communications, like Threema or Telegram), the majority of the consumer communications apps currently on the market do not compete (mainly) on privacy features (e.g. Facebook, Skype, WeChat, Line, etc.).[21]

8.18 The second argument, which the three Commission officials advanced, is that the majority of the consumer communications apps on the market did not compete (mainly) on privacy features. But this is perhaps too one-dimensional. Facebook's privacy policy may have offered too little protection to consumers—a result of what Professor Farrell has called a 'dysfunctional equilibrium':

> If firms perceive that few consumers shift their demand in response to actual privacy policies, then the firm's incentives are to make its policy noncommittal and/or non-protective.... It would then be tempting to design disclosures so as not to

---

[19] Ibid, para 104.

[20] Ibid, para 105. Between December 2013 and April 2014, 'between [20–30]% and [50–60]% of WhatsApp users already used Facebook Messenger and between [70–80]% and [80–90]% of WhatsApp users were Facebook users and were therefore already within the reach of Facebook Messenger. Conversely, over the same period 60% to 70% of Facebook Messenger active users already used WhatsApp.' Ibid, para 140.

[21] Ocello et al, above note 5, p 6.

really communicate the choice of policy, if it is possible to obfuscate for the minority of consumers while retaining the ability to claim that the policy was disclosed. Meanwhile, if consumers perceive that firms behave in this kind of way, they will not expect attentive reading of privacy policies to be a rewarding activity. These patterns of conduct and expectations would reinforce each other, which is what makes them a game-theoretic or economic equilibrium.

It is often difficult to escape a dysfunctional equilibrium if there are large numbers of players involved. A consumer can't simply decide to start reading privacy policies—or rather, she can, but it won't do a lot of good, since firms will still expect that few consumers do so, so the consumer is apt either to learn little (noncommittal or vague policies) or be confirmed in her wary cynicism (policies that reveal a lack of protection—the rational choice for the firm when it expects that few consumers' behavior will be affected). A small firm, likewise, can't simply decide to break out of the equilibrium by adopting more protective policies and clearer disclosures, because its demand won't shift by much. . . . Escape from a dysfunctional equilibrium often, and probably here, requires action by large and powerful players, and/or concerted action by groups of players.[22]

Here, WhatsApp may have been the maverick seeking to disrupt this 'dysfunctional **8.19** equilibrium' that benefitted the industry leader, Facebook, and the smaller texting apps, all of which opted for a revenue model that values the needs of behavioural advertising over users' privacy needs. And, at least before the merger, WhatsApp may have been succeeding, at least based on evidence of its popularity.

Competition law reaches this theory of harm. The agencies consider whether a **8.20** merger may lessen competition by eliminating a 'maverick' firm, ie, 'a firm that plays a disruptive role in the market to the benefit of customers'.[23] One traditional antitrust concern is when 'one of the merging firms has a strong incumbency position' (ie, Facebook) and the other merging firm 'threatens to disrupt market conditions with a new . . . business model'.[24] Here, WhatsApp sought to shake things up with a different business model that did not harvest users' personal data to target them with behavioural ads. WhatsApp offered a different business model that strongly signalled how protecting users' data and privacy was in its corporate DNA. This theory of harm is within antitrust's framework.[25]

It seems, instead, that the Commission relied on the conventional antitrust theory **8.21** that dissimilar products compete less fiercely. Products and/or services with nearly identical physical, technical, or privacy characteristics are lumped together as close competitors. Because the texting apps had different business models and privacy

---

[22] Joseph Farrell, 'Can Privacy Be Just Another Good?', 10 *J on Telecomm & High Tech L* (2012): pp 251, 258–9.
[23] US Horizontal Merger Guidelines, above note 7, s 2.1.5.
[24] Ibid.
[25] Ibid, s 6.4.

policies, this suggested that they were not close competitors. Although this heuristic may work with other differentiated goods (such as premium versus discount shampoos), its shortcomings are revealed where a key parameter of competition is privacy protection. Instead, the competition agency should consider whether the incumbent is seeking to eliminate a maverick that offers greater privacy protections, and thus the merger would likely lessen competition and harm consumers.

C. Substitutability of Data

8.22 Competition policy deals often with the cross-elasticity of demand, which 'measures the responsiveness of the demand for one product to changes in the price of a different product'.[26] If the price of one increased, all else remaining equal, would a sufficient number of consumers switch to the other product to defeat the price increase? Indeed, the agencies and courts determine the boundaries of a product and geographic market by the reasonable interchangeability or cross-elasticity of demand.[27] Reasonable interchangeability and cross-elasticity of demand also help 'evaluate the extent competition constrains market power and are, therefore, indirect measurements of a firm's market power'.[28] As the European Commission states, '[t]he higher the degree of substitutability between the merging firms' products, the more likely it is that the merging firms will raise prices significantly.'[29]

8.23 Often the debate is whether products or services outside the proposed market are interchangeable with products inside the market (such as should the market for English muffins include bagels). Fatal to an antitrust claim is when the market is defined so broadly to include products that are not substitutable. As one example, consider what happened to the plaintiffs in *Golden Gate Pharmacy Services, Inc v Pfizer, Inc*, where the antitrust complaint was dismissed for failing to sufficiently allege a relevant product market.[30] The plaintiffs alleged a relevant product market of 'the pharmaceutical industry', which included the 'manufacture, sale, and innovation of all pharmaceutical products, prescription pharmaceutical products, non-prescription pharmaceutical products, brand name pharmaceutical products and particular pharmaceutical products and therapies specifically noted and identified

---

[26] *US Horticultural Supply v Scotts Co*, 367 F App'x 305, 309 (US Ct of Apps (3rd Cir), 2010); EC Horizontal Merger Guidelines, above note 10, para 29 n 38.

[27] Form CO, above note 6, p 39 (market definition depends on 'substitutability, conditions of competition, prices, cross-price elasticity of demand or other factors relevant for the definition of the product markets (for example, supply-side substitutability in appropriate cases)'); *United States v Archer-Daniels-Midland Co*, 866 F2d 242, 246 (US Ct of Apps (8th Cir), 1988).

[28] *Archer-Daniels-Midland Co*, above note 27, p 246.

[29] EC Horizontal Merger Guidelines, above note 10, para 28.

[30] *Golden Gate Pharmacy Services, Inc v Pfizer, Inc*, 433 F App'x 598 (US Ct of Apps (9th Cir), 2011).

by Pfizer and Wyeth in their annual reports'.[31] The court dismissed the complaint because not all pharmaceutical products are interchangeable for the same purpose. 'The failure to allege a product market consisting of reasonably interchangeable goods' rendered the complaint 'facially unsustainable'.[32]

At times, the competition agencies define the market as a cluster of products and **8.24** services offered by the merging parties.[33] With these products markets, the market reality is that companies to compete effectively must offer all or nearly all types of products and services in that cluster.[34] No one contends that component products and services of the 'cluster' are interchangeable with each another. Even though the components are not interchangeable, the clusters themselves are.[35]

Consequently, substitutability plays a key role in competition law. Issues of market **8.25** definition and market power often hinge on the degree of interchangeability, which 'implies that one product is roughly equivalent to another for the use to which it is put; while there might be some degree of preference for the one over the other, either would work effectively'.[36] As the FTC observed, the 'identification of substitutes is at the core of product market definition'.[37] And the primary purpose of defining a relevant market is 'to facilitate the analysis of competitive effects of a transaction'.[38]

Data-driven mergers may involve issues of substitutability of the free products, such **8.26** as the extent to which Waze's navigation app was an effective substitute for Google Maps. Data-driven mergers or joint ventures, at times, involve issues of substitutability of the underlying data. Google and Waze, for example, both collected users' geo-location data necessary in improving their mapping technologies. Microsoft and Yahoo! in their joint venture sought to combine data on their users' search behaviour to improve the quality of the search results. Here we see how issues of substitutability can apply to both the free products and the underlying data collected.

---

[31] Ibid, p 599.

[32] Ibid.

[33] *United States v Philadelphia National Bank*, 374 US 321, 356–7, 83 S Ct 1715, 1736–8 (1963) (relevant product market consisting of various kinds of credit products and services (eg checking accounts and trust administration) offered by commercial banks); *Federal Trade Commission v Sysco Corp*, Case No 1:15-CV-00256 (APM), 2015 WL 3958568, p *10, 12 (US Dist Ct (D DC), 23 June 2015) (FTC alleging, and the court accepting, that the relevant product market was 'broadline foodservice distribution'; what was relevant for the court's consideration was not any particular food item sold or delivered by the merging firms, 'but the full panoply of products and services offered by them that customers recognize as "broadline distribution"').

[34] *United States v Grinnell Corp*, 384 US 563, 572, 86 S Ct 1698, 1703 (1966) ('We see no barrier to combining in a single market a number of different products or services where that combination reflects commercial realities.').

[35] *Philadelphia National Bank*, above note 33.

[36] *US Horticultural Supply*, above note 26, p 309, quoting *Allen-Myland, Inc v International Business Machines Corp*, 33 F3d 194, 206 (US Ct of Apps (3rd Cir), 1994).

[37] *In re Promedica Health System, Inc*, 2012 WL 1155375 (FTC, 22 March 2012).

[38] Ibid.

8.27   But one of the four critical 'V's of Big Data is the *variety* of data. Google in acquiring Nest Labs was not necessarily seeking data that was substitutable with the voluminous personal data that it already amassed through its search engine (Google), video platform (YouTube), browser (Chrome), mapping applications (Google Maps and Waze), email service (Gmail), and operating system for mobile devices (Android). The value in acquiring Nest Labs was not getting more of the same type of personal data Google already had, but rather other data, such as our offline behaviour in our homes, which Google in turn could incorporate in its existing free services and to increase advertising revenue.

8.28   Nor does it make sense, as we saw in Chapter 6's discussion of Facebook/WhatsApp to treat all data as fungible, and roughly calculate how much data each company controls. So the real issue in data-driven mergers like Google/Nest Labs is not whether Google's data is substitutable with the data collected from the thermostats and surveillance cameras. Instead, the issue is whether the merger, in enabling the firm to amass a greater *variety* of data, may likely increase the firm's ability to maintain its dominant position, to leverage its dominance into another market, or to otherwise lessen competition in any side of the multi-sided market. Would a combined Google/Nest Labs reduce actual or potential rivals' ability or incentive to compete, which in turn would reduce the competitive pressure on the merged entity? Suppose Google changes the privacy policy and starts using the data from Nest Labs' home security cameras for its other operations. Google can better see what users are doing away from their computer, smartphones, or tablets. Google, with this data, could refine its user profiles for behavioural advertising, helping maintain its dominance in search advertising.

8.29   Likewise, suppose Facebook acquired a dominant health insurer and could, in that country, use the health data for behavioural advertising. Again, Facebook's cluster of products and services are not a substitute to the products or services offered by the health insurance companies. Nor are Facebook's and the health insurer's databases substitutes. Nonetheless, the merger may substantially lessen competition by increasing entry barriers for any other platform seeking to provide an advertising-supported social network. It would lack many users' medical history information, which is attractive to behavioural advertisers. From the user's health records, texting, search inquiries, and interactions on its social network, Facebook has a superior view of the user's interests, behaviour, medical concerns, and risks.

8.30   Thus courts generally require the agencies to provide economic evidence that the merging parties' products are 'good substitutes' and therefore in the same market.[39] Data-driven mergers at times defy this logic. The value of the target firm's data lies in its variety and non-substitutability with the data that the acquirer already

---

[39] *DSM Desotech Inc v 3D Systems Corp*, 749 F3d 1332, 1340 (US Ct of Apps (Fed Cir), 2014).

possesses. Nonetheless, in acquiring the data, the firm can attain or maintain significant market power. Also the merger's effect will not necessarily impact one particular side of the market or even one service: 'As the data provided will typically be used for different purposes (e.g. across multi-sided markets), market concentration will need to be assessed in most cases across all sides of the market.'[40] In effect, data-driven mergers may enable a super-platform, such as Google's, to control key portals of data, which helps it attain or maintain its power across many products.

D. Defining a New Category

Nothing in the US or EU competition law requires that the merging parties' products or services be substitutes. The US Clayton Act requires sufficient evidence that the merger may substantially lessen competition or tend to create a monopoly. The Commission must assess whether or not a concentration would significantly impede effective competition, in particular as a result of the creation or strengthening of a dominant position in the common market or a substantial part of it.[41] One analogy, perhaps, is the foreclosure theory used to challenge vertical mergers, whereby 'actual or potential rivals' access to supplies or markets is hampered or eliminated as a result of the merger, thereby reducing these companies' ability and/or incentive to compete'.[42]   **8.31**

As one US court stated, '[t]he primary vice of a vertical merger or other arrangement tying a customer to a supplier is that, by foreclosing the competitors of either party from a segment of the market otherwise open to them, the arrangement may act as a "clog on competition" which "deprive[s] ... rivals of a fair opportunity to compete".'[43] Another US court provided this helpful road map: **8.32**

> In a Section 7 [of the Clayton Act] analysis of vertical mergers, the competitive significance of a vertical merger results primarily from the degree, if any, to which it may increase barriers to entry into the market or reduce competition by (1) foreclosing competitors of the purchasing firm in the merger from access to a potential source of supply, or from access on competitive terms, (2) foreclosing competitors of the selling firm from access to the market or a substantial portion of it, or (3) forcing actual or potential competitors to enter or continue in the market only on a vertically integrated basis because of advantages unrelated to economies attributable solely to integration.[44]

---

[40] OECD, *Data-Driven Innovation for Growth and Well-Being: Interim Synthesis Report*, October 2014, p 59, http://www.oecd.org/sti/inno/data-driven-innovation-interim-synthesis.pdf.

[41] EC Non-Horizontal Merger Guidelines, above note 1, para 1.

[42] Ibid, para 18.

[43] *Geneva Pharmaceuticals Technology Corp v Barr Labs Inc*, 386 F3d 485, 511 (US Ct of Apps (2d Cir), 2004) (internal quotation marks omitted).

[44] *Yankees Entertainment & Sports Network, LLC v Cablevision Systems Corp*, 224 F Supp 2d 657, 673 (Dist Ct (SD NY), 2002); *Fruehauf Corp v FTC*, 603 F2d 345, 352 (US Ct of Apps (2d Cir), 1979).

A vertical merger's competitive significance results primarily from the degree, if any, to which it may reduce competition by increasing entry barriers or rivals' costs, foreclosing suppliers, customers, or inputs, or facilitate collusion.

8.33   One example involved Google's acquisition of ITA Software, Inc.[45] The vertical merger affected two markets: the downstream *comparative flight search service* market, which enables consumers to search online for flight prices, schedules, and seat availability on multiple airlines simultaneously (think Kayak or Orbitz), and the upstream market for *airfare pricing and shopping systems* which involve 'a continuously-updated database of airline pricing, schedule and seat availability information, and a software algorithm used to search the database for flight options that best match consumers' search criteria' (think a search engine for flight data).[46] Google was entering the comparative flight service market. ITA was the most popular airfare pricing and shopping system, given the speed at which its algorithms could find seat availability. The concern was that post-merger Google could foreclose or disadvantage its downstream rivals such as Orbitz, Kayak, and Microsoft's Bing Travel. Google could refuse to renew existing ITA software contracts, refuse to enter into new ITA software contracts, enter into software contracts on less favourable terms than ITA would have, or degrade the speed or quality of ITA's services offered to Google's rivals.[47] The DOJ also alleged that the merger would raise entry barriers in the downstream market, and that vertical expansion upstream was unlikely. Indeed, 'Google looked at developing its own [airfare pricing and shopping] system as an alternative to acquiring ITA, but concluded it would take several years and require numerous engineers due to the complexity of the algorithms.'[48]

8.34   The DOJ's consent decree required Google post-merger to continue licensing—and improve—ITA's software, license a new flight search technology that ITA was developing, and erect a firewall at its business regarding the use of competitively sensitive information gained through ITA's services.[49] Access to airline seat and booking class data was a critical input to an airfare pricing and shopping system. To ensure that Google did not restrict access to this crucial data, the consent decree also limited Google from agreeing with an airline to restrict the airline's right to share seat and booking class data with Google's downstream rivals (unless an airline entered into exclusive agreement with a competitor). Google also had to make available to its downstream rivals any seat and booking class information it obtained for use in its new flight search service.

---

[45] *United States v Google Inc*, Case No 1:11-cv-00688 (US Dist Ct (D DC) 2011), Complaint filed 8 April 2011 ('Google Complaint'), http://www.justice.gov/file/497686/download.

[46] Ibid, para 24.

[47] Ibid, para 38.

[48] Ibid, para 42.

[49] *United States v Google Inc*, Case No 1:11-cv-00688 (US Dist Ct (D DC) 2011), Competitive Impact Statement filed 8 April 2011, http://www.justice.gov/file/497671/download.

Here the DOJ got the theory right. Moreover, as in *Bazaarvoice*, the DOJ recog- **8.35**
nized how data was a critical input for the algorithms. But its decree was incomplete. Google's rivals feared that after purchasing the travel search engine, Google
would use ITA data to feed details of specific flights directly to users of its search
engine, rather than pointing them to Expedia's and other competitors' web pages.[50]
And that is what happened.

In the Google/ITA merger, Google was not yet in the market. Its comparative flight **8.36**
search service was forthcoming. One problem is that the vertical foreclosure theory
generally presupposes an existing (or imminent) buyer–seller relationship between
the acquirer (and its competitors) and the acquired (and its competitors).[51]

Another possible problem, mainly in the US, is that agencies' guidelines for verti- **8.37**
cal mergers are dated. The US competition agencies, while updating the horizontal
merger guidelines five times,[52] have not updated their vertical mergers guidelines
since 1984.[53] The US agencies infrequently rely on them. Moreover, the last time
they litigated a vertical merger was in 1979.[54] One reason is that there is not the
same level of consensus on vertical mergers as horizontal mergers. As one US court
stated, 'respected scholars question the anticompetitive effects of vertical mergers
in general'.[55] Among the scholars cited were Robert Bork ('Antitrust's concern with
vertical mergers is mistaken. Vertical mergers are means of creating efficiency, not
of injuring competition....[The] foreclosure theory is not merely wrong, it is irrelevant.'[56]) and Herbert Hovenkamp ('Of all mergers, vertical acquisitions are the
most likely to produce efficiencies and the least likely to enhance the market power
of the merging firms.'[57]).

Nonetheless, as Professors Michael Riordan and Steven Salop observed 20 years **8.38**
ago, many economists have moved beyond the Chicago School; in 'apply[ing]
the newer methodology of modern industrial organization theory to more

---

[50] Richard Waters, 'How Diller's Google Prediction Came True', *Financial Times*, 15 April 2015,
http://www.ft.com/cms/s/0/121f171e-e2f8-11e4-aa1d-00144feab7de.html.
[51] *Brown Shoe Co v United States*, 370 US 294, 323, 82 S Ct 1502, 1522 (1962) ('Economic arrangements between companies standing in a supplier-customer relationship are characterized as
"vertical".'); EC Non-Horizontal Merger Guidelines, above note 1, para 4 ('[v]ertical mergers involve companies operating at different levels of the supply chain').
[52] DOJ, Merger Enforcement, http://www.justice.gov/atr/merger-enforcement.
[53] DOJ, Non-Horizontal Merger Guidelines, 14 June 1984, http://www.justice.gov/atr/
non-horizontal-merger-guidelines.
[54] James A Keyte and Kenneth B Schwartz, 'Getting Vertical Mergers Through the
Agencies: "Let's Make A Deal"', *Antitrust* (Summer 2015): p 10, citing *Fruehauf Corp v FTC*, 603
F2d 345 (US Ct of Apps (2d Cir), 1979).
[55] *Alberta Gas Chemicals Ltd v EI du Pont de Nemours & Co*, 826 F2d 1235, 1244 (US Ct of Apps
(3rd Cir), 1987).
[56] Robert Bork, *The Antitrust Paradox* (New York: Free Press, 1978), pp 226, 237.
[57] Herbert Hovenkamp, 'Merger Actions for Damages', 35 *Hastings LJ* (1984): pp 937, 961.

realistic market structures', they find that vertical mergers can have anticompetitive effects.[58] Likewise, the competition agencies' theories have evolved, incorporating post-Chicago School theories. Two antitrust practitioners noted that the agencies' consent decrees focus on

> (1) whether the post-merger entity will have the incentive to foreclose downstream competitors from obtaining key inputs by, inter alia, raising those competitors' costs of obtaining such inputs—an inquiry to which barriers of entry are not only relevant but critical; (2) whether the merger will result in customer foreclosure; and/or (3) whether the merger will facilitate collusion in the upstream or the downstream product market.[59]

8.39 Moreover, in considering whether the merger may substantially lessen competition, the competition agency can consider the increased risk of other anticompetitive behaviour, such as 'monopoly leveraging'.[60] Alternatively, the merger can be seen as monopoly maintenance (if it helps insulates the product with market power) or attempted monopolization (if it affects the adjacent market).

8.40 Nonetheless, some courts and competition agencies may be reluctant to condemn data-driven mergers under a vertical foreclosure theory. This is especially so when 'data' appears to be ubiquitous and when the competition authorities have not developed the tools to assess these types of anticompetitive risks.

---

[58] Michael H Riordan and Steven C Salop, 'Evaluating Vertical Mergers: A Post-Chicago Approach', 63 *Antitrust LJ* (1995): pp 513, 515.

[59] Keyte and Schwartz, above note 54, p 13.

[60] Monopoly leveraging 'involves a firm using its market power in one market to gain more market share in another market, other than by competitive means'. *AstroTel, Inc v Verizon Florida, LLC*, Case No 8:11-CV-2224-T-33TBM, 2012 WL 1581596, p *5 (US Dist Ct (MD Fla), 4 May 2012); *see also Verizon Commc'ns Inc v Law Offices of Curtis V Trinko, LLP*, 540 US 398, 415, 124 S Ct 872, 883 (2004) ('monopoly leveraging' theory requires a 'dangerous probability of success' in monopolizing a second market and anticompetitive conduct). In Europe, a firm with a dominant position on one market cannot engage in anticompetitive practices on a second market, even if the company does not enjoy a dominant position on the second market. *Tetra Pak v Commission* [1994] ECR II-755, [1997] 4 CMLR 726 (CFI), aff'd [1996] ECR I-5951, [1997] 4 CMLR 662 (ECJ); Scott M Kareff, '*Tetra Pak International SA v. Commission (Tetra Pak II)*: The European Approach to Monopoly Leveraging', 28 *Law & Pol'y Int'l Bus* (1997): pp 549, 550.

9

BELIEF THAT PRIVACY CONCERNS
DIFFER FROM COMPETITION
POLICY OBJECTIVES

A third reason why competition agencies have not fully considered the implications **9.01** of Big Data is the difficulty at times in incorporating the intangible, non-economic injury from invasions of privacy interests into their competition analysis. The intersection of privacy and competition law raises several looming, unresolved issues. As we will see, one unresolved issue is defining privacy. Another issue is whether and when there is a need to show harm, and if so, what type of harm. Even if competition authorities could identify the privacy interest and harm, a third unresolved issue is how the competition agencies and courts should balance the privacy interests with other interests. Privacy interests are rarely absolute. Once we add competition policy to the mix, privacy interests at times can be difficult to reconcile with other interests, such as promoting economic efficiency.

A. Defining Privacy in a Data-Driven Economy

A competition authority will likely inquire what is privacy in a data-driven economy. **9.02** Even in the brick-and-mortar economy, privacy scholars and courts have not recognized a single unifying privacy interest. Privacy, as Professor Anita Allen noted, has multiple dimensions, including:

- **Physical Privacy** (protection against physical intrusions and right to seclusion at home and bodily integrity);
- **Informational Privacy** (limiting access to personal data and rights against unwanted publication of intimate facts);
- **Decisional Privacy** (freedom from government interference with personal life, for example abortion rights, right to die, right to marry);
- **Proprietary Privacy** (rights of celebrities and others to control the attributes of their personal identities, their likeness, names, monikers, voices, trademarks, DNA, and Social Security number);

- **Associational Privacy** (seeking membership, inclusion, or access to an otherwise closed group; ability to meet alone with selected individuals of one's own choosing); and
- **Intellectual Privacy** (mental repose; ability to think forbidden thoughts).[1]

9.03 As Professor Rosa Brooks noted, '[s]cholars have killed trees and sacrificed unknown megabytes of disk space on the altar of privacy, attempting to define it, defend it, subdivide it, excoriate it, and occasionally even deny it.'[2] Meanwhile, competition officials are still debating the meaning of *consumer welfare* and the goals of competition law.[3] Thus, if 'privacy' is 'a grab bag of unrelated goodies',[4] competition officials may be reluctant to add privacy to antitrust's grab bag of unresolved issues, such as defining competition and the goals of competition law.

B. Whether and When There Is a Need to Show Harm, and If So, What Type of Harm

9.04 A second unresolved privacy issue is whether there is a need to show harm from a privacy invasion, and if so, what type of harm.[5] In many competition cases outside the realm of per se illegal offences, the agency focuses on how a challenged restraint or merger has substantially lessened competition or its probable effect is to substantially lessen competition.[6] Moreover, private antitrust plaintiffs in the US can only recover upon showing an antitrust injury, where the plaintiffs' loss 'stems from a competition-reducing aspect or effect of the defendant's behavior'.[7] Thus competition violations often involve tangible economic harms, such as sellers

---

[1] Anita L Allen, *Privacy Law and Society* (2nd edn, St Paul, MN: West, 2011); *see also* Executive Office of the President, President's Council of Advisors on Science and Technology, *Report to the President, Big Data and Privacy: A Technological Perspective*, May 2014, p 4 ('PCAST Report'), https://www.whitehouse.gov/sites/default/files/microsites/ostp/PCAST/pcast_big_data_and_privacy_-_may_2014.pdf; The Executive Office of the President, *Big Data: Seizing Opportunities, Preserving Values*, May 2014, p 11 ('White House Big Data Report'), https://www.whitehouse.gov/sites/default/files/docs/big_data_privacy_report_may_1_2014.pdf (noting that privacy is 'not a narrow concept, but instead addresses a range of concerns reflecting different types of intrusion into a person's sense of self, each requiring different protections'); Benjamin Shmueli and Ayelet Blecher-Prigat, 'Privacy for Children', 42 *Colum Hum Rts L Rev* (2011): pp 759, 767 (noting calls to stop trying to find 'a unitary common denominator for privacy', and recognize privacy as 'an umbrella term that refers to a wide and disparate group of related things') (quoting Daniel J Solove, *Understanding Privacy* (Cambridge, MA: Harvard University Press, 2008), p 82).

[2] Rosa Ehrenreich, 'Privacy and Power', 89 *Georgetown LJ* (2001): pp 2047, 2062.

[3] For an overview of the debate over the meaning of consumer welfare and goals of competition law, *see* Maurice E Stucke, 'Reconsidering Antitrust's Goals', 53 *BC L Rev* (2012): p 551.

[4] Laurence H Tribe, *American Constitutional Law* (2nd edn, Mineola, NY: Foundation Press, 1988), p 1303.

[5] *Remijas v Neiman Marcus Grp, LLC*, 794 F3d 688, 695 (US Ct of Apps (7th Cir), 2015).

[6] *McWane, Inc v FTC*, 783 F3d 814, 836 (US Ct of Apps (11th Cir), 2015).

[7] *Atlantic Richfield Co v USA Petroleum Co*, 495 US 328, 344, 110 S Ct 1884, 1894 (1990).

receiving too little money when dealing with buyer cartels and buyers paying too much to seller cartels.

For privacy violations, however, the individual harm often is non-economic and less **9.05** tangible, such as a loss of personhood or autonomy. Take, for example, the privacy tort of intrusion upon seclusion. Can the landlord be liable for secretly placing a recording device in the tenants' bedroom? Absolutely.[8] The injury here is 'injury to personality', the quality of being a person, which includes personal freedom and human dignity. The tenants need not show any economic gain by the defendant (such as the landlord publishing the recording and profiting thereby) or any economic loss they personally suffered.

But even here, courts disagree over whether the landlord should be liable if he **9.06** never listened to or heard the sounds or voices from the tenants' bedroom. Many US courts would find the landlord liable when he performed an act that had the potential to impair a person's peace of mind and comfort associated with the expectation of privacy.[9] Other courts would require others to actually see or hear the tenants' private activities.[10] As one court observed, '[t]he point of disagreement among courts across the nation essentially boils down to whether the harm sought to be remedied by the tort is caused by accessing information from the plaintiff in a private place or by placing mechanisms in a private place that are capable of doing so at the hand of the defendant'.[11] This issue also arises in the online world. If an algorithm reads my email to decide what ads to serve, has my privacy been violated?

In the Google 'Right to be Forgotten' case, a Spanish citizen lodged a complaint **9.07** with the National Data Protection Agency against a Spanish newspaper, Google Spain, and Google Inc.[12] When someone searched the citizen's name on Google, she would have found links to two pages of La Vanguardia's newspaper, which mentioned the citizen's name in a real-estate auction connected with attachment proceedings for the recovery of social security debts.[13] The citizen complained that the auction notice infringed his privacy rights because the proceedings concerning him had been fully resolved for a number of years; hence the reference was irrelevant. The

---

[8] *Hamberger v Eastman*, 106 NH 107, 206 A2d 239 (1964).

[9] *Hernandez v Hillsides, Inc*, 47 Cal 4th 272, 294, 211 P3d 1063, 1078 (2009); *Kohler v City of Wapakoneta*, 381 F Supp 2d 692, 704 (US Dist Ct (ND Ohio), 2005); *Amati v City of Woodstock*, 829 F Supp 998 (US Dist Ct (ND Ill), 1993); *Harkey v Abate*, 131 Mich App 177, 346 NW2d 74, 76 (1983).

[10] *Meche v Wal-Mart Stores, Inc*, 692 So 2d 544, 547 (La Ct of Apps, 1997); *Oliver v Pacific Northwest Bell Tel Co*, 53 Or App 604, 609–10, 632 P2d 1295, 1299 (1981); *Marks v Bell Tel Co of Pa*, 460 Pa 73, 86–7, 331 A2d 424, 431 (1975).

[11] *Koeppel v Speirs*, 808 NW2d 177, 184 (Iowa, 2011).

[12] Case C-131/12 *Google Spain SL v Agencia Española de Protección de Datos (AEPD)*, ECLI:EU:C:2014:317, 13 May 2014 ('Google Spain').

[13] Ibid, para 14.

citizen requested, first, that the newspaper either remove or alter the pages in question so that the personal data relating to him no longer appeared; and second, that Google Spain or Google Inc remove the personal data relating to him, so that it no longer appeared in the search results.

9.08 The Spanish Data Protection Agency upheld the citizen's complaint only against Google Spain and Google Inc, and ordered Google Inc to adopt the measures necessary to withdraw personal data relating to the citizen from its index and to prevent access to the data in the future. Google Spain and Google Inc appealed to Spain's National High Court, which in turn referred several questions to the Court of Justice of the European Union (CJEU) for a preliminary ruling regarding the interpretation of EU law (Directive 95/46) on the right to privacy (and consequently, of the Spanish data protection legislation).[14] One issue was whether individuals have the right to request that their personal data be removed from accessibility via a search engine (the 'right to be forgotten'). The CJEU held yes. Individuals can—under certain conditions—ask search engines to remove links with personal information about them. This applies where the information is inaccurate, inadequate, irrelevant, or excessive for the purposes of the data processing.

9.09 So European law 'seeks to ensure a high level of protection of the fundamental rights and freedoms of natural persons, in particular their right to privacy, with respect to the processing of personal data'.[15] As the CJEU noted, 'Article 7 of the Charter [of Fundamental Rights of the European Union] guarantees the right to respect for private life, whilst Article 8 of the Charter expressly proclaims the right to the protection of personal data.'[16] Thus the privacy right applies even to information that was lawfully obtained, truthful, and at one time in the public interest. Nor must the complainant show that including the information in the list of Google search results causes him prejudice.[17] So, the CJEU held that the person seeking to delist the information need not show any specific harm in having the information posted.

9.10 It is hard to see how competition lawyers could incorporate, in an effects-based analysis, privacy's often non-economic, less tangible harm. Ordinarily, one assesses under competition law the restraint's likely pro- and anticompetitive effects. But an individual asserting his privacy interest in Europe (and for some privacy claims in the US) does not even have to show any economic harm or prejudice. Moreover, the CJEU noted that a search engine can significantly affect the fundamental rights to privacy and to the protection of personal data; in light of the potential seriousness

---

[14] Directive 95/46/EC of the European Parliament and of the Council of 24 October 1995 on the protection of individuals with regard to the processing of personal data and on the free movement of such data [1995] OJ L 281/31.

[15] *Google Spain*, above note 12, para 66.

[16] Ibid, para 69.

[17] Ibid, para 96.

of that interference, the CJEU added, 'it is clear that it cannot be justified by merely the economic interest which the operator of such an engine has in that processing'.[18]

So let us return to *Facebook/WhatsApp*, where the European Commission officials **9.11** noted that if a website, post-merger, 'would start requiring more personal data from users or supplying such data to third parties as a condition for delivering its "free" product' then this 'could be seen as either increasing its price or as degrading the quality of its product' and infringe competition law.[19] That is an easy case. The companies merge; they now exercise market power by degrading quality below levels that consumers prefer. But often the agency has to predict competitive effects. Suppose the merging parties promise not to increase price or reduce quality post-merger. That should be irrelevant. Normally, a merger to monopoly is illegal even if the company promises not to exercise its market power. As the US Supreme Court observed, the legal authorities 'support the view that the material consideration in determining whether a monopoly exists is not that prices are raised and that competition actually is excluded but that power exists to raise prices or to exclude competition when it is desired to do so'.[20] It is unnecessary that the company actually exercise the market power it obtained; the existence of its power is sufficient.[21] So if the merger gives a company the *power* to raise price, it is illegal even though the company chooses to price reasonably.

But does the same apply to consumers' personal data? A merger, such as Facebook/ **9.12** WhatsApp or Google/Nest Labs, gives the combined entity going forward a significant volume and variety of data. The company may promise not to publish or use the data for behavioural advertising. But if the merger increases its market power, the company could backtrack on its privacy promises, without fear of competitive reprisals. Conceivably the concentration of data post-merger could raise an antitrust concern. Namely if the merger increases the company's market power, it can degrade the level of privacy protection.

Suppose WhatsApp collected data on its users, but used it internally for limited **9.13** technical performance purposes. WhatsApp users are concerned that post-merger Facebook could at any time access this data. Here Facebook, like our landlord, performed an act (namely acquired WhatsApp) that had the potential to impair a person's peace of mind and comfort associated with the expectation of privacy. Are these privacy concerns cognizable under the privacy laws (would the plaintiffs even have standing to bring such a claim), and if so, are these privacy claims relevant for

---

[18] Ibid, para 81.
[19] Eleonora Ocello, Cristina Sjödin, and Anatoly Suboč s, 'What's Up with Merger Control in the Digital Sector? Lessons from the Facebook/WhatsApp EU Merger Case', 1 *Competition Merger Brief* (February 2015): p 6.
[20] *American Tobacco Co v United States*, 328 US 781, 811, 66 S Ct 1125, 1139–40 (1946).
[21] Ibid, p 811.

the antitrust analysis? Must the competition authority show a tangible economic harm to consumers if the company used personal data, contrary to its customers' wishes? Or is the monopoly's collection and use of data alone enough? Both issues remain unresolved. Consequently, competition officials may find it difficult, at times, to incorporate the intangible, non-economic injury from invasions of privacy interests into their analysis.

C. How Should the Competition Agencies and Courts Balance the Privacy Interests with Other Interests?

9.14 Even if competition authorities could identify the privacy interest and a tangible economic harm (or fundamental privacy right), a third unresolved privacy issue is how to balance the privacy interest with other interests.

9.15 The CJEU in the 'right to be forgotten' Google case reaffirmed an EU objective to protect the fundamental rights and freedoms of natural persons (in particular the right to privacy).[22] Although the complainant did not have to show how Google's including the information in question in its search results caused him prejudice, his privacy interest was not absolute.[23] The 'fundamental' privacy right must be balanced against other rights, such as the freedom of expression, and the legitimate interest of Internet users and the media in accessing that information. Thus the CJEU called for a case-by-case assessment, considering the type of information in question; its sensitivity for the individual's private life; the interest of the public in having access to the information; the amount of time passed; and the role of the person in public life. The balancing between the privacy interest in being forgotten and the other societal interests was left initially to Google.

9.16 Thus the third open issue is how the competition agency balances the privacy right against other fundamental rights, such as the freedom of expression and the media. The US Supreme Court has purposefully left unresolved whether the Constitution protects informational privacy, and if so, the contours of any such right.[24] The lower

---

[22] CJEU, 'An Internet Search Operator is Responsible For the Processing It Carries Out of Personal Data Which Appear on Web Pages Published by Third Parties', Press Release No 70/14, 13 May 2014, http://curia.europa.eu/jcms/upload/docs/application/pdf/2014-05/cp140070en.pdf.

[23] European Data Protection Supervisor (EDPS), *Privacy and Competitiveness in the Age of Big Data: The Interplay Between Data Protection, Competition Law, and Consumer Protection in the Digital Economy*, Preliminary Opinion (26 March 2014), p 13 ('EDPS Preliminary Opinion'), https://secure.edps.europa.eu/EDPSWEB/webdav/shared/Documents/Consultation/Opinions/2014/14-03-26_competitition_law_big_data_EN.pdf ('The right to the protection of personal data is not an absolute right but "must be considered in relation to its function in society".').

[24] *Nat'l Aeronautics & Space Admin v Nelson*, 562 US 134, 135, 131 S Ct 746 (2011) (assuming, without deciding, that some constitutional privacy interest in avoiding disclosure of personal

courts weigh the litigant's privacy interest against other societal interests, such as freedom of speech and expression, freedom of the press, national security, law enforcement, and public health.

One risk with such free-form balancing is inconsistent, unpredictable results. Take, for example, a case when a US public employer may conduct a warrantless search of an employee's effects. This raises 'thorny Fourth Amendment issues because employees have reasonable expectations of privacy at work, but employers have legitimate interests that may sometimes justify warrantless searches of the workplace'.[25] In *O'Connor v Ortega*, state hospital officials placed a doctor on administrative leave for suspected improprieties, and conducted a warrantless search of his office, desk, and filing cabinets.[26] The government used the seized personal items from the doctor's desk and filing cabinets in administrative proceedings resulting in the doctor's discharge. The US Supreme Court tackled two issues: first, does a public employee have a reasonable expectation of privacy in his office, desk, and filing cabinets at his place of work? If so, what is the appropriate Fourth Amendment standard for a search that a public employer conducts in areas where a public employee is found to have a reasonable expectation of privacy? Four Justices proposed a case-specific, context-dependent totality of circumstances standard, which the deciding fifth Justice refused to join. Instead, Justice Scalia criticized the plurality for adopting a case-by-case standard 'so devoid of content that it produces rather than eliminates uncertainty in this field'.[27]

9.17

When it comes to competition cases, the concern is that the agencies, courts, and juries are not very good in balancing a restraint's net economic effects.[28] This is ironic, given that an effects-based, 'rule of reason' analysis is the prevailing, usual, and accepted standard for evaluating many competitive restraints. Under the rule of reason, balancing is the final step where the antitrust plaintiffs must show that, and the fact-finder concludes whether, the restraint's anticompetitive effects outweigh its pro-competitive benefits.[29] But the conventional wisdom is that courts 'almost never explicitly balance the procompetitive and anticompetitive effects of

9.18

---

matters exists, but 'whatever the scope' of this constitutional interest, it does not prevent the federal government from asking reasonable questions of the sort included in the employment background investigation forms that are subject to the Privacy Act's safeguards against public disclosure).

[25] *United States v Chandler*, 197 F3d 1198, 1200 (US Ct of Apps (8th Cir), 1999).

[26] 480 US 709, 717, 107 S Ct 1492 (1987).

[27] Ibid, p 730 (Scalia, J, concurring).

[28] *See, eg, Credit Suisse Sec (USA) LLC v Billing*, 551 US 264, 281, 127 S Ct 2383, 2395 (2007) (noting the 'unusually' high risk of inconsistent results by antitrust courts); *Northern Pacific Railway Co v United States*, 356 US 1, 5, 78 S Ct 514, 518 (1958) (stating that per se rule provides certainty and avoids lengthy and complex inquiries into history of particular industries to determine reasonableness of actions).

[29] *Geneva Pharmaceuticals Technology Corp v Barr Lab, Inc*, 386 F3d 485, 507 (US Ct of Apps (2d Cir), 2004).

an alleged restraint'.[30] Courts and agencies rarely reach the last stage of balancing, as they make policy trade-offs in the preceding steps when determining whether plaintiffs suffered an antitrust injury and have standing to bring an antitrust claim, what is pro- and anticompetitive in the first place, and the existence of less restrictive alternatives.[31]

9.19 So if the belief is that competition officials, courts, and juries have difficulties in balancing pro- and anticompetitive *economic* effects, then balancing becomes even more difficult when privacy's incommensurable benefits and harms are added to the mix.

9.20 Privacy interests at times are difficult to reconcile with economic efficiency. Safeguarding privacy could increase the sellers' costs in identifying purchasers, and perhaps keep socially valuable information out of the hands of people who could benefit from it. So if personal data can help producers more readily identify consumers who may need their product, courts and competition officials may be uncertain how to balance the lower search costs (and perhaps lower prices for the product) with the loss of privacy.[32] How then should courts and agencies balance the benefits to advertisers (and some consumers) from more targeted behavioural advertisements against the privacy harms? The agency and court may find it difficult to assess the net value when the product or service is offered for free (and privacy is the cost), especially when the benefit is direct and immediate (free search engine) and the harm is indirect, gradual, and also obscured.[33]

---

[30] William J Kolasky, Jr, 'Reinvigorating Antitrust Enforcement in the United States: A Proposal', 22 *Antitrust LJ* (2008): pp 85, 87; *see also* American Bar Association (ABA), Antitrust Section, *The Rule of Reason*, Monograph No 23 (1999), p 126 (balancing rarely undertaken); Herbert Hovenkamp, *Antitrust Law*, vol 11 (New York: Aspen Publishers, 2005), p 339 para 1912 ('[The] set of rough judgments we make in antitrust litigation does not even come close to this "balancing" metaphor. Indeed, most courts do not define a unit of measurement in which the quantities to be balanced can be measured.... To the best of our knowledge, this has never been done in any antitrust case.'); Michael A Carrier, 'The Real Rule of Reason: Bridging the Disconnect', *BYU L Rev* [1999]: pp 1265, 1268 (noting 84% of rule-of-reason cases examined were disposed after the plaintiff failed to make a prima facie showing of the restraint's actual anticompetitive effects or likely effects using the defendants' significant market share; the fact-finder reached last stage of balancing pro- and anticompetitive effects in only 20 of 495 rule-of-reason cases studied).

[31] Massimo Motta, 'The European Commission's Guidance Communication on Article 82', 30(12) *ECLR* (2009): pp 593–9, 599.

[32] McKinsey Global Institute, *Big Data: The Next Frontier for Innovation, Competition, and Productivity*, June 2011, p 11 ('McKinsey Report'), http://www.mckinsey.com/insights/business_technology/big_data_the_next_frontier_for_innovation (noting how '[p]ersonal data such as health and financial records are often those that can offer the most significant human benefits, such as helping to pinpoint the right medical treatment or the most appropriate financial product', how 'consumers also view these categories of data as being the most sensitive', and 'that individuals and the societies in which they live will have to grapple with trade-offs between privacy and utility').

[33] OECD, *Exploring the Economics of Personal Data: A Survey of Methodologies for Measuring Monetary Value*, OECD Digital Economy Papers, No 220 (2013), p 17, http://dx.doi.org/10.1787/5k486qtxldmq-en.

D. Courts' Acceptance of Prevailing Defaults, in Lieu of Balancing

Rather than weigh these competing interests, courts may simply go along with **9.21** the default option set by the industry participants. In doing so, they are implicitly weighing the privacy interest against the other interests.

The default option, as we have seen, can play a critical role. Thus one debate in the **9.22** privacy world is over whether individuals have to opt in or opt out of the data collection. As one privacy expert discussed,

> The traditional complement to 'notice' had long been 'consent', and the problem that attracted privacy scholars and policymakers was to determine what would constitute adequate or meaningful consent. Under the EU privacy regime, meaningful consent typically required 'opt-in', i.e., in the absence of affirmative action by the individual, the company simply could not make use of personal information for purposes unrelated to the transaction at hand. U.S. privacy law also followed an opt-in regime, particularly in the medical records field. However, industry groups and the Direct Marketing Association in particular urged the less burdensome 'opt-out' regime, which allows businesses to go forward with various uses of personal data as long as there are some means (however burdensome or inefficient) for consumer objections. In the United States, the opt-out regime was typically viewed as what industry was prepared to do and not what the public wanted done.[34]

One example is the default option in the *Boring v Google* case.[35] Aaron and Christine **9.23** Boring's privacy claims arose from Google's 'Street View' service, a feature on Google Maps that offers free access on the Internet to navigable views of streets in and around major cities. To create its Street View service, Google attached panoramic digital cameras to passenger cars and drove around cities photographing the areas along the street.

The Borings lived on a private road. Their home was not visible to the public eye, **9.24** being surrounded by trees. As the Borings alleged, Google drove on the private road ('1,000 feet of crunching gravel and potholes'), past the clearly marked 'Private Road No Trespassing' sign, and onto the Borings' driveway.[36] With its vehicle's cameras, in close proximity to their residence, garage, and swimming pool, Google 'recorded the secluded surroundings'.[37] The Borings alleged that Google's photographs, which were published worldwide, were highly offensive and disregarded

---

[34] Marc Rotenberg, 'Fair Information Practices and the Architecture of Privacy (What Larry Doesn't Get)', *Stan Tech L Rev* [2001]: pp 1, 29.

[35] *Boring v Google Inc*, 362 F App'x 273 (US Ct of Apps (3rd Cir), 2010).

[36] *Boring v Google Inc*, 2009 WL 4900242 (US Ct of Apps (3rd Cir), filed 25 August 2009), Appellant's Brief.

[37] Ibid.

their privacy interests. They purchased their home 'for a considerable sum of money, and privacy and seclusion of the home was a major component to purchase the property'.[38]

9.25 Google admitted photographing the exterior of the Borings' home, and making those 'unremarkable' photographs available through its Street View service.[39] But Google's mission, it told the court, 'is to organize the world's information and make it universally accessible and useful'.[40] Towards this end, Google told the court of the benefits of its actions—namely how it 'develops products that let its users more quickly and easily find, create, organize and share information', 'maintains the world's largest and most comprehensive index of web sites and other online content', and makes the information it organizes freely available to 'anyone with an Internet connection'.[41]

9.26 So Google pitched the societal benefits of its mission, of 'Street View', and in offering Internet users free 'panoramic street-level navigable views of streets and roads in major cities in the United States'. Out of respect for individuals' preferences, Google stated that residents, like the Borings, could opt out by requesting the automatic removal of any image available on Street View, 'whether it is entitled to privacy protection under the law or not'. Rather than using Google's opt-out mechanism, the Borings instead sued Google, seeking in excess of USD 25,000 on each count other than the injunction, plus punitive damages and attorneys' fees.

9.27 The US district court did not weigh the plaintiffs' right to be left alone against the societal interests from Street View. It dismissed the invasion of privacy claim because the Borings failed to show that Google's conduct was highly offensive to a person of ordinary sensibilities.[42] The US Court of Appeals for the Third Circuit agreed:

> No person of ordinary sensibilities would be shamed, humiliated, or have suffered mentally as a result of a vehicle entering into his or her ungated driveway and photographing the view from there.... [T]he privacy allegedly intruded upon was the external view of the Borings' house, garage, and pool—a view that would be seen by any person who entered onto their driveway, including a visitor or a delivery man.[43]

Likewise, the Third Circuit did not perceive any legal significance between seeing the plaintiffs' house versus posting a picture of the plaintiffs' house on the Internet: 'The

---

[38] Ibid.

[39] *Boring v Google Inc*, 2009 WL 4900244 (US Ct of Apps (3rd Cir), filed 24 September 2009), Appellee's Brief.

[40] Ibid.

[41] Ibid.

[42] *Boring v Google, Inc*, 598 F Supp 2d 695, 699–700 (US Dist Ct (WD Pa), 2009).

[43] *Boring*, above note 35, p 279.

existence of that image, though, does not in itself rise to the level of an intrusion that could reasonably be called highly offensive.'[44] Ultimately, the Borings recovered USD 1 for their surviving trespass claim against Google.[45]

Although the exterior image of the Borings' home may indeed have been unremark-able, Google's actions were highly offensive to the Borings. But the court implic-itly accepted the social utility of Google's behaviour and expressed no qualms of Google's requiring citizens to opt out of Street View. **9.28**

Another court could very well have recognized the Borings' right to be left alone as the default, and required Google to obtain permission. If the default switched so that Google could not use the exterior of the Borings' (or anyone else's) house unless the residents expressly opted in—namely by providing their consent to having their residences posted on Street View—then Google's transaction costs would have increased significantly. If the transaction costs became too high, Google and the other map providers could not provide this 'free' service. Thus, courts implicitly trade off the social utility of the defendant's actions versus the plaintiff's privacy interest in agreeing (or disagreeing) with the default option (most likely opt-out if set by the industry participants). **9.29**

Suppose Google or another company went further, and provided live street web-cams. Now, instead of one snapshot of your home on the Internet, someone could continuously monitor online your home's exterior. Would this continuous surveil-lance be highly offensive to a person of ordinary sensibilities? The court would assess the nature of the information in question, its sensitivity for the data subject's privacy interest, and the public's interest in having that information. How would courts assess the public's interest in a 'Surveillance' Street View? To what extent should the public's interest in getting the data trump the individual's privacy right? Moreover, suppose Google combines the 'Surveillance' Street View data with other data for its consumer profiling and behavioural advertising efforts. We have seen that companies may increase data's value through data fusion. Does that tilt the balance, and to what extent should a citizen's privacy interest subsidize a dominant firm's business interest? **9.30**

E. Setting the Default in Competition Cases

A competition official, witnessing this debate, would likely want to avoid the fray. 'What does the Borings' home have to do with competition?', the official asks. But **9.31**

---

[44] Ibid.
[45] Chloe Albanesius, ' "Boring" Family Gets $1 in Google Street View Trespass Case', *PC Magazine*, 2 December 2010, http://www.pcmag.com/article2/0,2817,2373754,00.asp.

the privacy default can play at times a key role in competition cases. The European Commission and other competition agencies are starting to recognize that data can be a key competitive asset. Competitors at times will want to access a monopolist's dataset on its customers, and the agency and court will have to balance the likely increase in competition against a reduction in privacy.

9.32 Such was the case where a dominant French electricity provider used the personal data it collected as a regulated monopoly to compete in another market. Since 2007, French gas customers could drop the incumbent GDF Suez monopoly for other gas supply offers.[46] Consumers could choose either (1) GDF Suez offers at the regulated tariffs or (2) market offers, which all suppliers including GDF Suez provided. Despite the government's hope to inject competition into this concentrated market, by 2014, the new gas suppliers' market shares remained low (5–13 per cent) for individuals and for industrial and commercial customers.

9.33 In 2014, a competitor Direct Energie complained that GDF Suez was seeking to drive its competitors out of the market with anticompetitive practices. One practice was GDF Suez's using its voluminous data of customers on the regulated tariffs (that it acquired as a regulated monopoly) to offer them deals on gas and electricity. The customer data, the rival alleged, gave the monopoly an incomparable advantage for maintaining its dominant position in the gas market and acquiring new customers in the electricity market.

9.34 The French competition authority investigated whether GDF Suez abused its dominant position in the gas market 'by using the infrastructure dedicated to regulated tariffs (i.e. customer database, website, customer platform…), which is in the realm of a public service activity, to market its gas and electricity offers, which are marketed in a competitive market'.[47] The competition agency found that GDF Suez improperly used its customer data 'to facilitate customer switching from regulated to unregulated offers, and to "win back" customers who had switched to competing unregulated offers'.[48] The regulated monopoly had an unfair competitive advantage, the competition authority found, 'since no database exists that would allow competitors to precisely locate gas consumers and know their consumption level, in order to propose them offers that are better suited to their profile'.[49] This was not competition on the merits because the database was not the 'product of a specific

---

[46] Autorité de la Concurrence, 'Gas Market', Press Release, 9 September 2014, http://www.autoritedelaconcurrence.fr/user/standard.php?id_rub=592&id_article=2420.

[47] Ibid.

[48] Peter Willis, 'French Competition Authority Orders GDF Suez to Give Competitors Access to Customer Data', Bird & Bird, 22 September 2014, http://www.twobirds.com/en/news/articles/2014/france/french-competition-authority-orders-gdf-suez-to-give-competitors-access-to-customer-data.

[49] Autorité de la Concurrence, Gas Market, above note 46.

innovation that GDF Suez may have introduced, but [was] merely inherited from its former status as monopolistic gas supplier'.[50]

So now the smaller competitors wanted access to the monopolist's data on its con-   **9.35**
sumers. Here, the competition agency was confronted with a trade-off: increasing competition versus privacy. In allowing competitors' access to the voluminous dataset, the playing field hopefully would become more level, as competition increased. But releasing this data to other companies would potentially infringe the consumers' privacy interest. The competition agency first must decide whether the monopoly should disclose the data to its rivals. If so, the agency next must assess the privacy default. Presumably the monopoly would want consumers to opt in, specifically it would release the data for only those consumers who provided the monopoly or a third party with authorized written consent. An opt-in, the smaller competitors would respond, rewards the monopoly, as many consumers would forget (or are too lazy) to opt in. Instead, the smaller competitors would prefer customers to opt out, namely the monopoly would disclose the customer's data, unless the particular customer expressly says no.

So if you were the competition authority would you order the regulated monopoly   **9.36**
to disclose the data? If so, would you set the default as opt-out or opt-in? Should the default vary with the facts of each case, so that the next case might differ?

Here the French competition agency ordered the disclosure of data 'strictly neces-   **9.37**
sary to ensure effective competition among suppliers, i.e. the customer name and address and the technical characteristics of his consumption'.[51] The agency also recognized that some consumers may not want their personal information disseminated. So the agency chose the opt-out default, ie, the data can be disclosed, unless the customer disagrees.

This was interesting as the privacy interest of protecting personal data is a funda-   **9.38**
mental right in Europe.[52] A competitive market, by itself, is not recognized as a fundament right. But the case highlights that with status quo bias, the choice of the default option will often be critical. And competition officials cannot always avoid privacy issues.

F. Conclusion

It would seem, after the discussion in Part III, that competition authorities have sev-   **9.39**
eral incentives to ignore or downplay the implications of Big Data on competition

---

[50] Ibid.
[51] Ibid.
[52] Charter of Fundamental Rights of the European Union [2012] OJ C 326/02, Art 8 'Protection of personal data'.

policy. They have not independently developed the legal and economic tools to assess non-price competition, along the parameters of quality and privacy protection. Data-driven mergers often defy their current horizontal, vertical, and conglomerate classifications. Under their effects-based analysis, the competition official cannot always identify the privacy interest at stake, observe and measure the harm to that privacy interest, and balance—with sufficient predictability, objectivity, and transparency—the privacy and economic efficiency interests. Privacy and competition policy interests are not always coextensive: advancing the privacy interest can undermine antitrust's objectives, such as promoting economic efficiency.

9.40 Thus competition officials may punt the privacy issues to other regulatory bodies or common law courts. While ignoring or downplaying the competitive significance of Big Data is an easy route, it raises, as the next part discusses, significant risks and harms.

PART IV

WHAT ARE THE RISKS IF COMPETITION AUTHORITIES IGNORE OR DOWNPLAY BIG DATA?

Competition policy and privacy are not coextensive. Thus, privacy, consumer pro- **IV.01** tection, and competition law will each play an important independent role. For example, privacy law requires firms without market power to undertake the necessary precautions to prevent the inadvertent disclosure of sensitive personal data. Another example is how enforcement of privacy and consumer protection laws can help foster more privacy competition, an important goal given that consumer cynicism about privacy promises has contributed to a 'dysfunctional equilibrium' where firms undersupply privacy. Competition policy at times will be a poor vehicle to advance different privacy interests. Indeed, as we saw in Chapter 9, competition interests (a regulated monopolist disclosing its customer data to rivals) may conflict with privacy values (limiting the disclosure of one's personal data).

The fact that competition policy and privacy are not coextensive does not mean **IV.02** they are distinct and unrelated. At times privacy and competition policy interests overlap. As Part I has discussed, consumer data is becoming a key mechanism for companies to secure a competitive advantage. If companies undertake data-driven strategies to secure and sustain their competitive advantage, it stands to reason that some companies will devise data-driven strategies that exclude competitors and potential entrants and reduce our welfare. Companies may use traditional measures (such as mergers, tying, exclusive dealing) to maintain or attain market power. Dominant firms may engage in otherwise illegal practices (such as deceiving the public on their privacy policies) or violating citizens' legal rights regarding the privacy of their personal data. Deception is not an antitrust violation per se. But deception can violate the competition laws when it appears reasonably capable of making a significant contribution to defendant's maintaining or attaining monopoly power.[1] Consequently competition officials must understand the antitrust implications of these data-driven mergers and business strategies, and have the tools to effectively and timely prevent consumer harm.

IV.03 This part explores the risks and costs in ignoring or downplaying the competitive significance of Big Data. As the following chapters explain, data-driven markets through several network effects can become dominated by a few firms. In effect, the big get bigger, controlling more personal data of our daily activities. They ultimately know more about what we are doing (and will likely do), than what we think they know. As the data-driven economy expands, and as companies seek data to obtain and sustain a competitive advantage, competition authorities must understand the implications of a few firms' unparalleled system of harvesting and monetizing their data trove.

---

[1] Maurice E Stucke, 'How Do (and Should) Competition Authorities Treat a Dominant Firm's Deception?', 63 *SMU L Rev* (2010): p 1069.

10

IMPORTANCE OF ENTRY BARRIERS IN ANTITRUST ANALYSIS

Outside of per se illegal antitrust offences, like price-fixing, antitrust analysis gener- **10.01** ally considers the ease of entry.[1] The belief is that companies cannot exercise market power for long when entry into these markets would be timely (generally under two years), likely (profitable for the entrants), and sufficient (the entrants would attain sufficient business to prevent the exercise of market power by the incumbent firms).[2] As the European Commission stated, '[w]hen entering a market is sufficiently easy, a merger is unlikely to pose any significant anti-competitive risk.'[3] If a firm degraded quality below competitive levels, entrants would seize the opportunity to profit and competition would be fully restored. Whether this is empirically true is another matter.[4] But there is little dispute that market power can be sustained in markets with significant entry barriers, and 'entry analysis constitutes an important element of the overall competitive assessment'.[5]

---

[1] *United States v Microsoft Corp*, 253 F3d 34, 51 (US Ct of Apps (DC Cir), 2001) (absent direct evidence, monopoly power 'may be inferred from a firm's possession of a dominant share of a relevant market that is protected by entry barriers'). Entry barriers 'are factors (such as certain regulatory requirements) that prevent new rivals from timely responding to an increase in price above the competitive level'. Ibid.

[2] US Department of Justice (DOJ) and Federal Trade Commission (FTC), Horizontal Merger Guidelines, 19 August 2010, s 9, https://www.ftc.gov/sites/default/files/attachments/merger-review/100819hmg.pdf.

[3] European Commission, *Guidelines on the Assessment of Horizontal Mergers Under the Council Regulation on Control of Concentrations Between Undertakings* [2004] OJ C 31/03, para 68 ('EC Horizontal Merger Guidelines'), http://eur-lex.europa.eu/legal-content/EN/TXT/?uri=celex: 52004XC0205%2802%29 ('For entry to be considered a sufficient competitive constraint on the merging parties, it must be shown to be likely, timely and sufficient to deter or defeat any potential anti-competitive effects of the merger.').

[4] Maurice E Stucke, 'Behavioral Economists at the Gate: Antitrust in the Twenty-First Century', 38 *Loyola U Chicago LJ* (2007): pp 513, 563–72.

[5] EC Horizontal Merger Guidelines, above note 3, para 68; *see also US Auto Parts Network, Inc v Parts Geek, LLC*, 494 F App'x 743, 745 (US Ct of Apps (9th Cir), 2012) (affirming summary judgment on antitrust counterclaims when Parts Geek failed inter alia to offer evidence such that a jury could reasonably find significant entry barriers in that market).

10.02   Thus, under US and EU competition law, a key issue is whether entry barriers are sufficiently low to alleviate concerns about adverse competitive effects.

A.   Entry Barriers in Data-Driven Markets

10.03   Some argue that data does not lend itself to entry barriers. This at times is true. The Organisation for Economic Co-operation and Development (OECD), for example, noted three trends underlying data-driven innovation:

> (i) the exponential growth in data generated and collected, (ii) the widespread use of data analytics including by start-ups and small and medium enterprises (SMEs), and (iii) the emergence of a paradigm shift in knowledge creation and decision-making.[6]

10.04   Others, however, go further in claiming that '[o]nline markets are notable for their low entry barriers and typically do not require big data for entry'.[7] Google's chairman, for example, stated that 'the barriers to entry are negligible, because competition is just one click away'.[8] The chairman of one of the world's largest collectors of personal data told a room full of executives, economists, and scientists that, 'Our experience is that you don't need data to compete online.'[9]

10.05   There is no empirical support for concluding that entry barriers are invariably low or high across online markets. The reality is that entry analysis for data-driven markets, as in other markets, will likely be fact-specific.

B.   Looking Beyond Traditional Entry Barriers

10.06   But the merging parties or dominant firm may use the traditional factors that the agencies consider to argue that entry barriers are generally low in that online industry. So under these traditional factors, the entry barriers may seem low, obviating the need for intervention.

10.07   For example, many online industries are dynamic and fast-growing. The General Court, in upholding the European Commission's decision to not intervene in Microsoft's acquisition of Skype, observed how the consumer communications

---

  [6] OECD, *Data-Driven Innovation for Growth and Well-Being: Interim Synthesis Report*, October 2014, p 35, http://www.oecd.org/sti/inno/data-driven-innovation-interim-synthesis.pdf.

  [7] Darren S Tucker and Hill B Wellford, 'Big Mistakes Regarding Big Data', *Antitrust Source* (December 2014): p 1.

  [8] Eric Schmidt, Executive Chairman of Google, 'Why Google Works', *Huffington Post*, 20 January 2015, http://www.huffingtonpost.com/eric-schmidt/why-google-works_b_6502132.html.

  [9] Eric Schmidt, Executive Chairman of Google, 'The New Gründergeist', Google Europe Blog, Posted: 13 October 2014, http://googlepolicyeurope.blogspot.com/2014/10/the-new-grundergeist.html.

sector was 'a recent and fast-growing sector which is characterised by short innovation cycles in which large market shares may turn out to be ephemeral'.[10] In such a dynamic context, the Court noted, 'high market shares are not necessarily indicative of market power and, therefore, of lasting damage to competition which Regulation No 139/2004 seeks to prevent'.[11]

Also data-driven mergers often involve free products. For the General Court, this **10.08** was relevant in assessing the merging parties' market power:

> In so far as users expect to receive consumer communications services free of charge, the potential for the new entity to set its pricing policy freely is significantly restricted. The Commission rightly observes that any attempt to make users pay would run the risk of reducing the attractiveness of those services and of encouraging users to switch to other providers continuing to offer their services free of charge.[12]

This statement has several important implications. What we want to mention here is that firms can have market power even though their product or service is free of charge. Companies, like Facebook and Google, have tremendous market power for free products (such as social network and search), and free might be *supra*-competitive when a competitive market offers a negative price (ie, the company pays you to toil on its social network providing information to attract others users).

Other historical entry factors are any 'technical or economic constraints which **10.09** might prevent users from switching providers'.[13] Customers generally are not locked-in if they can easily switch to other free products or services. The General Court did not find any 'technical or economic constraints' when users could download several communications applications on their operating device, and the software was free, easy to download, and took up little space on their hard drives.[14]

Finally launching a competing app may not require a lot of time and investment. **10.10** And the requisite technology to enter may be standardized.

Focusing on these traditional factors, the agency or court may conclude that entry **10.11** barriers are low. Take for example search engines, like Google, Bing, Yahoo!, and DuckDuckGo. They are free and easy to use. Users can easily switch from one search engine to another. Seemingly users are not locked-in by any data portability

---

[10] Case T-79/12 *Cisco Systems Inc v Commission*, ECLI:EU:T:2013:635, 11 December 2013, para 69.
[11] Ibid.
[12] Ibid, para 73.
[13] Ibid.
[14] Ibid.

issues. Moreover, search engines do not display the classic direct network effects that the courts and agencies have identified.

10.12 If this were true, then the low entry barriers and switching costs should prevent any search engine from intentionally degrading quality (in terms of the relevance of the response to a search inquiry). As the European Commission's statement of objections involving Google reflects, that is not the case.[15]

10.13 So in focusing on traditional entry barriers, the agency or court will likely miss other important entry barriers, namely data-driven network effects.

10.14 The next three chapters outline four potential network effects: classic network effects in Chapter 11; network effects arising from the scale of data in Chapter 12; and in Chapter 13, network effects from the scope of data and how network effects on one side of a multi-sided platform can spill over to the other side.

10.15 The observation by the General Court in *Cisco Systems* that free constrains an entrant's ability to price (either positively or negatively) has important implications. When consumers become accustomed to 'free', it is very hard for a new entrant to charge even a small amount for the same or a similar service, even if the quality is higher. Similarly, just because something is 'free' does not mean that the competitive price should be zero rather than negative. But transaction costs may prevent an entrant from 'paying' customers for their information. So the result seems to be that once the market price is set at zero, entrants likely have to live with this constraint. But that may be hard, as we shall see, if they cannot quickly ramp up to scale to attract users and advertisers.

10.16 We want to emphasize at the outset that markets susceptible to network effects do not always lead to dominance.[16] For example, Waze, as the UK competition authority recognized, failed to achieve sufficient scale to represent a significant competitive threat in Great Britain. Google, while dominant in certain markets, has not always leveraged its dominance to other markets. As the European Commission aptly stated, '[t]he existence of network effects as such does not a priori indicate a competition problem in the market affected by a merger'.[17] Instead, the extent to which network effects have increased entry barriers must 'be assessed on a case-by-case basis'.[18]

---

[15] European Commission, 'Fact Sheet: Commission Sends Statement of Objections to Google on Comparison Shopping Service', 15 April 2015, http://europa.eu/rapid/press-release_MEMO-15-4781_en.htm; Maurice E Stucke and Ariel Ezrachi, 'When Competition Fails to Optimize Quality: A Look at Search Engines', 18 *Yale J L & Tech* (2016): p 70.

[16] *Cisco Systems Inc*, above note 10, para 76 (observing that 'the existence of network effects does not necessarily procure a competitive advantage for the new entity').

[17] *Facebook/WhatsApp* (Case Comp/M.7217), Commission Decision C(2014) 7239 final, 3 October 2014, para 130.

[18] Ibid.

Our point here is that competition authorities in assessing mergers and monopolistic abuses will have an incomplete picture of the market realities if they consider only the traditional entry barriers and traditional network effects. They must be aware of several additional data-driven network effects, which can lead to market concentration and dominance.

11

ENTRY BARRIERS CAN BE HIGHER IN MULTI-SIDED MARKETS, WHERE ONE SIDE EXHIBITS TRADITIONAL NETWORK EFFECTS

11.01 Competition officials and scholars recognize that network effects in online markets potentially could allow the dominant firm 'to foreclose competitors and make more difficult for competing providers to expand their customer base'.[1] As several European Commission officials observed, '[m]any digital services are prone to network effects because they are based on the interaction of users (or different sets of users) through a platform.'[2]

11.02 Competition authorities are familiar with traditional network effects, which can be direct or indirect. Direct network effects arise when a consumer's utility from a product increases as others use the product.[3] A classic example is the telephone. As more people have telephones, the more people one can call, the greater one's utility

---

[1] European Commission, 'Commission Seeks Feedback on Commitments Offered by Google to Address Competition Concerns—Questions and Answers', Memo, 25 April 2013, p 1, http://europa.eu/rapid/press-release_MEMO-13-383_en.htm (noting that in 'high-tech markets in particular, network effects may lead to entrenched market positions' and its preliminary view that Google 'is dominant in the European Economic Area (EEA) both in web search and search advertising' and the 'significant barriers to entry and network effects in both markets'); Lisa Kimmel and Janis Kestenbaum, 'What's Up with WhatsApp?: A Transatlantic View on Privacy and Merger Enforcement in Digital Markets', 29(1) *Antitrust* (Fall 2014): pp 48, 52 (noting 'the prevalence of network effects in many digital markets, if the information necessary to compete on equal footing is not readily available from alternative sources, the potential competitive harm from data-driven entry barriers raises a cognizable theory of competitive harm under the antitrust laws').

[2] Eleonora Ocello, Cristina Sjödin, and Anatoly Suboès, 'What's Up with Merger Control in the Digital Sector? Lessons from the Facebook/WhatsApp EU Merger Case', 1 *Competition Merger Brief* (February 2015): pp 3, 4.

[3] Marina Lao, 'Networks, Access, and "Essential Facilities": From Terminal Railroad to Microsoft', 62(1) *SMU L Rev* (2009): pp 557, 560–1; *see also United States v Microsoft Corp*, 84 F Supp 2d 9, 20 (US Dist Ct (D DC), 1999) (discussing the 'positive network effect' of Windows); Case T-201/04 *Microsoft Corp v Comm'n* [2007] ECR II-3601 ('*CFI Microsoft*') (discussing the indirect network effects of streaming media players).

in having a telephone. Indirect network effects arise when people increasingly use a product or technology. Microsoft's desktop computer operating system is a classic example: the more people that use Microsoft's platform, 'the more there will be invested in developing products compatible with that platform, which, in turn reinforces the popularity of that platform with users'.[4]

Firms still compete in markets with network effects. But these markets, given **11.03** the network effects, can tip towards one or two products or platforms. As the US Court of Appeals for the DC Circuit stated in *Microsoft*, as a product or standard increases in popularity, it trends towards dominance precisely 'because the utility that a user derives from consumption of the good increases with the number of other agents consuming the good'.[5] As another court observed, 'once dominance is achieved, threats come largely from outside the dominated market, because the degree of dominance of such a market tends to become so extreme'.[6] This chapter examines the traditional network effects in the Facebook/WhatsApp merger.

A. Traditional Network Effects in Facebook/WhatsApp

Facebook and WhatsApp argued that entry barriers were generally low in the fast- **11.04** paced texting industry: 'In particular, should the merged entity introduce or raise its prices or stop innovating, customers could easily switch to competing services which are available free of charge and which will provide new features and better quality services.'[7]

The European Commission recognized that there were no significant 'traditional' **11.05** barriers to enter the consumer communications app market.[8] The market was 'dynamic and fast-growing'.[9] Developing and launching a consumer communications app did not require 'a significant amount of time and investment',[10] and the requisite technology to enter was 'increasingly standardized'.[11]

---

[4] *CFI Microsoft*, above note 3, para 1061; *see also Microsoft (I)* (Case Comp/C-3/37.792), Commission Decision C(2008) 764 final, 21 April 2004, para 449 ('the more popular an operating system is, the more applications will be written to it and the more applications are written to an operating system, the more popular it will be among users').

[5] *United States v Microsoft Corp*, 253 F3d 34, 49 (US Ct of Apps (DC Cir), 2001).

[6] *Novell, Inc v Microsoft Corp*, 505 F3d 302, 308 (US Ct of Apps (4th Cir), 2007); *see also United States v Microsoft Corp*, above note 5 ('Once a product or standard achieves wide acceptance, it becomes more or less entrenched. Competition in such industries is "for the field" rather than "within the field".').

[7] *Facebook/WhatsApp* (Case Comp/M.7217), Commission Decision C(2014) 7239 final, 3 October 2014, para 94.

[8] Ibid, para 117.

[9] Ibid, para 118.

[10] Ibid, para 119.

[11] Ibid, para 120.

11.06 Despite the absence of traditional entry barriers, the Facebook/WhatsApp merger did raise the traditional direct network effects with which enforcers and courts are most comfortable. The merger involved classic direct network effects in two different product markets: texting apps and social networking. Recognizing how the texting apps could be susceptible to these direct network effects, the European Commission did not end its analysis on the 'traditional' entry barriers.

11.07 The value of a texting app, the European Commission found, increases the more one's friends and acquaintances use that particular texting app:[12]

> The market investigation revealed that the size of a communications app's user base is important for consumers. Consumers value the inclusion of their friends and relatives in an app's network—the people they communicate with most frequently. In addition, the overall size of the app's network is also important for consumers, because it determines their chances to reach people with whom they may communicate occasionally (for example, colleagues or new acquaintances).[13]

11.08 So if your family and friends use WhatsApp to text, you will more likely use WhatsApp as well. Likewise, as more people join the social network Facebook, it becomes easier to connect and communicate with friends and acquaintances (and befriend others). Thus, Facebook and WhatsApp both enjoy traditional network effects, whereby one's utility from the product increases as others use the product.

11.09 Given these direct network effects, the European Commission discussed how a few firms can dominate these markets. The more users a texting or social network has, the more attractive it becomes to new members looking to connect with them, the greater the likelihood of joining the larger network, which makes the texting or social network more attractive to other potential users:

> As the number of users of a particular service grows, more new users are attracted to the same service, in a positive feedback loop. Once a product reaches a 'tipping point' in the number of users, its network may make it the most attractive alternative to consumers, and it may end up dominating the market. This is why some companies offer digital services for free—to generate a critical mass of users. Competitors with smaller networks may find it difficult to grow or even to protect their existing customer base from migration to the largest and most attractive network. The negative impact of network effects on competition can be aggravated by the lack of interoperability with the products of competitors (i.e. resulting in a 'walled-off

---

[12] Ibid, para 88 ('consumer communications service can offer utility to customers if the people they want to communicate with are also users of that service. Therefore, the relevance of the user base appears to be more important than its overall size.').

[13] Ocello et al, above note 2, p 4; *see also* Monopolkommission, *Competition Policy: The Challenge of Digital Markets*, Summary of the Special Report by the Monopolies Commission Pursuant to Section 44(1)(4) of the Act Against Restraints on Competition, 1 June 2015, p 7, http://www.monopolkommission.de/index.php/en/home/84-pressemitteilungen/285-competition-policy-the-challenge-of-digital-markets.

network of the winner) and by high customer switching costs (monetary, contractual, know-how, etc.).[14]

Thus where the merging parties already have vast user bases, smaller competitors **11.10** may find it harder to attract and retain users. Facebook and WhatsApp were the two leading consumer communications apps on Apple's iOS and Google Android smartphones between November 2013 and May 2014.[15] By 2014 WhatsApp had nearly 600 million users, and Facebook Messenger had 'close to [250–350] million users'.[16] Moreover, the network effects would likely be more pronounced given the 'lack of interoperability between the parties' communications apps and those of their competitors'.[17] Unlike email, WhatsApp users could not text Facebook Messenger users.

B. The Commission's Reasoning Why the Merger Was Unlikely to Tip the Market to Facebook

So the merging parties, by far, had the two most popular texting apps, in a market **11.11** where given the lack of interoperability, users had to choose the app their friends, family, and acquaintances use. The merger conceivably could tip the market to Facebook. Why then didn't the European Commission block the merger? In concluding that the merger was unlikely to tip the market to Facebook, the Commission relied on several factors.

First, consumers would not be locked in post-merger with Facebook. Consumers **11.12** could easily switch between different consumer communications apps.[18] In short, the merger was unlikely to increase consumers' switching costs. Communications app users normally 'multi-home', which means that they frequently use two or more apps to text.[19] For example, consumers may use WhatsApp to communicate with one set of friends in Europe, and Viber to communicate with friends at home.

Second, the Commission found that status quo bias (where consumers stick with **11.13** the default option) was unlikely: 'neither Facebook Messenger nor WhatsApp are

---

[14] Ocello et al, above note 2, p 4.
[15] *Facebook/WhatsApp*, above note 7, para 96. The Commission's public version of the decision replaces actual market shares with ranges: WhatsApp [20–30]% and Facebook Messenger [10–20]%.
[16] Ibid, para 128.
[17] Ocello et al, above note 2, p 5.
[18] *Facebook/WhatsApp*, above note 7, para 109.
[19] Ibid, para 110 (noting that 'approximately [80–90]% of EEA users of consumer communications apps use more than one service per month, and approximately [50–60]% use more than one such service on a daily basis' and 'users have installed on their smart-phones three or more consumer communications apps and on average use two or more apps every month').

pre-installed on a large basis of handsets'[20] and 'users normally have to actively download both Facebook Messenger and WhatsApp'.[21]

11.14 Third, the merging parties did not control the smartphone, its operating system, or other essential parts of the network. This had several implications. Facebook, post-merger, could not 'make it more burdensome for users to switch between different consumer communications apps'.[22] Users remained 'in control of their smartphones, email addresses and phone numbers, which they can use for joining other communications apps'.[23] Facebook could not 'foreclose access to the final user of the consumer communications service'.[24]

11.15 Fourth, data portability was not a significant factor for texting apps. Users cannot always easily port their data across networks (say migrate all their Facebook social network data and contact information to another platform). At times, one can communicate across platforms (such as email), but changing email accounts can be difficult when one's contact information (email address) is widespread, effectively communicating to others one's new email address is difficult, and one stores important information and attached documents in the email account. In Facebook/WhatsApp, several telecom operators told the Commission 'that switching costs for consumers would be represented by the loss of all data and interaction history when changing consumer communications app'. [25] But the Commission did not find 'any evidence suggesting that data portability issues would constitute a significant barrier to consumers' switching in the case of consumer communications apps', as the text messages tend 'to consist to a significant extent of short, spontaneous chats, which do not necessarily carry long-term value for consumers'.[26] Competitors could recreate a user's network of contacts on WhatsApp simply by accessing the user's phone book. Thus, users, with the available technology, could easily port their contact data across apps.[27]

11.16 Accordingly, the Commission concluded that, on balance, the network effects 'would not constitute an insurmountable barrier for competitor entry or expansion post-merger'.[28] But the Commission cautioned against inferring any broad rule. Its findings were limited to the 'specific facts and characteristics of the companies and markets involved and should in no way be interpreted as a general line of the

---

[20] Ibid, para 111.
[21] Ibid.
[22] Ibid, para 112.
[23] Ocello et al, above note 2, p 5.
[24] Ibid.
[25] *Facebook/WhatsApp*, above note 7, para 113.
[26] Ibid.
[27] Ibid.
[28] Ocello et al, above note 2, p 5.

Commission ruling out the possible negative impact of network effects on competition in all digital markets'.[29]

C. Strengths and Weaknesses of the Commission's Analysis of Network Effects

One insight from the Facebook/WhatsApp merger is that direct network effects **11.17** can be localized. Your choice of texting app will likely depend on which app your friends, family, and acquaintances use. The fact that Tencent's WeChat has over 500 million monthly active texting users, with about 85 per cent in China, does not necessarily increase its market power in Europe and the US.[30] Even within Europe, a popular texting app in Germany may not be popular in the UK. Thus, texting app developers cannot readily leverage this network effect and accompanying market power across geographic markets. In contrast, as we shall see in the next two chapters, some data-driven network effects, such as learning-by-doing, can be leveraged across geographic markets.

The Commission looked primarily at multi-homing, where users had Facebook **11.18** Messenger, WhatsApp, and perhaps another (free) texting app on their smartphone:

> The market investigation produced extensive evidence of consumers switching between different communications apps on a regular basis, for example depending on the addressee or type of communication. According to the data on the file, approximately 80–90% of EEA users of consumer communications apps use more than one service per month, and approximately 50–60% of them use more than one such service on a daily basis.[31]

The Commission felt that 'active multi-homing in communications apps ensures that the merged entity will not become an exclusive provider to its users' and that 'competitors will be able to gain users even though those users don't abandon the merged entity's network.'[32]

After this merger, however, the big got even bigger. Facebook's Messenger app, by **11.19** June 2015, had 700 million active users, up from 600 million users just three months earlier. WhatsApp by early 2016 grew to over one billion users.[33] Collectively,

---

[29] Ibid.

[30] Daniel Van Boom, 'Four Mega Popular Messaging Apps You've Probably Never Heard Of', cNet, 7 September 2015, http://www.cnet.com/news/four-megapopular-messaging-apps-youve-probably-never-heard-of/.

[31] Ocello et al, above note 2, p 5.

[32] Ibid.

[33] Deepa Seetharaman, 'WhatsApp Joins the Billion Users Club', *Wall Street Journal*, 1 February 2016, http://blogs.wsj.com/digits/2016/02/01/whatsapp-joins-the-billion-users-club/.

Facebook/WhatsApp have far more monthly active users than QQMobile (603 million users), WeChat, and remaining smaller texting apps.[34]

11.20 Even if Facebook and WhatsApp are getting bigger post-merger, for the Commission, these network effects do not translate into market power. The Commission's outlook might have differed if Apple or Google were the acquiring party. Presumably there is a greater risk of foreclosure if a dominant smartphone operating system pre-installs the texting app on the smartphone, and the texting app is so integrated with the smartphone's operating system that it delivers functions that the rival apps cannot replicate. But even here, the switching costs are low, as texting apps are easy to use, and many do not care about saving old texts. (Indeed, with SnapChat the text disappears after you read it.)

11.21 But the Commission may have missed an important issue, namely how competition can be dampened when the tyranny of the majority dictates the privacy choices of the minority. If you want to join a group chat with many members, then you must join the platform which that group already uses. If your group chat consists of two family members, arguably, you can convince them to try another texting app with greater privacy protections. But if many of your high school, college, or adult friends are using Messenger or WhatsApp, and you are concerned about Facebook's privacy policy, what are your options? You can try to persuade them to switch to another texting app. Or you relent. So if you want to group chat with your friends on Facebook Messenger, you use that app. If you wanted to communicate with your friends on WhatsApp, you use WhatsApp.

11.22 The fact that users multi-home among communication apps does not necessarily mean that each app acts as a competitive constraint on the other. To illustrate, many people in Ireland in August 2015 had both Facebook Messenger (46 per cent of those surveyed) and Skype (43 per cent). But those with a Messenger account used the app far more frequently (49 per cent used the app daily) than Skype (9 per cent of its account holders used it daily).[35] WhatsApp had slightly fewer users in Ireland (37 per cent of those surveyed), but more of its users used the texting app daily (56 per cent).

11.23 Thus, your son and daughter might share a photo through Snapchat with their friends, group chat on Messenger with their other friends, Skype their relatives abroad, and text their parents using Apple's Messages. The choice may not reflect personal preference, but the degree of market power, through network effects,

---

[34] Statista, 'Most Popular Global Mobile Messenger Apps as of August 2015, Based on Number of Monthly Active Users', http://www.statista.com/statistics/258749/most-popular-global-mobile-messenger-apps/.

[35] Ipsos MRBI, @IpsosMRBI, Twitter, 17 September 2015, 9:01 AM, https://twitter.com/IpsosMRBI/status/644496283999277056/photo/1?ref_src=twsrc%5Etfw.

that each app has within that social group. Granted, users can migrate to other networks, but this takes time. WhatsApp, as Chapter 6 discussed, had significant privacy issues post-merger, but the privacy failures did not prompt a significant exodus of users. As WhatsApp differentiated itself pre-merger on its robust privacy protections, we can assume that users valued privacy. But they did not organize any migration to another app. Thus multi-homing is significant only if the exercise of market power by one app would cause many users in many geographic markets to switch to other texting apps on their smartphone.

In this context, a particular app, at times, can exercise market power, despite users **11.24** multi-homing; direct network effects confer this market power. As Chapter 8 discusses, there is reason to believe that WhatsApp acted as a competitive restraint on Facebook (perhaps more so than other texting apps). Facebook, post-merger, now might have less incentive to protect consumers' privacy and improve quality along this dimension since it knows that users will continue to use WhatsApp and Messenger. Indeed, many people within the group may dislike Facebook's privacy policy and its use of data to support its advertising-based revenue model. But they do not have the time or resources to poll everyone in the group, and get enough of them to shift to another group texting/messenger platform. In the interim, Facebook collects user data it would not otherwise obtain absent this direct network effect, especially from more privacy-aware users.

Nor is it clear how easy it will be for another privacy-focused texting app to increase **11.25** its user base to effectively challenge the dominant texting apps, which in many communities, are Facebook and WhatsApp. In effect, the merger created a protective moat around the leading apps, thereby raising entry barriers for alternative, more privacy-focused texting apps in communities where many are already actively using Messenger or WhatsApp.

12

SCALE OF DATA: TRIAL-AND-ERROR, 'LEARNING-BY-DOING' NETWORK EFFECTS

12.01   This chapter explores a second network effect, which arises from the scale of data: the more people who actively or passively contribute data, the more the company can improve the quality of its product, the more attractive the product is to other users, the more data the company has to further improve its product, which becomes more attractive to prospective users. Unlike the traditional network effects (such as a texting app or telephone), one may not think at first that one's utility increases as others use the product. After all, one may not care if, and how many, other people use Google to search the web. But, as we shall see, one can benefit (and one's utility can increase) when others use the same search engine, since the quality of the search results can increase. As more people use the search engine, the more trial-and-error experiments, the more likely the search engine's algorithms can learn of consumer preferences, the more relevant the search results will likely be, which in turn will likely attract others to use the search engine, and the positive feedback continues.

12.02   As the Organisation for Economic Co-operation and Development (OECD) found, there are increasing returns to scale from data:

> The accumulation of data can lead to significant improvements of data-driven services which in turns can attract more users, leading to even more data that can be collected. This 'positive feedback makes the strong get stronger and the weak get weaker, leading to extreme outcomes' [Carl Shapiro and Hal R Varian, *Information Rules: A Strategic Guide to the Network Economy* (Boston, MA: Harvard Business Press, 1999)]. For example, the more people use services such as Google Search, or recommendation engines such as that provided by Amazon, or navigation systems such as that provided by TomTom, the better the services as they become more accurate in delivering requested sites and products, and providing traffic information, and the more users it will attract.[1]

---

[1] OECD, *Data-Driven Innovation for Growth and Well-Being: Interim Synthesis Report*, October 2014, p 29, http://www.oecd.org/sti/inno/data-driven-innovation-interim-synthesis.pdf.

We will consider this data-driven network effect in three contexts: Waze's navigation app, search engines, and Facebook's digital assistant 'M'.

A. Waze's Turn-by-Turn Navigation App

Waze's business model, as Chapter 6 discusses, was built on this data-driven network effect. As its former CEO remarked, Google had money, Waze had people. Rather than drive along the roads (as Google and Tele Atlas did) to obtain traffic and mapping data for its navigation systems, Waze community-sourced the traffic information. The more people that actively or passively contributed data to Waze, the more accurate and fresher the mapping data became (including real-time traffic patterns for that city), and the more likely others would use the app.[2] As Waze described its network:

> After typing in their destination address, users just drive with the app open on their phone to passively contribute traffic and other road data, but they can also take a more active role by sharing road reports on accidents, police traps, or any other hazards along the way, helping to give other users in the area a 'heads-up' about what's to come.

> In addition to the local communities of drivers using the app, Waze is also home to an active community of online map editors who ensure that the data in their areas is as up-to-date as possible.[3]

12.03

As more people actively or passively contribute data (eg, driving with the app open in their smartphones), then Waze has a greater variety of data (as people drive along different roads), which it can quickly collect and process to depict near-real-time traffic patterns. As more people in a locale use Waze, its quality improves, as does one's utility in using the app to navigate roads to avoid accidents, road construction, and police speed traps.

12.04

Here the data-driven network effects are localized. Waze's popularity in Costa Rica, for example, increases the value of the real-time mapping data and navigation system in that country. Volunteers used Waze to map the entire island. According to one 2014 report, 'The app is especially popular in the capital, San Jose, boasting

12.05

---

[2] Office of Fair Trading (OFT), *ME/6167/13: Completed Acquisition by Motorola Mobility Holding (Google, Inc.) of Waze Mobile Limited*, 11 November 2013, para 45 (OFT, *Google/Waze*), http://webarchive.nationalarchives.gov.uk/20140402142426/http:/www.oft.gov.uk/shared_oft/mergers_ea02/2013/motorola.pdf ('Waze was a map building company which used a community based application to develop its maps. Creating a community has demand-side network effects, since users receive more value from a community if they can interact with more users, which in turn attracts more users. Similarly, the OFT was told that mapping is a "positive feedback business", where the more users there are the more data is created, which improves the experience and attracts yet more users.').

[3] Waze, 'About Us', https://www.waze.com/about.

300,000 active users. On one day earlier this month—Oct. 17—users reported nearly 47,000 incidents, which include things such as a traffic jam, an accident or hazard.'[4] Indeed, this data-driven network effect complements the traditional direct network effects we saw with texting. The same article noted how in Costa Rica, '[i]f inviting friends over for a party, it's common to share a Waze hyperlink to one's address through a WhatsApp group or a Facebook event.'[5] Nonetheless, Waze, while successful in attracting users in some geographic markets (such as Costa Rica), could not easily leverage these network effects and market power to other markets, like the UK.

12.06 Waze sought to take advantage of these network effects to compete against Google. Waze offered its turn-by-turn navigation app for free. Its app was easy to download. Users could easily switch to it. Its interface was straightforward, and Waze was well-known (especially after Apple's missteps with its mapping service). The number of Waze registered users increased significantly between its 2010 launch and 2013.[6] Despite its growth, Waze did not have a first mover advantage that secured dominance (or even significant market power) in every market.[7] The UK competition authority agreed. Waze, at least in the UK, did not attract enough users to attain the scale needed for its map navigation system to threaten Google's and Apple's dominance.[8] For traffic information, Waze's model required 'a minimum number of registered users for it to have a good understanding of prevailing traffic conditions on major routes at peak commuting times within a given territory', which Waze still lacked in the UK.[9] So here Waze's insufficient scale hindered its competitive significance against Google and Apple.[10]

B. Search Engines

12.07 This data-driven network effect can extend beyond local markets. Search engines are an example. Google, Yahoo!, Microsoft's Bing, and DuckDuckGo do not

---

[4] Matt McFarland, 'Why Navigation App Waze Is Popular in Costa Rica', *Boston Globe*, 27 October 2014, https://www.bostonglobe.com/business/2014/10/27/why-navigation-app-waze-popular-costa-rica/11w2NwPSYdLjpObS1p1KaP/story.html.

[5] Ibid.

[6] OFT, *Google/Waze*, above note 2, para 41 ('Data provided by the parties shows that Waze's registered users increased from a little over [1,000–100,000] when it was launched in January 2010 to [500,000–four million] by August 2013, of which over [50,000–two million] are active users.') (brackets in the original).

[7] Ibid, para 46.

[8] Ibid, para 39 ('the evidence before the OFT does not indicate that Waze had been successful in attracting sufficient users to build a UK map that would currently be considered to have good coverage and detailed accuracy and features compared to that of alternative providers of map data').

[9] Ibid, para 48.

[10] Ibid, para 49.

charge users for searching the web with their search engine. Search engines therefore compete for users based on quality. One important dimension of quality is to quickly provide relevant search results.[11] The search engine's commercial model relies on its intermediary role, connecting 'content providers (who want users), users (who want content), and advertisers (who want users)'.[12] As the Federal Trade Commission (FTC) Staff Report in the Google case found, '[a]lthough a user does not pay for the web search service, the user's focused interest—or intent—is very valuable to advertisers, because users are effectively identifying themselves as potential customers through the content of their queries.'[13]

A search engine cannot read the user's mind. It does not know when the user types **12.08** 'apple' and 'orange', whether she is searching for fruit or technology companies. When a consumer types 'orange' and 'apple', the search engine quickly generates an opinion as to what information the user will find most useful. Trial-and-error, or learning-by-doing, means that more searches increase the search engine's likelihood of identifying relevant results. As Google's Executive Chairman testified:

> When a consumer enters search terms, those terms are processed by the search engine's mathematical algorithms, which determine the probability that any given webpage will be responsive to the search. The user then receives results that are rank-ordered based on the search engine's judgment of the likelihood that each result matches what the user was seeking in entering the search terms. This process necessarily depends on multiple variables and constant refinement.[14]

The search engine first has the benefit of observing which links, if any, its users actu- **12.09** ally choose. If many choose a link that was originally offered down the list (say on the third or fourth page of results), the search engine's algorithm can harvest that information to move that link up the list; the search engine's algorithm demotes less frequently tapped suggested links down the list.[15] Thus, as more people use the

---

[11] *Microsoft/Yahoo! Search Business* (Case Comp/M.5727), Commission Decision C(2010) 1077, 18 February 2010, para 101 (competition takes place of the quality of the search results—ie, their relevance and speed—and the user interface); Teresa Vecchi, Jerome Vidal, and Viveca Fallenius, 'The Microsoft/Yahoo! Search Business Case', 2 *Competition Policy Newsletter* (2010): p 46 (EC finding that the 'quality and relevance of the algorithmic search engine' as 'the most important factor in attracting users to a particular search engine').

[12] Ioannis Lianos and Evgenia Motchenkova, 'Market Dominance and Search Quality in the Search Engine Market', 9(2) *J Competition L & Econ* (2013): p 421.

[13] FTC, Bureau of Competition, *Report re Google Inc*, 8 August 2012, p 8 ('FTC Staff Report'), http://graphics.wsj.com/google-ftc-report/.

[14] *The Power of Google: Serving Consumers or Threatening Competition?*, Hearing Before the Subcommittee on Antitrust, Competition Policy and Consumer Rights, US Senate Judiciary Committee, 112th Congress, 21 September 2011, p 2 (Testimony of Eric Schmidt, Executive Officer, Google Inc).

[15] FTC Staff Report, above note 13, p 14, quoting Google's former chief of search quality Udi Manber:

> The ranking itself is affected by the click data. If we discover that, for a particular query, hypothetically, 80 percent of people click on Result No 2 and only 10 percent click on

search engine and the more searches they run, the more trials the search engine's algorithm has in predicting consumer preferences, the more feedback the search engine receives of any errors, and the quicker the search engine can respond with recalibrating its offerings.[16] Increased traffic volumes make more experiments possible, thereby improving search results.[17] The product improvement in turn attracts additional users to that search engine compared to rival search engines. In effect, the more users and searches, the larger (and more heterogeneous) the sample size, and the better the search engine can identify relevant responses for both popular and less frequent queries ('tail' queries).[18] The European Commission aptly coined it 'greater relevance through greater scale'.[19]

12.10   Entry barriers into the search engine market are already high.[20] Microsoft reportedly invested in 2010 'more than $4.5 billion into developing its algorithms and building the physical capacity necessary to operate Bing'.[21] A new entrant can hire tech talent, but it would still lack the scale of this trial-and-error experimentation.[22] Microsoft argued, and the European Commission found, that 'scale is an important element to be an effective competitor'.[23] As Microsoft's then CEO said, 'it turns out there's a feedback loop in the search business, where the most searches you serve, or paid ad searches you serve, the more you learn about what people click on, what's

---

Result No 1, after a while we figure out, well, probably Result 2 is the one people want. So we'll switch it.

Other Google executives confirmed that 'click data is important for many purposes, including, most importantly, providing "feedback" on whether Google's search algorithms are offering its users high quality results'. Ibid, p 14.

[16] Steve Lohr, 'Can These Guys Make You "Bing"?', *New York Times*, 31 July 2011, p 3 ('Consumer testing is key to the algorithm refining process, and Google uses both human reviewers and samples of real search traffic in order to measure whether a proposed algorithm change improves the user experience or not.'); US Department of Justice (DOJ), 'Statement of the Department of Justice Antitrust Division on Its Decision to Close Its Investigation of the Internet Search and Paid Search Advertising Agreement Between Microsoft Corporation and Yahoo! Inc.',18 February 2010, http:// www.justice.gov/atr/public/press_releases/2010/255377.pdf.

[17] FTC Staff Report, above note 13, p 14 (stating '[t]he more search users there are at any given time, the more experiments can be run, the faster they can be completed, and the more improvements that can be made to the search algorithms' and how 'search providers run experiments on large volumes of users'); Vecchi et al, above note 11, pp 44, 46; *Microsoft/Yahoo! Search*, above note 11, para 223 ('the effects of scale are likely to allow the merged entity to run more tests and experiments on the algorithm in order to improve its relevance').

[18] FTC Staff Report, above note 13, p 14; *Microsoft/Yahoo! Search*, above note 11, para 162 (noting Microsoft's claim).

[19] *Microsoft/Yahoo! Search*, above note 11, para 225.

[20] FTC Staff Report, above note 13, p 76 ('Along with specialized algorithms, search and search advertising platforms require enormous investments in the technology and infrastructure required to crawl and categorize the entire Internet.').

[21] Ibid.

[22] Ibid.

[23] *Microsoft/Yahoo! Search*, above note 11, para 153; *see also* FTC Staff Report, above note 13, p 76 (noting that Internet search, search advertising, and search syndication are 'markets characterized by substantial scale effects').

relevant, and it turns out that scale drives knowledge which then can turn around and redrive innovation and relevance'.[24] With fewer trials by fewer users, entrants have fewer opportunities to experiment and predict search terms (through an auto-complete) or the relevant results in response to the search query. Entrants have fewer opportunities to observe subsequent errors and to perceive trends. Their ability to identify websites that consumers prefer is likely to remain inferior, so the entrant remains at a competitive disadvantage in attracting consumers (and, as we will see in Chapter 13, advertisers).[25]

Recognizing this, a smaller search engine can specialize in specific functions, such **12.11** as travel and flight options on travel-specific Internet sites, like Kayak and Expedia. However, one downside in becoming a niche player is that the search engine can lose an important segment of the population.[26] As Microsoft observed,

> there's this kind of inverse power loss, where 39 percent of the users account for 66 percent of all the searches. I think of them as the heavy searchers. Ourselves and Yahoo! and others have been losing heavy searchers for the last number of years. Since the Bing launch, we've actually inverted that, we're actually growing heavy searchers. And when you look at the demographics, we are over-indexed on 18 to 24 year olds now as a result of those heavy users. Before that, we were over-indexed on 65-year plus in terms of demographics, which is our MSN base.[27]

If a search engine's audience skews to users over 65 years old, its search results may start skewing to their preferences, which may differ from younger audiences, and make the search engine less attractive to younger users.

Interestingly, increased market usage and share correlates with increased quality. **12.12** Each person's utility from using the search engine increases as others use it as well. As more people use the search engine, the more trial-and-error experiments, the more likely the search engine can learn consumers' preferences, the more relevant the search results will likely be, which in turn will likely attract others to use the search engine, and the positive feedback continues.

---

[24] Transcript from Remarks from the Conference Call Held by Steve Ballmer, Chief Executive Officer, Microsoft, and Carol Bartz, Chief Executive Officer, Yahoo!, to Announce the Search Engine Agreement Between Yahoo! and Microsoft, Microsoft News Center, 29 July 2009, http://news.microsoft.com/speeches/steve-ballmer-carol-bartz-microsoft-yahoo-search-agreement/.

[25] Pamela Jones Harbour and Tara Isa Koslov, 'Section 2 in a Web 2.0 World: An Expanded Vision of Relevant Product Markets', 76 *Antitrust LJ* (2010): p 784 ('Google search engine has become further entrenched as the dominant search site, and the firm has accumulated even more search data. Given the role of network effects, one might wonder whether any other firm will be able to chip away at Google's search supremacy without access to a comparable trove of data.') (internal footnotes omitted).

[26] Yusuf Mehdi, Senior Vice President, Online Audience Business, Microsoft, Remarks at the Credit Suisse Annual Technology Conference, Scottsdale, AZ, 1 December 2009.

[27] Ibid.

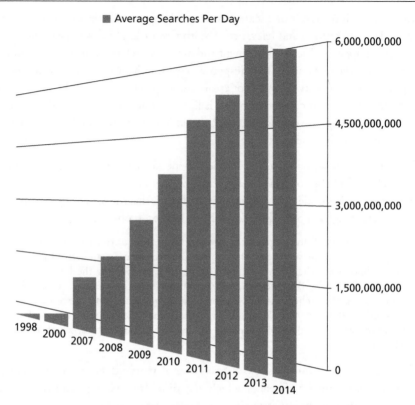

■ Average Searches Per Day

Figure 12.1 Growth of Google in average searches per day

Source: *Google Annual Search Statistics*, Statistic Brain Research Institute, 9 January 2015, http://www. statisticbrain.com/google-searches/.

12.13 Figure 12.1 reflects Google's increase in scale, growing from an average of 9,800 searches per day in 1998 to over 5.7 billion searches per day in 2014.

12.14 Contrast Google with DuckDuckGo. As Figure 12.2 reflects, DuckDuckGo has also grown since 2010 in the average number of daily searches, especially in 2014 when both Safari and Firefox added the search engine.

12.15 But as Table 12.1 reflects, DuckDuckGo's growth over the four years is miniscule relative to Google's.

12.16 Table 12.1 reveals a couple of things. First, Google scaled up a lot quicker than DuckDuckGo, which after four and a half years still has not reached the level that Google reached in three years. Second, Google is in the billions of daily searches while DuckDuckGo is still in the low millions. To put this in perspective, using the 2014 averages, the number of daily searches on Google is slightly more than one

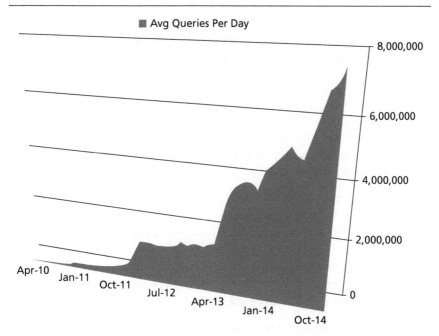

Figure 12.2 Growth of DuckDuckGo in average searches per day

Source: 'DuckDuckGo Direct queries per day (1y avg)', https://duckduckgo.com/traffic.html.

Table 12.1 Comparison of growth of Google and DuckDuckGo

	Google Average Searches Per Day	DuckDuckGo Average Searches Per Day
1998	9,800	
2000	60,000,000	
2007	1,200,000,000	
2008	1,745,000,000	
2009	2,610,000,000	
2010	3,627,000,000	59,886
2011	4,717,000,000	272,229
2012	5,134,000,000	1,355,469
2013	5,922,000,000	2,927,999
2014	5,740,000,000	5,398,752

search by every person in the 40 most populous countries.[28] DuckDuckGo's daily average is slightly more than one search by every resident of the Houston, Texas

---

[28] *Countries of the World*, World Atlas, http://www.worldatlas.com/aatlas/populations/ctypo-pls.htm (equalling 5,712,085,060 people).

metropolitan area.[29] Google's popularity enables more trial-and-error experiments, which in turn increases its popularity.[30] Google with its massive number of search users can 'tap into the "wisdom of the users"' to identify the most relevant websites for any given query.[31]

12.17 Consequently, there are, as the competition authorities and OECD found, non-linear, increasing returns to scale from searches and personal data. But at what point do the returns to scale taper off? How many more daily search inquiries would DuckDuckGo need to be as good as Google in terms of the quality of its search results? That issue remains unresolved.

12.18 A simple illustration is to assume that the returns to scale uniformly level off at a specific level—say 100,000 search inquiries per day per relevant geographic market. Google, Yahoo!, Bing, and DuckDuckGo will have more relevant search results over a new entrant (for example, Apple), but that advantage will disappear as soon as Apple averages 100,000 daily inquiries in those locales. Under this scenario, network effects exist, but are readily surmountable by Apple and any other entrant that can attract 100,000 search queries per day.

12.19 Now suppose that the returns to scale taper off for different types of searches. Suppose Google and DuckDuckGo attract a random cross-section of the population for search queries. DuckDuckGo averages five million daily searches and Google five billion. Suppose 1 per cent of the daily searches involve a hot topic (such as a scandal involving a celebrity). The smaller search engine DuckDuckGo has 50,000 searches from which to experiment, Google 50 million. For the more popular search, both search engines may have a sufficiently large sample to identify the more popular, relevant sites, even though the larger website might do a better job identifying and ranking the second or third tier results. However, the results are different for esoteric 'tail' queries. Suppose a search, such as *'law and economics professors' and NCAA*, averages one per 10 million searches. The smaller search engine will get one search every two days, the larger search engine gets 500 queries per day.

---

[29] *Populations of the World's 100 Largest Cities*, World Atlas, http://www.worldatlas.com/city-pops.htm (5,383,000 people).

[30] Harbour and Koslov, above note 25, pp 777–8 (noting how 'Google's popularity has exploded, however, because the accuracy and relevance of Google search results actually improves as more and more searches are conducted. This improved performance, in turn, has attracted even more searchers to Google, which further improves the search results, and so on, in a continually self-reinforcing loop.'); OECD, *Supporting Investment in Knowledge Capital, Growth and Innovation*, 10 October 2013, p 171, http://dx.doi.org/10.1787/9789264193307-en ('Supply-side economies of scale may also occur in digital markets, most notably in the context of search engines, where increased data from users allows for the development of more accurate search algorithms.').

[31] *Power of Google*, US Senate Hearing, above note 14, p 2 (Testimony of Eric Schmidt, Executive Officer, Google Inc).

Consequently, to identify relevant responses for frequent, popular queries, the **12.20** search engine might need fewer average daily searches (say 100,000) than for less frequent, esoteric tail inquiries. The smaller search engine may perform as well in terms of quality for popular searches, but struggle for less frequent tail inquiries, where its sample size is much smaller than the larger search engines. If new searches are a significant component of daily searches (say 20 per cent),[32] then the larger search engine will enjoy an inherent advantage. In averaging five billion searches per day, a leading search engine is likely to provide more relevant results across the board—from esoteric 'tail' to popular queries—than a search engine averaging five million searches per day. Under this scenario, the larger search engine's results will continually improve as more people use the search engine for all of their searches, but the incremental benefits from scale (increase in relevance) will taper off as the sample size approaches all users.

Microsoft and Yahoo! advanced this argument to the European Commission to **12.21** justify their ten-year partnership. In December 2009, Microsoft partnered with Yahoo! to provide the exclusive algorithmic and paid search platform for the Yahoo! websites. Microsoft believed its joint venture with Yahoo! would allow it over time to improve the effectiveness and increase the value of its 'search offering through greater scale in search queries and an expanded and more competitive search and advertising marketplace'.[33] Before the partnership, fewer people used Microsoft's and Yahoo!'s search engines compared to Google. In attaining greater scale, Microsoft and Yahoo! could produce more relevant search results to better compete against industry leader Google. As the parties argued, their incentive was to increase the number of queries and users to attain similar scale with Google, which lessened their incentive to shade quality.[34]

This argument, of course, assumes that the benefits from scale had not already **12.22** levelled off for Microsoft and Yahoo! For if Microsoft, Yahoo!, and Google were all operating at or above the minimum efficient scale for search queries, if the other network effects were not involved, and if the quality of the algorithms were similar, then the quality of their search results would be roughly similar.

---

[32] *Google Search Statistics*, Internet Live Stats, http://www.internetlivestats.com/google-search-statistics/#ref-4 (noting that 16% to 20% of queries that get asked every day on Google have never been asked before).

[33] Microsoft Corporation, 2011 Annual Report, p 6, https://www.sec.gov/Archives/edgar/data/789019/000119312511200680/d10k.htm.

[34] *Microsoft/Yahoo! Search*, above note 11, paras 211, 213. Moreover, Microsoft argued that the structure of its transaction with Yahoo! provided 'a large incentive to innovate on the search experience because, according to the definitive Agreements, the publishing businesses of Microsoft and Yahoo will remain separate, and the revenue attributable to either Yahoo or Microsoft depends on the source of the search query'. Ibid, para 208. Yahoo! and Microsoft would only earn revenue from ads that appear on their respective websites (and those of its publisher affiliates), so each would have a strong incentive to attract users to their own entry points. Ibid, para 208.

12.23   In closing its investigation, the US Department of Justice described how the benefits from scale might enable a combined Microsoft/Yahoo! to better compete against the dominant search engine:

> The search and paid search advertising industry is characterized by an unusual relationship between scale and competitive performance. The transaction will enhance Microsoft's competitive performance because it will have access to a larger set of queries, which should accelerate the automated learning of Microsoft's search and paid search algorithms and enhance Microsoft's ability to serve more relevant search results and paid search listings, particularly with respect to rare or 'tail' queries. The increased queries received by the combined operation will further provide Microsoft with a much larger pool of data than it currently has or is likely to obtain without this transaction. This larger data pool may enable more effective testing and thus more rapid innovation of potential new search-related products, changes in the presentation of search results and paid search listings, other changes in the user interface, and changes in the search or paid search algorithms. This enhanced performance, if realized, should exert correspondingly greater competitive pressure in the marketplace.[35]

12.24   The European Commission also found scale to be an important factor to effectively compete,[36] with a caveat: 'While the Commission notes that Google appears to perform better in terms of relevance especially for [deleted in original] queries, this does not provide evidence that scale leads to higher relevance for users, since the above studies do not take into account the technology of the different search engine which are not related to scale.'[37] The Commission found that the search platform's revenue per search increased with the volume of search queries.[38] Market participants who responded to the Commission's market investigation indicated 'almost unanimously that scale is important in order to be an effective competitor in search advertising'[39] and that 'Microsoft did not have enough traffic to compete effectively with Google'.[40] Google was the exception. It argued that 'while scale is an important and necessary ingredient of having a successful search engine, its degree of importance has been largely overstated'.[41] The Commission did not elaborate. Both Google and Microsoft acknowledged that 'the value of incremental data decreases as the amount of data increases'.[42] The issues of when that happens, for which types of searches, and the quality differential were left unresolved.

---

[35] DOJ, *Advertising Agreement*, above note 16.

[36] *Microsoft/Yahoo! Search*, above note 11, para 153; Vecchi et al, above note 11, pp 46–7 (noting that the EC's market investigation 'confirmed that scale is an important aspect in the economics of the industry').

[37] *Microsoft/Yahoo! Search*, above note 11, para 168.

[38] Ibid.

[39] *Microsoft/Yahoo! Search*, above note 11, para 173.

[40] Vecchi et al, above note 11, p 46.

[41] *Microsoft/Yahoo! Search*, above note 11, para 174.

[42] Ibid.

Likewise, the FTC in its investigation of Google tackled the issue of the scale **12.25**
curve. Google acknowledged 'the importance of scale in the abstract'.[43] Moreover,
Google's internal documents, according to the FTC, were 'replete with references
to the "virtuous cycle" among users, advertisers, and publishers'.[44] Google's executives, however, testified of the diminishing returns from scale, and that Google has
'enough users already that more users don't make it much better'.[45] Google also
argued that Microsoft's search engine had reached optimal scale: 'Bing's query and
advertiser volume have passed the point at which scale should—or would—matter
significantly to Microsoft, and that any volume gains made by Bing would yield
minimal improvements in either Bing's search quality or its monetization ability.'[46]
Microsoft agreed that there were generally diminishing returns to scale,[47] but disagreed that it reached the optimal scale. As the FTC Staff observed,

> [the] main bone of contention between Google and Microsoft is where on this
> scale curve Microsoft currently operates. This is an important question, but one
> which evades easy answers. This is, in part, because neither party can identify a
> fixed number of queries or ads that constitutes the 'minimum efficient' point of
> operation.[48]

Here, again, the competition agency and market participants recognized the power **12.26**
of scale, but at what point this network effect loses its power was left unresolved.
No competition agency, as of early 2016, has publicly stated when this data-driven
network effect tapers off.

C. Facebook

Learning-by-doing underlies not only search algorithms but artificial intelligence **12.27**
generally. After its WhatsApp acquisition, Facebook in 2015 announced a beta
version of 'M', its 'digital assistant' that can replace most of one's web searches
and apps with a chat app on Facebook Messenger.[49] Like Apple's Siri, Microsoft's
Cortana, and Google's voice-recognition systems, Facebook's technology relies on
machine learning.

Here, too, the entry barriers may appear low if one does not consider the data-driven **12.28**
network effects. M's underlying code and algorithms are largely open source.[50] Thus,

---

[43] FTC Staff Report, above note 13, p 16.
[44] Ibid.
[45] Ibid, p 124 n 77 (quoting Schmidt).
[46] Ibid, p 16.
[47] Ibid.
[48] Ibid.
[49] Christopher Mims, 'Ask M for Help: Facebook Tests New Digital Assistant: Single Interface
Could Replace Web Searches and Apps on Mobile Devices', *Wall Street Journal*, 9 November 2015,
http://www.wsj.com/articles/ask-m-for-help-facebook-tests-new-digital-assistant-1447045202.
[50] Ibid.

the key asset is the scale of data, and the ability of the algorithm to learn by trial-by-error. As the *Wall Street Journal* reported, 'Facebook Messenger already has more than 700 million users', which yields it the following advantage: 'with access to so many users, Facebook has a plausible way to get the gigantic quantity of conversational data required to make a chat-based assistant sufficiently automated'.[51] M watches humans handle requests that M 'itself isn't yet smart enough to handle, and every day it learns a little more and gets a little better at handling those requests'.[52] With more users making more requests, Facebook's M can quickly process more tasks easily. In effect, users help the company's algorithm learn by noting and correcting mistakes.

12.29 Now thanks to the WhatsApp acquisition, Facebook has over one billion WhatsApp users. Granted there is some overlap between Facebook Messenger and WhatsApp users. But the acquisition significantly increased Facebook's user base and enables Facebook's self-learning algorithms to ramp up a lot quicker than DuckDuckGo or an entrant. So while the European Commission considered the traditional direct network effects, it failed to see how combining the two largest texting apps can raise entry barriers for any technology where the scale of data is important. Previously, to compete against Facebook, an entrant seeking the scale necessary to improve quality through machine-learning might have partnered with WhatsApp. That option is now lost.

12.30 The stakes are huge. Google, Apple, and Facebook are all jockeying as to 'who gets to control the primary interface of mobile devices'.[53] Google was, and remains as of 2015, the primary portal for the web through its search engine. Google dominates through its search engine 'direct response' advertising, 'which is the kind of ad that pops up when we are searching for an airline ticket, a new laptop or any other purchase'. [54] Facebook is now seeking with chat, both through voice and over a text-based interface, to become the first place where users go on mobile devices.[55]

D. Reflections

12.31 The consensus among the competition authorities and OECD is that search engines have exhibited this data-driven network effect. Thus, it should be uncontroversial when market participants or competition authorities identify this network effect in other data-driven industries.[56]

---

[51] Ibid.
[52] Ibid.
[53] Ibid.
[54] Ibid.
[55] Ibid.
[56] OECD, *Data-Driven Innovation*, above note 1, p 58 (noting that 'the more people use services such as Google search, a recommendation engine such as provided by Amazon, or a navigation system by TomTom, the better the services become as they become more accurate in delivering requested sites and products, and providing traffic information, and the more users

This scale-based network effect can be output enhancing. Our Google example **12.32** shows that it can enhance quality. Our Facebook example shows it can drive innovation (development of artificial intelligence (AI)). Netflix, for example, in tracking its subscribers' viewing habits can predict other movies and shows that the subscriber may enjoy. As more people with diverse backgrounds subscribe to Netflix, the more data Netflix has on consumer preferences, the better able Netflix can predict entertainment that would capture consumers' interest, the more strategic it can be in licensing its entertainment. Amazon also uses personal data for its recommendation engine 'you may also like...' based on a type of predictive modelling technique called 'collaborative filtering'.[57] Amazon reported 'that 30 percent of sales were due to its recommendation engine'.[58] As the management consultants McKinsey & Company found, this data mining can yield state-of-the-art cross-selling, which 'uses all the data that can be known about a customer, including the customer's demographics, purchase history, preferences, real-time locations, and other facts to increase the average purchase size'.[59]

But learning-by-doing can also entrench dominance. This has been notable in **12.33** online search, where Google has been dominant for years. Despite Microsoft's significant investment, its venture with Yahoo!, and its long-standing dominance of the personal computer operating system platform, Microsoft's Bing has not threatened Google's dominance. In May 2015, Google continued to lead the US 'explicit core search market' for desktop searches with a 64.1 per cent market share, followed by Microsoft Sites (20.3 per cent), Yahoo! Sites (12.7 per cent), Ask Network (1.8 per cent), and AOL, Inc (1.2 per cent).[60] As Figure 12.3 reflects, Google's desktop share of search in the US has stabilized in the 60 per cent range.

In US search inquiries on mobile phones and tablets, Google, helped by its **12.34** Android operating system and being the default search engine on Apple, has an even greater share. In May 2015, Google had an 86 per cent share, with Yahoo! (8 per cent) and Microsoft (4.92 per cent) trailing behind.[61]

---

they will attract. Where data linkage is possible, the diversification of services can lead to further positive feedbacks.').

[57] McKinsey Global Institute, *Big Data: The Next Frontier for Innovation, Competition, and Productivity*, June 2011, p 23, http://www.mckinsey.com/insights/business_technology/big_data_the_next_frontier_for_innovation.

[58] Ibid, p 67.

[59] Ibid.

[60] comScore, 'comScore Releases May 2015 US Desktop Search Engine Rankings', 16 June 2015, http://www.comscore.com/Insights/Market-Rankings/comScore-Releases-May-2015-US-Desktop-Search-Engine-Rankings.

[61] *See* StatCounter, 'StatCounter Global Stats: Top 5 Mobile & Tablet Search Enginees [sic] in the United States from June 2014 to May 2015', http://gs.statcounter.com/#mobile+tablet-search_engine-US-monthly-201406-201505.

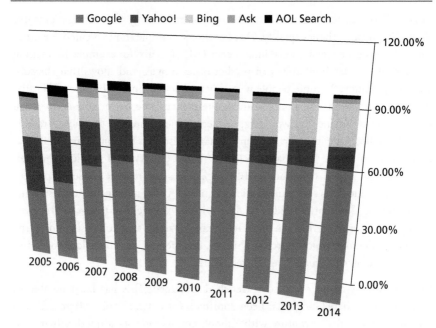

Figure 12.3 Desktop share of search in the United States

Source: Statistic Brain Research Institute, 'Search Engine Market Share', 9 January 2015, http://www. statisticbrain.com/search-engine-market-share/ (using comScore data).

12.35 In Europe, Google has an even larger share of the search market. In 2013, the European Commission observed how Google 'has been holding market shares in web search well above 90% in most European countries for several years now, a level which is higher than in many other parts of the world'.[62] The Commission also stated that it did 'not seem likely that another web search service will replace it as European users' web search service of choice'.[63]

12.36 In response, one claim is that people are conducting fewer search inquiries on general search engines, and are instead turning to mobile apps and spending more time on smartphones and tablets. The data does not support this assertion. General search inquiries in the US are growing overall.[64] For local search query volume, mobile has overtaken desktops.[65] As consumers shift their digital activity to mobile,

---

[62] European Commission, 'Commission Seeks Feedback on Commitments Offered by Google to Address Competition Concerns—Questions and Answers', 25 April 2013, p 1, http://europa.eu/ rapid/press-release_MEMO-13-383_en.htm.

[63] Ibid.

[64] Adam Lella and Andrew Lipsman, *2015 US Digital Future in Focus*, comScore, 26 March 2015, p 16, https://www.comscore.com/Insights/Presentations-and-Whitepapers/2015/2015-US-Digital-Future-in-Focus ('total US multi-platform web search market grew 5 percent in query volume in Q4 2014 vs. the previous year').

[65] Mike O'Brien, 'Mobile Surpasses Desktop in Search Queries', Search Engine Watch, 1 June 2015, http://searchenginewatch.com/sew/news/2411038/mobile-surpasses-desktop-in-search-queries (market research firm found that 66.5 million local search queries were made via mobile devices versus desktop's 65.6).

'growth in the search market is being driven by both smartphones (up 17 percent from the prior year) and tablets (up 28 percent)', while desktop search 'has declined marginally during the same period'.[66] Moreover, Google's 'strong leadership on both smartphones and tablets boosts its share of the multi-platform search market by several percentage points vs desktop alone'.[67] Thus there are no signs that Google will be knocked off its perch.

[66] Ibid.

[67] Ibid ('Google remains the leader in the US explicit core search market with 66 percent market share of search queries conducted in Q4 2014, followed by Bing at 20 percent and Yahoo at 11 percent. Bing increased its market share in 2014, while Yahoo's recent search partnership with Firefox has also bolstered its share.'). Moreover, smartphone users, in one 2014 survey, spent more time with apps they've downloaded from Facebook and Google than with any other company: 'Of the apps they chose to download, users spent 13% of their total time in Facebook's apps', and 12% of their time with Google apps. Matt Rosoff, 'Facebook and Google Are Winning the App War', *Business Insider UK*, 29 June 2015, http://uk.businessinsider.com/facebook-and-google-are-winning-the-app-war-2015-6?r=US.

13

TWO MORE NETWORK EFFECTS: SCOPE OF DATA AND SPILL-OVER EFFECTS

A. Scope of Data

13.01 In addition to scale, companies can enjoy network effects from the scope of data. Here we see how the feedback loop is accelerated when the company harnesses the *variety* of data across its platform to improve the quality of its product or service, which attracts more users (including to its search engine), which provides the company with more data to further improve its product (and to target them with behavioural ads). We will consider this network effect with Facebook's new digital assistant 'M' and search engines.

1. Facebook's digital assistant 'M'

13.02 Returning to Facebook's digital assistant 'M', the quality of its results can improve as the social network collects a greater variety of personal data on its users. If people use, besides the digital assistant, Facebook's other services (such as its social network, texting, pictures on Instagram, etc), Facebook can use the variety of data to refine M's algorithms and its user profiles to better predict individual tastes and interests, and better target the person with more probative organic and sponsored results.

13.03 Here we see how the second and third data-driven network effects can reinforce one another. Under the second network effect, with more inquiries, the digital assistant, through learning-by-doing, can identify the likely universe of relevant responses. Under the third network effect, the more that users rely on the platform's other services, the greater the variety of personal data on particular users, the better the digital assistant can segment results by user profiles, and the better the digital assistant can personalize results.

13.04 So the feedback loop adds a dimension: it is no longer the trial-and-error, learning-by-doing from earlier queries, but trial-and-error in predicting individual tastes and preferences from the variety of personal data the company collects across its platform (such as the person's email, geo-location data, social network, browser history) and Internet (from the cookies placed when the person visits a website). Now the digital assistant—in personalizing results—can target users with specific sponsored advertisements that they will more likely click (thereby generating more revenue for the platform operator). The more time people invest on the company's platform, the greater their loyalty to the platform, the more the digital assistant may learn about user preferences and improve its results' relevance and quality. As the Organisation for Economic Co-operation and Development (OECD) discussed,

> The diversification of services leads to even better insights if data linkage is possible. This is because data linkage enables 'super-additive' insights, leading to increasing 'returns to scope'. Linked data is a means to contextualise data and thus a source for insights and value that are greater than the sum of its isolated parts (data silos).[1]

Suppose the digital assistant provides an array of services, including navigation apps and maps. The digital assistant, in collecting users' geo-location data, knows where its users typically walk or drive each week. With the other data collected on the user, the platform can now target the user with responsive information: while the user is driving home, for example, the digital assistant can target specific nearby restaurants within the user's price range (based on inferences of where the user works, lives, and shops) that the user likely would enjoy (based on what the user's friends recommend in the user's social networks). As more people use the company's platform of services, the more data the company collects, the more refined the user profile, the more likely the company can target users with information they might find relevant at critical purchasing moments, and the more opportunities the platform can observe consumer behaviour and refine its algorithms accordingly. **13.05**

Besides launching its digital assistant 'M', Facebook is also improving users' ability to search its social network.[2] Here the responses for your queries can be personalized based on who your friends are on the social network: 'Starting with authoritative sources like news organizations, the search results will become more granular as you scroll down to what your friends are saying, liking and commenting on and then finally to strangers discussing the same topic.'[3] Facebook is highlighting how its search engine is tailored to each individual user: 'Facebook says every single action you've taken on the social network, from who you've become friends with to every page you like, will inform the search results.'[4] So here we see how the first network effect (traditional direct network effects) amplifies this data-driven network effect. **13.06**

---

[1] OECD, *Data-Driven Innovation for Growth and Well-Being: Interim Synthesis Report*, October 2014, p 29, http://www.oecd.org/sti/inno/data-driven-innovation-interim-synthesis.pdf (internal footnote omitted).

[2] Nick Statt, 'Facebook Is Unleashing Universal Search Across Its Entire Social Network: Indexing 2 Trillion Posts', *The Verge*, 22 October 2015, http://www.theverge.com/2015/10/22/9587122/new-facebook-search-all-public-posts.

[3] Ibid.

[4] Ibid.

2. Search engines

13.07   Another example of how the *variety* of personal data can help amplify the other net-work effects is Google.[5] Google, as we saw in the last chapter, benefits from the scale of search inquiry data. But even after those benefits taper off (the minimum efficient scale), Google can still benefit from the scope of data it collects and analyses across its platform.[6] Google can aggregate and analyse the variety of data it collects across its platform of services (such as learning of a person's travel plans from an email to a friend, a search query, a video watched on YouTube, a site visited via the company's browser, or information in the user's calendar) to add parameters to its algorithm that can better predict more personalized search results.

13.08   Google, for example, scans the email received or sent by its Gmail to create user profiles and provide targeted advertising.[7] As one FTC Commissioner observed, '[t]ype the search term 'apple' into the Google search engine, and Google will "know" whether the user is focusing on food (apple recipes) or technology products (Apple computers), depending on which websites the user recently visited (Cooking Light versus MacWorld) as well as what searches she recently conducted (Golden Delicious versus iPod).'[8] Using the geo-location data from the user's mobile phones, the search engine knows when the person arrived at the destination. As the OECD discussed,

> As Newman (2013)[9] highlights in the case of Google: "It's not just that Google collects data from everyone using its search engine. It also collects data on what they're

---

[5] *Microsoft/Yahoo! Search Business* (Case Comp/M.5727), Commission Decision C(2010) 1077, 18 February 2010, para 40 (noting that a 'growing number of both search and non-search ads are also behaviourally targeted').

[6] Public Citizen, *Mission Creep-y: Google Is Quietly Becoming One of the Nation's Most Powerful Political Forces While Expanding Its Information-Collection Empire*, November 2014, p 11, https://www.citizen.org/documents/Google-Political-Spending-Mission-Creepy.pdf ('Google personalizes results based on information about users, sometimes taking advantage of information it has gleaned from its customers' use of other services in Google's growing constellation of information-based product lines. The company also uses, information based on what ads and content users view and interact with.'); p 14 ('Not only does Google customize ads based on user profiles, but it apparently provides different search results to different users. The firm also appears to be customizing search results in a manner intended to increase its revenue.'); Federal Trade Commission (FTC), *In the Matter of Google/Double-Click FTC File No 071-0170: Dissenting Statement of Commissioner Pamela Jones Harbour*, 20 December 2007, p 7, https://www.ftc.gov/enforcement/cases-proceedings/071-0170/proposed-acquisition-hellman-friedman-capital-partners-v-lp.

[7] Frank Pasquale, *The Black Box Society: The Secret Algorithms That Control Money and Information* (Cambridge, MA: Harvard University Press, 2015), p 78; *In re Google Inc*, Case No 13-MD-02430-LHK, 2013 WL 5423918 (US Dist Ct (ND Cal), 26 September 2013), pp *1–2, *8, *11 (noting that 'Google's alleged interceptions are neither instrumental to the provision of email services, nor are they an incidental effect of providing these services').

[8] FTC, *In the Matter of Google/Double-Click*, above note 6, p 7.

[9] Nathan Newman, 'Taking on Google's Monopoly Means Regulating Its Control of User Data', *The Huffington Post*, The Blog, 24 September 2013, http://www.huffingtonpost.com/nathan-newman/taking-on-googles-monopol_b_3980799.html.

interested in writing in their Gmail accounts, what they watch on YouTube, where they are located using data from Google Maps, a whole array of other data from use of Google's Android phones, and user information supplied from Google's whole web of online services." This diverse data set allows the company to create even more detailed profiles about its users that were not possible with each single service.[10]

Other search engines, which do not operate such broad platforms, lack the variety **13.09** of user data that Google acquires, and accordingly cannot leverage the data to better target users with personalized sponsored and organic search results.

B. Spill-Over Effects: How Networks Effects on One Side of Multi-Sided Platforms Can Increase Market Power on the Other Sides

Under the three network effects examined, the growth of users increases the prod- **13.10** uct's quality or appeal, prompting more users to use the product. In the fourth network effect, the growth of users on one side of the multi-sided platform can attract more advertisers or suppliers on the other side of the platform, which in turn attracts more users, advertisers, and suppliers. We will first look at traditional spill-over effects, and then see how personal data can amplify the network effect.

1. Traditional spill-over effects in multi-sided online platforms

As the UK competition authority observed, '[g]enerally, where there is a two-sided **13.11** platform, there is more value to both sides of having more users'.[11] For example, as more people use the car service app Uber in a particular town, more drivers will be attracted to Uber's platform, which increases the utility of users as the waiting time for cars decreases. As more customers in a community use Uber, the drivers' utility increases, as the downtime waiting for passengers decreases. As more drivers are attracted to the platform, more users are drawn to the platform, thereby increasing the platform operator's market power in that local geographic market.

Likewise, the traditional spill-over network effects can span geographic markets. **13.12** For example, Airbnb in early 2016 had over 2 million temporary residential listings in over 34,000 cities in over 190 countries.[12] As more travellers turn to Airbnb for housing in a particular city, more accommodation owners will list on the site, which can increase each guest's utility, with greater variety of accommodation and price

---

[10] OECD, *Data-Driven Innovation*, above note 1, p 29 (internal footnote omitted).
[11] Office of Fair Trading (OFT), *ME/6167/13: Completed Acquisition by Motorola Mobility Holding (Google, Inc.) of Waze Mobile Limited*, 11 November 2013, para 19 (OFT, *Google/Waze*), http://webarchive.nationalarchives.gov.uk/20140402142426/http://www.oft.gov.uk/shared_oft/mergers_ea02/2013/motorola.pdf.
[12] Airbnb, Inc, *About Us*, https://www.airbnb.co.uk/about/about-us.

points—such as downtown lofts, midtown studios, uptown duplexes, outer bor-ough townhouses, and suburban single-family houses—for a particular weekend. As the online platform attracts more guests, the utility of accommodation owners also can increase: they have a better sense of the market price for their accommoda-tion and a greater variety of guests to choose from for a greater range of dates.

13.13 This spill-over effect occurs with traditional media. As more people watch the World Cup, more advertisers will want to reach these viewers and advertising rates increase. The same applies for newspapers and commercial radio stations. Relying on the work of economists Jean-Charles Rochet, Jean Tirole, and David Evans on multi-sided markets, the OECD identified this spill-over effect as one of the three fundamental aspects of multi-sided platforms:

> . . . the value that a customer on one side realizes from the platform increases with the number of customers on the other side. (There could also be an 'externality in use': a customer and a merchant benefit when each of them takes the same tender type regardless of how many other people do.) A search platform is more valuable to advertisers if it is more likely that it will reach a larger number of potential buyers. It is more valuable to users looking to buy something if there are more advertisers attracted to the platform because that makes it more likely that the user will see a relevant advertisement. It is often the strength of these indirect network effects that determines whether the two-sidedness matters enough to have a substantive effect on the results of economic analysis, or whether it is only an interesting curiosity.[13]

13.14 So what is true for traditional media platforms, like television, radio, and news-papers, is also found on online platforms, like YouTube, Facebook, and search engines. But unlike television, radio, and newspaper advertisers, online plat-forms can collect personal data, create user profiles, target users with specific ads, and even enlist users to endorse products. Thus as we explore below, this data-driven network effect can be more dynamic than a popular television show, which attracts more advertising dollars as its viewership among key demograph-ics increases.

2. Data-driven spill-over effects

13.15 With online platforms, the operator can tailor the ads for each individual based on the profile it has on the individual. 'As a result', the UK competition authority recognized, 'the value of online advertisements can be enhanced, because they are more likely to be of interest to the consumers in question and thus more likely to

---

[13] OECD, *Policy Roundtables: Two-Sided Markets*, 17 December 2009, p 29, http://www.oecd. org/daf/competition/44445730.pdf. The other fundamental elements of two-sided platforms are 'the existence of two distinct groups of customers, who need each other in some way, and who rely on the platform to intermediate transactions between them' and the 'non-neutrality of the price structure', whereby the 'platform can affect the volume of transactions by charging more to one side of the market and reducing the price paid by the other side by an equal amount'. Ibid.

successfully prompt them to purchase the item'.[14] Personal data, as the OECD found, can amplify the spill-over effect: 'The reuse of data generates huge returns to scale and scope which lead to positive feedback loops in favour of the business on one side of the market, which in turn reinforces success in the other side(s) of the market'.[15]

3. Coupons.com

One illustration is Coupons.com. The online platform delivers digital coupons and **13.16** promotions from 700 consumer packaged goods companies (including household goods suppliers Clorox and Procter & Gamble, consumer packaged goods providers General Mills and Kellogg's, and North American retailers Albertsons-Safeway, CVS, Dollar General, Kroger, and Walgreens) to roughly 17 million people a month.[16] Its platform, according to its annual report, seeks 'to engage consumers at the critical moments when they are choosing which products they will buy and where they will shop'.[17] To engage users, the platform relies on personal data. For example, it offers a popular mobile phone app that serves as a grocery shopping list. The application automatically finds relevant coupons based on the customer's grocery list. It also uses consumer data to personalize its digital coupons, 'based on which offers the consumer has clicked on and what searches the consumer may conduct on our network as well as the coupons that the consumer previously activated by printing or loading to their loyalty cards and redeeming'.[18]

We can see the online platform's data-advantage over paper coupons distributed in **13.17** newspapers or by direct mail. Although both paper and online coupons can target households, the online platform benefits in the velocity of data (targeting consumers who are about to shop with relevant coupons) and volume and variety of data (tracking consumer behaviour across the Internet and past purchasing behaviour). Thus, Coupons.com identifies its '[p]roprietary data on consumer behaviour from intent to purchase' as a 'key strength'.[19]

We can see how personal data accelerates the spill-over effects on both sides of this **13.18** online platform. The more data Coupons.com collects on customers, the better it

---

[14] UK Competition and Markets Authority, *The Commercial Use of Consumer Data: Report on the CMA's Call for Information*, June 2015, para 2.77, https://www.gov.uk/government/uploads/system/uploads/attachment_data/file/435817/The_commercial_use_of_consumer_data.pdf.

[15] OECD, *Data-Driven Innovation*, above note 1, p 29.

[16] Quotient, 'Coupons.com Incorporated Changes Corporate Name to Quotient', Press Release, 6 October 2015, http://www.quotient.com/coupons-com-incorporated-changes-corporate-name-to-quotient/.

[17] Coupons.com Incorporated, 2014 Annual Report ('Coupons.com 2014 Annual Report'), p 3, https://www.sec.gov/Archives/edgar/data/1115128/000156459015001837/coup-10k_20141231.htm. The company changed its name to Quotient Technology Inc, *see* Quotient, 'Coupons.com Incorporated Changes', above note 16.

[18] Coupons.com 2014 Annual Report, above note 17, p 5.

[19] Ibid, p 4.

can target them with relevant coupons when they are shopping, and the more likely customers will use the coupons. In leveraging the scope and scale of personal data to predict what coupons would interest its users, the platform can increase the level of coupon redemption. This attracts consumer goods manufacturers and retailers seeking to increase sales (by better price discriminating in reaching and enticing price-sensitive shoppers). As more manufacturers and retailers join the platform, the online platform has a greater variety of discounts to offer consumers. With more consumers, the online platform can harvest even more personal data to identify relevant coupons and, based on the customer's price sensitivity, the magnitude of the discount. This in turn attracts more manufacturers and retailers to the platform. Not surprisingly, Coupons.com also identifies '[p]owerful network effects' as one of its 'key strengths':

> The large and growing base of retailers using our platform has allowed us to attract, retain and grow the digital promotion spending of leading [consumer packaged goods companies]. The breadth of our offerings from these leading brands enables us to attract and retain a growing and more diverse range of retailers, publishers and consumers.[20]

13.19 Fuelling these network effects is personal data. The company's 2014 annual report nicely captures the interplay of these data-driven network effects:

> We use the data flowing through our platform to understand shopper behavior and intent and use those insights for advertising targeting and analytics. Our data processing systems are able to provide consumer intent to various advertising networks and extend our reach, which effectively increases advertising sales. We can reach users through web, mobile and social channels. For example, we can target consumers on Facebook who have used a particular category of coupon with advertising for that category of product. The quality and real-time nature of our data network enables us to offer campaigns that exceed our clients' expectations, even as the number of their promotions increases. As our platform and network and audience grows, the value of our data and analytics increases.[21]

13.20 Because of the scale of its platform, the online company can tap into its 'significant differentiated data on the associated searches, activations, redemptions, shopping list building and social sharing of coupons' which it can use to target consumers with specific promotions by Procter & Gamble, other consumer packaged goods companies, and retailers.[22] As Coupons.com monetizes its data by influencing consumer purchasing behaviour (even when consumers are offline[23]), its market power increases. It may be easy for an entrant to create a website that delivers coupons, but

---

[20] Ibid, p 4.
[21] Ibid, p 6.
[22] Ibid, p 4.
[23] Coupons.com Presentation at Deutsche Bank Technology Conference, 16 September 2015, https://cc.talkpoint.com/deut001/091615a_ae/?entity=31_Q6GBLRJ (log-in required).

it lacks the personal data. Consequently, as the OECD observed, the data-driven network effects on the free side can spill over to the paid side, and each can reinforce the other: 'The reuse of data generates huge returns to scale and scope which lead to positive feedback loops in favour of the business on one side of the market, which in turn reinforces success in the other side(s) of the market.'[24]

4. Facebook

Facebook, we saw, exhibits traditional network effects on the free side (ie, as more **13.21** people use the social network, the utility of Facebook users increases and its appeal to potential users increases as people want to join the larger social network that has most of their family, friends, and acquaintances). About 1.01 billion people checked the social network at least once a day in September 2015.[25]

Facebook's growth in active users on the free side can spill over by attracting more **13.22** advertisers who want to reach these users. Here again data can amplify the network effect. First, Facebook does not create much, if any, original content. It relies on the free labour of its users to post information to attract others to the site. In August 2011, 'Facebook said the average user created 90 pieces of content a month, including news stories and photo albums'.[26] In 2014, users shared 50 billion pieces of content from other apps and websites.[27] Facebook noted how it was '"vital" to encourage a broad range of users to contribute content'.[28] Thus, when users slow down in providing data, Facebook nudges them. In the third quarter of 2015, people were not posting as much: '34% of Facebook users updated their status, and 37% shared their own photos, down from 50% and 59%, respectively, in the same period a year earlier'.[29] So Facebook began nudging people to post more. Using individuals' likes and location, Facebook began placing 'prompts related to ongoing events at the top of some users' news feeds, aiming to spur conversations'.[30] Facebook's effort to prod its users to post updates to attract others (and get them to post updates) seems to be working.[31]

---

[24] OECD, *Data-Driven Innovation*, above note 1, p 2.
[25] Deepa Seetharaman, 'Facebook Earnings Rise Despite Higher Costs: Revenue Jumps as Companies Spend More to Advertise Across the Social Network', *Wall Street Journal*, 4 November 2015, http://www.wsj.com/articles/facebook-earning-rise-despite-higher-costs-1446671622 (in its third quarter of 2015, Facebook had 1.55 billion people tap the social network at least once a month (up from 1.49 billion in the second quarter)).
[26] Deepa Seetharaman, 'Facebook Prods Users to Share a Bit More: Amount of New Content Posted Has Slipped, Leading Social Network to Try to Prompt Conversation', *Wall Street Journal*, 2 November 2015, http://www.wsj.com/articles/facebook-prods-users-to-share-a-bit-more-1446520723.
[27] Ibid.
[28] Ibid.
[29] Ibid.
[30] Ibid.
[31] Ibid.

13.23 Second, besides providing data to attract others to spend time on the social network, users (knowingly or not) provide the social network data so that advertisers can better target them with behavioural ads.[32] As the *New York Times* noted, '[e]verything you do on Facebook can be used by marketers.'[33] Indeed, the volume, velocity, variety, and value of personal data can accelerate significantly as the social network grows.

13.24 Third, many Facebook users, besides passively providing their personal data, effectively become endorsers when they 'like' a product, advertisement, or company. They can be part of the advertisement effort to induce others to buy, including their friends and family.[34] The more users toil on Facebook's platform, the more data they provide to attract other users to the social network, and the more likely they will help sell ads to themselves, their friends and family, and other Facebook users.[35]

13.25 Fourth, the overall volume and variety of the personal data, the President's Council of Advisors on Science and Technology found, can help advertisers identify trends and trendsetters:

> In the realm of commerce, it is well-understood that what a person's friends like or buy can influence what he or she might buy. For example, in 2010, it was reported that having one iPhone-owning friend makes a person three times more likely to own an iPhone than otherwise. A person with two iPhone-owning friends was five times more likely to have one. Such correlations emerge in social-network analysis and can be used to help predict product trends, tailor marketing campaigns towards products an individual may be more likely to want, and target customers (said to have higher 'network value') with a central role (and a large amount of influence) in a social network.[36]

---

[32] John Gantz and David Reinsel, 'Extracting Value from Chaos', International Data Corporation (IDC) View, June 2011, p 6, https://www.emc.com/collateral/analyst-reports/idc-extracting-value-from-chaos-ar.pdf ('Social media solutions such as Facebook, Foursquare, and Twitter are the newest new data sources. Essentially, they have built systems where consumers (consciously or unconsciously) are providing near continuous streams of data about themselves, and thanks to the "network effect" of successful sites, the total data generated can expand at rapid logarithmic rates.').

[33] Vindu Goel, 'Flipping the Switches on Facebook's Privacy Controls', *New York Times*, 29 January 2014, http://www.nytimes.com/2014/01/30/technology/personaltech/on-facebook-deciding-who-knows-youre-a-dog.html.

[34] Ibid.

[35] European Data Protection Supervisor (EDPS), *Privacy and Competitiveness in the Age of Big Data: The Interplay Between Data Protection, Competition Law and Consumer Protection in the Digital Economy*, Preliminary Opinion, March 2014, p 35, https://secure.edps.europa.eu/EDPSWEB/webdav/shared/Documents/Consultation/Opinions/2014/14-03-26_competition_law_big_data_EN.pdf ('Successful online providers persuade increasing numbers of customers to provide more personal information which increases the value of the service to advertisers, thus generating "network effects" whereby yet more customers are attracted to the service.').

[36] Executive Office of the President, President's Council of Advisors on Science and Technology, *Report to the President, Big Data and Privacy: A Technological Perspective*, May 2014, p 29, https://www.whitehouse.gov/sites/default/files/microsites/ostp/PCAST/pcast_big_data_and_privacy_-_may_2014.pdf.

As Facebook tells its investors, '[t]he size of our user base and our users' level of **13.26** engagement are critical to our success'.[37] Thus a key metric for Facebook is daily active users: 'Trends in the number of users affect our revenue and financial results by influencing the number of ads we are able to show, the value of our ads to marketers, the volume of Payments transactions, as well as our expenses and capital expenditures.'[38]

With Facebook prompting users to post data to attract others, and with over a bil- **13.27** lion people checking Facebook at least once a day in September 2015, Facebook's advertising revenue are increasing. In September 2015, Facebook had 2.5 million advertisers (25 per cent more than in February 2015), who seek to target 'specific groups of people and deliver ads to their news feed, especially on mobile phones'.[39] In its third quarter of 2015, Facebook's revenues rose to USD 4.5 billion, a 41 per cent increase from the same period a year earlier.[40] In its fourth quarter, Facebook's quarterly profit for the first time broke the USD 1 billion mark; mobile ads accounted for 80 per cent of Facebook's ad revenue, which climbed to USD 5.84 billion.[41] As one analyst commented, 'Facebook is your first port of call if you're a digital advertiser and if you have money to spend'.[42]

Thus, Facebook benefits from network effects on the demand side; it also benefits **13.28** on the supply side in collecting a greater *volume* and *variety* of data, which it can quickly analyse and use for advertising purposes and new products and services. Thus, both traditional and new forms of network effects can help the social network attain and maintain market power on both the 'free' and 'paid' side of its multi-sided platform. As the OECD observed, many 'data-driven services and platforms such as social networking sites are characterized by large network effects (demand side economies of scale) where the utility of the services increases over proportionately with the number of users', and this in turn 'reinforces the increasing returns to scale and scope on the supply side'.[43]

---

[37] Facebook Inc, 2014 Annual Report, p 9 ('Facebook 2014 Annual Report'), http://files. shareholder.com/downloads/AMDA-NJ5DZ/650609882x0xS1326801-15-6/1326801/filing.pdf. Facebook's average revenue per user (ARPU) has steadily increased since 2010. Statista, 'Facebook's Average Revenue per User from 2010 to 2014, by Region (in US Dollars)', http://www.statista. com/statistics/251328/facebooks-average-revenue-per-user-by-region/. In 2014, Facebook's worldwide ARPU was USD 9.45, an increase of 39% from 2013—with significant increases in the US and Canada (approximately 53%), Europe (44%), and Asia-Pacific (42%). Facebook 2014 Annual Report, p 38.

[38] Facebook 2014 Annual Report, above note 37, p 3.

[39] Seetharaman, above note 25.

[40] Ibid.

[41] Steve Rosenbush, 'The Morning Download: Facebook Results Show Soaring Influence of Mobile', *Wall Street Journal*, 28 January 2016, http://blogs.wsj.com/cio/2016/01/28/the-morning-download-facebook-results-show-soaring-influence-of-mobile/.

[42] Seetharaman, above note 25.

[43] OECD, *Data-Driven Innovation*, above note 1, p 2.

13.29 Professors Whittington and Hoofnagle suggest that consumers who provide information to social network services are making investments specific to the firms to which they provide information.[44] The firms have an incentive to engage in opportunistic behaviour, such as changing privacy policies or making such policies difficult to enforce.[45] And consumers may not easily exit these transactions and can rarely (if ever) reclaim their investment or transfer it elsewhere.[46] They argue that these characteristics create an online version of customer lock-in.[47]

5. Search engines

13.30 Search engines also reflect how the inflow of many users with heterogeneous search inquiries will attract a greater variety of advertisers to the platform prompting a snowball effect: more users generate more search queries, which generate more trial-and-error, which yields better search results, which attracts more users and advertisers to the search platform, which enables better profiling of users and greater likelihood of users clicking the ads, which generates more advertising revenue to enable the search engine to offer even more free services,[48] which enables consumers to spend more time on the company's platform, and which allows it 'to gather even more valuable data about consumer behaviour, and to further improve services, for (new) consumers as well as advertisers (on both sides of the market)'.[49]

13.31 Google and Yahoo! derive nearly all of their revenue from advertising.[50] For example, in 2013, 91 per cent of Google's revenues came from advertisers,[51] and 79 per cent of Yahoo!'s total revenue came from display and search advertising.[52] In 2014, 89 per cent of Google revenues came from advertising.[53]

---

[44] Jan Whittington and Chris Jay Hoofnagle, 'Unpacking Privacy's Price', 90 *North Carolina L Rev* (2012): p 135.

[45] Ibid, pp 134–6.

[46] Ibid, p 135.

[47] Ibid.

[48] OECD, *Data-Driven Innovation*, above note 1, p 29 (noting how these 'self-reinforcing effects may increase with the number of applications provided on a platform, e.g. bundling email, messaging, video, music and telephony as increasing returns to scope kicks in and even more information becomes available thanks to data linkage').

[49] Ibid, p 29; *see also* FTC, Bureau of Competition, *Report re Google Inc*, 8 August 2012, p 76 (discussing this 'virtuous cycle' and how it represents a 'significant barrier for any potential entrant').

[50] *Microsoft/Yahoo! Search*, above note 5, para 3.

[51] Google Inc, Annual Report Pursuant to Section 13 or 15(D) of the Securities Exchange Act of 1934 for the fiscal year ended December 31, 2013, p 9 ('Google 2013 Annual Report'), http://www.sec.gov/Archives/edgar/data/1288776/000128877614000020/goog2013123110-k.htm.

[52] Yahoo! Inc, Annual Report Pursuant to Section 13 or 15(D) of the Securities Exchange Act of 1934 for the fiscal year ended December 31, 2013, p 13, http://www.sec.gov/Archives/edgar/data/1011006/000119312514077321/d636872d10k.htm. '

[53] Google Inc, Annual Report Pursuant to Section 13 or 15(D) of the Securities Exchange Act of 1934 for the fiscal year ended December 31, 2014, p 7, http://www.sec.gov/Archives/edgar/data/1288776/000128877615000008/goog2014123110-k.htm.

The search engines' algorithms provide users with 'sponsored' results and **13.32** 'organic' results.[54] Most advertisers pay on a cost-per-click basis, whereby the advertiser pays the search engine when a user clicks on its sponsored search result.[55] Since they are paid only when users click on a 'sponsored search' result, search engines generate 'revenues primarily by delivering relevant, cost-effective online advertising'.[56] Indeed, the goal of Google's AdWords, its main auction-based advertising program, 'is to deliver ads that are so useful and relevant to search queries or web content that they are a form of information in their own right'.[57]

Here we see how data can amplify the network effects. Platforms compete for **13.33** advertisers on the return on investment they can deliver. One metric is how many users click the ad; another metric is how many people that click the ad buy the product.[58] As the company attracts more users on the free side of its platform (such as search, texting, video, email, mapping, etc), it also collects a greater variety of personal data to develop user profiles.[59] With detailed user profiles, the platform can better target users with personalized sponsored search results. As users spend more time on the platform, the company—besides collecting more data—has more opportunities to target users with behavioural ads across media (such as on their personal computers, smartphones, tablets, and, soon, household appliances) and across its expanding platform (such as free texting apps, maps, videos, etc).

Google's Waze, as we saw, relies on network effects to improve the quality of their **13.34** navigation apps. But the network effect can spill over to the advertising side. In attracting more users, the mapping app has more geo-location data for firms interested in location-based advertising on Waze or elsewhere.[60] Moreover, advertisers can target

---

[54] *Microsoft/Yahoo! Search*, above note 5, para 100.

[55] Google 2013 Annual Report, above note 51, p 53. Google also offers advertising on a cost-per-impression basis, whereby advertisers pay based on the number of times their ads display on Google websites and its Google Network Members' websites as specified by the advertisers. Ibid; *Microsoft/Yahoo! Search*, above note 5, paras 35, 45.

[56] Google 2013 Annual Report, above note 51, p 3; *Microsoft/Yahoo! Search*, above note 5, para 10; Andrea Amelio and Dimitrios Magos, 'Economic Background of the Microsoft/Yahoo! Case', 2 *Competition Policy Newsletter* (2010): p 50 (discussing how search platforms use a 'quality' score of an advertiser, that reflects the expected likelihood that users will click on the ad, also known as the Click Through Rate).

[57] Google 2013 Annual Report, above note 51, p 4.

[58] *Microsoft/Yahoo! Search*, above note 5, para 106.

[59] *See, eg, In re Google Inc*, 2013 WL 5423918, above note 7, p *2 (complaint alleging that although some Google apps users, whether through the educational programme or the partner programme, 'did not receive content-based ads', their emails were 'nevertheless intercepted to create user profiles').

[60] *See* AOL Inc, *How Waze Makes Money* [Video], http://on.aol.com/video/how-waze-makes-money-518485894.

users while driving, for example by telling them of nearby Taco Bells and other fast-food restaurants.[61]

13.35   The platform—in amassing more data on users' preferences, behaviour, and interests—can target users with behavioural ads that consumers will likelier click (which generates revenue for the platform on a cost-per-click basis) or watch a display ad (which generates revenue on a cost-per-impression basis).[62] As users click or watch more ads, the platform delivers significant value for advertisers, thereby attracting more advertisers who want to reach the increasing number of users likely to click their ads.[63] The platform becomes a must-have for advertisers.[64]

13.36   With a greater variety of advertisers on the paid side, users can benefit with more relevant sponsored search results. Advertisers can benefit in targeting specific users in the moments that matter for a purchasing decision.[65] Advertisers also can benefit when the search engine's broad platform of services (such as texting, video, etc) reduces the advertisers' fixed costs of managing multiple ad campaigns.

13.37   The platform can benefit several ways. First, its advertising revenues increase. Second, increasing the variety of advertisers enables the platform to further fine-tune its behavioural advertising. It can, for example, identify relevant sponsored search results for particular search queries, and thereby increase its advertising revenue and profits. Third, as more users and advertisers are drawn to its platform of products, the search engine can invest its increasing profits in acquiring (or developing) other free products and services, which enable users to spend more time on

---

[61] 'Taco Bell Promotes New Appetizers With Digital & Social Media, Custom Apps', The Realtime Report, 26 December 2012, http://therealtimereport.com/2012/12/26/taco-bell-promotes-new-appetizers-with-digital-social-media-custom-apps/.

[62] Teresa Vecchi, Jerome Vidal, and Viveca Fallenius, 'The Microsoft/Yahoo! Search Business Case', 2 *Competition Policy Newsletter* (2010): p 46 (noting that the search business 'is subject to network effects in that scale can improve the quality of the search results and the quality of the matching of the ads with the queries').

[63] Pamela Jones Harbour and Tara Isa Koslov, 'Section 2 in a Web 2.0 World: An Expanded Vision of Relevant Product Markets', 76 *Antitrust LJ* (2010): p 781; Public Citizen, *Mission Creep-y*, above note 6, p 10 ('The more narrowly and accurately Google can target an ad to a user to match her interests, the more it can charge advertisers for each view or click').

[64] *Microsoft/Yahoo! Search*, above note 5, para 157 (all of the advertisers responding to the market investigation highlighted that Google's query volume was one of the main reasons why Google was a 'must have' for search advertising campaigns); ibid, para 163 ('Higher query volume in turn generate ad inventory.'); Vecchi et al, above note 62, p 44.

[65] Google 2013 Annual Report, above note 51, p 25 ('The main focus of our advertising programs is to help businesses reach people in the moments that matter across all devices with smarter ads that are relevant to their intent and context, reflecting our commitment to constantly improve their overall web experience.'); comScore, *The 2015 U.S. Mobile App Report*, 22 September 2015, p 52, https://www.comscore.com/Insights/Presentations-and-Whitepapers/2015/The-2015-US-Mobile-App-Report (finding that '[m]obile ads caused point lifts 2–3x greater than ads on desktop across four key brand metrics and performed strongest in bottom-funnel metrics, such as intent to buy and likelihood to recommend. Less ad clutter and proximity to point of purchase may be driving better effectiveness for mobile ads.').

the platform and the platform to collect even more personal data, which provides more opportunities to target users with more tailored behavioural ads from the growing list of advertisers. The platform also has more money to invest in gateways to the Internet to increase the likelihood of consumers using (and spending time on) its platform of services. This includes ensuring that its products (including search engine) are the default options, such as paying rival browsers to set its search engine as the default option.[66] It includes developing a mobile phone operating system, which is pre-loaded with the company's own browser (to better track which websites consumers are visiting), video app, mapping and navigation app, email, texting app, and search engine. The platform will continue to expand to other ventures, such as driverless cars, which besides collecting more data on its users' behaviour, enables the passengers to spend more time on the platform, and be targeted with ads. It allows ventures into the Internet of Things, to collect the personal data from household appliances and deliver behavioural ads on thermostats, doorbells, refrigerators, etc.

Then FTC Commissioner Harbour noted how her fellow commissioners ignored this data-driven network effect when analysing the *Google/DoubleClick* merger: **13.38**

> On the search side, Google is able to charge a premium for search advertising because Google has the highest volume of searches. More searches translate to more incoming data, which enables Google to enhance the quality of the underlying algorithms used to process searches and match them to relevant advertisements. Google's search methodology and advertisement targeting become even better as consumers use Google's search engine more. Improved searches drive still more traffic to the site, which further increases the value of search advertising on Google.[67]

Commissioner Harbour asked, 'If advertisers and publishers have to channel their online advertising through Google/DoubleClick in order to access the best dataset that supports targeted advertising, will any other firms have the ability or incentive to compete meaningfully in this market?'[68]

We have seen how data can amplify and reinforce the network effects on the free and paid side of multi-sided platforms. Here again big platforms will likely become bigger; entry barriers will increase, which help the leading company attain and maintain its dominant position. We reflect on the implications in the next chapter. **13.39**

---

[66] Google, for example, is the default engine on Apple's Safari Internet browser. Google reportedly paid Apple USD 82 million in 2009, and USD 1 billion in 2013 and 2014 for this partnership. 'Apple Working on Its Own Search Engine; Aims to Take on Google: Report', IBN Live, 10 February 2015, http://ibnlive.in.com/news/apple-working-on-its-own-search-engine-aims-to-take-on-google-report/527597-11.html; Joel Rosenblatt and Adam Satariano, 'Google Paid Apple $1 Billion to Keep Search Bar on iPhone', BloombergBusiness, 21 January 2016, http://www.bloomberg.com/news/articles/2016-01-22/google-paid-apple-1-billion-to-keep-search-bar-on-iphone.

[67] FTC, *In the Matter of Google/Double-Click*, above note 6, p 6 (internal footnotes omitted).

[68] Ibid, p 8 (internal footnotes omitted).

14

REFLECTIONS ON DATA-DRIVEN NETWORK EFFECTS

14.01 If competition authorities and courts consider only traditional entry barriers, then they may easily conclude that online markets are easy to enter. The European Commission in the Facebook/WhatsApp merger, for example, identified five factors that suggested low entry barriers:

> First, all consumer communications apps are offered for free or at a very low price. Second, all consumer communications apps are easily downloadable on smartphones and can coexist on the same handset without taking much capacity. Third, once consumer communications apps are installed on a device, users can pass from one to another in no-time. Fourth, consumer communications apps are normally characterised by simple user interfaces so that learning costs of switching to a new app are minimal for consumers. Fifth, information about new apps is easily accessible given the ever increasing number of reviews of consumer communications apps on app stores.[1]

14.02 This may be true, but on account of the four network effects, the market may be difficult to enter and susceptible to dominance by one or two firms. Network effects are not necessarily bad. After all, users' utility can increase as others join the platform. But these data-driven network effects raise several competition issues.

A. Ten Implications of Data-Driven Network Effects

14.03 First, the increasing returns to scale from data can foster a positive feedback loop, whereby an increase in the *volume* of data (eg, traffic and road conditions; search queries) by a diverse population group (*variety*) can enable the company in near-real time (*velocity*) to increase the *value* of its services and products (relevancy of sponsored ads/traffic patterns), which in turn attracts more users and advertisers.

---

[1] *Facebook/WhatsApp* (Case Comp/M.7217), Commission Decision C(2014) 7239 final, 3 October 2014, para 109 (footnotes omitted).

Second, the quality of the algorithm may be less important than accessing a lot of **14.04** data.[2] As Google's Alon Halevy, Peter Norvig, and Fernando Pereira observed, 'invariably, simple models and a lot of data trump more elaborate models based on less data'.[3] An entrant might have a superior algorithm. But only a few platforms—like Google's, Apple's, Facebook's, and Amazon's—will have the scale of users and their data and thus the competitive advantage. Their many users, when interacting with the platform's self-learning algorithm, can ramp up the quality of the algorithm's results. For example, Facebook users post a lot of pictures: '4.4 million labeled faces harvested from the Facebook pages of 4030 users'.[4] Facebook took advantage of this data to train its algorithm's facial recognition capacity: 'The more faces the system trains on, the more accurate the guesses'.[5] Its DeepFace machine-learning system is now as accurate as humans in recognizing faces with 'an accuracy of 97.35%—a full 27% better than the rest of the field'.[6] Thus, the disruptive innovation here is likely to come from the same firms, whose dominance is maintained in part through these data-driven network effects.

Accordingly, companies that operate and control the platform can collect a large **14.05** volume and variety of personal data that may have significant value. Having control over and being able to quickly analyse the personal data at times will provide the platform operator a critical competitive advantage. The technology for the app may be off the shelf. But data is the key input—whether traffic data for Waze, search inquiries for Google, Bing, and Yahoo!, or personal data for Coupons.com, Facebook, and Google.

Third, the data-driven network effects in these online markets can amplify the **14.06** stakes of gaining and losing users. Depending on the network effect, the loss of users can degrade the product's quality and reduce the likelihood of attracting (and retaining) users, advertisers, or sellers. With each user the platform acquires relative to its competitors, a quality gap emerges. If the quality differences become apparent to users, the feedback loop can accelerate—attracting both new users and users of rival products.

---

[2] Viktor Mayer-Schönberger and Kenneth Cukier, *Big Data: A Revolution That Will Transform How We Live, Work, and Think* (London: John Murray, 2013), pp 36–9 (discussing how more data trumps better algorithms in the area of better language processing).

[3] Alon Halevy, Peter Norvig, and Fernando Pereira, 'The Unreasonable Effectiveness of Data', *IEEE Intelligent Systems*, March/April 2009, p 9, http://research.google.com/pubs/archive/35179. pdf ('Similar observations have been made in every other application of machine learning to Web data: simple n-gram models or linear classifiers based on millions of specific features perform better than elaborate models that try to discover general rules. In many cases there appears to be a threshold of sufficient data.').

[4] John Bohannon, 'Unmasked: Facial Recognition Software Could Soon ID You in Any Photo', 347 *Science* (30 January 2015): pp 492, 493.

[5] Ibid, p 493.

[6] Ibid.

14.07 To illustrate, let us compare the toothpaste and search engine markets. Both can be characterized as zero-sum competition. But the stakes differ. For toothpaste, the winner captures a sale and extra profit; the losers lose a potential toothpaste sale. If you purchase Colgate instead of Crest, the quality of either toothpaste is unaffected. But in markets with data-driven network effects, such as search engines, social networks, and community-sourced navigation apps, the winner not only gains potential revenue, for example when the user clicks on sponsored ads; that user's data actually helps improve the quality of the product itself (such as the navigation app or Google's or Facebook's self-learning algorithms), which affects the product's likelihood of attracting future users and advertisers. So the stakes are much greater each time Bing or Yahoo! loses a search query to Google: they lose the potential advertising revenue (ie, fewer users clicking on sponsored ads); they lose an opportunity for their algorithms to experiment (learning by doing), which can adversely affect the quality of their search results; and they lose consumer data, which reduces their ability to personalize search results and target users with behavioural ads. With each net loss, the quality gap widens. So the more people 'google', the less attractive Bing and Yahoo! become to users and advertisers.

14.08 Fourth, quality under the data-driven network effects will continually improve as more people use the product, but the incremental increase in quality will taper off as the sample size (N) approaches *all*. The debate will turn to what is the minimum efficient scale in that industry. The minimum efficient scale can be quite large in some industries. The competition agencies, for example, believed that neither Microsoft nor Yahoo! were at the minimum efficient scale at the time of their joint venture. In September 2009, according to comScore, Americans conducted 13.8 billion searches, of which Google sites accounted for 9 billion searches, followed by Yahoo! sites (2.6 billion), Microsoft sites (1.3 billion), Ask Network (541 million), and AOL LLC (416 million).[7] Thus, even though Yahoo! and Microsoft averaged over 80 and 40 million searches per day, respectively, they were still at a disadvantage.

14.09 Fifth, the scale curve may not be uniform. For search, the scale curve depends not only on the number of queries per se, but on other factors, such as the representativeness of the search users, the type of search inquiry ('tail' versus popular), and its nature (seeking an objective, clear-cut answer, such as *number of days in a year* versus an open-ended inquiry). Thus, the search engine needs a robust sample that reflects the universe of potential users, not simply of a particular kind of search or from a particular demographic. Likewise, Waze, to accurately depict road and

---

[7] comScore, 'comScore Releases September 2009 US Search Engine Rankings', Press Release, 14 October 2009, http://www.comscore.com/Insights/Press-Releases/2009/10/com Score-Releases-September-2009-U.S.-Search-Engine-Rankings.

traffic conditions, will need enough drivers on both the popular roads and highways as well as the less frequented, but important, secondary roads.

Sixth, the data-driven network effect in some markets will be localized, while in other markets can be leveraged across a broader region. If many New Yorkers use Waze, this does not benefit those stuck in traffic in Los Angeles. But for search engines, these network effects can be broader geographically. Californians benefit when others in the US use the same search engine. Although people can access Microsoft Bing, Yahoo!, and Google anywhere in the world (where the site is not blocked by the government), companies may be unable to fully leverage the network effects across languages; users likely want the search results in their own language. For example, in China, Baidu accounts for over 80 per cent of the search engine market by revenue.[8] Google has been unable to leverage its dominance in Europe and the US to China; nor has Baidu been able to leverage its dominance to Europe or the United States. **14.10**

A dominant search engine can seek to leverage its quality advantage across countries. Locals in a particular country may better identify which resources on the web are more relevant for a particular search query (such as finding images of a place, object, animal, or person within their country). So when one searches on Google for images of Big Ben, one can benefit with better images—thanks to the search activity of UK residents, where Google also dominates.[9] Users from different countries can help with other applications, such as Google Translate, which encourages bilingual users to edit and correct translations into their native language.[10] Search queries at times transcend local preferences (such as searching relevant academic papers through Google Scholar). Finally, the search engines, the European Commission found, 'strive to index the whole internet and are accessible from anywhere in the world'.[11] Thus local businesses and websites are likelier to use the dominant search engine's tools to index their website (and devote efforts to optimize their ranking for relevant search inquiries), thereby lowering the costs of the dominant search engine to find new websites and index them. **14.11**

Seventh, there is the potential, as one competition authority found, for the market to ' "tip", so whilst there may still be competition from other suppliers, there is one leading supplier'.[12] Thus in markets where no platform is yet dominant, competition **14.12**

---

[8] iResearch Consulting Group, *Q1 2015 China Search Engine Revenues Attain 15.64 Bn Yuan*, 8 June 2015, http://www.iresearchchina.com/views/6477.html.

[9] *See* The E Word, *Search Engine Market*, http://theeword.co.uk/info/search_engine_market/ (accessed 12 November 2015).

[10] *See generally* Google Translate: Translate Community, https://translate.google.com.au/community?source=desktop-new-promo.

[11] *Microsoft/Yahoo! Search Business* (Case Comp/M.5727), Commission Decision C(2010) 1077, 18 February 2010, para 96.

[12] UK Office of Fair Trading (OFT), *ME/6167/13: Completed Acquisition by Motorola Mobility Holding (Google, Inc.) of Waze Mobile Limited*, 17 December 2013, para 44 n 28 ('OFT,

can be fierce to prevent the market from tipping to a rival. Search engines will compete to attract users to their platform and retain existing users on their platform and monetize (or generate revenues from) the traffic on their platform.[13]

14.13   Eighth, once the market tips, it will be harder for smaller competitors to scale up to dethrone the dominant platform.[14] To illustrate, suppose a search engine only has one thousand daily queries. Its algorithms have less data to learn and predict responsive search results (other than more straightforward inquiries) and fewer related searches that it can suggest to users. With poorer quality search results, it will unlikely attract many users from the larger search engines; with fewer users, the search engine will attract fewer advertisers, and will have fewer relevant 'paid' search results to offer, which means fewer occasions for users to click on paid search results and less advertising revenue and profits to expand its platform.

14.14   Ninth, since data-driven network effects will not necessarily reward the first mover in every market, the incentives for both anticompetitive and procompetitive behaviour increase. When the stakes are so great, competition can be fierce, and consumers can benefit. But the incentives also increase for online platforms to resort to anticompetitive practices and mergers to tip the market in their favour. The feedback loop can reinforce dominance and prevent the sales of a rival's platform from gaining momentum. Now the strong will likely get stronger both on the free and advertising sides of the multi-sided market.[15]

14.15   Tenth, these four network effects (traditional, scale of data/trial-by-error, scope of data, and spill-over) provide dominant online firms' breathing room to engage in anticompetitive behaviour to illegally maintain their monopoly.

Google/Waze'), http://webarchive.nationalarchives.gov.uk/20140402142426/http:/www.oft.gov.uk/shared_oft/mergers_ea02/2013/motorola.pdf.

[13] Google Inc, Annual Report Pursuant to Section 13 or 15(D) of the Securities Exchange Act of 1934 for the fiscal year ended December 31, 2014, p 15 ('Google 2014 Annual Report'), http://www.sec.gov/Archives/edgar/data/1288776/000128877615000008/goog2014123110-k.htm.

[14] UK Competition and Markets Authority, *The Commercial Use of Consumer Data: Report on the CMA's Call for Information*, June 2015, para 3.51, https://www.gov.uk/government/uploads/system/uploads/attachment_data/file/435817/The_commercial_use_of_consumer_data.pdf (receiving 'a number of comments from firms that did not have access to consumers to collect data directly themselves, and commented that a lack of access to data at a particular scale, or of sufficient breadth to equal that of an incumbent was a barrier. Respondents' comments related to a variety of markets including online search, advertising and marketing. One respondent noted that the challenges posed by a lack of access to data were magnified by the two-sided nature of the markets and the presence of large established firms.').

[15] Organisation for Economic Co-operation and Development (OECD), *Data-Driven Innovation for Growth and Well-being: Interim Synthesis Report*, October 2014, p 58, http://www.oecd.org/sti/inno/data-driven-innovation-interim-synthesis.pdf (concluding that the feedback loops, 'which are also characteristic for markets with network effects, finally reinforce the market position of the service provider and have a tendency to lead to its market dominance or at least to market concentration').

To illustrate, let consider how Uber and Lyft might rely on exclusivity provi- **14.16** sions that prohibit sellers from using rival platforms. In 2015, drivers can use both Uber's and Lyft's car service app. Indeed, a driver can switch between platforms throughout the day, picking up a passenger using Uber at noon, and someone using Lyft an hour later. Suppose Uber becomes the dominant trans- portation app in one geographic market, say Nashville, Tennessee. To main- tain its dominance, suppose Uber also requires drivers on its platform not to drive for any competing platforms, such as Lyft. Thus drivers can only pick up Uber passengers.

This exclusivity provision could harm not only competitors but ultimately users. **14.17** Although customers could continue to choose any transportation app, they will likely choose the one with the best mix of wait time, service, and price. If Uber has more drivers (on account of its having more users), a particular user will likely remain with Uber if its prices remain competitive, its service is good, and the wait time is minimal. Drivers accordingly would likely stick with Uber, if most custom- ers use that app. The other transportation service apps, like Lyft, may continue courting customers and drivers. But Uber could match their discounts, and still have an advantage in terms of wait time (with more drivers).

If most users continue to use Uber, then the rivals will have a harder time recruiting **14.18** drivers. Drivers would have to forego the opportunity of picking up Uber custom- ers, who constitute the lion's share of potential business. As the rival transportation services apps have greater difficulty in retaining and recruiting drivers, they will have fewer drivers. With fewer drivers on the road, the existing users' average wait time will increase, thereby reducing the app's appeal among potential users. After all, why wait 20 minutes for a Lyft car, when an Uber car is only five minutes away? More users migrate to Uber, which makes it harder for competitors to retain drivers, quickening the downward cycle.

Once its rivals are weakened, Uber could exercise its market power. One way **14.19** is to squeeze from the drivers a greater share of their revenues. The drivers will likely protest. But they have fewer outside options. Unless they formed a union, they would unlikely undertake joint action, such as collectively agreeing among themselves to boycott Uber and migrate to a competitor. (Indeed, a group boycott may subject the drivers to antitrust liability.) No driver could afford to unilater- ally switch to any rival in order to punish Uber. On the user side, Uber may ex- ercise market power along less visible, non-price parameters. For example, it may collect their geo-location data even when they are not using the app, and their contact data, and use that information for advertising purposes.[16]

---

[16] Uber, Privacy Statement, 15 July 2015, https://www.uber.com/legal/privacy/users/en.

B. Why Controlling the Operating System Gives the Platform a Competitive Advantage Over an Independent App

14.20   As the above ten points reflect, the network effects encourage a data arms race. But not everyone starts from the same starting line. Companies that control an operating system with a large installed base of users—such as Google's Android and Apple's iOS for smartphones—will often have an inherent data (and competitive) advantage.

14.21   To illustrate, let us consider Waze, Google, and Apple. All three offer navigation apps for free. But, unlike Google's or Apple's map applications, Waze was not pre-installed on smartphones which, the UK competition authority found, placed it at a competitive disadvantage:

> ... the strongest competitive constraints in the market may be expected from applications which are "native" and have access to a large user base. Integration of a map application into the operating system creates opportunities for operating system developers to use their own or affiliated services (for example search engines and social networks) to improve the experience of users and it allows for the collection of real-time traffic information.[17]

There are several reasons why controlling the operating system gives the platform a data-advantage over an independent app.

14.22   The independent app has to get on the smartphone. One important gateway is through the platform's app store, such as Apple's App Store and Google Play. Apps, such as Disconnect that threaten the platform's advertising-based revenue model, can be kicked out of the store, making it harder for users to find and download the app.[18] Thus the platform operator, in denying access, can effectively kill an app.

14.23   Even when the app, along with millions of other apps, is available in Apple's App Store and Google Play, the dominant operating system developer benefits from status quo bias. The user still has to know of Waze, find it in the app store, download it, and use it. In contrast, Google through its licensing agreements with smartphone makers and Apple in manufacturing its iPhone have their mapping app pre-installed on the smartphone. Having the mapping app pre-installed increases the likelihood

---

[17] OFT, *Google/Waze*, above note 12, para 57.
[18] Complaint of Disconnect, Inc, Regarding Google's Infringement of Article 102 TFEU Through Bundling into the Android Platform and the Related Exclusion of Competing Privacy and Security Technology (Case Comp/40.099), June 2015, https://assets.documentcloud.org/documents/2109044/disconnect-google-antitrust-complaint.pdf.

that consumers will use the default option, even when another app is one or two clicks away.

We do not mean to overplay status quo bias. Many consumers are more comfortable **14.24** downloading apps in 2015 than they were in the early 2000s, when the Commission found that Microsoft abused its dominant position in the personal computer operating system market by tying its Windows Media Player product with its Windows PC operating system.[19] But pre-installing an app on an Android or Apple smartphone gives the app immediate access to a large user base (and the positive feedback loop that can arise from it).

Moreover, status quo bias is likelier when the operating system developer integrates **14.25** its pre-installed app with the platform's other services, such as its search engine and browser. By integrating its mapping app with other pre-loaded apps on the smartphone, the operating system developer can make switching more burdensome to users. For example, Apple's voice-driven personal assistant software Siri can help drivers navigate to their destination. But Siri automatically connects with Apple Maps.[20] So if one wants to use Siri while driving, one is unlikely to turn to MapQuest or Waze, but instead will rely on Apple Maps. Thus combining the company's map application with other products (such as search results and social networks) can increase the likelihood that users stick with the default option. Another option is to start with an open platform and then close it after achieving dominance, which is what Google is alleged to have done with Android.[21]

Consumers are unlikely to actively provide traffic information to multiple turn-by- **14.26** turn navigation apps. They will likely provide traffic information to either Waze or another community-sourced mapping app, not both.[22] For active data collection, the operating system can make it easier for smartphone users to report traffic information for its pre-installed navigation app, as opposed to other apps. Apple, in 2014, for example, was working on developing Siri, so that users can provide and receive traffic alerts in real-time.[23]

---

[19] European Commission, 'Microsoft Case: The Commission Investigation', http://ec.europa.eu/competition/sectors/ICT/microsoft/investigation.html.

[20] Fred Zahradnik, 'Getting the Most from Siri for Navigation, GPS, and Location-based Services: Road Testing the Apple iPhone 4S Siri Personal Assistant Software', About Tech, http://gps.about.com/od/mobilephonegps/a/Siri-GPS-Navigation-Travel.htm.

[21] Fair Search, The Google Playbook, http://fairsearch.org/google-playbook-open-dominate-close/.

[22] *TomTom/Tele Atlas* (Case Comp/M.4854), Commission Decision C(2008) 1859 [2008] OJ C 237/53, p 25.

[23] Jordan Kahn, 'Apple Maps to Expand Community Crowdsourcing Features, Siri + Passbook Integration', 9to5Mac, http://9to5mac.com/2014/12/04/apple-maps-crowdsourcing-siri-passbook-feedback/ (reporting how Apple was developing its frameworks and plugins to enable its Apple Maps to 'integrate deeply and seamlessly with parts of the system such as Siri and Passbook, to extend and enhance the feedback experience').

14.27 For passive data collection, operating system developers have an inherent advantage over independent apps. Companies can acquire geo-location data from one's computer, smartphone, or any type of radio or network-connection-enabled device.[24] The geo-location data identifies the phone's or computer's actual physical location. Operating systems already capture users' geo-location data for various uses, such as automatically tagging the location of photos or helping with searches queries (such as *good restaurants near me*). The company that controls the operating system and these other apps (such as photo, browser, and search engine) automatically collects their users' geo-location data, regardless of which mapping app the user primarily uses. Thus Apple and Google will likely have greater access to, and collect more of, smartphone users' trace data (such as tracking the smartphone user's geo-location) than independent app developers. They can use the trace data for, among other things, real-time traffic information.

14.28 To illustrate, suppose 1 per cent of Apple iPhone users primarily rely on MapQuest Navigation App and 2 per cent rely on Waze.[25] While MapQuest and Waze collect a lot of geo-location data, they are at a disadvantage relative to Apple, which can collect 100 per cent of its smartphone users' geo-location data. On the other hand, Waze and MapQuest, unlike Apple, can collect data from Android users; nonetheless, depending on their share of Google users for particular cities, the independent apps may still be at a disadvantage. Google has a significant data-advantage over independent navigation app developers, as it too can collect 100 per cent of the geo-location data from Android users as well as from those Apple iPhone users who enable location services for Google Maps app.[26] So whatever passive data that MapQuest and Waze collect from their app users, Google and Apple will likely have a greater volume and variety of data. Moreover, users may opt to not disclose their geo-location when the navigation app is closed, but opt for security reasons (such as to locate one's smartphone) to allow the operating system to collect their geo-location data all (or most of) the time.

---

[24] ISACA, *Geolocation: Risk, Issues, and Strategies* (2011), http://www.isaca.org/Groups/Professional-English/wireless/GroupDocuments/Geolocation_WP.pdf.

[25] One statistic gave information on 'the most popular mobile apps worldwide as of third quarter 2013, ranked by the percentage of global smartphone users who have accessed the app during the past month'. Neither Waze nor MySpace was among the 17 apps listed, with the 17th having a 3% share. Statista, 'Most Popular Mobile Social Apps Worldwide as of 4th Quarter 2013, Sorted by Reach', http://www.statista.com/statistics/263919/most-popular-mobile-apps-worldwide-sorted-by-reach/.

[26] Chris Foresman, 'Google Faces $50 Million Lawsuit over Android Location Tracking', *Ars Technica*, 1 May 2011, http://arstechnica.com/tech-policy/2011/04/google-faces-50-million-lawsuit-over-android-location-tracking/.

C. Independent App Developers' Dependence on Google and Apple

Developers may compete to get their smartphone app out first and for free to scale **14.29** up quicker than rivals and benefit from these data-driven network effects. This strategy is inherently risky. The company incurs significant development and investment costs upfront to offer the product or service for free, with the hope that its app will attract enough users and data to monetize for advertising purposes.[27] This strategy is even riskier when the independent app will likely compete with the apps pre-loaded on the operating system and integrated with other pre-loaded apps (such as the browser and search engine).

So we can see why Waze had several disadvantages under these data-driven net- **14.30** work effects: it was an independent, stand-alone app competing against Apple's and Google's pre-installed apps on their popular mobile operating systems; its mapping quality depended on reaching sufficient scale of users and accessing their geo-location data; and its viability depended on the amount of breathing room Apple and Google provided.

Waze was not alone. Independent apps Uber and Lyft must wonder to what extent **14.31** Google and Apple will grant them breathing room to develop their platforms on Android and iOS (and rely on their mapping technologies). Indeed, it would be unsurprising if Google extended its super-platform into this space—given its mapping technology, its investment in driverless cars, and the attractiveness in collecting additional valuable user data (and targeting them with advertisements). Uber's acquisition of Microsoft's mapping technology may be seen as an interim defensive measure.[28]

D. How Google Benefits from These Network Effects

If the controller of the operating system has several competitive advantages over **14.32** many independent app developers, why don't more independent apps launch their own operating systems? Why doesn't Uber displace Google and Apple by

---

[27] *See* OFT, *Google/Waze*, above note 12, para 20 (noting 'that, although some suppliers of mobile applications provide their applications for free, these suppliers are actively competing to attract users (and hence advertisers)', that 'an important early stage in the development of mobile applications, such as those of the parties, is often to build a sufficient user base', and that this 'occurs before seeking to monetise the user base. As a result, significant development and investment is made up-front before advertising revenues may be generated in later periods').

[28] Ben Popper, 'Uber Acquires Mapping Tech and Talent from Microsoft: Around 100 Bing Engineers Are Headed to Uber', *The Verge*, 29 June 2015, http://www.theverge.com/2015/6/29/8863687/uber-acquires-mapping-data-tech-and-talent-from-microsoft-bing.

coming out with its own mobile operating system, on which its navigation app is integrated with other apps? As the EU and US courts found in *Microsoft* the operating system itself is subject to network effects. The more people that use a software operating platform, 'the more there will be invested in developing products compatible with that platform, which, in turn reinforces the popularity of that platform with users'.[29]

14.33 Thus it is hard for Uber and other independent app developers to enter the operating system market. The Federal Trade Commission (FTC) thought otherwise in 2010 when it did not challenge Google's acquisition of AdMob, which combined the two leading mobile advertising networks. The FTC believed that entry into the mobile operating system market was likely:

> [A]s has been reported in the financial press, a number of firms appear to be developing or acquiring smartphone platforms to better compete against Apple's iPhone and Google's Android. Because of the importance of advertising-supported content to the success of smartphone platforms, these firms would have a strong incentive to facilitate competition among mobile advertising networks, including through self-supply.[30]

The FTC predicted wrongly. Apple and Google continue to dominate the mobile operating system market. No meaningful entry has occurred. For new shipments of smartphones, Google's Android continued, as of 2015, to dominate (80.7 per cent of worldwide shipments), with Apple trailing (17.7 per cent of shipments), and the remainder collectively comprising 1.5 per cent of shipments.[31] Of all smartphones and tablets currently in use as of February 2016, Google's Android is the leader (59.65 per cent), followed by Apple (32.28 per cent).[32]

14.34 Network effects helped Android become the biggest operating system for mobile devices. Network effects also helped Google become the largest search engine, the largest video platform (YouTube), and the largest mapping app

---

[29] Case T-201/04 *Microsoft Corp v Comm'n* [2007] ECR II-3601, para 106; *see also United States v Microsoft Corp*, 253 F3d 34, 49 (US Ct of Apps (DC Cir), 2001) (discussing network effects in dynamic technological markets).

[30] Statement of the Federal Trade Commission Concerning Google/AdMob, FTC File No 101-0031, 21 May 2010, p 2 ('FTC Google/AdMob Statement'), https://www.ftc.gov/sites/default/files/documents/closing_letters/google-inc./admob-inc/100521google-admobstmt.pdf.

[31] Gartner Inc, 'Gartner Says Worldwide Smartphone Sales Grew 9.7 Percent in Fourth Quarter of 2015', Press Release, 18 February 2016, http://www.gartner.com/newsroom/id/3215217; *see also* IDC, Smartphone OS Market Share 2015 Q2, http://www.idc.com/prodserv/smartphone-os-market-share.jsp; comScore, 'comScore Reports April 2014 US Smartphone Subscriber Market Share', Press Release, 3 June 2014, http://www.comscore.com/Insights/Press-Releases/2014/6/comScore-Reports-April-2014-US-Smartphone-Subscriber-Market-Share.

[32] Netmarketshare, Mobile/Tablet Top Operating System Share Trend—April, 2015 to February, 2016, https://www.netmarketshare.com/operating-system-market-share.aspx?qprid=9&qpcustomb=1.

Table 14.1 **Top ten smartphone apps of adult US mobile media users**
              (iOS and Android)

1	Facebook (Mobile App)	74.1%
2	**Google Play (Mobile App)***	**50.9%**
3	YouTube (Mobile App)	49.7%
4	**Google Search (Mobile App)**	**48.3%**
5	Pandora Radio (Mobile App)	44.9%
6	**Gmail (Mobile App)**	**41.6%**
7	**Google Maps (Mobile App)**	**41.5%**
8	Yahoo! Stocks (Mobile App)	30.0%
9	Instagram (Mobile App)	29.3%
10	Facebook Messenger (Mobile App)	26.7%

* Google apps are in bold.

Source: comScore, 'comScore Reports April 2014 US Smartphone Subscriber Market Share', Press Release, 3 June 2014, http://www.comscore.com/Insights/Press-Releases/2014/6/comScore-Reports-April-2014-US-Smartphone-Subscriber-Market-Share; *see also* comScore, 'The 2015 U.S. Mobile App Report', p 19 (2015) (Google controlling 5 of the top 10 apps, based on unique visitors).

(Google Maps). As shown in Table 14.1, of the top ten smartphone apps of adult US mobile media users (iOS and Android platforms), Google in April 2014 controlled half.

One 2014 survey of nearly 2,000 US smartphone users asked them about the time **14.35** spent on apps they downloaded. Users spent most of their time on Facebook apps (13 per cent) and Google apps (12 per cent).[33] That figure under-represented Google as it excluded the time spent on Google apps pre-loaded on its Android system.

Controlling the largest online platform, Google is considered the world's largest **14.36** media owner. According to one estimate of 2013 media revenues, which include advertising revenues and other revenues generated by businesses that support advertising, such as circulation revenues, Google was 136 per cent larger than the second-largest media owner Disney, and 'bigger than Disney and the third-largest media owner, Comcast, combined'.[34]

---

[33] Alistair Barr, 'Google Mobile Apps Grab Almost as Much User Time as Facebook's Apps', *Wall Street Journal* Digits blog, 29 June 2015, http://blogs.wsj.com/digits/2015/06/29/google-mobile-apps-grab-almost-as-much-user-time-as-facebooks-apps/.

[34] Nathalie Tadena, 'Google Expands Lead as World's Largest Media Owner', *Wall Street Journal* CMO Today blog, 11 May 2015, http://blogs.wsj.com/cmo/2015/05/11/google-expands-lead-as-worlds-largest-media-owner/.

14.37 Google's online advertising revenue far outdistances Facebook, Yahoo!, and Microsoft.[35] Google's net income in 2014 was USD 14.4 billion.[36] Google was forecasted to get '$2 of every $5 marketers spend in 2015 on digital advertising in the United States'.[37] Google's search advertising revenue was forecasted 'to reach $19.21 billion in 2015, or 72.4% of net US search ad revenue'.[38] Google also represents nearly one-third of net mobile ad revenue.[39] As Figure 14.1 reflects, Google's advertising revenue has increased significantly.

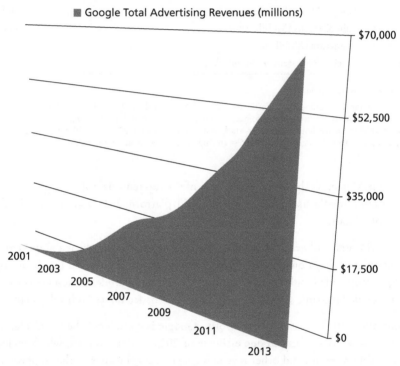

Figure 14.1 Growth in Google's total advertising revenue

Source: Google Inc, Investor Relations: 2015 Financial Tables, https://investor.google.com/financial/tables.html.

---

[35] Overall, in 2013, Google was 'expected to capture 33.2% of the world's $117 billion in digital ad spending, up from 31.5% in 2012', far ahead of Facebook (5% of the market, up from 4.1% in 2012), Yahoo! (3.1%, down from 3.4% in 2012), and Microsoft (1.8% in 2013, up from 1.6% in 2012). Amir Efrati, 'In Online Ads There's Google—Then Everybody Else,' *Wall Street Journal* Digits blog, 13 June 2013, http://blogs.wsj.com/digits/2013/06/13/in-online-ads-theres-google-and-then-everybody-else/.

[36] Google 2014 Annual Report, above note 13, p 22.

[37] Laurie Sullivan, 'Google Will Get $2 Of Every $5 Marketers Spend This Year On Digital Advertising In US', *Search Marketing Daily*, 8 September 2015, http://www.mediapost.com/publications/article/257894/google-will-get-2-of-every-5-marketers-spend-thi.html.

[38] Ibid.

[39] Ibid.

Google attributed its 2013 and 2014 increase in advertising revenues from an in- **14.38** crease in the number of paid clicks through its advertising programmes.[40] The increase in the number of paid clicks came from, among other things, 'new and richer ad formats', greater traffic across all of its platforms, the continued global expansion of Google products, advertisers, and user base, and more Google Network Members.[41] (Google's average revenue per user in the first quarter of 2014 was six times higher than Facebook's.[42])

Although Google argues that competition is one click away, we have seen how it **14.39** benefits from several data-driven network effects: the trial-by-error, scope of data, and spill-over. As one industry expert observed, '[a]pps are worth millions. Platforms are worth billions. If you want to make money in mobile, build a killer platform.'[43] Google has a killer platform. As one 2015 report stated, 'No single company comes close to commanding that level of market share.'[44]

E. Domination is not Guaranteed

One final caveat. Controlling an operating system can help tip the network ef- **14.40** fects in one's favour. But it does not ensure domination. Google's social network, Google+, for example, while growing, has not surpassed Facebook.[45]

Another example is when the FTC predicted (incorrectly) in 2010 that Apple's **14.41** iAd mobile ad network 'quickly will become a strong mobile advertising network competitor'.[46] Here the FTC reasoned that in controlling the iOS platform, Apple had four advantages. First, Apple 'has extensive relationships with application

---

[40] Google 2014 Annual Report, above note 13, p 24; Google Inc, Annual Report Pursuant to Section 13 or 15(D) of the Securities Exchange Act of 1934 for the fiscal year ended December 31, 2013, p 28 ('Google 2013 Annual Report'), https://www.sec.gov/Archives/edgar/data/1288776/000128877614000020/goog2013123110-k.htm.

[41] Google 2014 Annual Report, above note 13, p 24; Google 2013 Annual Report, above note 40, p 28.

[42] Digital Strategy Consulting, 'How Much Are You Worth? Average Revenue Per User at Google, Facebook, and Twitter', 18 June 2014, http://www.digitalstrategyconsulting.com/intelligence/2014/06/ad_revenue_per_user_google_facebook_twitter.php.

[43] Barr, above note 33.

[44] Sullivan, above note 37.

[45] One metric, social log-in preferences, showed that 45% of users opted for Facebook as their log-in, and 37% used Google+ in the first quarter of 2015. Far fewer people used other networks—eg Twitter (5%), Yahoo! (3%), and LinkedIn (3%)—to log in. Alexandra Larralde, 'Social Log-in Trends Across the Web: Q1 2015', Janrain, 3 April 2015, http://janrain.com/blog/social-log-in-trends-across-the-web-q1-2015/. Google+'s penetration in selected countries as of 4th quarter 2014 varies, ranging from a high of 83% of the online population having an account on Google+ in Indonesia to a low of 17% in Japan. Statista, 'Google Plus Penetration in Selected Countries as of 4th Quarter 2014', http://www.statista.com/statistics/376341/google-plus-penetration-countries/.

[46] FTC Google/AdMob Statement, above note 30, p 1.

developers and users'.[47] Second, Apple collected a lot of data from its users. Third, Apple could offer targeted ads (heretofore a strength of AdMob) 'by leveraging proprietary user data gleaned from users of Apple mobile devices'.[48] Finally, Apple's ownership of the iPhone software development tools, and its control over the developers' licence agreement, gave 'Apple the unique ability to define how competition among ad networks on the iPhone will occur and evolve.'[49]

14.42   But even Apple, with these strengths, could not displace Google. Several years after the FTC's erroneous prediction, Apple had just a 2.6 per cent share of the US mobile ad market, lagging behind industry leader Google (37.7 per cent).[50] With its small market and revenue share, Apple announced that as of 30 June 2016 its iAd App network will be discontinued.[51]

14.43   Microsoft is another example. It remains the largest operating system for personal computers with a worldwide share of 90.85 per cent as of June 2015.[52] Yet Microsoft has been unable to leverage its historic dominance in personal computers to mobile phones, where its market share of operating systems is tiny. Only 1.1 per cent of the 403.1 million smartphones shipped worldwide in the fourth quarter of 2015 had the Windows operating system.[53] Moreover, Microsoft's significant advantage in personal computer operating systems does not provide the data to compete in the app world. Microsoft's Bing maps at the time of the UK competition authority's investigation did not provide 'turn-by-turn navigation', but the competition authority recognized that would change with its partnership with Nokia. Nonetheless, the UK competition authority accurately predicted that even if Bing maps were pre-installed on Nokia smartphones, and even if Bing maps were tied with Bing search, that still might be insufficient to topple Google or Apple: 'given that iOS and Android account for over 80 per cent of the new sales of smartphones, these alternative providers may be at a competitive disadvantage by having access to a smaller user base than either Google or Apple to update their respective maps'.[54] As discussed above, Microsoft in 2015 divested its mapping technology to Uber.

14.44   While network effects can help insulate the dominant firm from competitive pressures, they do not immunize them from competition altogether. The network effects

---

[47] Ibid.

[48] Ibid.

[49] Ibid.

[50] Lara O'Reilly, 'Apple Is Planning To Turn Around iAd By Venturing Into Programmatic For The First Time', *Business Insider UK*, 19 November 2014, http://uk.businessinsider.com/apple-iad-programmatic-partnership-with-rubicon-project-2014-11.

[51] Apple Inc, 'iAd App Network Will Be Discontinued', Press Release, 15 January 2016, https://developer.apple.com/news/?id=01152016a&1452895272.

[52] Netmarketshare, 'Desktop Top Operating System Share Trend August, 2014 to June, 2015', https://www.netmarketshare.com/operating-system-market-share.aspx?qprid=9&qpcustomb=0.

[53] Gartner Inc, above note 31.

[54] OFT, *Google/Waze*, above note 12, para 61 (internal footnote omitted).

do not assure that every firm that is dominant early in the product's lifecycle will remain dominant throughout. Facebook, for example, displaced the early social network leader MySpace. Google displaced Yahoo!

But it may be easier to topple the dominant firm earlier in the product's lifecycle, **14.45** when none of the firms have significantly scaled up. MySpace, at its peak, was attracting around 100 million monthly users, which is tiny relative to Facebook's 1.39 billion monthly users at the end of 2014.[55] Moreover, MySpace's decline, according to one executive, was attributable to greed, overreach, and a poor product.[56]

Another factor is poor corporate strategy. Yahoo!, for example, early on neither **14.46** developed its own search algorithm nor saw the importance of doing so. Instead, Yahoo! relied on Google to power its search engine, and 'this 4 year arrangement gave Google so much exposure that people eventually bypassed Yahoo! altogether'.[57]

Dominance based on these network effects will depend on multiple factors, includ- **14.47** ing the data involved, whether the merged entity will likely control key platforms for accessing the data, the extent to which others will be foreclosed from timely accessing such data, and the 'the level of investments required for building comparable datasets'.[58]

Our point here is that data-driven network effects can both benefit and harm con- **14.48** sumers. As we saw with learning-by-doing, data-driven network effects can improve quality (such as more relevant search results and better navigation maps).

Data-driven network effects, however, can also increase entry barriers, leading to **14.49** a few firms dominating the market. They can play in the favour of the companies that control the popular operating systems, when users stick with the default option (such as browser and search engine), the operating system's large user base can help the algorithm learn quicker than rivals with a smaller user base, and the operating system has a relative advantage in scooping up valuable data (such as users' geo-location).

As we will explore further in Chapter 18, data-driven network effects can enable **14.50** the dominant platform to engage in anticompetitive practices, even when competition is a click away. The dominant platform operator can degrade quality

---

[55] Stuart Dredge, 'MySpace—What Went Wrong: "The Site Was a Massive Spaghetti-Ball Mess"', *The Guardian*, 6 March 2015, http://www.theguardian.com/technology/2015/mar/06/myspace-what-went-wrong-sean-percival-spotify.
[56] Ibid.
[57] Search Engine Directory, History of Yahoo! Search—The Original Search Engine, http://searchenginedirectory.biz/search-engine-histories/history-of-yahoo-search-engine/.
[58] OECD, *Data-Driven Innovation*, above note 15, p 58.

(including privacy protections afforded to users). It can use its market power and customer lock-in to extract even more personal data than the firm otherwise could in a competitive market. The dominant platform can offer worse terms for sellers and stifle consumers' ability to experiment with other platforms (and privacy-enhancing technology).

14.51 Accordingly, competition authorities want to account for these network effects so as to not overstate potential entrants' ability to prevent the exercise of market power.

15

RISK OF INADEQUATE MERGER ENFORCEMENT

We saw in Chapter 6 several shortcomings in the way the competition agencies **15.01** have analysed data-driven mergers, and how they have not fully considered the implications of a data-driven economy. Some officials, we saw, believe that 'the antitrust principles are the same' for data-driven mergers and other conventional mergers.[1] This chapter identifies four significant risks if the agencies continue along the same path. First, it is questionable whether the competition agencies are accurately predicting many mergers' competitive effects in concentrated markets. The second risk is when the competition agencies consider only the merger's impact on the 'paid' side of multi-sided platforms and ignore the free side. To illustrate, the chapter uses the merger wave of US commercial radio stations in the 1990s–2000s, where the Department of Justice (DOJ) considered in its consent decrees only the mergers' effects on advertising, and not on listenership. The third risk is that even if the agency reviews the merger's likely effect on each side of the multi-sided platform, their price-centric tools are ill suited for evaluating the free side. Finally, the network effects, we discussed in the preceding chapters, can magnify the likely consumer harm.

A. The Prediction Business

For mergers, competition agencies are often in the prediction business. In many ju- **15.02** risdictions, like the US and EU, the merger, if it exceeds certain thresholds, cannot occur unless the merging parties notify the competition authority, and the waiting period passes (or is terminated early by the competition authority).[2] The pre-merger

---

[1] Lisa Kimmel and Janis Kestenbaum, 'What's Up with WhatsApp?: A Transatlantic View on Privacy and Merger Enforcement in Digital Markets', 29(1) *Antitrust* (Fall 2014): p 55 n 63.

[2] *See eg* European Commission, *Merger Control Procedures*, 13 August 2013, http://ec.europa.eu/competition/mergers/procedures_en.html (must receive notice of any merger 'with an EU dimension', where the merging firms 'reach certain turnover thresholds'); Hart–Scott–Rodino Antitrust Improvements Act of 1976, 15 USC s 18a.

notification regime is designed to strengthen antitrust enforcement. It gives the agency time to investigate large mergers before they are consummated and to preserve an effective remedy.[3]

15.03 With the pre-merger notification regime, the competition agency predicts the merger's likely effects. In assessing whether the merger may substantially lessen competition or tend to create a monopoly, the competition authority does not have the benefit of economic realities—namely, to allow the merger to occur, assess its competitive impact, and challenge the merger if it proves to be anticompetitive. The competition agency can always challenge a consummated merger. But as the Hart–Scott–Rodino Antitrust Improvements Act's (HSR) legislative history reflects, the remedy will often be ineffectual. By the time the agency assesses the merger's competitive effects several years later, among other things, production facilities will likely be closed, employees will likely be fired (or have left), and brands will likely be discontinued or repositioned. Moreover, the company, post-merger, knowing that its behaviour is under review may wait a couple of years longer before exercising its market power.

15.04 So the competition authority does not have the luxury of a wait-and-see approach. The closest thing pre-merger is an analogous historical event or 'natural experiment'. Here agencies 'examine the impact of recent mergers, entry, expansion, or exit in the relevant market' or 'similar' markets to assess the merger's likely impact.[4]

15.05 Absent natural experiments and consummated mergers, the agencies typically rely on economic theory to predict a merger's likely competitive effects. This entails predicting several likelihoods, including the 'likelihood that a merger would have anti-competitive effects in the relevant markets, in the absence of countervailing factors', the 'likelihood that buyer power would act as a countervailing factor to an increase in market power resulting from the merger', the 'likelihood that entry would maintain effective competition in the relevant markets', and the 'likelihood that efficiencies would act as a factor counteracting the harmful effects on competition which might otherwise result from the merger'.[5]

---

[3] *United States v Computer Associates Int'l, Inc*, Case No 01-02062(GK), 2002 WL 31961456 (US Dist Ct (D DC), 20 November 2002).

[4] US Department of Justice (DOJ) and Federal Trade Commission (FTC), *Horizontal Merger Guidelines*, 19 August 2010, s 2.1.2 ('US Horizontal Merger Guidelines'), http://www.justice.gov/atr/public/guidelines/hmg-2010.html.

[5] European Commission, *Guidelines on the Assessment of Horizontal Mergers under the Council Regulation on the Control of Concentrations Between Undertakings* [2004] OJ C 31/03, para 11 ('EC Horizontal Merger Guidelines'), http://eur-lex.europa.eu/legal-content/EN/TXT/?uri=celex:52004XC0205%2802%29.

B. Most Mergers are Cleared

The agencies do not have the luxury to review mergers at a leisurely pace. They **15.06**
often are under time constraints. So they must predict quickly (in antitrust time)—
typically within six to nine months for the mergers they review.

The US and EU clear most mergers. For example, between 1990, when its Merger **15.07**
Regulation came into force, and 2012, the European Commission cleared over
4,600 deals and blocked only 22 mergers.[6] Or, as Commissioner Joaquín Almunia
exclaimed, 'Fewer than five in every thousand cases!'[7]

In 2011, the Commission received 309 notifications, and blocked only one merger.[8] **15.08**
Over 90 per cent of its merger cases are typically resolved early on (in its Phase I),
generally without remedies.[9]

Likewise, the DOJ investigates few mergers. As Figure 15.1 reflects, between 1990 **15.09**
and 2010 the DOJ investigated, on average, 4.4 per cent of all HSR filings. It issued

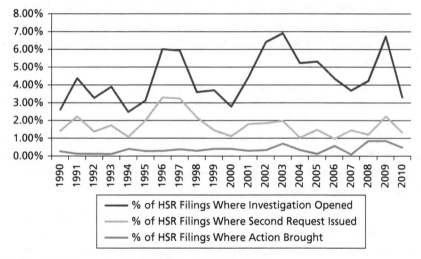

Figure 15.1 Requests for HSR filings, 1990–2010

Source: DOJ, Antitrust Division Workload Statistics FY 1990–2010, http://www.justice.gov/atr/
division-operations.

---

[6] Joaquín Almunia, Vice President of the European Commission responsible for Competition
Policy, 'Merger Review: Past Evolution and Future Prospects', Speech given at Conference on
Competition Policy, Law and Economics, Cernobbio, Italy, 2 November 2012, http://europa.eu/
rapid/press-release_SPEECH-12-773_en.htm.
[7] Ibid.
[8] Ibid.
[9] European Commission, *Merger Control Procedures*, above note 2. A Phase I review may involve
'[r]equests for information from the merging companies or third parties' and '[q]uestionnaires to
competitors or customers seeking their views on the merger, as well as other contacts with market
participants, aimed at clarifying the conditions for competition in a given market or the role of the
merged companies in that market.' Ibid.

on average a Second Request for 1.74 per cent of all HSR filings, and challenged 0.37 per cent of all HSR filings.

15.10 The Federal Trade Commission (FTC) challenges roughly the same percentage of mergers.[10] Consequently, of the many pre-merger notifications they receive annually, the EU and US competition agencies investigate a small percentage of mergers; an even smaller percentage reach the Second Request or Phase II stage. Even fewer mergers are challenged. And of those few mergers challenged, rarely do the merging parties go to trial; most settle with divestitures.

C. The Big Mystery: How Often Do the Competition Agencies Accurately Predict the Mergers' Competitive Effects?

15.11 One cannot fault the competition agencies for allowing so many mergers to sail through unchallenged (often without any scrutiny) if their analytical tools accurately screen anticompetitive mergers from the benign and procompetitive mergers. After all, in assessing the merger's likely competitive effects, the competition agencies, one prior European Commissioner noted, rely on 'sophisticated qualitative and quantitative analyses'.[11]

15.12 So how often do the agencies predict the mergers' competitive effects accurately? No one really knows. Ask any competition authority, and they cannot provide their batting average, namely the percentage of mergers where they accurately predicted the likely competitive effects. Competition agencies are often evaluated on how quickly they assess mergers, the predictability of their review, and the cost imposed on firms. The agencies are not assessed on how often they accurately predict the mergers' likely competitive effects.

15.13 What we do know is that over the past 45 years the US competition agencies have increased the concentration thresholds, permitting more and more mergers in concentrated industries.[12] Originally, the DOJ consistent with the Clayton Act, applied 'an additional, stricter standard in determining whether to challenge mergers occurring in any market, not wholly unconcentrated, in which there is a significant

---

[10] FTC Competition Enforcement Database, Merger Enforcement Actions, http://www.ftc. gov/competition-enforcement-database (reporting 351 merger actions (which includes both HSR and non-HSR transactions, and mergers that were abandoned during the review process) between 1996 and 2011).

[11] Almunia, above note 6.

[12] Compare DOJ, *1968 Merger Guidelines* (1968), s 6 ('US 1968 Merger Guidelines'), http:// www.justice.gov/sites/default/files/atr/legacy/2007/07/11/11247.pdf with DOJ, *1982 Merger Guidelines* (1982) ('US 1982 Merger Guidelines'), http://www.justice.gov/sites/default/files/atr/ legacy/2007/07/11/11248.pdf.

Table 15.1 Concentration levels of mergers challenged by the US competition agencies, 1999–2003

		\multicolumn{9}{c}{Change in the HHI}
		0–99	100–199	200–299	300–499	500–799	800–1,199	1,200–2,499	2,500+	Total
Post-Merger HHI	0–1,799	0	17	18	19	3	0	0	0	57
	1,799–1,999	0	7	5	14	14	0	0	0	40
	2,000–2,399	1	1	7	32	35	2	0	0	78
	2,400–2,999	1	5	6	18	132	34	1	0	197
	3,000–3,999	0	3	4	16	37	63	53	0	176
	4,000–4,999	0	1	3	16	34	30	79	0	163
	5,000–6,999	0	2	4	16	9	14	173	52	270
	7,000+	0	0	0	2	3	10	44	223	282
	Total	2	36	47	133	267	153	350	275	1,263

Source: FTC and DOJ, *Merger Challenges Data, Fiscal Years 1999–2003*, 18 December 2003, http://www.justice.gov/atr/merger-challenges-data-fiscal-years-1999-2003.

trend towards increased concentration'.[13] The Reagan administration dropped that, mentioning only 'the congressional intent that merger enforcement should interdict competitive problems in their incipiency'.[14] The US competition agencies, in the ensuing years, challenged mergers mostly in highly concentrated industries, as reflected in the Herfindahl–Hirschman Index (HHI).[15] Table 15.1 gives a snapshot showing the concentration levels of mergers that the agencies challenged between fiscal years 1999–2003.[16]

By 2010, to reflect their enforcement activity, the US competition agencies pushed the permissible concentration levels higher.[17]

The agencies' increasing tolerance for concentrated industries post-merger is not **15.14** due to empirical analysis. Although the HHI figures appear precise, there is no

---

[13] US 1968 Merger Guidelines, above note 12, s 7.

[14] US 1982 Merger Guidelines, above note 12, s 1.

[15] The HHI is calculated by summing the squares of the individual market shares of every firm in the relevant market. So the HHI of a market equally divided among ten firms would be 1,000.

[16] FTC and DOJ, *Merger Challenges Data, Fiscal Years 1999–2003*, 18 December 2003, http://www.justice.gov/atr/merger-challenges-data-fiscal-years-1999-2003.

[17] US Horizontal Merger Guidelines, above note 4, s 5.3.

scientific basis for the agencies' cut-offs. Neither the FTC nor DOJ calibrated the likelihood of anticompetitive effects with actual post-merger risks. They do not know whether, and the extent to which, mergers with post-merger HHIs below 2,000 are less likely to cause harm than those below 3,000.

15.15 How can we state this so confidently? Because the competition agencies in the US and elsewhere generally do not revisit the mergers in either highly or moderately concentrated industries to see whether their predictions were accurate.[18] In one survey, 43 per cent of the competition agencies said that they had not done in the prior five years *any ex-post* evaluations for *any* competition interventions.[19] Outside hospital and petroleum mergers, the US competition agencies typically do not revisit the industries post-merger to assess whether they predicted correctly.[20] The European Commission does *ex-post* reviews for only 'a small number of cases'.[21] Most notable was its 2005 merger remedies study.[22]

15.16 So why don't the agencies revisit mergers to see if they predicted correctly (especially when they permit many more mergers in moderately or highly concentrated industries)? Cost is one reason. The European Commission said 'ex post evaluations can require substantial econometric expertise and detailed datasets, which render them costly'.[23] The FTC said it was 'limited by agency resource constraints and the costly, time consuming nature of such research'. [24] It is interesting that it is easier for the agencies to confidently predict the merger's likely competitive effects (and to increase the concentration thresholds) than to see if their predictions are accurate. Granted it may be hard to compare the post-merger world with a competitive counterfactual,[25] but it is not impossible.

---

[18] Tomaso Duso and Peter Ormosi, 'Capacity Building Workshop on the Ex-Post Evaluation Of Competition Authorities' Enforcement Decisions: A Critical Discussion', Prepared for the OECD, Directorate for Financial and Enterprise Affairs Competition Committee, Working Party No 2 on Competition and Regulation, 26 October 2015, p 2, http://www.oecd.org/officialdocuments/publicdisplaydocumentpdf/?cote=DAF/COMP/WP2%282015%298&doclanguage=en ('quite a few of the over 110 competition authorities around the world are yet making use' of *ex-post* reviews).

[19] International Competition Network, Advocacy Working Group, *Interim Report on the Explaining the Benefits of Competition Project*, April 2012, p 56, http://www.internationalcompetitionnetwork.org/uploads/2011-2012/interim_benefits%20project%20report%20-%20final.pdf.

[20] Daniel Hosken, Deputy Assistant Director, Bureau of Economics, US Federal Trade Commission, 'Ex-Post Evaluation in the US: Lessons Learned', http://www.oecd.org/daf/competition/workshop-expost-evaluation-competition-enforcement-decisions.htm ('Since 1983, the FTC Economists have conducted more than 20 ex-post evaluations.').

[21] Ibid, pp 58 and 64 ('owing to the costs involved, ex post evaluations cannot be systematic; they should only cover a select number of cases').

[22] DG Competition, European Commission, *Merger Remedies Study*, October 2005, http://ec.europa.eu/competition/mergers/legislation/remedies_study.pdf.

[23] Hosken, above note 20, p 58.

[24] Ibid.

[25] The most widely used method has been difference-in-differences, where one compares 'the change in prices in a market affected by the analysed practice (cartel, merger or abuse of dominance) with the change in prices for the same period in a different market unaffected by the analysed practice.' Duso and Ormosi, above note 18, p 10.

D. The *Ex-Post* Merger Reviews Paint a Bleak Picture

In 2013 Professor John Kwoka collected all the recent post-merger reviews. The **15.17** available post-merger reviews, he concluded, suggest that the US competition agencies are inadequately enforcing the competition laws. Of the 53 post-merger reviews with price estimates in 16 different industries, '40 or 75.5 per cent report postmerger price increases'.[26] Of the mergers for which data on the agency's actions were available, the agency opposed five mergers, cleared eight mergers, and obtained remedies in ten mergers.[27] As Kwoka concluded, '[c]ollectively, these results suggest that merger control in these studied cases may overall be too permissive, that the remedies chosen may be inadequate to the task of preserving competition, and that conduct and conditions remedies may be especially ineffective.'[28]

Granted, the finding of a price increase in one case does not necessarily mean that **15.18** the agency's predictive tools are inadequate. There might have been intervening, unforeseen events (such as a competitor's plant closing due to weather, changes in consumers' tastes) that caused the price increase.[29] But it is questionable that 75 per cent of the industries studied involved natural disasters or other unforeseen events. Or perhaps the old management did not price its goods to maximize profits, negotiated poorly, or otherwise left money on the table, while the new management understood the market better and was more capable. Again, it is unlikely that this explains the price increases Kwoka found. It is absurd to think that all the acquired firms are amateurish while all acquiring firms are professional. Still, as Kwoka cautioned, 'the number of observations is not especially large, classifications are sometimes difficult, the data have other limitations, and selection issues abound'.[30] Perhaps as more post-merger reviews are undertaken, we will obtain a clearer picture of markets or mergers where the agencies' tools work well and where they do not.

Based on what we do know, three out of four mergers for which we have post-merger **15.19** analysis led to price increases. A 0.250 batting average may suffice for a mediocre

---

[26] John E Kwoka, Jr, 'Does Merger Control Work? A Retrospective on US Enforcement Actions and Merger Outcomes', 78 *Antitrust LJ* (2013): pp 619, 631–2 (the average increase was 9.40%, ranging from a 0.06% up to a high of 28.4%; with 13 transactions (24.5% of the total) found to result in price decreases, which average 4.29% and range from 0.04% to 16.3% in absolute value; the survey included three joint ventures and four airline code-shares; of the three joint ventures '(all in petroleum), two reported price increases while one reported a decrease. The magnitudes are all small, and average a positive 0.43 per cent. On the other hand, all four of the studied airline code-sharing arrangements are found to have resulted in price decreases.').

[27] Ibid, p 638.

[28] Ibid, p 641.

[29] Duso and Ormosi, above note 18, p 15.

[30] Kwoka, above note 26, p 644.

minor league baseball team, but not for mergers that affect trillions of dollars of commerce. It may be that selection bias abounds—namely the 53 post-merger studies involved the more contentious, problematic mergers. Perhaps the agencies predicted accurately for most other mergers. But as the next chapter explores, that is unlikely. If Kwoka's survey of post-merger reviews even approximates the agencies' track record (a big *if*, we concede), then the agencies and courts are simply not enforcing the competition laws well. If the agencies' price-centric analytical tools are often wrong (at least for the industries covered in the merger retrospectives), then there is no reason to assume that these price-centric tools somehow work well in assessing data-driven mergers in multi-sided markets, where the products on one side are free.

E. The High Error Costs When the Agencies Examine Only One Side of a Multi-Sided Platform

15.20 The risk of inadequate merger enforcement increases when the competition agencies focus only on one side (eg, advertising) of a multi-sided platform. For example, the European Commission in broadcast TV cases 'considered only the market for advertising' and 'did not consider the "free" TV side to be a market'.[31] Likewise, as we shall see, the DOJ considers only the advertising side in commercial radio mergers.

15.21 It is unclear why any competition agency today would consider only one side of a multi-sided platform. Perhaps the assumption is that the anticompetitive effects are linked: namely, the merger, in lessening competition on the paid side, must also lessen competition on the free side. This, at times, is true. A newsweekly that monopolizes the advertising market may also lack meaningful competition on the free side. A search engine may dominate both the free and advertising sides.

15.22 The fallacy is to assume that if anticompetitive effects are unlikely on the paid side (eg, unlikely that the merged entity could raise advertising rates), then anticompetitive effects are also unlikely on the free side. One assumption is that given the spillover network effects, the platform to attract advertisers may 'subsidize' the other side, by offering the product for free. Thus, the platform has little incentive to exert market power on the free side. This may be true if one platform competes against other platforms offering similar products, which users view as substitutes, and users frequently switch among the platforms. But this is not always true.

---

[31] Teresa Vecchi, Jerome Vidal, and Viveca Fallenius, 'The Microsoft/Yahoo! Search Business Case', 2 *Competition Policy Newsletter* (2010): p 45, http://ec.europa.eu/competition/publications/cpn/2010_2_8.pdf.

We can see this with newspapers, magazines, commercial television, and com- **15.23** mercial radio. They compete for an audience to read their articles, and listen and watch their programmes, which often are offered for free or a nominal subscriber fee, and for advertisers that seek to target this audience. But the advertising competition and advertising rates do not necessarily capture the editorial competition. Today a free newspaper in the US likely competes against Google and Craigslist for advertising revenue. But Google, while aggregating the news, does not produce in-depth local journalism. Craigslist does not gather the news. Google and Craigslist, while formidable competitors to the traditional media for certain advertisers, are not competitive threats for newsgathering. If Craigslist entered a local geographic market, the increase in classified advertising competition will not translate into better local journalism. Thus, competition on the paid advertising side may lower the newspapers' advertising rates, but it will not necessarily improve the news content's quality on the free side. Likewise, if two competing newsweeklies merge, readers will likely be worse off with fewer choices for local investigative journalism, while classified advertisers, given online alternatives, may be less affected.

Thus a merger can lessen non-price competition on the free side (eg, editorial com- **15.24** petition and diversity of viewpoints needed for an effective democracy), without lessening competition on the paid side, and vice versa.

The emerging consensus is that competition authorities must consider the merger's **15.25** impact on each side of a multi-sided platform. For mergers in data-driven industries, the Organisation for Economic Co-operation and Development (OECD) warned, 'focussing on one side of market will rarely lead to a proper market definition'.[32] It also cautioned that '[m]echanical market definition exercises that exclude one side usually lead to errors.'[33] At a minimum, the competition authority must understand the linkages and interrelationships among the sides.[34] The fact that assessing the merger's impact on one side of the platform is more difficult, the OECD counselled, does not warrant ignoring it:

> The difficulties inherent in measuring diversity and quality, and in predicting how a merger might affect them is not a good justification for ignoring them in merger review. This is especially true if there is little or no sector regulation dealing with these matters.
>
> The non-price effects of media mergers can have just as significant an impact on economic welfare in media markets as they have in other markets. It is

---

[32] OECD, *Data-Driven Innovation for Growth and Well-being: Interim Synthesis Report*, October 2014, p 59, http://www.oecd.org/sti/inno/data-driven-innovation-interim-synthesis.pdf (noting that in multi-sided markets, as enabled by data, one cannot focus only on one side of the market, since one side will often exert an externality on the other side).

[33] OECD, *Policy Roundtables: Two-Sided Markets*, 17 December 2009, p 11, http://www.oecd.org/daf/competition/44445730.pdf.

[34] Ibid.

quality-adjusted changes in prices that are pertinent for determining effects on economic welfare.

There could be jurisdictions where diversity and quality are so tightly regulated, through detailed content rules for instance, that competition authorities can justifiably assume that media mergers will leave diversity and quality unchanged or even improved. Absent such regulation, there is no a priori reason why the diversity and quality effects of media mergers should not be examined by competition authorities when diversity and quality changes have a direct effect on economic welfare.[35]

15.26 In evaluating commercial radio mergers, however, the DOJ erred in considering the merger's impact solely on the paid side (namely advertisers and the rates they paid), and did not account the mergers' impact on the free side (namely non-price competition regarding programming quality, listener choice, or the likely impact of these mergers on the marketplace of ideas).[36] As a result, both consumers and advertisers have paid the price.

15.27 Nothing in the Clayton Act restricts the DOJ from considering solely advertising competition. For other media markets, like free or paid newspapers, the DOJ for decades has examined both sides of the platform.[37] Nor can one claim that the listenership side is best left to the Federal Communications Commission (FCC). This is contrary to Congress's intent in enacting the Telecommunications Act of 1996.[38] And, we discuss elsewhere, the FCC's 'public interest' standard and restrictions on common ownership do not adequately address a media merger's impact on the marketplace of ideas.[39]

---

[35] OECD, *Policy Roundtables: Media Mergers*, 19 September 2003, p 9, http://www.oecd.org/competition/mergers/17372985.pdf.

[36] *See, eg, United States v Entercom Communications Corp*, Case No 1:15-cv-01119 (US Dist Ct (D DC), 14 July 2015), Complaint (alleging that acquisition likely would substantially lessen competition for the sale of radio advertising to advertisers targeting English-language listeners); *United States v Cumulus Media Inc*, Case No 1:11CV01619 (US Dist Ct (D DC), 8 September 2011), Complaint, para 9; *United States v CBS Corp*, Case No 98CV00819, 1998 US Dist LEXIS 10292, pp *1–2 (US Dist Ct (D DC), 30 June 1998); *United States v Westinghouse Elec Corp*, Case No 96 2563, 1997 US Dist LEXIS 3263, pp *1–2 (US Dist Ct (D DC), 10 March 1997); *United States v Bain Capital, LLC*, Case No 1:08-cv-00245 (US Dist Ct (D DC), 13 February 2008), Competitive Impact Statement, pp 5–7; *United States v Clear Channel Communications, Inc & AMFM Inc*, Case No 00-2063 (US Dist Ct (D DC), 29 August 2000), Complaint, pp 2–3 (complaint filed with consent decree); Joel I Klein, Acting Assistant Attorney General, DOJ, 'DOJ Analysis of Radio Mergers', Speech, Washington DC, 19 February 1997, http://www.justice.gov/atr/public/speeches/1055.pdf.

[37] OECD, *Policy Roundtables: Two-Sided Markets*, above note 33, p 149 (United States) ('In some markets, the network interactions between the two sides are so significant that both sides of the market are important for economic analysis. In newspaper markets, methods that account for network interactions between newspaper readers and advertisers have been used in economic analysis for decades.'); *United States v Village Voice Media LLC & NT Media LLC*, Case No 1:03CV0164, 2003 WL 22019516 (US Dist Ct (ND Ohio), 2003).

[38] Maurice E Stucke and Allen P Grunes, 'Antitrust and the Marketplace of Ideas', 69 *Antitrust LJ* (2001): pp 249, 288–91.

[39] Ibid, pp 291–5.

So what happened after the 1996 Telecommunications Act, which weakened owner- **15.28**
ship limits on radio stations nationally and locally,[40] and the DOJ's examining only
the advertising side of the two-sided platform? There was not surprisingly a merger
wave, and radio ownership became significantly more concentrated. Between
March 1996 and March 2007, the number of commercial radio stations increased
6.8 per cent, but the number of radio owners declined by 39 per cent.[41] This trend
was already apparent in 2001, by which time the number of radio owners had already declined 25 per cent from when the 1996 Act commenced.[42] Over the same
period and until 2007, the nation's largest radio group owners grew even bigger: 'In
1996, the two largest radio group owners controlled 62 and 53 stations, respectively.
By March 2007, the leading radio group, Clear Channel Communications, owned
over 1,100 radio stations.'[43]

The ensuing merger wave, not surprisingly, had an adverse impact on non-price **15.29**
competition, including on programming quality and programming choices for
listeners.[44] One complaint, the Project for Excellence in Journalism reported, was
'that Clear Channel's domination was diminishing the quality of the AM/FM
radio dial by monopolizing key markets and homogenizing content'.[45] A frequent
complaint was that the deregulation 'allowed for unprecedented consolidation in
commercial radio, which has resulted in a homogeneity that is often out-of-step
with artists, entrepreneurs, media professionals and educators—not to mention
listeners'.[46] An FCC Commissioner observed how '[r]espected media watchers

---

[40] Telecommunications Act of 1996, Pub L No 104-104, 110 Stat 56 (codified in scattered sections of 47 USC). Section 202 of the 1996 Act abolished the Federal Communications Commission's
(FCC) limits on the number of radio stations a single entity could own nationally. In 1996, the FCC
in revising s 73.3555 of its rules (47 CFR s 73.3555) eliminated the national multiple radio ownership rule and relaxed the local ownership rule. FCC Order, *In re* Implementation of Sections 202(a)
and 202(b)(1) of the Telecommunications Act of 1996 (Broadcast Radio Ownership), 47 CFR s
73.3555 (7 March 1996), http://www.fcc.gov/Bureaus/Mass_Media/Orders/1996/fcc96090.txt.

[41] George Williams, FCC, *Review of the Radio Industry 2007*, p 1, http://hraunfoss.fcc.gov/
edocs_public/attachmatch/DA-07-3470A11.pdf.

[42] FCC, *Review of the Radio Industry 2001*, September 2001, p 3, http://www.fcc.gov/mb/policy/
docs/radio01.pdf.

[43] Williams, above note 41, p 1. In 2008, Clear Channel controlled 833 US radio stations, '508
of which were located' in the largest 100 Arbitron markets. *Bain Capital*, Competitive Impact
Statement, above note 36, p 4.

[44] *See* Maurice E Stucke and Allen P Grunes, 'Toward a Better Competition Policy for the
Media: The Challenge of Developing Antitrust Policies That Support the Media Sector's Unique
Role in Our Democracy', 42 *Connecticut L Rev* (2009): pp 101, 111 n 43, 123 (discussing decline
in the amount of local news by radio stations and noting how increased concentration has not increased the average number of formats across markets).

[45] Project for Excellence in Journalism, State of the News Media 2007, Radio Ownership, http://
www.stateofthemedia.org/2007/radio-intro/ownership/.

[46] *On the 'Future of Radio': Hearing Before the Senate Committee on Commerce, Science, & Transportation*,
110th Cong 3, 24 October 2007, Testimony of Mac McCaughan, co-founder of Merge Records, http://
commerce.senate.gov/public/?a=Files.Serve&File_id=f83d2199-70b0-4633-9fc6-1db93c1d71bd.

argue that this concentration has led to far less coverage of news and public interest programming', how one multiyear study found a homogenization of music that got air play, and how radio served more 'to advertise the products of vertically integrated conglomerates than to entertain Americans with the best and most original programming'.[47] Mel Karmazin, the former head of commercial radio for Infinity Broadcasting and CBS and former CEO of Sirius XM, recognized that commercial radio after the 1996 Act became 'totally homogenized'.[48] Karmazin advocated for radio consolidation '[s]trictly for business reasons. No one asked [him] if it was good for consumers'.[49]

15.30 Sometimes, prices increases and quality degradation on one side of the platform are offset with discounts and quality improvements on the platform's other side. So to 'evaluate the market power of a platform one has to look at the markups on both sides'.[50] Here consolidation, brought by ineffective antitrust enforcement, harmed both radio listeners and advertisers.

15.31 As a consequence of the radio merger wave, the largest firms often dominated the market in terms of audience and revenue share. By 2012, the largest commercial radio firms, as the FCC found, 'enjoy[ed] substantial advantages in revenue share—on average, the largest firm in each Arbitron Metro market ha[d] a 45 per cent share of the market's total radio advertising revenue, with the largest two firms accounting for 73 per cent of the revenue'.[51] In over a third of all Arbitron Metro markets, 'the top two commercial station owners control[led] at least 80 per cent of the radio advertising revenue'.[52] Not surprisingly, radio advertising rates nearly doubled during this period of consolidation[53]—suggesting that even on this advertising dimension, the DOJ's antitrust review may have been inadequate. So anticompetitive effects were seen on both sides of many commercial radio markets.

---

[47] Michael J Copps, FCC Commissioner, 'Remarks to the NATPE 2003 Family Programming Forum', New Orleans, La, 22 January 2003, http://www.fcc.gov/Speeches/Copps/2003/spmjc301.pdf.

[48] Phil Rosenthal, 'Homogenized Radio Stations Bottle Up Growth', *Chicago Tribune*, 11 November 2007, Business, p 3.

[49] Ibid.

[50] OECD, *Policy Roundtables: Two-Sided Markets*, above note 33, p 220.

[51] FCC, *Further Notice of Proposed Rulemaking and Report and Order*, adopted 31 March 2014; released 15 April 2014, para 92 ('2014 Quadrennial Regulatory Review') in *In re 2014 Quadrennial Regulatory Review—Review of the Commission's Broadcast Ownership Rules and Other Rules Adopted Pursuant to Section 202 of the Telecommunications Act of 1996*, MB Docket No 14-50.

[52] Ibid, para 92; Williams, above note 41, p 2.

[53] 2014 Quadrennial Regulatory Review, above note 51, para 92 n 237 (also noting that while the Consumer Price Index increased approximately 3% per year between the 1996 Act and June 2011, the annual growth rate in radio advertising rates was approximately 6.5%); Williams, above note 41, p 16.

F. How Data-Driven Mergers Increase
the Risks of False Negatives

If the competition agencies ignore or downplay data-driven mergers, then they will   **15.32**
allow mergers that could significantly harm consumers.

First, as Kwoka and others found, it is questionable whether the competition agen-   **15.33**
cies are generally reaching the right outcome in assessing the mergers' likely effect
on prices in concentrated markets.[54] The belief is that the competition authorities
have more sophisticated tools for assessing mergers' price effects (in particular unilateral price effects). If the competition authorities' batting average in predicting
price effects is a mediocre 0.250, then their batting average in predicting the data-
driven mergers' effects on non-price competition is not likely to be any better.

Second, even when the agencies accurately predict the merger's price effects on the   **15.34**
advertising side of a multi-sided platform, there remains the significant risk of false
negatives when they ignore the platform's other sides (such as the harm US radio
listeners suffered when the merger wave degraded quality).

Third, even if the agencies review the merger's likely effect on each side of the multi-   **15.35**
sided platform, their price-centric tools are ill suited for free services. The agencies,
like the European Commission, already have a hard time assessing a merger's net
effect in multi-sided platforms where each side has a positive price:

> The complexity primarily arises from the presence of two (or more) unique, but
> interdependent, classes of agents or customers. The analysis needs to account for
> (1) the responses of two (or more) distinct sets of agents to platform owners (2) plat-
> form owners responses to two sets of agents, and (3) the responses of one set of agents
> to changes in the others' behaviour and vice versa—particularly as demand condi-
> tions change on each side. This pattern of cross-responses will generally affect each
> step of standard antitrust analysis, from product market definition, the competitive
> assessment, entry, efficiencies, etc. However, as argued in this contribution, this
> does not imply a need to abandon the typical tools that one applies in the analysis of
> single-sided markets, only to adapt them.[55]

It will be even harder for the agency with its price-centric tools to assess (i) the effect   **15.36**
of a price increase (or decrease) on the paid side of the platform on the quality of (and

---

[54] Orley Ashenfelter et al, 'Did Robert Bork Understate the Competitive Impact of Mergers?
Evidence from Consummated Mergers', 57(S3) *J L & Econ* (2014): pp S67, S69 ('While we agree
with some of Bork's critique of merger enforcement circa 1970, we believe that he went too far in
dismissing likely competitive harm resulting from mergers that fell short of creating a monopoly or
dominant firm. Subsequent empirical studies examining the price effects of consummated mergers have shown that, contrary to what Bork believed, mergers in oligopolistic markets can increase
prices and harm consumers.').
[55] OECD, *Policy Roundtables: Two-Sided Markets,* above note 33, p 158.

demand for) the 'free' side; (ii) the effect of quality degradation on the free side on the demand for the paid side; and (iii) the effect either has on the platform's overall profitability.[56]

15.37 Say, for example, the Facebook/WhatsApp merger benefits advertisers in enabling Facebook to amass even more data on us to better target us with behavioural ads. But many of us who do not like being tracked are worse off, when there is no viable alternative social platform/texting app. Suppose the merger increases advertisers' welfare by USD 100 million (in lowering the costs to target us with behavioural ads), but significantly reduces our privacy protections. Suppose the agency cannot quantify the consumer harm. Whose interest should prevail: the advertisers' or ours? How does the competition authority assess the trade-off? One concern is that when it is easier to assess and quantify the benefits or harm to advertisers, that trumps any privacy harms to individuals that are more difficult to quantify.

15.38 With the Facebook/WhatsApp example, the agency can at least inquire how users of texting apps would react to the degradation in quality of the texting app. The problem in the Alliance/Conversant merger is that individuals do not always interact with the merging parties. We may not even know how, and the extent to which, they are tracking us and using our personal data. So do we count? The competition authorities often proclaim how antitrust should promote consumer welfare. Thus the competition agency should be especially vigilant regarding mergers like Alliance/Conversant, as we may not even know of the merging companies, the data they collect on us, and how the merger will affect our welfare.

15.39 Finally, many single-sided markets are not characterized with network effects. But with data-driven mergers, network effects can arise with a vengeance. One may see the traditional direct and spill-over network effects, amplified by the data-driven network effects (learning-by-doing and scope of data). Where such substantial economies of scale exist, the European Commission noted, 'the typical market structure is likely to consist of a few large firms each with significant market power'.[57] So the data-driven network effects increase the cost of false negatives. With these market realities, firms will strive to tip the market to their advantage, including through mergers. Thus the harm when the agencies get it wrong is not just market power, but *monopoly* power, which market forces will not quickly correct.

15.40 Consequently if the competition authorities continue to assess a merger's *price* effects (where, if the post-merger reviews are a guide, their batting average is 0.250)

---

[56] Ibid, p 168.
[57] Ibid, p 169.

because they lack a solid analytical framework for evaluating 'free' products and services in multi-sided platforms, and if data-driven mergers often fall outside the agencies' pre-existing horizontal, vertical, and conglomerate merger categories, many data-driven mergers will continue to pass through without any significant scrutiny. For the anticompetitive ones, consumers will bear the brunt, which, as the next chapter discusses, can be severe.

16

THE PRICE OF WEAK
ANTITRUST ENFORCEMENT

16.01 Chapter 15 explores the risks of the competition agencies' clearing anticompetitive data-driven mergers, especially ones involving multi-sided platforms. This chapter explains why the societal harm is too great to ignore data-driven mergers and abuses by dominant firms. The costs from the agencies' and courts' getting it wrong can be very high, going to the heart of many democratic systems. Anticompetitive data-driven mergers and monopolistic abuses can affect not only consumers' economic interests but also their privacy interests and the values that underlie these privacy interests, such as individual autonomy and freedom of expression and association.[1] The chapter also explains why the privacy and consumer protection agencies and laws—through behavioural remedies and fines—will not necessarily prevent these harms.

A. The Chicago School's Fear of False Positives

16.02 Cartels are generally condemned. We do not care if the particular cartel was successful or unsuccessful in imposing harm. But for everything else—mergers and exploitive, predatory, and exclusionary conduct—the concern is whether under the current legal framework, the competition authority finds procompetitive or benign business activity to be anticompetitive (false positives/type I errors) or finds anticompetitive behaviour to be benign or procompetitive (false negatives/type II errors).

---

[1] *See, eg*, Public Citizen, *Mission Creep-y: Google Is Quietly Becoming One of the Nation's Most Powerful Political Forces While Expanding Its Information-Collection Empire*, November 2014, p 7, https://www.citizen.org/documents/Google-Political-Spending-Mission-Creepy.pdf (warning that 'the amount of information and influence that Google has amassed is now threatening to gain such a stranglehold on experts, regulators and lawmakers that it could leave the public powerless to act if it should decide that the company has become too pervasive, too omniscient and too powerful').

The Chicago School made much ado about false positives—namely the risk of ag- **16.03**
gressive antitrust enforcement chilling procompetitive business activity. Much less
has been said about false negatives—namely the risks of weak antitrust enforcement. As one Department of Justice (DOJ) official said in 2002, '[i]n designing
decision rules, it is important therefore that we take into account the relative costs of
type I (false positive) and type II (false negative) errors. Because markets tend to be
self correcting, we in the United States tend to put more emphasis on reducing false
positives in order not to chill competition.'[2] Likewise, the US Supreme Court, since
1980, has been more concerned over false positives, noting for example that the
'cost of false positives counsels against an undue expansion of § 2 liability', which
involves monopolization and attempt to monopolize claims.[3]

The Chicago School's underlying belief is that when the agencies get it wrong, by **16.04**
not intervening, market forces often will correct the mistake. Market forces often
cannot correct the harm when the government erroneously intervenes.

This is far from empirically true. A former DOJ colleague observed how the US **16.05**
merger review process is so concerned with preventing erroneous challenges that it
is systematically skewed to under-enforcement:

> If the agency determines that a merger is anticompetitive, that decision is subject
> to review by a federal court, since to 'enforce' its determination that the merger is
> anticompetitive the agency must typically seek an injunction in federal court. On
> the other hand, if the agency determines that the merger is not anticompetitive (or
> even that it is anticompetitive, but other factors, such as opportunity costs or litiga-
> tion risks are sufficiently high as to make a challenge unwise), that is typically the
> end of the matter: there is no judicial review. Thus, the prospect of correction of an
> error made by the reviewing agency depends upon the type of error. If the reviewing
> agency's determination is a false positive, error correction via judicial review is avail-
> able. If the agency's determination is a false negative, it is not; the error will almost
> certainly go uncorrected. Assuming the reviewing agency is not significantly more
> prone to false positives or false negatives, the inevitable result of the entire process
> (including any available judicial review), would be significantly more false negatives
> than false positives.

> Indeed, the effect of this asymmetry is not simply limited to the fact that agency false
> positives may be corrected whereas false negatives are not. A rational entity, know-
> ing that a decision in one direction is subject to review (which entails significant
> costs and perhaps an embarrassing reversal that might undermine future enforce-
> ment efforts) and a decision in the opposite direction is final (and thus, essentially
> costless) would have some incentive to choose the latter. Although it is impossible to

---

[2] William J Kolasky, Deputy Assistant Attorney General, US Department of Justice (DOJ),
Antitrust Division, 'What Is Competition?', Address Before the Seminar on Convergence,
Sponsored by the Dutch Ministry of Economic Affairs, The Hague, Netherlands, 28 October 2002,
http://www.justice.gov/atr/speech/what-competition.
[3] *Verizon Communications Inc v Law Offices of Curtis V Trinko, LLP*, 540 US 398, 414, 124 S
Ct 872, 882 (2004).

estimate the magnitude or importance of this incentive on agency decision making, logically, the asymmetrical nature of judicial review would tend to encourage the reviewing agency, particularly in close cases, to err in favor of closing investigations rather than undertaking enforcement actions.[4]

16.06 It gets worse. As Larry Frankel notes, the agencies, under 'a nondeferential standard', must persuade a generalist court 'with less expertise, information, and resources'.[5] Although this reduces false positives, it 'will also inevitably lead to true positives being converted into false negatives'.[6] A string of agency defeats may further skew the error mix towards more false negatives than false positives.[7] The net result, Frankel notes, 'is systematic underenforcement'.[8]

16.07 Likewise, economist Jonathan Baker has argued that contemporary antitrust commentators employing an 'error cost' framework have made a series of erroneous assumptions: 'These assumptions systematically overstate the incidence and significance of false positives, understate the incidence and significance of false negatives, and understate the net benefits of various rules by overstating their costs.'[9]

16.08 As an example, the claim that markets self-correct rests in part on an economic premise: if entry is easy, the exercise of market power will prompt new competitors to emerge. The proponents move from that premise to the conclusion that errors of under-enforcement will 'self-correct' as well. Baker notes that this requires reliance on a second, unstated premise, namely 'that entry will generally prove capable of policing market power in the oligopoly settings of greatest concern in antitrust—or at least prove capable of policing market power with a sufficient frequency, to a sufficient extent, and with sufficient speed to make false positives systematically less costly than false negatives'.[10] However, there is little reason to believe that is true. Dominant firms often persist for decades, and cartels often last more than a decade even when antitrust enforcement cuts short their duration. As Baker concludes,

> The many examples of long-lasting dominant firms and cartels, along with the theoretical reasons why the exercise of monopoly power need not be transitory or corrected by new rivals attracted by supracompetitive prices, make clear that the exercise of durable market power should be treated as a serious concern. One cannot simply presume that entry by new competitors will correct the instances of market power that antitrust courts identify.[11]

---

[4] Lawrence M Frankel, 'The Flawed Institutional Design of US Merger Review: Stacking the Deck Against Enforcement', *Utah L Rev* [2008]: pp 159, 171–2 (internal footnotes omitted).

[5] Ibid, p 180.

[6] Ibid.

[7] Ibid.

[8] Ibid.

[9] Jonathan B Baker, 'Taking the Error Out of "Error Cost" Analysis', 80 *Antitrust LJ* (2015): pp 1, 37.

[10] Ibid, p 9.

[11] Ibid, pp 11–12.

Moreover, as Chapter 7 discusses, neither the EU nor US competition agencies need **16.09** to predict perfectly. The US Clayton Act, for example, tilts the balance towards enjoining mergers. Congress intended the agencies to arrest trends towards concentration and anticompetitive harms therefrom in their incipiency. Built into the law is some tolerance of false positives, namely that some mergers may ultimately not lessen competition but are enjoined to prevent further concentration.

B. The United States as a Test Case of Weak Antitrust Enforcement

Historian Richard Hofstadter asked in the mid-1960s what happened to the anti- **16.10** trust movement in the US. '[O]nce the United States had an antitrust movement without antitrust prosecutions', observed Hofstadter.[12] By the 1960s, however, there were 'antitrust prosecutions without an antitrust movement'.[13] By 2015, the US has far fewer antitrust prosecutions without an antitrust movement.

Figure 16.1 shows the overall decline, since the mid-1970s, in the number of private **16.11** federal antitrust lawsuits brought in the US.

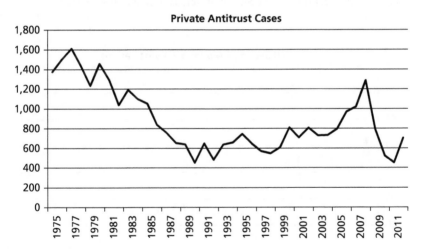

Private Antitrust Cases

Figure 16.1 Number of private federal antitrust lawsuits brought in the United States

Source: Sourcebook of Criminal Justice Statistics Online, Antitrust Cases Filed in US District Courts Antitrust Cases 1975–2012 (2012), Table 5.41, http://www.albany.edu/sourcebook/pdf/t5412012.pdf.

---

[12] Richard Hofstadter, 'What Happened to the Antitrust Movement?', in Richard Hofstadter, *The Paranoid Style in American Politics and Other Essays* (New York: Vintage Books, 2008), pp 188, 189.
[13] Ibid.

Figure 16.2 shows the steady decline in the number of DOJ investigations (civil and criminal) under section 1 of the Sherman Act.

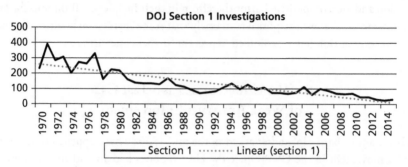

Figure 16.2 DOJ investigations (civil and criminal) under section 1 of the Sherman Act

Source: DOJ, Antitrust Division Workload Statistics FY 1970–2014, http://www.justice.gov/atr/division-operations.

The DOJ has investigated even fewer monopolization and attempted monopoly violations under section 2 of the Sherman Act, as shown in Figure 16.3.

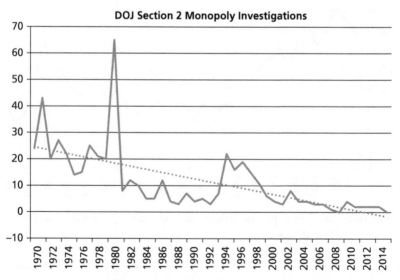

Figure 16.3 DOJ investigations of monopolization and attempted monopoly violations under section 2 of the Sherman Act

Source: DOJ, Antitrust Division Workload Statistics FY 1970–2014, http://www.justice.gov/atr/division-operations.

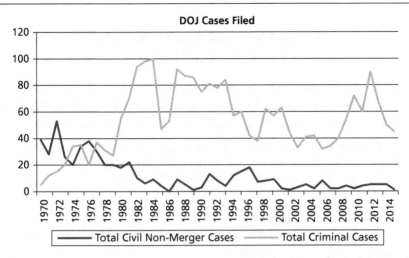

DOJ Cases Filed

Figure 16.4 Total DOJ civil non-merger cases and criminal cases filed, 1970–2014

Source: DOJ, Antitrust Division Workload Statistics FY 1970–2014, http://www.justice.gov/atr/
division-operations.

One possible explanation is that while the DOJ opened fewer investigations, it **16.12** brought more cases. As Figure 16.4 shows, aside from criminal price-fixing cases, that has not happened. Civil non-merger enforcement has dramatically declined. To put this in perspective, the Nixon administration brought more civil non-merger antitrust cases in one year (53 in 1972), than the DOJ brought collectively under the George W. Bush and Obama administrations.

Thus private antitrust actions, DOJ investigations, and DOJ civil non-merger en- **16.13** forcement are down. And as we saw in Chapter 15, the US agencies have challenged relatively few mergers, mainly in highly concentrated industries. So have markets effectively regulated themselves? Have the markets' self-policing powers prevented companies from inflicting significant harm and safeguarded our welfare?

Not surprisingly, with weak antitrust enforcement, markets have become more con- **16.14** centrated. 'In nearly a third of industries', the *Wall Street Journal* found in 2015, 'most US companies compete in markets that would be considered highly concentrated under current federal antitrust standards, up from about a quarter in 1996.'[14] Among the industries experiencing greater concentration is commercial radio, where we saw in Chapter 15 the harm from deficient merger review. Now we will look at the agricultural and financial industries.

---

[14] Theo Francis and Ryan Knutson, 'Wave of Megadeals Tests Antitrust Limits in US: Analysis shows that in many industries, most firms are competing in highly concentrated markets', *Wall Street Journal*, 18 October 2015, http://www.wsj.com/articles/wave-of-megadeals-tests-antitrust-limits-in-u-s-1445213306.

C. Costs of Weak Antitrust Enforcement in the Agricultural Industry

16.15 In 2010 the DOJ and US Department of Agriculture (USDA) examined buyer power in the seed, hog, livestock, poultry, and dairy industries.[15] The DOJ and USDA deserve credit for arranging the workshops. Professor Peter Carstensen noted:

> For years many of us who follow agricultural competition issues have lamented the failure of both antitrust enforcement and market facilitating regulation to deal with continuing problems that farmers and ranchers confront in both the acquisition of inputs and the marketing of their production.[16]

Over 4,000 people attended the public workshops in Iowa, Alabama, Wisconsin, Colorado, and Washington DC. The DOJ received over 18,000 public comments.

16.16 The DOJ heard many complaints about market concentration, monopsony, bid rigging, potential market manipulation, high input prices, and weak antitrust enforcement:

- how the 'lack of antitrust enforcement in recent decades' has resulted in 'a severely concentrated marketplace in which power and profit are limited to a few at the expense of countless, hard working family farmers';
- how one recent merger challenge was an 'anomaly', given 'a lot of mega-mergers' that 'have allowed a lot of concentration of market power' and finding it 'appalling that our antitrust enforcement has not been more vigorous than it has been in the past'; and
- how 'merger policy has been broken for 10 years, if not 20 or 30'.[17]

16.17 Participants complained that 'high input prices, low commodity prices, or other hardships, hav[e] invested particular suppliers or buyers with greater market power'.[18] Many participants at the workshops, the DOJ observed, 'specifically raised the issue of monopsony power'.[19] Some expressed concern that the enforcers, courts, and competition laws were 'inattentive to the monopsony problem'.[20]

---

[15] DOJ, 'From Farm to Fork: Antitrust Division and USDA Agriculture Workshops. Division Update Spring 2011', updated 15 July 2015, http://www.justice.gov/atr/public/division-update/2011/ag-workshops.html.

[16] Peter C Carstensen, 'Comments for the United States Departments of Agriculture and Justice Workshops on Competition Issues in Agriculture', University of Wisconsin Law School, Legal Studies Research Paper No 1103, 15 January 2010, pp 1–2, http://ssrn.com/abstract=1537191.

[17] DOJ, 'Competition and Agriculture: Voices from the Workshops on Agriculture and Antitrust Enforcement in our 21st Century Economy and Thoughts on the Way Forward' (2012), pp 4–5, ('DOJ Agriculture Workshops'), http://www.justice.gov/sites/default/files/atr/legacy/2012/05/16/283291.pdf.

[18] Ibid, p 5.

[19] Ibid, pp 8, 16.

[20] Ibid.

Participants complained how processors 'depress[ed] the prices of crops or animals below competitive levels'.[21] Participants 'pointed to retail concentration as an area of concern, charging that retailers are extracting a greater and greater share of the consumer food dollar, leaving producers with an ever decreasing share, and at the same time imposing price increases on consumers'.[22] Others raised social and moral concerns, such as the environmental toll from monopsonies.[23] The US livestock industry, observed several states, was more concentrated in 2010 than in 1921, when Congress enacted the Packers and Stockyards Act to respond to a market the 'Big Five' packers controlled 'and to ensure fair competition and fair trade practices in the marketing of livestock, meat and poultry'.[24]

One account of the hearings aptly summarized, '[w]hat applies across the board—in **16.18** cattle ranching and dairy and hog farming—is the stark and growing imbalance of power between the farmers who grow our food and the companies who process it for us, and how this imbalance enables practices unimaginable in any competitive market.'[25]

The DOJ had heard these complaints before. US Senator Kohl at a 2008 congres- **16.19** sional hearing on concentration in the agriculture industry observed:

> Disparity in market power between family farmers and large agribusiness firms all too often leaves the individual farmer and rancher with little choice regarding who will buy their products and under what terms....
>
> Unfortunately, it appears that the Justice Department's antitrust enforcement efforts, both in the ag sector and generally, have been much too weak and passive in recent years. In the opinion of many experts, the Justice Department has often failed to take effective action as merger after merger in the pork, milk, and seed markets have sharply increased concentration as well as reducing competition. Antitrust investigations in the dairy industry have languished, with no resolution. While the Justice Department sits largely on the sidelines, agriculture concentration rises, and food prices rise.[26]

---

[21] Ibid.

[22] Ibid, p 7.

[23] *See* ibid, p 8 ('[I]t's the monopsony power of these concentrated purchases of farm goods that are stressing the people and the natural systems that are producing food...' (internal quotation marks omitted)).

[24] Attorneys General of the States of Montana, Iowa, Maine, et al, Comments Regarding Competition in the Agriculture Industry, United States Department of Agriculture and United States Department of Justice Competition in the Agriculture Industry Workshops, 11 March 2010, p 6, http://www.justice.gov/atr/public/workshops/ag2010/016/AGW-15683.html (providing comments from the attorneys general of various states).

[25] Lina Khan, 'Obama's Game of Chicken', *Washington Monthly*, November–December 2012, pp 32, 35–6, http://www.washingtonmonthly.com/magazine/november_december_2012/features/obamas_game_of_chicken041108.php; *see also* David A Domina and C Robert Taylor, Organization for Competitive Markets, *The Debilitating Effects of Concentration in Markets Affecting Agriculture*, October 2009, p ii, http://farmfutures.com/mdfm/Faress1/author/2/OCM%20competition%20report.pdf.

[26] *Concentration in Agriculture and an Examination of the JBS/Swift Acquisitions: Hearing Before the Senate Committee on Antitrust, Competition Policy, and Consumer Rights*, 110th Cong 1,

16.20 Thus 2010 appeared to be a watershed. Recognizing 'that, historically, farmers and others have voiced concern about the level of merger enforcement in the agricultural sector', the DOJ under the Obama administration promised to redouble its efforts to prevent anticompetitive agricultural mergers and conduct.[27]

16.21 Other than one 2008 case,[28] the DOJ did not bring any significant enforcement actions in the agricultural sector.[29] Nor have the competition agencies, as Diana Moss and C Robert Taylor observed, systematically examined the 'increasingly concentrated agricultural supply chains and their implications for the two most vulnerable stakeholders: growers and consumers'.[30] One concern of the lax antitrust enforcement is that as a result farmers are being paid less, consumers are being charged more, and the middlemen are collecting a bigger profit.[31]

D. Costs of Weak Antitrust Enforcement in the Financial Sector

16.22 Given the importance of the financial services industries to the US economy, one priority of antitrust policy should be promoting the efficiency and competitiveness of the US financial markets. Before the financial crisis, the DOJ annually reviewed hundreds, if not thousands, of bank mergers.[32] The 1990s, one DOJ official said at the time, witnessed 'an explosion both in the number of mergers in banking and, in the past few years [late 1990s], in large deals that have caught the public imagination and concern'.[33]

---

8 May 2008), Statement of Sen Herb Kohl, Chairman, Senate Committee on Antitrust, Competition Policy, and Consumer Rights, http://www.gpo.gov/fdsys/pkg/CHRG-110shrg45064/html/CHRG-110shrg45064.htm.

[27] DOJ Agriculture Workshops, above note 17, p 16.

[28] *US and Plaintiff States v JBS SA and National Beef Packing Company, LLC*, Case No 08CV5992 (US Dist Ct (ND Ill), filed 20 October 2008), Complaint, http://www.justice.gov/atr/case-document/complaint-137.

[29] David Dayen, 'Bring Back Antitrust', *American Prospect*, Fall 2015, http://read.nxtbook.com/tap/theamericanprospect/theamericanprospectfall2015/bringbackantitrust.html.

[30] Diana L Moss and C Robert Taylor, 'Short Ends of the Stick: The Plight of Growers and Consumers in Concentrated Agricultural Supply Chains', *Wis L Rev* [2014]: pp 337, 338–9.

[31] Christopher R Leslie, 'Antitrust Law as Public Interest Law', 2 *UC Irvine L Rev* (2012): pp 885, 905.

[32] Between its fiscal years 2000 and 2009, the DOJ participated annually in 463 (2009) to 1,373 (2000) bank merger proceedings, with screenings requiring competitive analysis ranging between 342 and 945 mergers. DOJ, *Antitrust Division Workload Statistics FY 2000–2009*, http://www.justice.gov/sites/default/files/atr/legacy/2012/04/04/281484.pdf.

[33] Robert Kramer, Chief, DOJ, Antitrust Division, Litigation II Section, ' "Mega-Mergers" in the Banking Industry', Speech given at the American Bar Association Antitrust Section, Washington DC, 14 April 1999, http://www.justice.gov/atr/speech/mega-mergers-banking-industry. *See also* Robert E Litan, Deputy Ass't Attorney General, DOJ, Antitrust Division, 'Antitrust Assessment of Bank Mergers', Speech given at the American Bar Association Antitrust Section, 6 April 1994,

But what was the DOJ reviewing in these bank mega-mergers? Competition agen-   **16.23**
cies, as Chapter 7 explores, typically examine a merger's anticompetitive risks with
respect to the exercise of market power (ability to raise price) in narrowly defined
markets. So, absent the resurrection of the perceived potential entrant theory, the
DOJ would unlikely challenge a merger between a dominant bank in the western
US and a dominant bank in the eastern US.[34]

Here too, the post-merger reviews reflect a bleak picture, as six of seven studies found   **16.24**
evidence that bank mergers in the US (and abroad) resulted in price increases.[35] But
in focusing on the short-term static effects (such as whether the banks post-merger
may raise rates for specific categories of borrowers), the competition (and banking)
authorities failed to see or assess the long-term impact of the merger wave, such as
the mergers' impact on the efficiency, competitiveness, and stability of the overall
financial system.[36]

One lesson from the financial crisis is the role of systemic risk. The financial system,   **16.25**
when viewed as a complex adaptive system, can become more vulnerable when one
bank increases in size and becomes too big and too integral to fail.

The irony is that the DOJ and Federal Reserve heard these concerns during the   **16.26**
1990s merger wave in the financial services industry. One mega-merger was between Travelers Group Inc and Citicorp. In 1998, Travelers was a diversified financial services firm. With total assets of approximately USD 420 billion, it engaged
in various securities, insurance, lending, advisory, and other financial activities in
the United States and overseas.[37] Citicorp, with total assets of approximately USD

---

http://www.justice.gov/atr/public/speeches/litan.htm (noting that in the early 1990s the DOJ was
reviewing approximately 2,000 bank merger or acquisition applications annually).

[34] *See* Kramer, above note 33, p 7 (noting how the NationsBank and Bank of America mega-
merger 'was a classic market extension merger since NationsBank's operations focused generally on
the east coast and south and Bank of America was largely on the west coast' so the merger's competitive issues for the DOJ involved only two states—New Mexico and Texas).

[35] Orley Ashenfelter et al, 'Did Robert Bork Understate the Competitive Impact of Mergers?
Evidence from Consummated Mergers', 57 *J L & Econ* (2014): pp S67, S78.

[36] Janet L Yellen, Chair of the Federal Reserve Board, Speech at 'Finance and Society: A Conference
Sponsored by Institute for New Economic Thinking', Washington DC, 6 May 2015, 2015
WL 2152904, p *4 ('Yellen Speech'), http://www.federalreserve.gov/newsevents/speech/yellen20150506a.
htm (noting how the 'financial crisis revealed weaknesses in our nation's system for supervising
and regulating the financial industry. Prior to the crisis, regulatory agencies, including the Federal
Reserve, focused on the safety and soundness of individual firms—as required by their legislative
mandate at the time—rather than the stability of the financial system as a whole. Our regulatory
system did not provide any supervisory watchdog with responsibility for identifying and addressing
risks associated with activities and institutions that were outside the regulatory perimeter. The rapid
growth of the "shadow" nonbank financial sector left significant gaps in regulation.').

[37] Federal Reserve Board, Travelers Group, Inc, and Citicorp, Order Approving Formation of
a Bank Holding Company and Notice to Engage in Nonbanking Activities, 84 *Federal Reserve
Bulletin* (23 September 1998): p 985 ('Federal Reserve Citicorp Order'), http://www.federalreserve.
gov/boarddocs/press/BHC/1998/19980923/19980923.pdf.

331 billion, was the third-largest commercial bank in the US. The USD 70 billion merger created in 1998 the world's largest commercial banking organization, with total consolidated assets of approximately USD 751 billion.[38] During its merger review, a DOJ official said, the Antitrust Division 'heard numerous complaints that Citigroup would have an undue aggregation of resources— that the deal would create a firm *too big to be allowed to fail*'.[39] But the DOJ 'essentially viewed this as primarily a regulatory issue to be considered by the [Federal Reserve Board]'.[40]

16.27   The Federal Reserve Board, however, dismissed this and several other concerns, which presaged the financial crisis a decade later. Some commentators forewarned the Federal Reserve Board of Citicorp's anticompetitive abuses with subprime mortgagers.[41] A 'significant number of other commenters' said the merger violated the Glass–Steagall Act and 'urged the Board not to consider the proposal unless and until Congress amends the law to allow unlimited combinations of insurance, banking and securities businesses'.[42] Travelers CEO Sanford Weill had hoped his mega-merger would push Congress to remove the barriers under the Glass–Steagall Act of 1933.[43] Congress did so a year later. The Gramm–Leach–Bliley Act repealed the Glass–Steagall Act's restrictions on affiliations between bank and securities firms and amended the Bank Holding Company Act to permit affiliations

---

[38]   Ibid, p 4.

[39]   Kramer, above note 33 (emphasis added).

[40]   Ibid.

[41]   Federal Reserve Citicorp Order, above note 37, p 6 ('Travelers's marketing and sales practices for its subprime mortgage loans, personal loans and insurance products adversely affect consumers' and the merger 'would provide incentives for Citigroup to "steer" [low to moderate income] and minority consumers to its subprime lenders.'). In 2002, in the largest consumer protection settlement in the FTC's history, Citigroup Inc paid USD 215 million to resolve the FTC's charges of systematic and widespread deceptive and abusive lending practices by a company it acquired in 2000 and merged in its consumer finance operations. The FTC sued Citigroup Inc and CitiFinancial Credit Company as successor corporations to Associates First Capital Corporation and Associates Corporation of North America, which Citigroup acquired in 2000. Federal Trade Commission, 'Citigroup Settles FTC Charges Against the Associates Record-Setting $215 Million for Subprime Lending Victims', Press Release, 19 September 2002, https://www.ftc.gov/news-events/press-releases/2002/09/citigroup-settles-ftc-charges-against-associates-record-setting. Citigroup said that the alleged predatory lending practices happened before its 2000 acquisition and that it had taken corrective steps to prevent such abusive tactics. *See* Paul Beckett, 'Citigroup to Pay $215 Million to Settle Charges with FTC', *Wall Street Journal*, 20 September 2002, http://www.wsj.com/articles/SB103244794635808195. Despite these assurances, Citicorp and CitiFinancial Credit Company were fined USD 70 million in 2004 for their subprime lending practices in 2000 and 2001. Board of Governors of the Federal Reserve System, *In the Matter of Citigroup, Inc*, Order to Cease and Desist and Order of Assessment of a Civil Money Penalty Issued Upon Consent, 27 May 2004, http://www.federalreserve.gov/boarddocs/press/enforcement/2004/20040527/attachment.pdf. And in 2005, Citigroup acknowledged that it made hundreds of high-cost home loans to customers with poor credit histories in 2004. Eric Dash, 'Citigroup Units Kept Making Loans that Violated Policy', *New York Times*, 4 May 2005, http://www.nytimes.com/2005/05/04/business/citigroup-units-kept-making-loans-that-violated-policy.html.

[42]   Federal Reserve Citicorp Order, above note 37, p 6.

[43]   The NewsHour with Jim Lehrer: Financial Powerhouse, PBS television broadcast, 7 April 1998.

among financial services companies, including banks, securities firms, and insurance companies.[44]

Commentators also warned that the Citicorp/Travelers Group merger 'would result   **16.28**
in an undue concentration of resources and in an organization that is both "too big
to fail" and "too big to supervise" '.[45] In permitting the merger, the Federal Reserve
responded that the markets in which the merging parties competed were 'unconcentrated' and, in any market where one party had a significant presence, the other
party has a relatively small market share.[46]

The nation's largest corporate merger, predicted the Federal Reserve, 'would have   **16.29**
a *de minimis* effect on competition'.[47] The Federal Reserve rejected the argument
that the absolute or relative size of Citicorp would adversely affect the market
structure.[48] It saw no evidence that 'the size or breadth of Citicorp's activities
would allow it to distort or dominate any relevant market'.[49] Finally, the Federal
Reserve claimed it had 'extensive experience supervising Citicorp and, building
on that experience', it 'developed a comprehensive, risk-based supervision plan' to
effectively monitor Citibank; also other agencies, like the Securities and Exchange
Commission, would 'assist the Board in understanding Citigroup's business and
the risk profiles of those businesses'.[50]

Thus, during the 1990s, the DOJ and Federal Reserve heard concerns about mega-   **16.30**
mergers in the financial industry, including the concern that the Citibank–Travelers
merger would create an institution too big to fail. Over the next decade, Citigroup
senior management (and the Federal Reserve) demonstrated a lack of understanding
of the collateralized debt obligation (CDO) business and the risk profiles of that business. After Citigroup senior executives testified before the Financial Crisis Inquiry
Commission investigators on the cause of Citigroup's 2008 bailout, the Commission's
Chairman said, '[o]ne thing that is striking is the extent to which senior management
either didn't know or didn't care to know about risks that ultimately helped bring the
institution to its knees.'[51] As the Federal Reserve Chair Janet Yellen said,

> The crisis also revealed that risk management at large, complex financial institutions was insufficient to handle the risks that some firms had taken. Compensation

---

[44] Glass–Steagall Act (1933), *New York Times*, http://www.nytimes.com/topic/subject/glasssteagall-act-1933.
[45] Federal Reserve Citicorp Order, above note 37, p 74.
[46] Ibid, p 75.
[47] Ibid.
[48] Ibid, p 85.
[49] Ibid, p 86.
[50] Ibid.
[51] Bradley Keoun, Jesse Westbrook, and Ian Katz, 'Citigroup "Liquidity Puts" Draw Scrutiny from Crisis Inquiry', Bloomberg Business, 13 April 2010, http://www.bloomberg.com/news/2010-04-13/citigroup-s-14-billion-liquidity-put-loss-is-focus-of-u-s-crisis-panel.html.

systems all too frequently failed to appropriately account for longer-term risks undertaken by employees. And lax controls in some cases contributed to unethical and illegal behavior by banking organizations and their employees.[52]

16.31   A decade after its merger, Citibank, and other financial institutions considered too big to fail, were (or were perceived to be) failing, and received an implicit government guarantee. Citigroup, an early recipient of the government bailout, received a USD 45 billion emergency infusion and USD 301 billion of government asset insurance, which was the largest taxpayer bailout for any US bank.[53] In March 2010, Citigroup's CEO testified before Congress that no financial institution should be too big to fail, and that 'Citi owes a large debt of gratitude to American taxpayers' for bailing out his bank.[54]

16.32   So what are we left with after ineffectual antitrust and banking oversight during the 1980s–1990s merger wave? For one thing, a highly concentrated financial services industries in the US. Six bank holding companies—Citigroup, JPMorgan Chase, Bank of America, Wells Fargo Bank, Goldman Sachs, and Morgan Stanley— dominate the industry. By the third quarter of 2010, the assets of these six bank holding companies were worth 64 per cent of gross domestic product (GDP), which was higher than in 2006 (about 55 per cent of GDP) and 1995 (17 per cent of GDP).[55] As one point of comparison, the combined assets of *all* US commercial banks in 1978 were worth 53 per cent of GDP.[56]

16.33   As another measure of concentration, in 1990, the five largest banks accounted for 9.68 per cent of the US banking industry's total assets. By 2014, they controlled 44.19 per cent of the industry assets.[57] In 2011, the four largest US commercial banking firms (Bank of America, Wells Fargo, JPMorgan Chase, and Citigroup) accounted for 34 per cent of national deposits and 56.6 per cent of the market in general purpose credit card purchase volume; they originated 58.2 per cent of mortgage loans by volume in 2009 and serviced 56.3 per cent of such loans.[58]

---

[52] Yellen Speech, above note 36, p *3.

[53] *See* Keoun et al, above note 51; Pro Publica Inc, 'Where Is the Money?: Eye on the Bailout', http://projects.propublica.org/bailout/entities/96-citigroup.

[54] Eric Dash, 'Panelists Question Citigroup's "Government Guarantee"', *New York Times*, 4 March 2010, http://www.nytimes.com/2010/03/05/business/05tarp.html.

[55] Simon Johnson, 'The Bill Daley Problem', *Huffington Post*, 9 January 2011, http://www.huffingtonpost.com/simon-johnson/bill-daley-obama-chief-of-staff_b_806341.html.

[56] Simon Johnson and James Kwak, *13 Bankers: The Wall Street Takeover and the Next Financial Meltdown* (New York: Vintage Books, 2010), p 59.

[57] Chris Vanderpool, '5 Banks Hold More Than 44% of US Industry's Assets', SNL Financial, 2 December 2014, https://www.cbinsight.com/press-release/snl-financial-report-5-banks-hold-more-than-44-of-us-industrys-assets.auth=inherit#news/article?id=30025507&KeyProductLinkType=0&cdid=A-30025507-14130.

[58] Financial Stability Oversight Council, 'Study & Recommendations Regarding Concentration Limits on Large Financial Companies', January 2011, pp 13, 24, http://www.treasury.gov/initiatives/Documents/Study%20on%20Concentration%20Limits%20on%20Large%20Firms%2001-17-11.pdf.

As a point of reference, the 25 largest banks accounted for 29.1 per cent of deposits in 1980.[59]

So what has been the primary response to the bank merger wave that yielded a **16.34** handful of dominant financial institutions deemed too big to fail? The 2010 Dodd–Frank Wall Street Reform and Consumer Protection Act. It seeks to 'promote the financial stability of the United States by improving accountability and transparency in the financial system, to end "too big to fail" to protect the American taxpayer by ending bailouts, to protect consumers from abusive financial services practices, and for other purposes'.[60] Toward that end, the Act created a Financial Stability Oversight Council (Council), which, among other things, (1) monitors the financial services marketplace to identify potential threats to the financial stability of the United States; and (2) advises Congress and makes recommendations in such areas that will enhance the integrity, efficiency, competitiveness, and stability of the US financial markets.[61] (Conspicuously missing from the Council are any officials from the DOJ's Antitrust Division or the FTC.[62] Despite the DOJ's role in reviewing bank mergers and the DOJ's and FTC's role in preserving the competitiveness of the US financial markets, the antitrust agencies are on the sidelines with respect to this Council's fact-gathering and advising function.)

Interestingly, the Council studied a statutory measure to effectively curb the larger **16.35** financial institutions from getting any bigger by acquiring rivals. A financial company could not merge with, or acquire, another company if the resulting company's liabilities would exceed 10 per cent of the aggregate liabilities of all financial companies.[63] The Council studied how the statutory cap would affect financial stability, moral hazard in the financial system, the efficiency and competitiveness of US financial firms and financial markets, and the cost and availability of credit and other financial services to US households and businesses.

By barring very large bank mergers, a statutory cap, under the old Chicago School **16.36** beliefs, would raise significant concerns of false positives. Not true, the Council

---

[59] Stephen A Rhoades, Board of Governors of the Federal Reserve System, *Bank Mergers and Banking Structure in the United States, 1980–98*, Staff Study 174, August 2000, p 26, http://www.federalreserve.gov/pubs/staffstudies/2000-present/ss174.pdf.

[60] Pub L 111-203, 124 Stat 1376 (2010) ('Dodd–Frank').

[61] 12 USC s 5322(a)(2).

[62] 12 USC s 5321.

[63] Dodd–Frank, above note 60, s 622; 12 USC s 1852; *see also* Financial Stability Oversight Council (FSOC), *Study & Recommendations Regarding Concentration Limits on Large Financial Companies*, January 2011, p 4 ('FSOC Study'), http://www.treasury.gov/initiatives/fsoc/studies-reports/Documents/Study%20on%20Concentration%20Limits%20on%20Large%20Firms%2001-17-11.pdf (noting how s 622 would limit growth by acquisition more comprehensively than the pre-existing 10% nationwide deposit cap imposed by the Riegle–Neal Act because 'it also takes into account non-deposit liabilities and off-balance sheet exposures, limiting incentives to shift liabilities from deposits to potentially more volatile on- and off-balance-sheet liabilities').

found. Overall, the statutory cap would have a 'positive impact on US financial stability':

> Specifically, the Council believes that the concentration limit will reduce the risks to US financial stability created by increased concentration arising from mergers, consolidations or acquisitions involving the largest US financial companies. Restrictions on future growth by acquisition of the largest financial companies ultimately will prevent acquisitions that could make these firms harder for their officers and directors to manage, for the financial markets to understand and discipline, and for regulators to supervise. The concentration limit, as structured, could also have the beneficial effect of causing the largest financial companies to either shed risk or raise capital to reduce their liabilities so as to permit additional acquisitions under the concentration limit. Such actions, other things equal, would tend to reduce the chance that the firm would fail....

> Although the Council expects the impact of the concentration limit on moral hazard, competition, and the availability of credit in the US financial system to be generally neutral over the short- to medium-term, over the long run the Council expects the concentration limit to enhance the competitiveness of US financial markets by preventing the increased dominance of those markets by a very small number of firms.[64]

16.37 In 2014, the Federal Reserve implemented the financial sector concentration limit.[65] The rule, however, does not eliminate systemic risk.[66] But the statutory cap should limit *domestic* acquisitions by Bank of America, JPMorgan Chase, Citigroup, and Wells Fargo.[67]

16.38 Why should competition policy take bigness into account in one sector but not another? Or disregard lack of competitive overlaps sometimes but not always? We are not arguing for a statutory merger cap for every industry. There is a significant difference between financial mergers and many other mergers, such as when two large chains of fast-food restaurants merge. The key issue is the separation of risk

[64] FSOC Study, above note 63, p 4.

[65] 'Concentration Limits on Large Financial Companies', 79 *Fed Reg* 68095 (14 November 2014) (codified at Concentration Limit: Regulation XX, 12 CFR Part 251) ('Regulation XX').

[66] FSOC Study, above note 63, p 10 (finding 'firms with less than 10 percent of US financial liabilities can be sufficiently large or otherwise critical to the functioning of financial markets to raise systemic issues in the event of failure, the concentration limit alone is unlikely to sufficiently reduce the risks posed to financial stability by systemically important firms').

[67] Ibid, p 8. One loophole involves acquisitions by foreign banks. Section 622 provides that the liabilities of a ' "foreign financial company" equal the risk-weighted assets and regulatory capital attributable to the company's "US operations" '. Regulation XX, above note 65, p 68098. As a result, one law firm noted, the regulation would have the 'effect of favoring business combinations between US financial companies and foreign companies that are structured, as a legal matter, such that the foreign financial entity is the technical survivor of the merger, for example even where the US financial company is the larger counterparty or where the merger is a merger of equals'. Sullivan & Cromwell LLP, 'Dodd–Frank Act: Additional Concentration Limits on Large Financial Companies', 28 May 2014, p 7, https://www.sullcrom.com/siteFiles/Publications/SC_Publication_Dodd_Frank_Act_Additional_Concentration_Limits_on_Large_Financial_Companies.pdf.

and reward for these institutions deemed too big and too integral to fail. In creating a financial institution too big to fail, a merger can adversely affect consumers and other market participants by reducing the requisite degree of diversity for the financial network to remain stable. Moreover, in being deemed too big to fail, financial institutions can engage in risky behaviour with the confidence of a government bailout, and thus enjoy a competitive advantage over smaller rivals that are permitted to fail.[68]

The financial crisis exposed the significant harm that many large financial institutions inflicted on society. As the Fed Chairwoman observed, '[i]nstead of promoting financial security through prudent mortgage underwriting, the financial sector prior to the crisis facilitated a bubble in the housing market and too often encouraged households to take on mortgages they neither understood nor could afford.'[69] She noted how recent research has 'raised important questions about the benefits and costs of the rapid growth of the financial services industry in the United States over the past 40 years', including how trends in compensation in the financial sector contributes to the increase in income inequality in the United States in recent decades.[70]   **16.39**

One complaint is that the senior executives at these financial services firms were never prosecuted for any of the fraudulent activity leading up to the economic crisis.[71] Nor were any of the too-big-to-fail financial institutions criminally prosecuted. Then US Attorney General Eric Holder told Congress that the financial institutions were too big to criminally prosecute: 'It does become difficult for us to prosecute them when we are hit with indications that if you do prosecute—if you do bring a criminal charge—it will have a negative impact on the national economy, perhaps even the world economy'.[72]   **16.40**

And the concentrated financial sector continues to be fertile ground for illegal collusive behaviour. In May 2015, five banks—Citicorp, JPMorgan Chase, Barclays, the Royal Bank of Scotland, and UBS AG—pled guilty to felony charges of conspiring to manipulate the price of US dollars and euros exchanged in the foreign   **16.41**

---

[68] Johnson and Kwak, above note 56, p 205; FSOC, 2011 Annual Report, p 109, https://www.treasury.gov/initiatives/fsoc/Documents/FSOCAR2011.pdf (noting that credit rating agencies 'factor an explicit "uplift"' into the ratings of financial institutions perceived as too big to fail, how this support 'increased dramatically in 2008 and persists'; while the markets may not factor the ratings uplift into their evaluation of these companies' long-term debt, the uplift provides 'a direct benefit for the short-term funding rating for these firms' in accessing short-term wholesale funding markets that they would be unable to access with a lower rating).

[69] Yellen Speech, above note 36, p *2.

[70] Ibid.

[71] Jed S Rakoff, 'The Financial Crisis: Why Have No High-Level Executives Been Prosecuted?', *New York Review of Books*, 9 January 2014, http://www.nybooks.com/articles/archives/2014/jan/09/financial-crisis-why-no-executive-prosecutions/.

[72] Ibid.

currency exchange spot market. The banks agreed to pay criminal fines totalling over USD 2.5 billion.[73] Moreover, two banks—UBS and Barclays—had to pay an additional USD 203 million and USD 60 million, respectively, for breaching their 2012 non-prosecution agreements resolving the DOJ's investigation involving the London Interbank Offered Rate (LIBOR). The DOJ fined Citicorp (USD 925 million), Barclays (USD 650 million), JPMorgan (USD 550 million), and RBS (USD 395 million). The new US Attorney General noted how the financial penalties 'should deter competitors in the future from chasing profits without regard to fairness, to the law, or to the public welfare'.[74] That is optimistic. Since 2009, the large financial institutions have paid over USD 204 billion in 175 settlements (counting only settlements where the fine exceeded USD 100 million).[75]

16.42 Moreover, the concentrated financial sector now faces a new systemic threat, namely cyber-attacks. When Congress repealed the Glass–Steagall Act to allow different types of financial institutions—commercial banks, brokerage houses, and insurers—to merge, it also enabled the merging parties to amass a variety of personal data. The Gramm–Leach–Bliley Act required, among other things, the financial institutions to design, implement, and maintain reasonable safeguards to protect the security, confidentiality, and integrity of their customers' sensitive information.[76]

16.43 No doubt many companies and government agencies are subject to data breaches. But the large financial institutions are a treasure trove for hackers. Apparently hackers used off-the-shelf technology to steal in 2014 the personal data of 83 million JPMorgan Chase customers.[77] So the Council is grappling with preventing cyber-attacks from destabilizing the financial sector's stability (and undermining our privacy). It warns that '[m]alicious cyber activity is likely to continue, and financial sector organizations should be prepared to mitigate the threat posed

---

[73] DOJ, 'Five Major Banks Agree To Parent-Level Guilty Pleas: Citicorp, JPMorgan Chase & Co., Barclays PLC, The Royal Bank of Scotland plc Agree to Plead Guilty In Connection With The Foreign Exchange Market and Agree to Pay More Than $2.5 Billion In Criminal Fines', Press Release, 20 May 2015, http://www.justice.gov/opa/pr/five-major-banks-agree-parent-level-guilty-pleas.

[74] Ibid.

[75] Jeff Cox, 'Misbehaving Banks Have Now Paid $204B in Fines', CNBC, 30 October 2015, http://www.cnbc.com/2015/10/30/misbehaving-banks-have-now-paid-204b-in-fines.html (Bank of America USD 77.09 billion, JPMorgan Chase USD 40.12 billion, Citigroup USD 18.39 billion, Wells Fargo USD 10.24 billion, BNP Paribas USD 8.90 billion, UBS USD 6.54 billion, Deutsche Bank USD 5.53 billion, Morgan Stanley USD 4.78 billion, Barclays USD 4.23 billion, and Credit Suisse USD 3.74 billion).

[76] 15 USC ss 6801(b) and 6805(b)(2); 16 CFR Part 314; FTC, Financial Institutions and Customer Information: Complying with the Safeguards Rule, April 2006, https://www.ftc.gov/tips-advice/business-center/guidance/financial-institutions-customer-information-complying.

[77] 'What Lies Behind the JPMorgan Chase Cyber-attack: The Criminal Economy is Developing Faster Than the Lawful One Can Defend Itself', *The Economist*, 12 November 2015, http://www.economist.com/news/business-and-finance/21678214-criminal-economy-developing-faster-lawful-one-can-defend-itself-what-lies-behind.

by cyber attacks that have the potential to destroy critical data and systems and impair operations.'[78]

And the Federal Reserve Chairwoman in 2015 is still dissatisfied with changes made **16.44** by the largest US financial firms since the 2008 crisis. The Fed still sees 'substantial compliance and risk management issues' at the largest financial firms.[79]

E. Consumers' Overall Welfare

No one has calculated the costs of false negatives—namely the US government's **16.45** passivity in enforcing the competition laws. For too long, the focus has been on false positives. On a macro level, it is hard to see how competition policy has promoted consumer welfare over the past 35 years–given the bleak picture of America's stark income and wealth inequality, the stagnant living standards, the growing economic insecurity and poverty, and the decline in social mobility.

One recurring theme in 1890 (when the Sherman Act was enacted), in 1950 (when **16.46** the Clayton Act was amended), and today is the destabilizing effect from extreme wealth inequality. In 1890, inequality was high. Senator Sherman identified this inequality of condition, wealth, and opportunity as the greatest threat to disturbing social order: this inequality had 'grown within a single generation out of the concentration of capital into vast combinations to control production and trade and to break down competition'.[80] As the majority and dissent in the 1911 *Standard Oil* decision discussed, people were concerned about wealth concentrated in the hands of a few individuals and corporations.[81]

Economists have documented the distinctive 'U' shape of income disparity between **16.47** 1917 and 2014 in the US.[82] Peaking in 1928, income disparity sharply declined during the Great Depression. Thereafter, '[b]etween 1947 and 1973, economic growth was both rapid and distributed equally across income classes', reported the Economic Policy Institute. 'The poorest 20% of families saw growth at least as fast as the richest 20% of families, and everybody in between experienced similar rates of income growth.'[83] But in the late 1970s, income inequality in the US began

---

[78] FSOC, 2015 Annual Report, p 4, http://www.treasury.gov/initiatives/fsoc/studies-reports/Documents/2015%20FSOC%20Annual%20Report.pdf.
[79] Ryan Tracy et al, 'Yellen: Not Satisfied With Banks' Changes', *Wall Street Journal*, 5 November 2015, p C3.
[80] 21 *Congressional Record* 2455, 2460 (1890).
[81] *Standard Oil Co v United States*, 221 US 1, 50, 31 S Ct 502, 512 (1911); ibid, 83–4 (1911) per Harlan, J, concurring in part and dissenting in part.
[82] Thomas Piketty and Emmanuel Saez, 'Inequality in the Long Run', 344(6186) *Science* (23 May 2014): pp 838–43; Thomas Piketty, *Capital in the Twenty-First Century* (Cambridge, MA: Harvard University Press, 2014), p 24.
[83] State of Working America, Income Inequality, http://stateofworkingamerica.org/inequality/income-inequality/.

growing, reaching a record high in 2014.[84] In 2014, the official poverty rate in the US was 14.8 per cent, with 46.7 million people in poverty.[85]

16.48 The widening income inequality is not limited to the US. It is a worldwide issue. In a 2014 Pew Research Center survey, 'majorities in all 44 nations polled described the gap between rich and poor as a big problem for their country, and majorities in 28 nations said it was a very big problem'.[86]

16.49 The rise in income inequality beginning in the late 1970s corresponds with the period when antitrust enforcement began tapering off. Scholars are studying the implications of weak antitrust on wealth and income inequality.[87] For example, economist Joseph E Stiglitz discusses why the growing wealth and income inequality is not the natural by-product of a market economy, but the result of policy decisions.[88] Stiglitz's central thesis is that this bleak picture did not appear naturally. Rather economic policies entail choices. All economic policies have distributive consequences. Much of the inequality resulted from deliberate legal and enforcement decisions, whereby the government over the past 30 years failed to protect most Americans. Instead, the economically powerful used the government to enrich themselves at society's expense. Stiglitz provides a panorama of how various government policies increased wealth and income inequality, including the deregulation of the financial sector, various corporate welfare

---

[84] Carmen DeNavas-Walt and Bernadette D Proctor, US Census Bureau, *Income and Poverty in the United States: 2014*, Current Population Reports, P60-252, September 2015, p 8, https://www.census.gov/content/dam/Census/library/publications/2015/demo/p60-252.pdf (between 1999—the year that US household income peaked before the 2001 recession—and 2014, 'incomes at the 50th and 10th percentiles declined 7.2 percent and 16.5 percent, respectively, while income at the 90th percentile increased 2.8 percent'). Since 1999, the 90th to 10th percentile income ratio increased 23.1%. Ibid, pp 8–9.

[85] Ibid, p 12.

[86] Richard Wike, 'Inequality is at Top of the Agenda as Global Elites Gather in Davos', Pew Research Center, 21 January 2015, http://www.pewresearch.org/fact-tank/2015/01/21/inequality-is-at-top-of-the-agenda-as-global-elites-gather-in-davos/.

[87] *See, eg*, Anna Kingsbury, 'Competition Law and Economic Inequality: Distributional Objectives in New Zealand Competition Law', 33(5) *ECLR* (2012): pp 248, 248 (discussing the distributional goals in New Zealand competition law, in the context of rising economic inequality, and considering the relationship between competition law and inequality in New Zealand); Jonathan B Baker and Steven C Salop, 'Antitrust, Competition Policy, and Inequality', 104 *Geo LJ Online* (2015), http://georgetownlawjournal.org/glj-online/antitrust-competition-policy-and-inequality/; *see also* Greg Ip, 'Behind Rising Inequality: More Unequal Companies: More Competition Would Help Narrow the Gap Between the Highest- and Lowest-paid Employees', *Wall Street Journal*, 4 November 2015, http://www.wsj.com/articles/behind-rising-inequality-more-unequal-companies-1446665769 ('Mounting evidence suggests the prime driver of wage inequality is the growing gap between the most- and least-profitable companies, not the gap between the highest- and lowest-paid workers within each company. That suggests policies that have focused on individuals, from minimum wages to education, may not be enough to close the pay gap; promoting competition between companies such as through antitrust oversight may also be important.').

[88] Joseph E Stiglitz, *The Price of Inequality: How Today's Divided Society Endangers Our Future* (New York: WW Norton & Co, 2012).

programmes, the regulatory race to the bottom, the attack on unions, the biased tax and bankruptcy policies, the permissiveness towards predatory lending, and macro-economic policies that prized inflation over unemployment. What is interesting is how lax antitrust enforcement went hand-in-hand with these other policy choices. The wealthy devised better ways to attain, maintain, and exploit their market power. Stiglitz criticizes how judges and policymakers were 'educated' in the Chicago School ideologies of self-correcting, presumptively efficient and competitive markets, even when the economic literature was refuting these claims. Other factors that Stiglitz attributes to monopolies' durability are network effects and new business tactics to resist entry (such as Microsoft's notorious 'FUD' strategy of Fear, Uncertainty, and Doubt). But the rent-seeking problem ultimately for Stiglitz was weak enforcement of the competition laws.

Finally, Stiglitz articulates why the growing inequality matters. Society overall pays **16.50** a stiff price. We end up with a less stable, less efficient economy that generates less growth, less public investment, and less opportunity. Our democracy is weakened with greater voter disillusionment, greater distrust in our government, and greater disillusionment as many citizens are disempowered. Society ends up with more rent seeking, more lobbyists, and a greater misallocation of economic resources (as talented people flock to the financial sector to devise better ways to fleece consumers). Ultimately, there is an under-investment in human capital. The greatest cost imposed on society is 'the erosion of our sense of identity in which fair play, equality of opportunity, and a sense of community are so important'. Not surprisingly, among the various economic reforms Stiglitz advances are stronger and more effectively enforced competition laws.[89]

F. Why Ignoring Big Data Will Compound the Harm

With the rise of too-big-to-fail financial institutions, the complaints of excessive **16.51** concentration in other industries, like radio and agriculture, and Kwoka's meta-analysis of post-merger studies, one would think that the competition agencies are finally taking note. One would expect them to inquire whether their analytical tools for assessing mergers are up to par. One would also expect the agencies to revisit their merger guidelines assumptions and explore when actual marketplace behaviour deviates from their theories' predicted behaviour. The cost of weak antitrust enforcement is too great.

---

[89] Stiglitz's book complements other recent scholarship, such as Daron Acemoglu and James A Robinson's discussion of extractive and inclusive economies in *Why Nations Fail: The Origins of Power, Prosperity, And Poverty* (New York: Crown Business, 2012), and Adair Turner's critique in *Economics After the Crisis: Objectives and Means (Lionel Robbins Lectures)* (Boston, MA: MIT Press, 2012), of the simplistic beliefs about the objectives and means of economic activity that dominated the past few decades.

16.52   The cost of false negatives in data-driven industries will likely be even greater. Data-driven mergers, McKinsey and Company predicted, will only increase: 'the need for scale of data and IT infrastructure may become a critical driver toward consolidation, which can be both an opportunity and threat, in sectors where subscale players are abundant'.[90] Many of these industries, given the data-driven network effects, are ripe for consolidation. Thus the incentives for mergers and exclusionary behaviour increase to tip the market towards dominance. We are already hearing the warnings: 'Where companies acquiring massive proprietary data sets', the OECD observed, 'there is thus a higher risk that we're kind of heading toward data as a source of monopoly power.'[91] The OECD also noted how the 'economics of data favours market concentration and dominance' and how 'data-driven markets can lead to a "winner takes all" result where concentration is a likely outcome of market success'.[92]

16.53   So data-driven mergers coupled with network effects and sleepy (or intellectually captured) antitrust enforcers will likely yield highly concentrated markets. One long-standing premise of competition policy is that, absent strong economic evidence to the contrary for a specific industry, less concentrated markets are generally preferable over moderately and highly concentrated markets. In discussing the need for a statutory cap to prevent further mergers by large firms, the Financial Stability Oversight Council noted how a 'large body of theoretical and empirical work has found that less concentrated markets produce socially beneficial results compared to more concentrated markets'.[93] That is especially true in data-driven industries, where a few dominant firms can undermine many democratic systems. Of the many harms, the OECD noted, is the *loss of autonomy and freedom*:

> Advances in data analytics make it possible e.g. to infer sensitive information including from trivial data. The misuse of these insights can affect core values and principles, such as individual autonomy, equality and free speech, and may have a broader impact on society as a whole. Discrimination enabled by data analytics, for example, may result in greater efficiencies, but also limit an individual's ability to escape the impact of pre-existing socio-economic indicators....[94]

16.54   Second, the shift in power to a handful of dominant tech firms will exacerbate existing inequalities:

> Better data-driven insights come with a better understanding of the data objects and of how best to influence or control them. Where the agglomeration of data leads to

---

[90]   James Manyika et al, McKinsey Global Institute, *Big Data: The Next Frontier for Innovation, Competition, and Productivity*, June 2011, p 113, http://www.mckinsey.com/insights/business_technology/big_data_the_next_frontier_for_innovation.

[91]   OECD, *Data-Driven Innovation for Growth and Well-Being: Interim Synthesis Report*, October 2014, p 58, http://www.oecd.org/sti/inno/data-driven-innovation-interim-synthesis.pdf.

[92]   Ibid, p 7.

[93]   FSOC Study, above note 63, p 12 n 26.

[94]   OECD, *Data-Driven Innovation*, above note 91, p 7.

concentration and greater information asymmetry, significant shifts in power can occur away from: i) individuals to organisations (incl. consumers to businesses, and citizens to governments); ii) traditional businesses to data-driven businesses given increasing returns to scale and potential risks of market concentration and dominance; iii) governments to data-driven businesses where businesses can gain much more knowledge about citizens than governments can; and iv) lagging economies to data-driven economies.[95]

For example, Professors Lianos and Motchenkova discuss how search engines, **16.55** unlike other two-sided platforms, 'act as "information gatekeepers"': they not only provide information on what can be found on the web; they are 'an essential first-point-of-call for anyone venturing onto the Internet'.[96] Moreover, search engines 'detain an important amount of information about their customers and advertisers (the "map of commerce")'.[97]

As a gateway, a dominant search engine, one study found, could impact democratic **16.56** elections.[98] Many users trust and choose the search engine's higher-ranked results more than its lower-ranked results. The study inquired whether manipulating the search rankings could alter the preferences of undecided voters in democratic elections. Using 4,556 undecided voters representing diverse demographic characteristics of India's and the US's voting populations, the experiments found that '(i) biased search rankings can shift the voting preferences of undecided voters by 20% or more, (ii) the shift can be much higher in some demographic groups, and (iii) search ranking bias can be masked so that people show no awareness of the manipulation'.[99] As the authors concluded, 'Given that many elections are won by small margins, our results suggest that a search engine company has the power to influence the results of a substantial number of elections with impunity. The impact of such manipulations would be especially large in countries dominated by a single search engine company'.[100]

Moreover, as privacy erodes, so can trust. Consumers may be reluctant to share **16.57** personal data, including data for innovations that improve overall welfare. After hearing the 'widespread concerns about the effectiveness of the means by which consumers engage with the process of collecting data, including the use of privacy

---

[95] Ibid, p 7.

[96] Ioannis Lianos and Evgenia Motchenkova, 'Market Dominance and Search Quality in the Search Engine Market', 9(2) *J Competition L & Econ* (2013): pp 419, 422, doi: 10.1093/joclec/nhs037.

[97] Ibid.

[98] Robert Epstein and Ronald E Robertson, 'The Search Engine Manipulation Effect (SEME) and its Possible Impact on the Outcomes of Elections', 112(33) *PNAS* (2015): E4512–21; published ahead of print 4 August 2015, doi:10.1073/pnas.1419828112, http://www.pnas.org/content/112/33/E4512.full.pdf.

[99] Ibid.

[100] Ibid.

policies, terms and conditions and cookie notices', the UK competition authority expressed unease about how the deterioration in privacy competition could erode trust:

> Consumer trust could be fragile and at risk if negative perceptions about new technologies or the way firms manage data take hold. We are concerned that future changes in the way that data is collected and used (such as more passive collection via the [Internet of Things] could test how far consumers would be willing to continue to provide data.[101]

The OECD was likewise concerned. Many competition officials still are not fully acknowledging these privacy harms, and instead tend 'to direct the specific privacy issues to the privacy protection authorities; the latter however having no authority on competition issues'.[102] As the OECD concluded, '[t]he effective protection of privacy is therefore a key condition for preserving trust in data-driven innovation'.[103]

G. The Competition Agencies Cannot Assume that Other Agencies will Repair Their Mistakes

16.58 The DOJ in the radio merger wave might have assumed that the FCC would prevent any harm to listeners. Likewise, the DOJ assumed that the Federal Reserve would protect against increases in systemic risk during the bank merger wave. The problem was that the other agencies allowed these mergers to sail through. Even after consumers are harmed, the competition agency may point the finger at another agency. This is reminiscent of one quail hunt. The plaintiff was shot, but did not know which defendant had shot him. Under those circumstances, the court held, the burden shifted to the defendants to show who was responsible.[104]

16.59 We can safely say that many of the harms we identify for data-driven mergers and abuses are fairly traceable to weak antitrust. The privacy agencies typically are not notified of data-driven mergers. Nor can they enjoin the mergers. Privacy and consumer protection laws typically provide behavioural remedies and fines, which have been generally lower than antitrust penalties.[105] Fines will increase significantly

---

[101] UK Competition and Markets Authority, *The Commercial Use of Consumer Data: Report on the CMA's Call for Information*, June 2015, paras 21, 26, https://www.gov.uk/government/uploads/system/uploads/attachment_data/file/435817/The_commercial_use_of_consumer_data.pdf.

[102] OECD, *Data-Driven Innovation*, above note 91, pp 59, 62.

[103] Ibid.

[104] *Remijas v Neiman Marcus Grp, LLC*, 794 F3d 688, 696 (US Ct of Apps (7th Cir), 2015), discussing *Summers v Tice*, 33 Cal 2d 80, 199 P2d 1, 5 (1948).

[105] European Data Protection Supervisor (EDPS), *Privacy and Competitiveness in the Age of Big Data: The Interplay Between Data Protection, Competition Law, and Consumer Protection in the Digital Economy*, Preliminary Opinion, 26 March 2014, p 16 ('EDPS Preliminary Opinion'), https://secure.edps.europa.eu/EDPSWEB/webdav/shared/Documents/Consultation/Opinions/

in Europe for privacy violations.[106] But the privacy authorities still lack structural remedies. If a company uses anticompetitive tactics to tip the market in its favour, fines will unlikely reverse the network effects (or adequately deter given the likely monopoly profits).

Thus for anticompetitive data-driven mergers and restraints, the antitrust remedies **16.60** will often be critical and superior to attempts to regulate monopolies after the fact. US Senator Mike Lee (R-UT), for example, noted that 'antitrust enforcement may unlock beneficial competition for the protection of user privacy and avert the need for additional privacy regulation'.

Competition law accordingly can play an integral role in ensuring that we capture **16.61** the potential benefits of a data-driven economy while mitigating its associated risks. So what is to be done? Our next, and final, part identifies several steps the competition agencies can take.

2014/14-03-26_competitition_law_big_data_EN.pdf (noting that the sizes of potential sanctions for privacy law breaches 'vary widely between Member States' with 'the lower limit in Croatia is HRK 10 000 (EUR 1 131), while the UK authority may require penalties of up to GBP 500 000 (EUR 597 000)' and that in 'practice victims of unlawful processing are prevented from obtaining redress through the length and expense of proceedings and lack of unawareness of data protection rules and rights, although there have been some encouraging developments'). In contrast, fines for violating EU competition law are a percentage of the infringing company's relevant sales, which, depending on several factors, can be up to 30%; for cartels, 'the relevant percentage tends to be in the range of 15–20%.' European Commission, 'Fines for breaking EU Competition Law', November 2011, http://ec.europa.eu/competition/cartels/overview/factsheet_fines_en.pdf. In the US, the DOJ has obtained, as of 16 December 2014, criminal antitrust fines of USD 10 million or more 121 times, with fines reaching as high as USD 500 million. DOJ, 'Sherman Act Violations Yielding a Corporate Fine of $10 Million or More, updated 29 January 2016', http://www.justice.gov/atr/public/criminal/sherman10.html.

[106] Lisa Kimmel and Janis Kestenbaum, 'What's Up with WhatsApp?: A Transatlantic View on Privacy and Merger Enforcement in Digital Markets', 29(1) *Antitrust* (Fall 2014): pp 48, 50 (noting under proposed privacy regulation, violators 'could be subject to fines of up to 5 percent of its annual turnover or 100 million euros, whichever is greater—a dramatic increase from the maximum fines most individual data protection authorities may currently impose').

Part V

ADVANCING A RESEARCH AGENDA
FOR THE AGENCIES AND ACADEMICS

Although some argue that Big Data is a passing fad with no antitrust implications, **V.01** others, including the Organisation for Economic Co-operation and Development (OECD) and European Data Protection Supervisor (EDPS), recognize the need for a better understanding of the implications of a data-driven economy on competition policy, privacy law, and consumer protection.[1] Given the rise of data-driven business models, and the risks and costs in ignoring or downplaying data-driven mergers, abuses by dominant firms, and anticompetitive business strategies, we cannot afford our competition officials to remain ignorant.

Nor can competition agencies simply wait for the right case to present itself, which **V.02** presents a good theory of harm. If the agency does not understand the competitive significance of the four 'V's of data, the competitive benefits and risks of data-driven strategies, and the adequacy of its current tools, then it won't necessarily know which case is the right case, nor will it know what to do with the 'right' case

---

[1] EDPS, *Privacy and Competitiveness in the Age of Big Data: The Interplay Between Data Protection, Competition Law, and Consumer Protection in the Digital Economy*, Preliminary Opinion, 26 March 2014, https://secure.edps.europa.eu/EDPSWEB/webdav/shared/Documents/Consultation/Opinions/2014/14-03-26_competitition_law_big_data_EN.pdf; OECD, *Data-Driven Innovation for Growth and Well-Being: Interim Synthesis Report*, October 2014, p 7, http://www.oecd.org/sti/inno/data-driven-innovation-interim-synthesis.pdf; *see also* McKinsey Global Institute, *Big Data: The Next Frontier for Innovation, Competition, and Productivity*, June 2011, p 3, http://www.mckinsey.com/insights/business_technology/big_data_the_next_frontier_for_innovation (noting the challenge of ensuring 'that the right infrastructure is in place and that incentives and competition are in place to encourage continued innovation; that the economic benefits to users, organizations, and the economy are properly understood; and that safeguards are in place to address public concerns about big data') and p 23.

when its tools remain 'price-centric' for mainly single-sided markets. The competition agencies need to proactively increase their learning and refine their tools.

V.03 So where should the competition authorities begin? We do not argue for more enforcement, simply for its own sake. We do believe that some competition officials and judges have overemphasized false positives and discounted false negatives. Nonetheless, there is a significant risk of false positives when competition authorities simply enjoin every merger by large tech firms. If Google or Facebook were to acquire Twitter, for example, the data-driven merger would raise many concerns. But we cannot say that the merger on its face violates the competition law. Instead we must have a theory of how the merger may increase entry barriers, help maintain dominance, degrade privacy protections, or empower exclusionary behaviour.

V.04 So the first step is to recognize the antitrust implications of data-driven mergers and strategies. Competition agencies must avoid the ten myths and pitfalls that we examined in the earlier chapters, such as the temptation to examine the merger's likely effects only on the 'paid' side of a multi-sided market, consider only 'traditional' entry barriers, assume that privacy considerations are irrelevant, treat data as essentially fungible, or even worse, assume that data is ubiquitous and inexpensive.

V.05 Next the competition authorities must acknowledge that their price-centric analysis and categorization of mergers into horizontal, vertical, and conglomerate are ill-suited for data-driven mergers in multi-sided markets, where one side is free.

V.06 Third, the competition authorities must recognize that firms, in markets characterized with data-driven network effects, may use anticompetitive tactics to tip the market in their favour, and use exclusionary practices to maintain or attain their dominance.

V.07 Fourth, the competition authorities need to develop tools to screen data-driven mergers and identify categories of data-driven business strategies that likely yield significant procompetitive efficiencies.

V.08 This last part outlines several steps to help competition authorities, courts, lawyers, and economists towards this end.

17

RECOGNIZING WHEN PRIVACY AND COMPETITION LAW INTERSECT

Let us return to the European Commission's statement in closing its *Facebook/* **17.01**
WhatsApp investigation: '[a]ny privacy-related concerns flowing from the increased
concentration of data within the control of Facebook as a result of the transaction
do not fall within the scope of EU competition law'.[1] Then Commissioner Almunia
in promising a speedy merger review told journalists that the investigation would
not handle privacy concerns: 'while privacy "is a very important issue," it is not dealt
with by antitrust or merger rules in the EU'.[2] The Commissioner's response raises
the hotly contested issue of the objectives of competition policy.

At the outset, competition authorities must appreciate when privacy concerns are **17.02**
within the scope of competition law. Our concern is over the acquisition and use
of personal data to obtain significant market power. At times, data-driven business strategies will violate competition law, but not raise privacy concerns. At other
times, data-driven business strategies will raise privacy, but not antitrust, concerns.
Even when privacy concerns conceivably are within the scope of competition law,
the competition authorities and courts must appreciate whether their tools can advance the privacy interests, and whether doing so advances the antitrust objectives.
Even when a privacy concern arises from insufficient competition, competition law
does not always provide a remedy. Moreover, the competition officials must ensure
that they do not trample privacy and data protection concerns in their remedy.[3] This

---

[1] European Commission, 'Mergers: Commission Approves Acquisition of WhatsApp by
Facebook', Press Release, 3 October 2014, http://europa.eu/rapid/press-release_IP-14-1088_en.htm.
[2] Aoife White and Flavia Rotondi, 'Facebook's WhatsApp Takeover Faces Speedy Review
by EU', *Bloomberg*, 8 September 2014, http://www.bloomberg.com/news/print/2014-09-08/
facebook-s-whatsapp-takeover-faces-speedy-review-by-eu.html.
[3] Directive 95/46/EC of the European Parliament and of the Council of 24 October 1995 on
the Protection of Individuals with Regard to the Processing of Personal Data and on the Free
Movement of Such Data [1995] OJ L 281/31 ('EU Personal Data Directive') (noting that 'to
maintain a balance between the interests involved while guaranteeing effective competition,
Member States may determine the circumstances in which personal data may be used or disclosed
to a third party in the context of the legitimate ordinary business activities of companies and

chapter explains how privacy can be viewed as a parameter of quality competition. Moreover, the chapter discusses how antitrust in promoting citizens' welfare (and well-being) can promote privacy interests generally.

A. Promoting Consumers' Privacy Interests Can Be an Important Part of Quality Competition

17.03 To explore where privacy and competition intersect, we shall start with the emerging consensus of privacy protection as a parameter of non-price quality competition.[4] As several European Commission officials noted, if a website, post-merger, 'would start requiring more personal data from users or supplying such data to third parties as a condition for delivering its "free" product' then this 'could be seen as either increasing its price or as degrading the quality of its product' and infringe competition law.[5] Indeed, the vigour of privacy competition can signal an effective competitive process, like a singing canary signals to coal miners a safe air supply. As the UK competition authority observed, '[t]he presence of competition over privacy is a useful indicator, not only of firms' willingness to adapt to consumers' desires, but also consumers' understanding of the use of their data in that market, and the effectiveness of competition in the market in question'.[6] On the other hand, '[a]n absence of competition over privacy may indicate data markets failing to deliver what consumers want'.[7]

---

other bodies'). Professor Orla Lynskey noted, 'since 2009 data protection has been recognised as a fundamental right in the EU legal order, independently of the right to privacy. As such, it is binding on the EU institutions when enacting legislation or adopting decisions. Failure to respect this right will lead to the invalidity of the measure at stake (as we saw last week when the Data Retention Directive was declared invalid on the basis of its incompatibility with this Charter right).' Orla Lynskey, 'A Brave New World: The Potential Intersection of Competition Law and Data Protection Regulation', Chillin' Competition blog, 21 April 2014, http://chillingcompetition. com/2014/04/21/a-brave-new-world-the-potential-intersection-of-competition-law-and-data-protection-regulation-by-orla-lynskey/.

[4] Federal Trade Commission (FTC), 'Statement of the Federal Trade Commission Concerning Google/DoubleClick', FTC File No 071-0170, https://www.ftc.gov/system/files/documents/ public_statements/418081/071220googledc-commstmt.pdf, cited in Julie Brill, 'Commissioner Weaving a Tapestry to Protect Privacy and Competition in the Age of Big Data', Speech, European Data Protection Supervisor's Workshop on Privacy, Consumer Protection and Competition in the Digital Age, Brussels, 2 June 2014, http://www.ftc.gov/public-statements/2014/06/ weaving-tapestry-protect-privacy-competition-age-big-data-address-european.

[5] Eleonora Ocello, Cristina Sjödin, and Anatoly Suboĉs, 'What's Up with Merger Control in the Digital Sector? Lessons from the Facebook/WhatsApp EU Merger Case', 1 *Competition Merger Brief* (February 2015): p 6.

[6] UK Competition and Markets Authority, *The Commercial Use of Consumer Data: Report on the CMA's Call for Information*, June 2015, para 3.21 ('CMA Report'), https://secure.edps.europa. eu/EDPSWEB/webdav/site/mySite/shared/Documents/Consultation/Opinions/2015/15-09-11_ Data_Ethics_EN.pdf.

[7] Ibid, para 3.78.

Let us start with first principles. Competition includes price and non-price parameters. **17.04**
Within the latter, quality and innovation are fundamental aspects of competition.[8]
Quality drives innovation and economic growth, and a decrease in quality can be as
harmful to consumers (if not more harmful given health and safety concerns) as a price
increase.[9] Thus maintaining and improving quality are important competition policy
objectives.[10]

Quality is a broad concept that encompasses privacy protections.[11] Even **17.05**
though privacy harms can be subjective, so too are other quality degradations.
As the OECD concluded, quality is a 'multidimensional', 'relative' concept that
'incorporates a significant element of subjectivity, because certain quality aspects may be valuable only to some consumers, or more valuable to some than
others'.[12]

To illustrate the interplay between quality and competition, let us use safety. Suppose **17.06**
the domestic automobile manufacturers were producing unsafe cars. Suppose this

---

[8] Organisation for Economic Co-operation and Development (OECD), *The Role and Measurement of Quality in Competition Analysis*, 28 October 2013, p 5 (Executive Summary) ('OECD Quality Report'), http://www.oecd.org/competition/Quality-in-competition-analysis-2013.pdf (acknowledging that quality is a 'key non-price consideration that determines whether consumers will purchase a product').

[9] Ibid, p 5 (Executive Summary).

[10] Ibid, p 43 (Australia), pp 77 and 83 (EU) ('The Horizontal Merger Guidelines expressly state that one of the effects to be analysed in merger control is the effect on quality, putting the competitive harm caused by a reduction of quality on an equal footing with an increase of prices, or a reduction of output, choice of goods and services.') and p 89 (Japan).

[11] EDPS, *Privacy and Competitiveness in the Age of Big Data: The Interplay Between Data Protection, Competition Law, and Consumer Protection in the Digital Economy*, Preliminary Opinion, 26 March 2014, p 17 ('EDPS Preliminary Opinion'), https://secure.edps.europa.eu/EDPSWEB/webdav/shared/Documents/Consultation/Opinions/2014/14-03-26_competitition_law_big_data_EN.pdf ('It has even been argued that the ultimate purpose of competition law is to ensure that the internal market will satisfy all reasonable wishes of consumers for competition, including not only the wish for competitive prices but also the wish for variety, innovation, quality and other non-price benefits, including privacy protection.') (quoting Peter Swire, 'Protecting Consumers: Privacy Matters in Antitrust Analysis', Center for American Progress, 19 October 2007, https://www.americanprogress.org/issues/regulation/news/2007/10/19/3564/protecting-consumers-privacy-matters-in-antitrust-analysis). *See also* Robert H Lande, 'The Microsoft-Yahoo Merger: Yes, Privacy is an Antitrust Concern', FTC: Watch, No 714, University of Baltimore School of Law Legal Studies Research Paper No 2008-06 (2008), http://ssrn.com/abstract=1121934; Robert H Lande, Neil W Averitt, and Paul Nihoul, ' "Consumer choice" Is Where We Are All Going—So Let's Go Together', 2 *Concurrences* (2011): pp 1–3, http://papers.ssrn.com/sol3/papers.cfm?abstract_id=1856061; Lisa Kimmel and Janis Kestenbaum, 'What's Up with WhatsApp?: A Transatlantic View on Privacy and Merger Enforcement in Digital Markets', 29(1) *Antitrust* (Fall 2014): pp 48, 52 (recognizing that 'a combination of data associated with a merger can enhance market power and raise privacy concerns' and how in their analysis of Google/DoubleClick, 'both the FTC and the EC examined whether the combination of Google's customer search data with DoubleClick's browsing data would give AdSense an advantage that rivals could not match, restricting competition in online advertising intermediation service').

[12] OECD Quality Report, above note 8, p 6.

was attributable to insufficient competition. Although the poor quality is a competition issue,[13] the competition agency could not order the manufacturers to make safer cars. Competition officials lack the expertise to dictate how the cars should be improved. Here, poor safety—while a competition-related problem—cannot be easily remedied by the competition laws.

17.07 Now suppose a maverick enters the market and manufactures safer cars; the overall level of safety features increases. The incumbent car manufacturers grumble. Competition by the maverick has increased their cost in improving safety and overall quality. Weary from this competition, one of the entrenched car manufacturers seeks to acquire the maverick, and the competition authority uncovers compelling evidence that safety and other quality features would deteriorate post-merger. Now the competition laws could remedy the likely quality deterioration.[14] Here, the past competitive interaction provides the competition authority with 'an indication of the impact of the agreement on future competitive interaction'.[15] We also see how the merger 'may change the competitive incentives and capabilities of the competitor and thereby remove an important source of competition in the market'.[16] In the parlance of competition law, the merger would lead to an 'increase in market power', which 'refers to the ability of one or more firms to profitably increase prices, reduce output, choice or quality of goods and services, diminish innovation, or otherwise negatively influence parameters of competition'.[17] Ultimately, the merger would enable the entrenched car manufacturers to prevent effective competition from being maintained in the relevant market by giving them the opportunity to act to a

---

[13] *Nat'l Soc of Prof'l Engineers v United States*, 435 US 679, 695, 98 S Ct 1355, 1367 (1978): 'The assumption that competition is the best method of allocating resources in a free market recognizes that all elements of a bargain-quality, service, safety, and durability-and not just the immediate cost, are favorably affected by the free opportunity to select among alternative offers.' The engineers defended (unsuccessfully) their canon of ethics prohibiting competitive bidding on the ground that price competition would reduce safety and quality.

[14] European Commission, *Guidelines on the Assessment of Non-Horizontal Mergers Under the Council Regulation on the Control of Concentrations Between Undertakings* [2008] OJ C 265/07, para 85 ('EC Non-Horizontal Merger Guidelines'), http://eur-lex.europa.eu/LexUriServ/LexUriServ.do?uri=OJ:C:2008:265:0006:0025:en:PDF (noting that mergers may eliminate a maverick which 'is a supplier that for its own reasons is unwilling to accept the co-ordinated outcome and thus maintains aggressive competition'); European Commission, *Guidelines on the Assessment of Horizontal Mergers under the Council Regulation on the Control of Concentrations Between Undertakings* [2004] OJ C 31/03, para 42 ('EC Horizontal Merger Guidelines'), http://www.euchinacomp.org/attachments/article/12/12_Guidelines_on_the_assessment_of_horizontal_mergers_under_the_Council_Regulation_EN.pdf (how eliminating a maverick which 'has characteristics that gives it an incentive to favour different strategic choices than its coordinating competitors would prefer' may facilitate collusion).

[15] European Commission, *Guidelines on the Application of Article 101(3) of the Treaty on the Functioning of the European Union (formerly Article 81(3) of the Treaty Establishing the European Community)* [2004] OJ C 101/114, p 97, para 112.

[16] Ibid.

[17] EC Non-Horizontal Merger Guidelines, above note 14, para 10; EC Horizontal Merger Guidelines, above note 14, para 8.

considerable extent independently of their customers' wishes. As such, the competition authority would likely enjoin the merger.[18]

B. Some Simple Examples Where Privacy and Competition Law Intersect

If a reduction in automobile safety falls within the scope of competition law, it follows that mergers and restraints that affect other important dimensions of quality—such as privacy—should also fall within the scope of competition law. **17.08**

Suppose consumers desire the power to block certain ads and technology that prevent them from being tracked while on the Internet. The competition authority, as in our automobile safety example, cannot order the browser developers to provide the technology. Now suppose a maverick develops ad-blocking, anti-tracking technology that gives consumers such power. Suppose Apple, Google, and Microsoft agree to boycott the technology from their browsers Safari, Chrome, and Explorer. Here, the agreement among the undertakings violates EU and US competition law.[19] **17.09**

The browser developers may argue that their behaviour has not affected price competition. After all, their browsers remain free. But most competition lawyers would counsel otherwise. As competition authorities in a 2013 OECD roundtable warned, '[c]o-ordinated efforts between competitors to limit quality improvements or to degrade existing quality are generally most appropriately treated as equivalent to a cartel'.[20] **17.10**

---

[18] *T-Mobile Austria/tele.ring* (Case Comp/M.3916), Commission Decision C (2006) 1695 final [2006] OJ L 88/44.

[19] European Commission, 'Guidance on Restrictions of Competition "By Object" for the Purpose of Defining Which Agreements May Benefit from the *De Minimis* Notice', Staff Working Document SWD(2014) 198 final, 25 June 2014, s 2.5, http://ec.europa.eu/competition/antitrust/legislation/de_minimis_notice_annex.pdf (collective boycott 'occurs when a group of competitors agree to exclude an actual or potential competitor' and generally constitutes under Article 101(1) of the Treaty on the Functioning of the European Union 'a restriction by object'); *NW Wholesale Stationers, Inc v Pac Stationery & Printing Co*, 472 US 284, 290, 105 S Ct 2613, 2617 (1985) (stating that 'certain concerted refusals to deal or group boycotts are so likely to restrict competition without any offsetting efficiency gains that they should be condemned as per se violations of § 1 of the Sherman Act').

[20] OECD Quality Report, above note 8, p 8 (Executive Summary); *see also* ibid, p 77 ('Agreements that limit the quality of products or services fall within the prohibition of anticompetitive agreements.'); *National Macaroni Manufacturers Association v FTC*, 345 F2d 421 (US Ct of Apps (7th Cir), 1965) (charging the National Macaroni Manufacturers Association, its officers, and member manufacturers of macaroni and spaghetti products for illegally agreeing to fix and determine the quality of macaroni products 'for the purpose of depressing the price of durum wheat and preventing its price from being established in the open market by free competition, the effect being to eliminate quality competition in macaroni products'); *FTC v Indiana Fed'n of Dentists*, 476 US 447, 462–4, 106 S Ct 2009, 2020–1 (1986).

17.11 Suppose the browser developers argue that such anti-tracking, ad-blocking technology undermines their and many other Internet companies' advertising-dependent revenue model. If they cannot track consumers and target them with behavioural advertisements, they can no longer offer products or services for 'free'.

17.12 The US Supreme Court long ago rejected such defences to a group boycott. In a 1941 case, textile manufacturers, dress designers, and clothing distributors collectively agreed to boycott retailers that sold knock-off garments, namely dresses which other manufacturers copied from the boycotters' designs.[21] Defendants argued that their boycott and restraint of interstate trade 'were reasonable and necessary to protect the manufacturer, laborer, retailer and consumer against the devastating evils growing from the pirating of original designs'.[22] Irrelevant, replied the Court, 'for the reasonableness of the methods pursued by the combination to accomplish its unlawful object is no more material than would be the reasonableness of the prices fixed by unlawful combination'.[23]

17.13 Nor could the browser developers defend their boycott, on account of its affecting only one privacy app 'whose business is so small that [its] destruction makes little difference to the economy'.[24] As the US Supreme Court held in another case, '[m]onopoly can as surely thrive by the elimination of such small businessmen, one at a time, as it can by driving them out in large groups'.[25] Thus an anticompetitive restraint—here a group boycott—that thwarts non-price competition, namely, privacy protection, interferes with the natural flow of interstate commerce, and is subject to antitrust scrutiny.

C. Looking Beyond Privacy's Subjectivity

17.14 One response is that safety, unlike privacy, is more objective and easier to measure. To assess whether the merger may substantially lessen non-price competition, the competition authority needs objective uniform benchmarks of quality, and ways to measure small, but significant, non-transitory decreases in quality (SSNDQ). As Chapter 7 discusses, competition authorities have a difficult time applying an SSNDQ test to privacy, which is subjective and difficult to measure. Because some quality attributes are 'subjective, unobserved and dependent upon the perceptions of consumers', the 'multifaceted and indistinct nature of quality thus complicates the task of providing a robust definition of this concept'.[26]

---

[21] *Fashion Originators' Guild of Am v Fed Trade Comm'n*, 312 US 457, 461, 61 S Ct 703, 705 (1941).

[22] Ibid, 312 US 468.

[23] Ibid.

[24] *Klor's, Inc v Broadway-Hale Stores, Inc*, 359 US 207, 213, 79 S Ct 705, 710 (1959).

[25] Ibid.

[26] OECD Quality Report, above note 8, p 6.

This objection trumps quantification over importance. Privacy competition, while **17.15** not measurable, may be observed through consumer behaviour. To illustrate, let us return to Facebook and WhatsApp. Both companies offered users different privacy protections. Facebook offered its texting app for free, but collected individuals' data to profile and target them with behavioural ads. Unlike Facebook, WhatsApp did not sell advertising space or collect a lot of personal data on its mobile app users. Instead WhatsApp charged a small subscription fee to some users of its texting app.

Let us again assume WhatsApp's privacy protections were valuable to many of its **17.16** users, and Facebook offered the following defence for its acquisition: Facebook would reduce the privacy protections that WhatsApp had provided, but consumers would now get WhatsApp for free. As a result, its acquisition—Facebook argues—increases consumer surplus and welfare. A competition official interjects and asks about the quality degradation. Facebook responds: 'You can't consider the privacy protections, because they are subjective and non-quantifiable. Focus instead on price and those quality metrics that are measurable, objective and universally-accepted (such as speed, storage capacity, etc).' That response would be unsatisfactory. It is also contrary to the US Merger Guidelines, which state, 'purported efficiency claims based on lower prices can be undermined if they rest on reductions in product quality or variety that customers value'.[27] So the competition agency cannot consider only price and quantifiable quality metrics, as it will miss important parameters of competition.[28]

Thus, privacy can be part of the mix. The issue then is whether consumers have other **17.17** viable texting choices where their privacy is protected. If the answer is no, because of entry barriers and network effects, then WhatsApp users would be harmed by the lessening of competition, even though they would get the app for free.

The same competition-related privacy issues would arise if Google were to acquire **17.18** DuckDuckGo. The smaller search engine uses privacy to differentiate itself from its competitors. Its privacy policy is clear: 'DuckDuckGo does not collect or share

---

[27] US Department of Justice (DOJ) and Federal Trade Commission (FTC), *Horizontal Merger Guidelines*, 19 August 2010, s 10 ('US Horizontal Merger Guidelines'), http://www.justice.gov/atr/horizontal-merger-guidelines-08192010.

[28] *Facebook/WhatsApp* (Case Comp/M.7217), Commission Decision C(2014) 7239 final, 3 October 2014, para 87; *see also* ibid, para 174 (noting how '[p]rivacy concerns also seem to have prompted a high number of German users to switch from WhatsApp to Threema in the 24 hours following the announcement of Facebook's acquisition of WhatsApp'); Kimmel and Kestenbaum, above note 11, p 53 (recognizing that '[c]ustomers may choose products and services at least in part on the basis of privacy or other nonprice product attributes, such as quality and customer service', so both the EU and United States 'acknowledge the role of non-price competition in their merger guidelines', and how 'the FTC recognized privacy as a nonprice dimension of competition in Google/DoubleClick even before adopting new horizontal merger guidelines expressly recognizing nonprice competition').

personal information. That is our privacy policy in a nutshell.'[29] If Google were to acquire DuckDuckGo, it is highly unlikely that prices for search engines would increase. Instead, a key issue would be the degradation in privacy protection post-merger. One would be hard pressed to argue otherwise, unless one has a constricted view of the goals of competition law to protect only some parameters of competition (such as price or efficiency) and not others (such as the level of privacy protection afforded to consumers).

D. Developing Better Economic Tools to Address Privacy

17.19 Our illustrations offer a stark contrast in privacy protection. Competition agencies can use their current tools for mergers or restraints involving rapacious harvesters of data and privacy-protecting mavericks. But what about the remaining grey area?

17.20 Economist Keith Waehrer in a working paper lays out a framework for analysing the competitive effects from a merger of online services that compete in the level of privacy offered to consumers.[30] The paper fills a gap which we have identified throughout this book, namely the need for in-depth economic analysis of why Big Data issues are antitrust issues and should be solved not only by consumer protection and privacy laws but also by competition law.

17.21 Waehrer begins by noting that the US and European competition agencies appear to be open to analysing the loss of privacy as a potential anticompetitive effect in data-driven mergers, but face a number of challenges. One challenge is the subjectivity of consumer preferences about privacy. This is the same challenge the agencies have been facing for a long time when they think about quality. The element of subjectivity makes privacy (like quality more generally) harder to define and measure than price, and has led to the lack of a widely accepted framework and to, at best, superficial treatment by the agencies. Another challenge is that privacy issues generally come up in the context of two-sided advertising-supported platforms. This raises the question of how to balance benefits on the advertising side against harms on the consumer side. These difficulties might lead some competition agencies to regard privacy as incapable of measurement and to focus on the 'paid' advertising side of the market rather than on the 'free' consumer side.

17.22 The major contribution of Waehrer's work is to suggest a method to quantify the non-price effects of a merger (including privacy) that is analogous to the method

---

[29] Compare Google Privacy Policy, updated 15 August 2015, http://www.google.co.uk/policies/privacy/ with DuckDuckGo Privacy Policy, updated 11 April 2012, https://duckduckgo.com/privacy.

[30] Keith Waehrer, 'Online Services and the Analysis of Competitive Merger Effects in Privacy Protections and Other Quality Dimensions', Draft, 12 January 2016, http://waehrer.net/Merger%20effects%20in%20privacy%20protections.pdf.

economists already use to quantify upward pricing pressure.[31] Importantly, Waehrer's approach seeks to help the agencies avoid the likely subjectivity, measurement, and multi-sided platform pitfalls.

Assuming that consumers value some degree of privacy (which appears to be empirically supported), Waehrer observes that online firms compete to offer some amount of privacy protection in order to make their services more attractive to users. But for this competition, the firms would have preferred a lower level of privacy protection. It is intuitive why this is true. Privacy protection is costly to provide. It not only costs money to protect privacy, but it can also affect the revenues that a firm can make through targeted advertising or the sale of consumer information. Firms make a trade-off in deciding how much privacy protection to offer in order to attract or retain users to their 'free' online services. **17.23**

Waehrer bases his model on a hypothetical set of facts, but one that applies to a number of real world online mergers. He assumes that the advertising side of the market will remain competitive after the merger, as advertisers will continue to have other choices of where to spend their advertising dollars. This assumption is useful for two related reasons. First, if a merger leads to market power in an advertising market, the agencies already have tools available. On the basis of the merger's adverse effect on advertisers, the agency can block the merger or impose remedies that protect advertisers and consumers. Second, and importantly, if the advertising market remains competitive after the merger, then a loss of consumer privacy would not be protected by the proxy of looking solely at the advertising side. Competition in the advertising market would not necessarily protect users on the consumer side. **17.24**

Given that many online services in which privacy is an issue are priced at 'zero' on the consumer side, it is not reasonable to expect price effects from a merger on the consumer side, even in situations in which the services appear to be close substitutes. Waehrer observes that pricing to consumers is therefore constrained. This is borne out in reality. Although Microsoft offers consumers perks for using its Bing search engine,[32] online companies typically do not charge 'negative' prices (ie, pay consumers for their data or to use their service). Nor do online companies charge consumers a small amount for the use of the service. In a situation where price is constrained, it has long been recognized that quality competition becomes more important.[33] **17.25**

---

[31] US Horizontal Merger Guidelines, above note 27, s 6.1; *see also* Joseph Farrell and Carl Shapiro, 'Upward Pricing Pressure and Critical Loss Analysis: Response', *CPI Antitrust Journal* (February 2010).

[32] Microsoft, Bing Rewards, https://www.bing.com/rewards/levels.

[33] *Microsoft/Skype* (Case Comp/M.6281), Commission Decision C(2011)7279, 7 October 2011, para 81 (noting that '[s]ince consumer communications services are mainly provided for free, consumers pay more attention to other features' and '[q]uality is therefore a significant parameter

One need only think of airlines. In the era of US airline regulation when the Civil Aeronautics Board set prices, airlines tried to attract customers with food, empty seats, and frequency of flights.

17.26 Waehrer derives a formula for assessing downward quality pressure that is analogous to the upward pricing pressure calculation for unilateral effects. The formula assumes some loss (diversion) of users in response to lower privacy protection, and the possibility that a merger would allow the merged firm to recapture some of these users. In that way, a firm can profitably lower privacy protection unilaterally post-merger. It can be seen how this is similar to the unilateral effects analysis already familiar to antitrust enforcers. The elegance of the model is that it takes efficiencies into account, does not require the actual measurement of privacy (or quality more broadly), and has unambiguous results. If certain conditions are satisfied, the result of a merger of two online advertising-supported firms may be a reduction in consumer welfare. In sum, the paper is an important first step in developing new tools for the competition agencies in the era of Big Data.

E. Why Competition Policy Does Not Have an Efficiency Screen

17.27 Some may agree in part, and disagree in part. Alexander P Okuliar and FTC Commissioner Maureen K Ohlhausen agree with the emerging consensus that privacy represents a non-price dimension of competition and that consumer data is an increasingly important commercial good for digital platforms. While 'privacy issues may have some role in an antitrust analysis' they argue that 'role must be consistent with the goal of antitrust, which is to promote economic efficiency that enhances consumer welfare, not to address other types of harm'.[34] They claim that 'American competition law enforcement objectives are, and for a long time have been, primarily focused on economic efficiency'.[35]

---

of competition'); *Microsoft/Yahoo! Search Business* (Case Comp/M.5727), Commission Decision C(2010) 1077, 18 February 2010.

[34] Maureen K Ohlhausen and Alexander P Okuliar, 'Competition, Consumer Protection, and the Right (Approach) to Privacy', 80 *Antitrust LJ* (2015): pp 121, 150–1.

[35] Ibid, p 143. They cite in support of their claim former FTC Chairman Robert Pitofsky, who 'captured this view about the FTC's competition mandate from Congress when he said: "Oppressive, coercive, bad faith, fraud, and even contrary to good morals. I think that's the kind of roving mandate that will get the Commission in trouble with the Courts and with Congress."' (citing FTC, *Workshop on Section 5 of the FTC Act as a Competition Statute 67*, Transcript, 17 October 2008 (remarks of Robert Pitofsky), http://www.ftc.gov/bc/workshops/section5/transcript.pdf). This is weak support. While the FTC Chairman during the Clinton administration, Pitofsky referred to antitrust's non-economic goals. Robert Pitofsky, Chairman, FTC, 'Challenges of the New Economy: Issues at the Intersection of Antitrust and Intellectual Property', Speech given at the American Antitrust Institute Conference: An Agenda for Antitrust in the Twenty-First Century, Washington DC, 15 June 2000, https://www.ftc.gov/public-statements/2000/06/

There is no consensus, however, either in the US or worldwide, that competition **17.28**
law's sole, or primary, objective is to protect economic efficiency.[36] Scholars, as one
recent symposium on the goals of competition law reflects, continue to debate after
Robert H. Bork's influential book, *The Antitrust Paradox: A Policy at War With
Itself*,[37] over antitrust's goals. Even among those who advocate an economic welfare
objective, it is unsettled whether welfare should reflect consumer welfare or total
welfare, what those terms mean, and the extent to which it makes any difference.[38]
Professors Harry First and Spencer Weber Waller in their symposium piece took

---

challenges-new-economy-issues-intersection-antitrust-and-intellectual. Moreover, Pitofsky wrote
one of the leading articles on antitrust's non-economic goals, where he said, 'It is bad history, bad
policy, and bad law to exclude certain political values in interpreting the antitrust laws, and any
antitrust policy that excluded such political values would be unresponsive to the will of Congress.'
Robert Pitofsky, 'The Political Content of Antitrust', 127 *U Pa L Rev* (1979): pp 1051, 1051–2. One
political value underlying the Sherman Act, he noted, was a fear that excessive concentration of
economic power will breed antidemocratic political pressures.

[36] Daniel L Rubinfeld, 'On the Foundations of Antitrust Law and Economics', in Robert
Pitofsky (ed), *How the Chicago School Overshot the Mark: The Effect of Conservative Economic Analysis
on US Antitrust* (New York: Oxford University Press, 2008) pp 51, 56 (noting the disagreement
within the antitrust community over whether economic efficiency should be the sole norm in antitrust or whether efficiency should be balanced against other norms such as consumer welfare and/
or the promotion of small business); John B Kirkwood and Robert H Lande, 'The Chicago School's
Foundation Is Flawed: Antitrust Protects Consumers, Not Efficiency', in Pitofsky (ed), *How the
Chicago School Overshot the Mark*, pp 89, 93 94.

[37] New York: Free Press, 1978.

[38] Maurice E Stucke, 'Reconsidering Competition', 81 *Mississippi LJ* (2011): p 107. *See, eg*,
Roger D Blair and D Daniel Sokol, 'Welfare Standards in US and EU Antitrust Enforcement', 81
Fordham L Rev (2013): pp 2497, 2499 (arguing that 'total welfare rather than consumer welfare…
should drive antitrust analysis'); Herbert Hovenkamp, 'Implementing Antitrust's Welfare Goals',
81 *Fordham L Rev* (2013): pp 2471, 2471 ('One welfare concern that has dominated debates over US
antitrust policy over the last several decades is whether antitrust should adopt a "consumer welfare"
principle rather than a more neoclassical "total welfare" principle.'); David A Hyman and William E
Kovacic, 'Institutional Design, Agency Life Cycle, and the Goals of Competition Law', 81 *Fordham
L Rev* (2013): pp 2163, 2163–4 ('Post-Chicago School enthusiasts accept the importance of efficiency but argue that the antitrust laws also exist to achieve other economic ends, including the
protection of consumer choice and the prevention of unfair transfers of wealth from consumers
to producers.'); John B Kirkwood, 'The Essence of Antitrust: Protecting Consumers and Small
Suppliers from Anticompetitive Conduct', 81 *Fordham L Rev* (2013): pp 2425, 2453 (addressing
and critiquing total welfare standard); Robert H Lande, 'A Traditional and Textualist Analysis of
the Goals of Antitrust: Efficiency, Preventing Theft from Consumers, and Consumer Choice', 81
Fordham L Rev (2013): pp 2349, 2360 n 54 (noting Bork's 'deceptive use of the term "consumer
welfare", instead of the more honest term "total welfare", was a brilliant way to market the efficiency
objective'); Alan J Meese, 'Reframing the (False?) Choice Between Purchaser Welfare and Total
Welfare', 81 *Fordham L Rev* (2013): pp 2197, 2198 (noting how the term consumer welfare, while a
popular goal, 'means different things to different people'); Barak Orbach, 'How Antitrust Lost Its
Goal', 81 *Fordham L Rev* (2013): pp 2253, 2273 (noting that '[f]or Bork, the phrase "consumer welfare" meant "allocative efficiency"' but a 'few years after Bork presented his thesis of the legislative
intent of the Sherman Act, the phrase "consumer welfare" acquired a popular [and different] cultural meaning referring to the buyer's well being: the benefits a buyer derives from the consumption
of goods and services, or more casually, the individual's well being'); Joshua D Wright and Douglas
H Ginsburg, 'The Goals of Antitrust: Welfare Trumps Choice', 81 *Fordham L Rev* (2013): pp 2405,
2406 n 10 (arguing, on the one hand, that the 'promotion of economic welfare as the lodestar of
antitrust laws—to the exclusion of social, political, and protectionist goals—transformed the state

'as a given that antitrust has political goals and reflects political value judgments'.[39] Likewise, Professor Ezrachi's paper 'Sponge' considers the inherent properties of the law and questions the presence of a clear dividing line between competition law and external considerations. Ezrachi argues that 'the law, by its nature, provides for an absorbent and flexible platform which soaks up national values and interests—in short a sponge' and, accordingly, 'the inherent scope and nature of modern competition laws are not necessarily as consistent and objective as one might like them to be'.[40]

17.29 Nor did the drafters of the US competition laws seek to promote primarily efficiency.[41] Nor is there any consensus among competition agencies that efficiency is the primary objective. Enhancing efficiency, for example, has trailed two other goals— *ensuring an effective competitive process* and *promoting consumer welfare*—in one 2007 survey of competition agencies.[42] If efficiencies were the sole, or primary, objective, competition officials would face many significant operational and rule of law problems.[43] Finally, from a normative perspective, as Lionel Robbins noted, '[t]here is no penumbra of approbation around the theory of equilibrium. Equilibrium is just equilibrium'.[44]

---

of the law and restored intellectual coherence to a body of law', while declining, on the other hand, to elaborate 'whether the appropriate standard is aggregate economic efficiency, often referred to as the total welfare standard or "true" consumer welfare (in the economic sense of a consumer surplus) standard' and how policymakers would choose between the two welfare standards without referencing social and political goals (footnote omitted)).

[39] Harry First and Spencer Weber Waller, 'Antitrust's Democracy Deficit', 81 *Fordham L Rev* (2013): pp 2543, 2544.

[40] Ariel Ezrachi, 'Sponge', The University of Oxford Centre for Competition Law and Policy Working Paper CCLP (L) 42; Oxford Legal Studies Research Paper No 16/2015, 1 March 2015, http://ssrn.com/abstract=2572028.

[41] Historian Richard Hofstadter, for example, categorized antitrust's goals as (1) economic (competition maximizes economic efficiency), (2) political (antitrust principles intended to block private accumulations of power and protect democratic government), and (3) social and moral (competitive process was disciplinary machinery for character development). Richard Hofstadter, 'What Happened to the Antitrust Movement?', in Richard Hofstadter, *The Paranoid Style in American Politics and Other Essays* (New York: Vintage, 2008), pp 188, 199–200. *See also* Thomas J Horton, 'The Coming Extinction of Homo Economicus and the Eclipse of the Chicago School of Antitrust: Applying Evolutionary Biology to Structural and Behavioral Antitrust Analyses', 42 *Loyola U Chicago LJ* (2011): pp 469, 503–4; Frank Maier-Rigaud, 'On the Normative Foundations of Competition Law: Efficiency, Political Freedom and the Freedom to Compete', in Daniel Zimmer (ed), *The Goals of Competition Law* (Cheltenham: Edward Elgar, 2012), p 132.

[42] Unilateral Conduct Working Group, *Report on the Objectives of Unilateral Conduct Laws, Assessment of Dominance/Substantial Market Power, and State-Created Monopolies*, Presented at the 6th Annual Conference of the International Competition Network (ICN), Moscow, 2007, p 31 ('2007 ICN Report'), http://www.internationalcompetitionnetwork.org/uploads/library/doc353.pdf.

[43] Maurice E Stucke, 'Reconsidering Antitrust's Goals', 53 *Boston College L Rev* (2012): pp 551, 577–91.

[44] Adair Turner, *Economics After the Crisis, Objectives and Means* (Boston, MA: MIT Press, 2012), p 95.

F. Using a Consumer Well-Being Screen

Economic efficiency can inform competition policy, but it is not the sole, or pri-   **17.30**
mary, objective. As an initial premise, competition policy must improve our welfare or well-being.[45] Our theory of 'effective', 'fair', or 'perfect' competition must
serve our citizens. If, as a result of our competition policy, our overall physical and
mental health deteriorates, our isolation and distrust increase, and our freedom,
self-determination and well-being decrease, then whatever the competition policy
is promoting, it is not consumer welfare. So competition policy must promote—or
at least not impede—overall well-being. The same holds true for privacy and data
protection. The European Data Protection Directive makes this clear:

> Whereas data-processing systems are designed to serve man; whereas they must,
> whatever the nationality or residence of natural persons, respect their fundamental
> rights and freedoms, notably the right to privacy, and contribute to economic and
> social progress, trade expansion and the well-being of individuals.[46]

Accordingly, the issue is how can competition law (with other laws and informal
ethical, moral, and social norms) promote overall well-being.

On the one hand, part of competition policy's institutional soundness is its recogni-   **17.31**
tion that competition law cannot cure every societal ill. Competition law is at its
strongest when it focuses on preserving an effective competitive process and enforcing norms of free, fair, and open competition.

On the other hand, competition policy is not divorced from citizens' well-being.   **17.32**
One insight from the emerging economic literature is that well-being is promoted
along multiple dimensions, including (1) material well-being (income and wealth,
housing, and jobs and earnings) and (2) quality of life (health status, work and life
balance, education and skills, social connections, civic engagement and governance, environmental quality, and personal security).[47] A competition policy that
seeks primarily to promote price competition and greater consumer surplus makes
sense (i) in markets where price competition is paramount, and (ii) in developing
economies where many citizens cannot afford the most basic needs. After all, if
impoverished consumers must choose between milk and bread, then with all else
being equal, lowering the price of milk and bread significantly benefits consumers'

---

[45] OECD, 'Evaluation of Competition Interventions', http://www.oecd.org/competition/
evaluationofcompetitioninterventions.htm ('Ultimately, competition policy should be justified by
its beneficial effects on the economy and well-being (for example, its effects on growth, innovation,
or employment)'.).

[46] EU Personal Data Directive, above note 3.

[47] OECD, *Better Life Initiative: Compendium of OECD Well-Being Indicators* (2011), p 6, http://
www.oecd.org/std/47917288.pdf.

health and well-being. But if competition policy's sole or primary goal is to maximize consumer surplus in a post-industrial economy where many are materially well-off, then the competition policy has a minor, and at times inconsequential, role in maximizing overall well-being.[48] As the country's living standards increase and its citizens' basic material needs, such as food, clothing, and shelter, are met, then the citizens will likely place greater importance on quality-of-life factors associated with well-being, such as work and life balance, social connections, safety, and environmental quality.[49] Material well-being stills matters (especially employment) in promoting overall welfare. But there is less bang (in terms of increased well-being) for that extra buck of consumer surplus.[50]

17.33 If maximizing consumer welfare involves maximizing well-being, then it does not automatically follow that maximizing economic efficiency generally, or productive efficiency in particular, will necessarily promote overall well-being. There comes a point at which the marginal cost to our well-being from the incremental (productive) efficiency gain outweighs its benefit.

17.34 Moreover, aside from the utilitarian cost–benefit framework, citizens may want to preserve other rights and values (such as individual autonomy and economic freedom) for their own sakes. In rejecting a pure efficiency rationale for punitive damages, the US Supreme Court observed that '[c]itizens and legislators may rightly insist that they are willing to tolerate some loss in economic efficiency in order to deter what they consider morally offensive conduct, albeit cost-beneficial morally offensive conduct; efficiency is just one consideration among many.'[51] Thus, if citizens (1) do not prize efficiency for its own sake and (2) have different thresholds at which they prize other values over the incremental efficiency gain, then, competition policy, if it intends to promote consumer welfare, cannot consider only efficiency, while disregarding other more important, albeit non-quantifiable, harms. Basically, to assess whether consumers will be better or worse off as a result of the merger, competition authorities must

---

[48] Maurice E Stucke, 'Should Competition Policy Promote Happiness?', 81 *Fordham L Rev* (2013): pp 2575, 2626–8 (discussing some of the literature on wealth and well-being).

[49] *See, eg,* Turner, above note 44, pp 1–33.

[50] Jan Delhey, 'From Materialist to Post-materialist Happiness? National Affluence and Determinants of Life Satisfaction in Cross-national Perspective', 97 *Soc Indicators Res* (2010): pp 65, 74–7 (finding a shift from materialist to post-materialist well-being between poorer and wealthier countries). As countries become wealthier, individual well-being tends to become more post-materialist: 'The more widespread post-materialist values are in a society, the more the citizenry values personal autonomy, relative to income, as a source of [subjective well-being].' Ibid, p 73. People derive greater satisfaction from job creativity than income. Ibid. And '[i]n richer countries, personal autonomy drives life satisfaction—relative to income—more strongly.' Ibid, p 74.

[51] *Cooper Industries v Leatherman Tool Grp*, 532 US 424, 439–40, 121 S Ct 1678, 1687 (2001), quoting Marc Galanter and David Luban, 'Poetic Justice: Punitive Damages and Legal Pluralism', 42 *Am U L Rev* (1993): 1393, 1450.

better understand how data-driven mergers may affect both price and non-price parameters of competition.

Consequently, competition is not just about prices or efficiency. Instead, in post- **17.35** industrial economies, the social, political, and moral objectives of competition policy become more important.[52] We will develop this concept with media markets.

G. Media Mergers as an Example of a Consumer Well-Being Screen

Competition officials, judges, and citizens are not primarily concerned about pro- **17.36** moting economic efficiency in reviewing media mergers; nor are they primarily concerned about the price that consumers will pay for the news post-merger. Often, consumers pay nothing (such as commercial television and radio news). Instead, the aim is '[e]nsuring media pluralism' which 'implies all measures that ensure citizens' access to a wide variety of information, voices etc. in order to form their opinion without the undue influence of one dominant opinion forming power.'[53]

Media markets, like many data-driven markets, are subject to network effects. One **17.37** concern is that market forces, if left unchecked, will yield concentrated media markets that will hinder pluralism and the marketplace of ideas. News collection and production of media content often involve high fixed costs. For example, the cost to publish the 'first copy' of the *Wall Street Journal* or *Financial Times* newspapers would be in the millions of dollars, given the costs of the news bureaus and journalists. This fixed cost can be absorbed with each additional copy of the newspaper being sold above marginal cost. (The increase in readership can also bring more advertising revenue.) Thus media mergers can be an attractive option to reduce these fixed costs or to spread them over a wider audience.

Media markets also have a different form of market failure. With many com- **17.38** modities, market failure manifests in higher prices. The consumer pays more. But market failure in a media market may not manifest itself simply with higher prices. Increased concentration may lessen the competition among news providers and the quality of reporting. In highly concentrated media markets, private owners associated with the state or political parties—or protecting their business interests—can

---

[52] Benjamin M Friedman, *The Moral Consequences of Economic Growth* (New York: Vintage, 2005), p ix; *see also* ibid, pp 79–102 (discussing how economic growth can promote other values, such as 'openness of opportunity, tolerance, economic and social mobility, fairness, and democracy').

[53] Allen P Grunes and Maurice E Stucke, 'Plurality of Political Opinion and the Concentration of the Media', in Karen B Brown and David V Snyder (eds), *General Reports of the XVIIIth Congress of the International Academy of Comparative Law* (New York: Springer Publishing, 2012), p 573 (quoting European Commission).

shape or control the dissemination of information. Increased media concentration may also increase the risk of self-censorship.

17.39 In many countries, competition authorities have the power to apply their law to the media. Competition law comes into play in two primary ways: as a means of preventing abuse of a dominant position (monopolization), and as a means of preventing anticompetitive mergers. Many countries also appear to favour some coordination—either formal or informal—between the competition authority and the media sector regulator.

H. Conclusion

17.40 Thus in media (or data-driven) mergers, the primary concern is not economic efficiency, but other values, such as promoting a plurality of opinions (or privacy). Looking at these mergers through the prism of price effects will not be particularly meaningful. The actual 'cost' that individuals pay in anticompetitive media mergers is the loss of an independent voice and greater risk of censored (or biased) news. In data-driven mergers, the actual cost is the merging parties acting to a considerable extent independently of their customers' wishes by intruding into their personal life and using their personal data to better exploit them.[54] The consumer will unlikely know the exact toll.

17.41 On a macro level, competition in dispersing political and economic power can increase economic opportunity and personal autonomy, a key predictor of happiness. Citizens would not be resigned to a few dominant tech firms tracking them and collecting their personal data. When a firm engages in exploitative, unfair behaviour, a competitive market should provide real alternatives.[55] The invisible hand should be painful to companies that disregard or alter their privacy policies to consumers' detriment. As US Senator Herb Kohl stated:

> Some commentators believe that antitrust policymakers should not be concerned with these fundamental issues of privacy, and merely be content to limit their review to traditional questions of effects on advertising rates. We disagree. The antitrust laws were written more than a century ago out of a concern

---

[54] EDPS Preliminary Opinion, above note 11, p 6 ('Not all big data is personal, but for many online offerings which are presented or perceived as being "free", personal information operates as a sort of indispensable currency used to pay for those services.') and p 10 ('in fact individuals are required to surrender valuable personal information to enjoy them. Consumers provide richly detailed information about their preferences through their online activities which permits individuals, not groups, to be targeted with far greater precision than ever before.').

[55] *Ross v Bank of Am, NA (USA)*, 524 F3d 217, 223 (US Ct of Apps (2d Cir), 2008) (noting that antitrust injury includes '[c]oercive activity that prevents its victims from making free choices between market alternatives', quoting *Associated Gen Contractors of Cal, Inc v Cal State Council of Carpenters*, 459 US 519, 528, 103 S Ct 897, 903 (1983)).

with the effects of undue concentrations of economic power for our society as a whole, and not just merely their effects on consumers' pocketbooks. No one concerned with antitrust policy should stand idly by if industry consolidation jeopardizes the vital privacy interests of our citizens so essential to our democracy.[56]

There are also political and social costs in enabling a few companies to control so much data. For these companies, like Google, Facebook, and Conversant, whose business models are data-driven, greater privacy protections pose a threat.[57] These data-opolies have much to lose if we achieve greater control over our data, and will lobby fiercely to prevent this. Competition law historically was concerned about concentrated economic power. But if the privacy concerns fall outside competition law, who then has authority to review and enjoin mergers that would significantly infringe many individuals' privacy interests? Not the privacy officials, who typically do not receive the merger notifications and lack the power to enjoin mergers. **17.42**

Consequently, the overarching challenge for policymakers in post-industrial economies is assessing how competition policy can promote overall well-being. Although privacy, consumer protection, and competition law all seek to promote well-being, the laws are not coextensive. Privacy and consumer protection law will continue to play an important independent role in promoting individual autonomy and freedom. But competition authorities should not assume that competition policy and privacy are distinct, unrelated concepts. **17.43**

As this book discusses, a critical resource is data (not merely to target users with behavioural advertising, but also to optimize the products and services themselves). Firms with a significant competitive advantage in the four 'V's of data are not merely in the best position to dominate their own sectors, but are also poised to take over other fields as they expand their platforms into super-platforms. Even worse, to the extent such firms compile politically sensitive information about users, and mediate their experience of content, they also become powerful political actors. **17.44**

---

[56] Peter P Swire, Professor, Moritz College of Law of the Ohio State University and Senior Fellow, Center for American Progress, Submitted Testimony to the FTC Behavioral Advertising Town Hall, 18 October 2007, p 3.

[57] Chapter 5 of this volume; *see, eg*, Conversant, Inc, Annual Report Pursuant to Section 13 or 15(d) of the Securities Exchange Act of 1934 for the Year Ended December 31, 2013, filed 3 March 2014, p 18 ('Conversant 2013 Annual Report'), http://files.shareholder.com/downloads/AMDA-2MDMHL/3704485697x0xS1080034-14-14/1080034/filing.pdf (identifying tougher privacy regulation as potentially decreasing demand for its products and increasing its costs of doing business; and identifying the FTC's suggested 'Do Not Track' mechanism, whereby 'consumers can choose whether to allow the tracking of their online searching and browsing activities', as a threat to its business).

17.45 The first signpost of progress is when the agencies and courts recognize the competitive implications of data and how privacy protection can be an important parameter of non-price competition in a post-industrial economy. The next signpost is when they move beyond what is quantifiable to what is important, and beyond their price-centric tools to legal standards and presumptions that capture these important non-price parameters of competition.

18

DATA-OPOLY: IDENTIFYING DATA-DRIVEN EXCLUSIONARY AND PREDATORY CONDUCT

We have explored the acquisition and use of personal data to obtain significant **18.01** market power. Data-driven mergers and network effects, as we have seen, are two important ways to obtain power. A third way is data-driven anticompetitive exclusionary and predatory behaviour, our focus here.

This chapter cuts through the rhetoric of the virtues of monopolies and inapplica- **18.02** bility of antitrust in dynamic industries. The harm from data-driven monopolies can be greater and longer lasting. The chapter explores the issue of path depend- ence and *competitive portals*, namely critical inflection points when antitrust can make a key difference. Moreover, Big Data can provide some dominant firms with a 'Nowcasting Radar,' which makes them more dangerous than past monopolies. Thus another signpost of progress is when competition authorities, to protect society from these harms, become more proactive in identifying and challenging anticom- petitive data-driven strategies that monopolies use to maintain or attain their power.

A. In False Praise of Monopolies

Some within the tech industry praise monopolies: **18.03**

> A monopoly like Google is different. Since it doesn't have to worry about compet- ing with anyone, it has wider latitude to care about its workers, its products and its impact on the wider world. Google's motto—'Don't be evil'—is in part a branding ploy, but it is also characteristic of a kind of business that is successful enough to take ethics seriously without jeopardizing its own existence. In business, money is either an important thing or it is everything. Monopolists can afford to think about things other than making money; non-monopolists can't. In perfect competition, a business is so focused on today's margins that it can't possibly plan for a long-term future. Only one thing can allow a business to transcend the daily brute struggle for survival: monopoly profits.

... the world we live in is dynamic: We can invent new and better things. Creative monopolists give customers more choices by adding entirely new categories of abundance to the world. Creative monopolies aren't just good for the rest of society; they're powerful engines for making it better.[1]

18.04 Some large tech firms have joined the chorus for non-intervention in dynamic markets. They raise the risk of false positives. The Four Horsemen of the Apocalypse arising from governmental intervention are chilling innovation; chilling investment; protecting competitors, rather than competition; and public choice theory of how companies manipulate competition authorities to punish rivals or erect entry barriers. For some, these Four Horsemen are so scary, that the company gets a pass, whenever it can show any efficiency from its anticompetitive behaviour (even if the efficiency is as little as one dollar, euro, yen, or pound).

18.05 There is no empirical support that monopolies—whether in dynamic or static industries—are generally good for society.[2] As Professor Baker notes, the claim that monopoly enhances incentives to innovate ignores important ways that greater competition enhances these incentives. Thus firms often increase research and development investment in response to greater investment by their rivals. The claim also ignores the ability of firms exercising market power to restrict, deter, or eliminate new forms of competition through exclusionary conduct. 'To relax antitrust rules on the rationale that one firm is enough for competition, in rapidly changing high-technology markets or otherwise, would undermine innovation incentives under the guise of protecting them'.[3] Ensuring a multiplicity and diversity of independently innovating firms can promote the search for new problem solutions, safeguard the effectiveness of competition as a process of parallel experimentation and mutual learning, and enable faster adaptation to exogenous shocks.[4]

---

[1] Peter Thiel, 'Competition Is for Losers', *Wall Street Journal*, 12 September 2014, http://www.wsj.com/articles/peter-thiel-competition-is-for-losers-1410535536.

[2] Maurice E Stucke, 'Should the Government Prosecute Monopolies?', *U of Illinois L Rev* [2009]: p 497.

[3] Jonathan B. Baker, 'Taking the Error Out of "Error Cost" Analysis', 80 *Antitrust LJ* (2015): pp 1, 14.

[4] Wolfgang Kerber, 'Competition, Innovation and Maintaining Diversity Through Competition Law', in Josef Drexl et al (eds), *Competition Policy and the Economic Approach: Foundations and Limitations* (Cheltenham: Edward Elgar, 2011), pp 173, 174, 179; Grant Miles et al, 'Industry Variety and Performance', 14 *Strategic Mgmt J* (1993): pp 163, 166–72. Plus, competitors can mutually gain from localized competition, such as knowledge spill-overs, improving the quality of their labour pool, and strengthening their network of suppliers. Kenneth M Davidson, *Reality Ignored: How Milton Friedman and Chicago Economics Undermined American Institutions and Endangered the Global Economy* (Seattle, WA: CreateSpace Independent Publishing Platform, 2011), pp 96, 152–3; Michael E Porter, *The Competitive Advantage of Nations* (New York: Free Press, 1990), pp 662–9; Michael E Porter, 'Competition and Antitrust: A Productivity-Based Approach', in Charles D Weller et al (eds), *Unique Value: Competition Based on Innovation Creating Unique Value* (Ashland, OH: Innovation Press, 2004), pp 154, 161–5. By analogy, plant species compete for pollinators (bees). But in mutualistic networks, the more plant species that grow in a field, the

The US and EU competition laws seek to prevent mergers that create monopolies.   **18.06**
But in neither jurisdiction are monopolies guilty for being a monopoly: 'it is not in
itself illegal for an undertaking to be in a dominant position and such a dominant
undertaking is entitled to compete on the merits'.[5] To be liable, the monopoly
must monopolize, that is engage in unfair anticompetitive practices. The EU law
is arguably broader than the US law in that the dominant firm has 'a special responsibility not to allow its conduct to impair genuine undistorted competition
on the common market'.[6] Under EU law, unlike in the US, a dominant firm could
be liable for charging an excessively high price.[7] Nonetheless, in both jurisdictions, the emphasis is on 'safeguarding the competitive process' and ensuring that
dominant firms 'do not exclude their competitors by other means than competing
on the merits of the products or services they provide'.[8] Thus, both the US and EU
are mindful that 'what really matters is protecting an effective competitive process and not simply protecting competitors'.[9] The expectation is that competitors
'who deliver less to consumers in terms of price, choice, quality and innovation
will leave the market'.[10]

Nor is there any empirical support that many companies with market power are   **18.07**
now cowering in fear of improving their products so as to not raise antitrust concerns. Google and Apple, for example, were caught colluding. They agreed with
their competitors not to poach each other's employees in order to depress wages.[11]
So if they are violating antitrust's per se illegal offences, one wonders how seriously
they are worried about abusing their dominant position. Moreover, as we shall see,
the US, unlike the EU, has been less willing to intervene in technology markets and
pursue dominant companies for potential abuse.

---

more pollinators are attracted to the area; so, the different plant species stand to gain more when
they coexist. Jordi Bascompte, 'Disentangling the Web of Life', 325 *Science* (2009): pp 416, 418.

[5] European Commission, *Guidance on the Commission's Enforcement Priorities in Applying
Article 82 of the EC Treaty to Abusive Exclusionary Conduct by Dominant Undertakings* [2009] OJ C 45/7,
para 1 ('EC Article 82 Guidelines'), http://eur-lex.europa.eu/legal-content/EN/TXT/PDF/?uri=
CELEX:52009XC0224%2801%29&from=EN.

[6] Ibid.

[7] Ibid, para 7.

[8] Ibid, para 6; *Morrison v Murray Biscuit Co*, 797 F2d 1430, 1437 (US Ct of Apps (7th Cir),
1986) ('purpose of antitrust law, at least as articulated in the modern cases, is to protect the competitive process'); *see also Tal v Hogan*, 453 F3d 1244, 1258 (US Ct of Apps (10th Cir), 2006); *SCFC
ILC, Inc v Visa USA, Inc*, 36 F3d 958, 963 (US Ct of Apps (10th Cir), 1994).

[9] EC Article 82 Guidelines, above note 5, para 6.

[10] Ibid.

[11] US Department of Justice (DOJ), Office of Public Affairs, 'Justice Department Requires
Six High Tech Companies to Stop Entering into Anticompetitive Employee Solicitation
Agreements: Settlement Preserves Competition for High Tech Employees', Press Release,
24 September 2010, http://www.justice.gov/opa/pr/justice-department-requires-six-high-
tech-companies-stop-entering-anticompetitive-employee.

B. Debunking the Myth that Competition Law is Ill-Suited for New Industries

18.08　When competition authorities investigate new, technologically dynamic markets, one response is that the competition laws are inapposite. Microsoft argued—unsuccessfully—in the 1990s that the competition laws were ill-suited for its fast-moving tech market. The argument is that competition comes from surprising sources, so the monopolist needs to continually innovate for fear of the next competitive threat. Few, if any, anticipated Facebook's and Google's significance, when the US Department of Justice (DOJ) prosecuted Microsoft in the 1990s, just as few anticipated Microsoft's dominance when the DOJ prosecuted International Business Machines Corporation (IBM) in the 1970s. If innovation comes from unexpected sources, then competition officials and the public need not worry about monopolistic abuses, since the next disruptive innovator is currently tinkering away in some lab, garage, basement, or attic.

18.09　Dynamic industries, as the US Court of Appeals for DC Circuit observed in *Microsoft*, do present challenges for courts and the agencies:

> As the record in this case indicates, six years seems like an eternity in the computer industry. By the time a court can assess liability, firms, products, and the marketplace are likely to have changed dramatically. This, in turn, threatens enormous practical difficulties for courts considering the appropriate measure of relief in equitable enforcement actions, both in crafting injunctive remedies in the first instance and reviewing those remedies in the second. Conduct remedies may be unavailing in such cases, because innovation to a large degree has already rendered the anticompetitive conduct obsolete (although by no means harmless). And broader structural remedies present their own set of problems, including how a court goes about restoring competition to a dramatically changed, and constantly changing, marketplace.[12]

18.10　But these challenges, the DC Circuit added, did not mean that the competition laws no longer play an important role in curbing abuses by dominant firms in dynamic markets; nor should courts assume this in assessing the case's merits.[13]

18.11　One problem is that the dynamic disruption, especially in markets characterized by network effects, can take a long time. Suppose someone devises a better search engine or social network. With data-driven network effects, the innovations of 'one' will not immediately convert the many.

---

[12] *United States v Microsoft Corporation*, 253 F3d 34, 49 (US Ct of Apps (DC Cir), 2001).
[13] Ibid.

To illustrate, Microsoft benefits from network effects in the personal computer op- **18.12**
erating system market.[14] It still commanded in 2015 a worldwide share of 90.85 per
cent in that market. The threat to Microsoft's core business, which is built around
personal computers, comes not from other PC operating systems, but from mobile
phones and tablets. Benefitting from several data-driven network effects, Google
continues to dominate the search market, despite Microsoft's reportedly investing
in 2010 over USD 4.5 billion into developing its algorithms and building the physical capacity necessary to operate its rival search engine Bing. Facebook identifies numerous competitors, including Google+ and other, largely regional, social networks
that have strong positions in particular countries.[15] Nonetheless, benefitting from
several network effects, Facebook continues growing. In December 2014, it had on
average 890 million daily active users, an 18 per cent increase from December 2013;
on average, 745 million daily active users accessed Facebook from a mobile device, a
34 per cent increase from December 2013.[16] Both Google's and Facebook's average
revenue per user (ARPU) has steadily increased in the US, Canada, Europe, and
Asia.[17] Google's and Facebook's dominance on the free side enable both companies
to significantly profit from their advertising platforms: Google's net income in 2014
was USD 14.4 billion.[18] Facebook's net income was USD 2.925 billion.[19]

As new products or technologies are introduced and existing products evolve, the **18.13**
dominant platforms may become subject to additional competition. Nonetheless,
monopolies can persist, even in tech industries. There is no reason why consumers
should suffer from monopolistic abuses while waiting for the next big thing.

C. How the 'Waiting for Dynamic Competition' Argument Ignores Path Dependencies

Another assumption is that potential competitors will materialize and veer the **18.14**
market towards its natural competitive equilibrium (and what the market would
have looked like absent the monopolistic restraints). So, yes, the monopoly temporarily causes harm, but dynamic disruption will shepherd us to the new competitive
equilibrium where we would have been (but for the monopoly).

---

[14] Case T-201/04 *Microsoft Corp v Comm'n* [2007] ECR II-3601 (Ct First Instance), paras 558
and 1061.
[15] Facebook Inc, Form 10-K Annual Report, filed 29 January 2015, p 6 ('Facebook 2014 Annual
Report'), http://files.shareholder.com/downloads/AMDA-NJ5DZ/650609882x0xS1326801-15-
6/1326801/filing.pdf.
[16] Ibid, p 5.
[17] Chapter 13 of this volume.
[18] Google Inc, Annual Report Pursuant to Section 13 or 15(D) of the Securities Exchange Act
of 1934 for the fiscal year ended December 31, 2014, p 22 ('Google 2014 Annual Report'), http://
www.sec.gov/Archives/edgar/data/1288776/000128877615000008/goog2014123110-k.htm.
[19] Facebook 2014 Annual Report, above note 15, p 30.

18.15 This may be true for homogeneous goods, where price is the key parameter of competition. The monopoly elevates the price of bolts, entrants lower the price. The bolts remain the same, but their price differs. In tech industries, the assumption goes further: innovators will materialize whatever competition officials and monopolists do, or do not do, and bring us the innovations that would have occurred but for the monopoly. Indeed, the race may be for the entire market, not just a piece of it, so the incentives to derail a monopoly are said to be even greater.

18.16 The debate is akin to assuming that we have recreated all the cultural knowledge that was lost when the Library of Alexandria was destroyed. This was debated in Tom Stoppard's play, *Arcadia*:

> THOMASINA:...the enemy who burned the great library of Alexandria without so much as a fine for all that is overdue. Oh, Septimus!—can you bear it? All the lost plays of the Athenians! Two hundred at least by Aeschylus, Sophocles, Euripides—thousands of poems—Aristotle's own library!...How can we sleep for grief?

> SEPTIMUS: By counting our stock. Seven plays from Aeschylus, seven from Sophocles, nineteen from Euripides, my lady! You should no more grieve for the rest than for a buckle lost from your first shoe, or for your lesson book which will be lost when you are old. We shed as we pick up, like travellers who must carry everything in their arms, and what we let fall will be picked up by those behind. The procession is very long and life is very short. We die on the march. But there is nothing outside the march so nothing can be lost to it. The missing plays of Sophocles will turn up piece by piece, or be written again in another language. Ancient cures for diseases will reveal themselves once more. Mathematical discoveries glimpsed and lost to view will have their time again. You do not suppose, my lady, that if all of Archimedes had been hiding in the great library of Alexandria, we would be at a loss for a corkscrew?[20]

18.17 The exchange raises the issue of path dependence and competitive portals, namely critical inflection points when antitrust can make a difference. Under Septimus's perspective, high tech products and services are like bolts. Path dependencies play a minor role; we eventually arrive at the same competitive equilibrium and enjoy the same innovations (with or without the monopoly). So monopolies, like the destruction of the Library of Alexandria, do not impose any long-term harm. Thomasina is less confident. For her, under an evolutionary economic process, 'chance plays a significant role', and 'small, random (and therefore unpredictable) events may have severe long-run consequences'.[21] We may not recover what was lost (by the fire or abuses of a dominant firm).

---

[20] Alice Burton, 'Where We All Cry About the Library of Alexandria', Bookriot, 22 July 2015, http://bookriot.com/2015/07/22/cry-library-alexandria/.

[21] Bart Verspagen, 'The Use of Modeling Tools for Policy in Evolutionary Environments', 76(4) *Technological Forecasting & Social Change* (May 2009): p 455, http://www.sciencedirect.com/science/article/pii/S0040162508001121.

A personal observation are the three adjacent Connecticut rivers: the Housatonic, **18.18**
Shepaug, and Naugatuck. Over time, the persistence of random events—such
as a failed company, a leak in a canal, and the growth in demand for brass—
accumulated leading to completely different outcomes among the three rivers.[22]
Today, the bucolic Housatonic and Shepaug Rivers in northwestern Connecticut
attract trout anglers, kayakers, and hikers along their heavily wooded banks; the
Naugatuck is industrialized. If the history tape was rewound, and random events
unfolded differently (say the canal in Falls Village did not leak), the situation
today among the three rivers might differ, and walking along the Housatonic may
be less inspiring.

This may be especially true in complex adaptive industries, such as many tech **18.19**
industries. When the competitive portals are open, entry, expansion, or random
events during these periods of competitive opportunity can foster significant
innovation. On the other hand, a dominant firm may use its market power to
close the competitive portals. Thus abuse of dominance, if unchecked, may
have greater negative implications beyond that immediate industry and time-
frame. The long-run consequences of monopolistic practices may not simply be
higher prices, but foregone innovations. So, like some great works lost in the
Library of Alexandria that, contrary to Septimus's belief, were never recreated,
so too one price we may pay—when monopolies are unchecked—are innovations foregone.

D. How (Even Failed) Antitrust Enforcement Can Open Competitive Portals

Policymakers generally recognize the economist Joseph Schumpeter's 'creative **18.20**
destruction' thesis that capitalism 'is by nature a form or method of economic
change and not only never is but never can be stationary'.[23] Many accept that
competition from new commodities, technologies, sources of supply, and organizational structures can be more important than static price competition. The
difficulty lies in predicting where and when this innovation will emerge and what
motivates this innovation.

More recent economic theory (building on Schumpeter's disequilibrium dynam- **18.21**
ics) has identified the shortcomings of neoclassical economic theory in explaining industries where technological change drives economic growth. As economist

---

[22] George Black, *The Trout Pool Paradox: The American Lives of Three Rivers* (Boston, MA: Houghton Mifflin Harcourt, 2004), pp 10–11, 91–2.
[23] Joseph A Schumpeter, *Capitalism, Socialism, and Democracy* (3rd edn, New York: Harper, 1950), pp 82–3.

Douglass North noted in his Nobel Prize speech, 'Neoclassical theory is simply an inappropriate tool to analyze and prescribe policies that will induce development.'[24] Neoclassical economic theory assumes static equilibrium systems. When subject to an exogenous force (entry, government regulation, new technology, energy crisis), this equilibrium is disrupted temporarily. But neoclassical theory does not explain how markets develop.

18.22 Instead many markets may be complex adaptive systems. Firms, as individuals, make mistakes, readjust, and undertake new strategies. The competitive process 'is inherently a process of trial and error with no stable end-state considered by the participants in the process.'[25] And innovation and dynamic forces may need competitive portals, ie windows of opportunity.[26]

18.23 To illustrate competitive portals, let us consider whether the former AT&T and IBM monopolies still affect us today. Would our current technological developments exist if AT&T's and IBM's monopolies went unchallenged during the 1970s? Can we really say that the level of innovation would be the same today if the DOJ never prosecuted these monopolies?

18.24 The DOJ's break-up of AT&T is considered one of antitrust's success stories in unleashing innovation.[27] Less clear is IBM. The Reagan administration famously sacked the DOJ's 13-year-old investigation into the computer monopoly. In a memo to Reagan's Attorney General, John Roberts (before he was Chief Justice of the US Supreme Court) discussing an upset conservative's upcoming visit: he 'will doubtless arrive with many criticisms of the Department for not advancing conservative ideals'. Among the points Roberts mentioned: 'More reasonable [approach] to antitrust law, epitomized in the dropping of the IBM case'.[28] One scholar called the government's case 'the greatest waste of resources in the history of antitrust enforcement'.[29] Some might say that IBM's computer dominance (outside mainframes), with or without any antitrust investigation, was destined to be eclipsed—and cite the Wintel combination of Microsoft's Windows operating system and Intel microprocessors.

---

[24] Douglass C North, 'Economic Performance Through Time', 84 *Am Econ Rev* (1994): pp 359, 359.

[25] François Moreau, 'The Role of the State in Evolutionary Economics', 28 *Cambridge J Econ* (2004): pp 847, 851.

[26] Andrew I Gavil and Harry First, *The Microsoft Antitrust Cases* (Boston, MA: MIT Press, 2014), pp 324–4 (discussing importance of 'competitive movements').

[27] Tim Wu, *The Master Switch: The Rise and Fall of Information Empires* (New York: Alfred A Knopf, 2010) .

[28] Memorandum from John Roberts to Attorney General on Talking Points for Meeting with Lofton of Conservative Digest, 27 January 1982, http://www.archives.gov/news/john-roberts/accession-60-89-0372/ doc053.pdf.

[29] John E Lopatka, 'United States v IBM: A Monument to Arrogance', 68 *Antitrust LJ* (2000): pp 145, 146.

But one issue is whether the DOJ's antitrust investigation opened the competitive **18.25** portal that facilitated Microsoft's growth. In the late 1960s, IBM controlled about 70 per cent of the computer market. After the DOJ challenged IBM's practices, particularly its 'bundling' hardware and software, IBM changed course. This led to the development of the computer software industry. As IBM's second president Thomas J Watson, Jr wrote, '[p]recipitated by a massive antitrust complaint filed against IBM by the Justice Department in January 1969, the company reexamined its practices and decided to stop requiring customers to buy software, services, and hardware as one bundle in June of the same year. This pricing change opened up software markets to independent companies.'[30]

A decade later, when preparing to launch its personal computers, the still domi- **18.26** nant IBM approached the start-up Microsoft about creating a version of a BASIC computer program. Microsoft suggested that IBM talk to Digital Research, whose CP/M operating system had become the standard for computer hobbyists. One account is that Digital Research's president apparently disliked the arrogant IBM from his university days and was late in meeting the IBM executives. After the nego- tiations stalled, IBM returned to Microsoft to create an operating system for its per- sonal computer. When introducing its personal computer, IBM sold the Microsoft operating system for a much lower price than the CP/M-86 system.[31]

So one cannot assume that with or without antitrust enforcement, Microsoft (or **18.27** some other operating system) would have become dominant by the 1990s. If any- thing, the DOJ's investigation of IBM, it appears, opened a competitive portal, namely IBM's decision to unbundle software from its computers, which enabled software development to flourish.

E. The Nowcasting Radar—Why Some Data-opolies are More Dangerous than Microsoft in the 1990s

Before the Big Data era, dominant tech firms were less aware of what their cus- **18.28** tomers and rivals were doing (or planning to do). As Chapter 2 discusses, some platforms have a relative advantage in accessing and analysing data to discern con- sumer trends well before others. As we saw, companies can nowcast, ie, 'predict the present' by using search inquiries, social network postings, tweets, etc. Nowcasting

---

[30] R Lougee-Heimer, 'The Common Optimization INterface for Operations Research: Promoting Open-Source Software in the Operations Research Community', 47(1) *IBM J Research and Development* (2003): p 59, citing Thomas J Watson, Jr, *Father, Son, and Co: My Life at IBM and Beyond* (New York: Bantam, 1990).
[31] *See* Eric Beinhocker, *The Origin of Wealth: Evolution, Complexity, and the Radical Remaking of Economics* (Cambridge, MA: Harvard Business Review Press, 2006), pp 326–7; Gary Kildall Special, https://archive.org/details/GaryKild.

can yield a competitive advantage. Hedge funds, for example, are nowcasting to see in real-time how market forces are affecting portfolios, such as how many cars are in the Wal-Mart parking lots across the country.[32] In monitoring search queries, Google can predict flu outbreaks well before the government health agencies can. Twitter's data can help companies identify emerging trends. Google and Apple, in controlling the mobile phone app stores, immediately know when users download rivals' apps. As the UK competition authority observed,

> A number of third party firms also now offer tools and services that enable first parties to gain insights on how their brands and products are being discussed online (sometimes referred to as 'social listening', 'opinion mining' or 'sentiment tracking'). By analysing the extent to which they are mentioned in social media content (such as blogs, microblogs, forums, news sites and social network sites), whether trends are positive or negative and why, firms can adjust their marketing activity.[33]

18.29 Nowcasting represents a potent data-based weapon, not previously available for monopolies, to monitor new business models in real-time. The data-opoly can use its relative advantage in accessing and processing personal data (such as watching for trends in its proprietary data from posts on a social network, search queries, emails, etc) to quickly identify (and squelch) nascent competitive threats. The dominant firm can acquire entrants before they become significant competitive threats or blunt the entrant's growth (such as manipulating its search engine results to make it harder to find the company[34]). For example, Facebook warns its investors that its '[p]latform partners may use information shared by our users through the Facebook Platform in order to develop products or features that compete with us'.[35]

18.30 Thus, it is as if the monopoly invented a radar system to monitor in real-time the competitive portals. It can track nascent competitive threats shortly after they take off, and intercept or shoot them down long before they become visible to regulators and others. Moreover, the courts and agencies, if they follow the UK competition authority's logic in Google/Waze, will find that the distant planes

---

[32] Jessica Toonkel, 'BlackRock Betting Big Data Can Help Revive Its Active Equity Funds', *Reuters*, 6 August 2015, http://www.reuters.com/article/2015/08/06/us-blackrock-bigdata-equity-analysis-idUSKCN0QB0B520150806.

[33] UK Competition and Markets Authority, *The Commercial Use of Consumer Data: Report on the CMA's Call for Information*, June 2015, para 2.68 ('CMA Report'), https://www.gov.uk/government/uploads/system/uploads/attachment_data/file/435817/The_commercial_use_of_consumer_data.pdf.

[34] For example, Coupons.com identified search degradation as a significant risk. Coupons.com Incorporated, Annual Report Pursuant to Section 13 or 15(D) of the Securities Exchange Act of 1934 for the fiscal year ended December 31, 2014, p 18 ('Coupons.com 2014 Annual Report'), https://www.sec.gov/Archives/edgar/data/1115128/000156459015001837/coup-10k_20141231.htm; *see also* Maurice E Stucke and Ariel Ezrachi, 'When Competition Fails to Optimize Quality: A Look at Search Engines', 18 *Yale J L & Tech* (2016): p 70.

[35] Facebook Inc, Annual Report Pursuant to Section 13 or 15(D) of the Securities Exchange Act of 1934 for the fiscal year ended December 31, 2012, p 15 ('Facebook 2012 Annual Report'), http://www.sec.gov/Archives/edgar/data/1326801/000132680113000003/fb-12312012x10k.htm.

pose potential (yet speculative) threats, and will have insufficient evidence to prove that competition was likely harmed. The monopolist, however, is not troubled by the overall welfare effects in shooting down or intercepting the planes. Granted, the monopolist may damage its reputation, if it acts too brazenly, but reputational concerns generally do not inhibit some monopolies from raising prices. For entrants, there is the potential reward of being acquired. But there are also casualties when the monopoly shoots down others. If the blown-up planes come easier to mind, then some potential entrants (or funders), under the availability heuristic, may amplify the risk, and decide not to leave the runway. And the competition authority cannot force (or incentivize) entrants to fly towards the monopolist armed with this radar.

The European Data Protection Supervisor asked competition officials to consider (in   **18.31** coordination with privacy and consumer protection officials) the following issues:

- first 'how the control of personal information contributes to market power in the digital economy and the implications for data protection' and
- second 'the risks to the consumer posed by concentrations and the abuse of market dominance where firms process massive amounts of personal data'.[36]

Big Data can help prolong monopolies in at least two ways: data-driven network   **18.32** effects and this unique 'nowcasting' radar. In accessing consumer and other market data in real-time, some dominant firms can quickly detect and squelch competitive threats and close competitive portals.

F. Keeping the Competitive Portals Open

Competition law, when effectively enforced, can deter exclusionary and predatory   **18.33** practices and keep competitive portals open. After all, it is easier for the creative destruction to breeze through a window screen than topple a concrete wall.

Big Data, as we saw, can confer power and a durable competitive advantage.[37]   **18.34** Data-driven network effects can improve the product's or service's quality. Firms like Google thrive (and serve their users) by gathering as much data as possible to personalize search results. At times, consumers benefit from this competitive rivalry and drive to maintain a data-advantage. Companies innovate to expand their

---

[36] European Data Protection Supervisor, *Privacy and Competitiveness in the Age of Big Data: The Interplay Between Data Protection, Competition Law and Consumer Protection in the Digital Economy*, Preliminary Opinion, March 2014, p 8 ('EDPS Preliminary Opinion'), https://secure.edps.europa.eu/EDPSWEB/webdav/shared/Documents/Consultation/Opinions/2014/14-03-26_competitition_law_big_data_EN.pdf.

[37] Ibid, p 6 ('Extracting value from big data has become a significant source of power for the biggest players in internet markets.').

platform of services to secure a greater following. No one, for example, questions Google's investment in technology.[38]

18.35 But when the stakes are greater, so too are the incentives to engage in unfair practices to tip the market in one's favour and maintain a monopoly.[39] Consequently, competition authorities must be alert to dominant companies' unfair practices to thwart competitors and disruptive innovators. We outline below several potentially anticompetitive data-driven tactics.

1. Exclusive dealing to prevent rivals from accessing critical data

18.36 One historic concern is when a monopoly, through exclusive dealing, deprives its rivals of a needed resource. For example, aluminium producers to extract aluminium from alumina, require a 'very large amount of electrical energy, which is ordinarily, though not always, most cheaply obtained from water power'.[40] To foreclose other aluminium producers, Alcoa in its contracts with several hydro-power companies, illegally added covenants binding the power companies not to sell or let power to anyone else for the manufacture of aluminium.[41]

18.37 Likewise, the European Commission considers that 'such input foreclosure is in principle liable to result in anti-competitive foreclosure if the exclusive supply obligation or incentive ties most of the efficient input suppliers and customers competing with the dominant undertaking are unable to find alternative efficient sources of input supply'.[42]

18.38 Data in our industries is a critical input. Thus one obvious concern would be for a dominant firm to foreclose its rivals' timely access to critical data. The DOJ had this concern in the *Google/ITA Software* case, where it prevented Google post-merger from restricting, through exclusive dealing, its rivals' access to the airlines' seat and booking class data.[43] And in a merger between advertising firms, the European Commission inquired whether the competitors would still have access to 'big data' from other providers if post-merger, the merged entity were to develop its own 'big data' analytics platform, and deny access to its competitors.[44]

---

[38] Google 2014 Annual Report, above note 18, p 22 (far more of Google's 53,600 full-time employees are involved in research and development (20,832 employees), than in sales and marketing (17,621), general and administrative (7,510), or operations (7,637)).

[39] EC Article 82 Guidelines, above note 5, para 20 (noting incentive 'to "tip" a market characterised by network effects in its favour or to further entrench its position on such a market').

[40] *United States v Aluminum Co of Am*, 148 F2d 416, 422 (US Ct of Apps (2d Cir), 1945).

[41] These restrictive covenants and certain other practices were not the subject of the 1945 case, but a 1912 DOJ antitrust action. Ibid.

[42] EC Article 82 Guidelines, above note 5, para 32 n 4.

[43] *United States v Google Inc*, Case No 1:11-cv-00688 (US Dist Ct (D DC), filed 8 April 2011), Competitive Impact Statement, http://www.justice.gov/file/497671/download.

[44] *Publicis/Omnicom* (Case Comp/M.7023), Commission Decision C(2014) 89 final, 9 January 2014, para 625. A majority of competitors responded that if the merged entity developed its own

2. Exclusionary practices to prevent rivals from achieving scale

As the US Court of Appeals for the Eleventh Circuit noted in 2015, a monopoly can **18.39** violate section 2 of the Sherman Act when its exclusive dealing programme deprives smaller rivals of 'distribution sufficient to achieve efficient scale, thereby raising costs and slowing or preventing effective entry'.[45] So too a dominant data-driven company can use exclusionary tactics to prevent rivals from achieving the minimum efficient scale.[46] Scale, as Chapter 12 discusses, can be especially important in data-driven industries, such as search and search advertising. We saw, for example, how increasing the volume of both 'tail' and popular search queries can improve the quality of the search algorithm's results. In unfairly preventing smaller rivals and potential entrants from accessing critical data, the dominant firm can use the network effects (learning-by-doing, scope, and spill-over effects) to widen the quality gap over rivals, attract more users and advertisers, and expand its platform.[47]

The Federal Trade Commission (FTC) Bureau of Competition staff, from the re- **18.40** leased portions of its inadvertently produced report, recommended suing Google for several unfair practices. (The FTC Commissioners instead closed the investigation after Google voluntarily agreed to change some practices.) The FTC legal staff discussed the competitive significance of data and 'substantial scale effects' in the Internet search, search advertising, and search syndication markets.[48] One alleged anticompetitive practice was Google's use of exclusivity provisions to prevent its rival Microsoft from achieving scale, including the volume of search queries it received. Google used contractual restrictions, according to the FTC legal staff, to deny Microsoft critical scale and impair its ability to compete effectively in the markets for general search and search advertising.[49]

---

big data analytics platform and did not allow access to it, 'the impact will be limited as they are currently using their own data analytics platform or one from third parties'. Ibid, para 629.

[45] *McWane, Inc v FTC*, 783 F3d 838 (US Ct of Apps (11th Cir), 2015), citing FTC findings; *see also LePage's Inc v 3M*, 324 F3d 141, 159 (US Ct of Apps (3rd Cir), 2003) ('inquiry in *Microsoft* was whether the monopolist's conduct excluded a competitor (Netscape) from the essential facilities that would permit it to achieve the efficiencies of scale necessary to threaten the monopoly').

[46] Frank Pasquale, *The Black Box Society: The Secret Algorithms That Control Money and Information* (Cambridge, MA: Harvard University Press, 2015), p 67.

[47] CMA Report, above note 33, para 17 (noting that '[t]he ability and incentives to exclude competitors by denying access to data, and/or the barriers to entry arising from consumer data, will be stronger where the data is a significant input into the quality or other attributes of a product or service' and the concerns related to possible leverage of market power 'where consumer data obtained in one market is a significant input to products and services produced in a related but separate market'). A number of respondents highlighted market power as a potential concern, 'noting that a firm might be able to foreclose rivals by cutting off access to vital data'. Ibid, para 3.57.

[48] 'The FTC Report on Google's Business Practices', *Wall Street Journal*, 8 August 2012, p 76 ('FTC Staff Report'), http://graphics.wsj.com/google-ftc-report/.

[49] Ibid, pp 94, 96, 98, 100, 102, 104.

18.41   One can access a search engine in various ways, such as the browser one uses. Twenty companies (including AOL), the FTC legal staff found, account for 90 per cent of all search query volume. To steer users to its search engine, a search engine provider (like Google, Microsoft, or DuckDuckGo) can enter into distribution agreements with these entry points, namely hardware manufacturers, independent software vendors, and Internet service providers, 'to distribute toolbars and establish default settings that direct user searches to [its] search engine'.[50] Google, the FTC legal staff reported, had exclusive or restrictive agreements with four of the top five companies, and 12 of the top 20.[51] Google, for example, is the default engine on Apple's Safari Internet browser. Google reportedly paid Apple USD 82 million in 2009, and USD 1 billion in 2013 and 2014 for this partnership.[52] Google's internal documents, the FTC legal staff found, showed that 'Google's interest in renewing deals with some of its largest syndication customers may have been, in part, to keep Microsoft from gaining scale'.[53] Interestingly, Amazon decided it was in its long-term interest to funnel some query volume to Microsoft's Bing, even if it was losing money on each query.[54] One wonders why others did not do this. Perhaps, as the European Commission generally noted from its market investigation, the distributors' major concern was Google's bargaining power.[55]

3. Dominant firm leverages its data-advantage in a regulated market to another market

18.42   We saw in Chapter 9 how the regulated French energy monopoly GDF Suez was using its vast customer database to target customers in the unregulated market with deals on gas and electricity.[56] Since 2007, French gas customers could opt for the regulated tariffs, which only the incumbent operator GDF Suez offered, or the 'market' offers, which GDF Suez and its new rivals offered. In making its market offers, GDF Suez had an unfair advantage over its rivals. It was using the data it collected as a regulated monopoly to target customers with customized offers based on their usage. The personal data in question was commercially valuable.

---

[50]   *Microsoft/Yahoo! Search Business* (Case Comp/M.5727), Commission Decision C(2010) 1077, 18 February 2010, para 50.

[51]   FTC Staff Report, above note 48, p 104.

[52]   'Apple Working on Its Own Search Engine; Aims to Take on Google: Report', IBN Live, 10 February 2015, http://ibnlive.in.com/news/apple-working-on-its-own-search-engine-aims-to-take-on-google-report/527597-11.html; Joel Rosenblatt and Adam Satariano, 'Google Paid Apple $1 Billion to Keep Search Bar on iPhone', Bloomberg Business, 21 January 2016, http://www.bloomberg.com/news/articles/2016-01-22/google-paid-apple-1-billion-to-keep-search-bar-on-iphone.

[53]   FTC Staff Report, above note 48, p 108.

[54]   Ibid, p 112.

[55]   *Microsoft/Yahoo! Search,* above note 50, para 246.

[56]   *See* Autorité de la Concurrence, 'Gas Market', Press Release, 9 September 2014, http://www.autoritedelaconcurrence.fr/user/standard.php?id_rub=592&id_article=2420.

With the data a company could precisely locate gas consumers, identify their consumption level, and propose offers better suited to their profile.[57] The data was unavailable to the monopoly's competitors. Nor could the competitors replicate this data. Moreover, the database was not the 'product of a specific innovation that GDF Suez may have introduced' but was 'merely inherited from its former status as monopolistic gas supplier'.[58] GDF Suez was found in 2014 to have abused its dominant position.

In a similar case, the Belgian Competition Authority in 2015 fined the National **18.43** Lottery EUR 1,190,000 for abusing its dominant position when launching its sports betting product Scooore![59] Here, too, the defendant used the data it collected as a legal monopoly in organizing public lotteries to enter the sports betting market. The monopoly used the contact details of persons registered in its database to email them about launching Scooore! The National Lottery 'did not acquire these contact details following competition on the merits but in the context of its legal monopoly'.[60] Nor could competitors reproduce the data 'at reasonable financial conditions and within a reasonable period of time'.[61]

In both cases, the dominant firm acquired the data through its legal monopoly. **18.44** Monopolies in other industries may distinguish these cases. For example, they might have amassed the data following competition on the merits, such as an innovative app. That would be a closer call. But if the firm used other unfair tactics to attain or maintain its dominant position, then arguably using the valuable consumer data from its illegally maintained or attained monopoly is not competition on the merits. Even here, the competition authority must show why competitors could not reproduce the data under reasonable financial conditions and within a reasonable time period.

4. Increasing customers' switching costs

To maintain its data-advantage and prevent rivals from attaining scale, a monopoly **18.45** may make it harder for its customers to leave. Customers, if they are locked-in, will continue to supply the monopoly (rather than its competitors) with data. The basic

---

[57] The data in question involved the 'point de comptage and d'estimation' [metering and estimating point], 'consommations annuelles de référence' [annual reference consumption], consumption profiles, surnames and first names of customers, billing addresses and landline telephone numbers. Ibid.

[58] *See* ibid.

[59] Belgian Competition Authority, 'The Belgian Competition Authority Imposes a Fine of 1.190.000 EUR on the National Lottery for Having Abused Its Dominant Position when Launching Its Sports Betting Product Scooore!', Press Release No 15/2015, 23 September 2015, http://economie.fgov.be/en/binaries/20150923_Press_release_15_BCA_tcm327-272707.pdf.

[60] Ibid.

[61] Ibid.

premise is that as the time and cost needed to switch products or services increase, the greater the customer is locked-in, the harder it will be for rivals to attract users and achieve scale. This is especially the case where consumers cannot readily predict the long-run costs in using that platform or its quality levels over time.[62]

18.46 Network effects, as we saw, can increase users' switching costs. For example, users concerned over Facebook's privacy policies may want to switch to another social network. But unless they can get their friends, family, and acquaintances to switch, they will likely stick with Facebook (if they continue using a social network). This lock-in effect, by itself, does not violate the competition law. Other users' utility can increase as more join the social network, as they have more people to befriend online.

18.47 But a firm can abuse its dominant position by undertaking additional actions, the net effect of which is to increase users' switching costs and the firm's power. One way, in the European Commission's case against Microsoft, is to reduce the interoperability with other systems or platforms.[63] Likewise, in its Facebook/WhatsApp investigation, the Commission inquired, among other things, whether:

- users of the consumer communications apps were locked in to any particular physical network, hardware solution, or anything else that needed to be replaced in order to use competing products;
- the parties controlled and limited the portability of users' data; and
- the parties had any means to preclude competitors from recreating a user's network on the parties' applications.[64]

18.48 Presumably, if the answer was yes, the risk of anticompetitive unilateral conduct increases. Facebook and WhatsApp users, the European Commission concluded, could easily port their contact data to other texting apps. (Moreover, texting data, the Commission found, had little long-term value.) But if consumers invested a lot of time and effort in the service, such as a homepage with photos, timeline, updates, etc, and the dominant firm blocked customers' ability to port their data, when data portability was technologically feasible, that would raise antitrust concerns.

18.49 The switching cost can be as subtle as setting the app or service as the default option, thereby requiring consumers to opt out each time they want to use another service.

---

[62] *See, eg,* EC Article 82 Guidelines, above note 5, para 17; *Eastman Kodak Co v Image Tech Servs, Inc,* 504 US 451, 476, 112 S Ct 2072, 2087 (1992).

[63] Case T-201/04 *Microsoft Corp v Commission* [2007] ECR II-03601, para 650 (noting the 'lack of interoperability that competing work group server operating system products [could] achieve with the Windows domain architecture' that caused an increasing number of consumers to be locked into a homogeneous Windows solution at the level of work group server operating systems').

[64] *Facebook/WhatsApp* (Case Comp/M.7217), Commission Decision C(2014) 7239 final, 3 October 2014, para 134.

5. Vertical integration by a dominant platform operator

We saw in Chapter 14 why platforms are worth billions, while apps are worth mil- **18.50**
lions. Apple and Google have significant power in effectively controlling the respective mobile operating systems iOS and Android.[65] Both Google and Apple have
business interests in 'targeted advertising' and 'run the two biggest services, by revenue, for putting advertisements on mobile phones'.[66] Google especially relies on
personal data for maintaining a competitive advantage for advertising.[67] As such,
they have a greater incentive to prevent the personal data being diverted (as well
as individuals' using rival apps). To maintain and secure fresh sources of valuable
data, Apple and Google have greater opportunities to introduce their own applications and foreclose rival applications on their smartphone platforms. Thus there is a
greater risk of exclusionary behaviour.[68]

Competition authorities are sensitive to vertical integration by a dominant platform **18.51**
operator (ie where it also becomes a seller on its platform). The platform's incentives
now change, as it may earn greater profits by steering users and advertisers to its own
products and services to the detriment of rival sellers (and contrary to consumers'
wishes). The platform has a 'frenemy' relationship with the independent application developers.[69] The platform and independent apps are friends—in that both

---

[65] OECD, *Exploring the Economics of Personal Data: A Survey of Methodologies for Measuring Monetary Value*, OECD Digital Economy Papers, No 220 (2013), p 15, http://dx.doi.org/10.1787/5k486qtxldmq-en; *see also* Google Inc, Annual Report Pursuant to Section 13 or 15(D) of the Securities Exchange Act of 1934 for the fiscal year ended December 31, 2013, p 3, http://www.sec.gov/Archives/edgar/data/1288776/000128877614000020/goog2013123110-k.htm#s1EBF39222 B397626A1572E71A8B0E8ED (noting that its 'Android operating system continues to grow with more than a billion Android devices activated globally as of September 2013').

[66] OECD, *Exploring the Economics of Personal Data*, above note 65, p 15.

[67] Ibid, p 15 (noting that 'Google was the biggest recipient of data from smart phone apps in test run by the Wall Street Journal'; that 'Google's AdMob, AdSense, Analytics and DoubleClick units received information from 38 of the 101 apps tested'; and that Google's main mobile advertising network, AdMob, 'lets advertisers target phone users by location, type of device and demographic data, including gender or age group').

[68] *See, eg,* Public Citizen, *Mission Creep-y: Google Is Quietly Becoming One of the Nation's Most Powerful Political Forces While Expanding Its Information-Collection Empire*, November 2014, p 23, https://www.citizen.org/documents/Google-Political-Spending-Mission-Creepy.pdf:

> In the transition to Hangouts, Google made it harder for users to disable all chat histories from being recorded by Gmail. It also removed the ability of people to chat with others using different instant message services than Hangouts, or hosting their own chat serv-ers. Unlike before, people chatting through Google can now only chat with others if the others are chatting through Google, creating pressure for users of online chat programs to join the Google universe. Privacy experts say this is bad for users who want to be able to use chat programs that have better privacy protections and still be able to chat with others using Google's chat services.

[69] The frenemy relationship is discussed in Ariel Ezrachi and Maurice E Stucke, *Virtual Competition: The Promise and Perils of the Algorithm-Driven Economy* (Cambridge, MA: Harvard University Press, forthcoming 2016).

benefit as more users and complementary software developers are attracted to that platform, as opposed to rival platforms. Such will be the case when it is costly or time-consuming for independent software developers to customize, promote, and update their apps across multiple platforms or where one platform imposes greater restrictions on functionality, terms of sale, advertising, etc. The platform operator, however, is also competing with the independent software developer's app, and thus an enemy.[70] As the Organisation for Economic Co-operation and Development (OECD) warned, the platform owner 'may seek to exclude third-party applications developers, either to protect its own vertically integrated applications subsidiary or to prevent the emergence of a potentially competing platform'.[71]

18.52 Thus in its Facebook/WhatsApp investigation, the European Commission inquired whether:

- the parties controlled any essential parts of the network or any mobile operating system; and
- the parties' applications were pre-installed on a large base of mobile phones, tablets, or PCs, and if so whether 'status quo bias' could potentially affect consumers' choices.[72]

18.53 Likewise, Facebook in 2015 warned investors of the risk of the dominant mobile platforms inhibiting Facebook's apps or preferring their own programs or services.[73] So did Twitter, LinkedIn, Yelp, and smaller online platforms, like Coupons.com. They all noted their dependence on the Apple and Android mobile platforms.[74] They recognize that web usage is increasingly shifting to mobile platforms such as smartphones and other connected devices.[75] Their business growth and success depend on their interoperability with the popular mobile operating systems that they do not control.[76] So one significant business risk is if the mobile super-platforms—Apple

---

[70] OECD, *Supporting Investment in Knowledge Capital, Growth and Innovation*, 10 October 2013, p 173, http://dx.doi.org/10.1787/9789264193307-en.

[71] Ibid.

[72] *Facebook/WhatsApp*, above note 64, para 134.

[73] Facebook 2014 Annual Report, above note 15, p 11.

[74] Coupons.com 2014 Annual Report, above note 34, pp 15, 17; Twitter Inc, Quarterly Report Pursuant to Section 13 or 15(D) of the Securities Exchange Act of 1934 for the quarterly period ended June 30, 2015, p 44 ('Twitter June 2015 Quarterly Report'), http://www.sec.gov/Archives/edgar/data/1418091/000156459015006705/twtr-10q_20150630.htm; LinkedIn Corporation, Quarterly Report Pursuant to Section 13 or 15(D) of the Securities Exchange Act of 1934 for the quarterly period ended June 30, 2015, p 47 ('LinkedIn June 2015 Quarterly Report'), http://www.sec.gov/Archives/edgar/data/1271024/000127102415000020/a20150630-10qdocument.htm; Yelp Inc, Quarterly Report Pursuant to Section 13 or 15(D) of the Securities Exchange Act of 1934 for the quarterly period ended June 30, 2015, p 33 ('Yelp June 2015 Quarterly Report'), http://www.sec.gov/Archives/edgar/data/1345016/000120677415002479/yelp_10q.htm.

[75] Coupons.com 2014 Annual Report, above note 34, p 17; Yelp June 2015 Quarterly Report, above note 74, p 33; LinkedIn June 2015 Quarterly Report, above note 74, p 47.

[76] Facebook 2014 Annual Report, above note 15, p 11; Twitter June 2015 Quarterly Report, above note 74, p 44.

and Google (and to a much lesser extent Microsoft)—change the mobile operating systems that degrade the functionality of the independent apps and online platforms—like Twitter, Yelp, or Coupons.com—or give preferential treatment to their own similar services or competitive services.

Facebook identified several potential anticompetitive measures by the mobile super-platforms including: **18.54**

- degrading the independent app's functionality,
- reducing or eliminating the independent app's ability to distribute its products,
- giving preferential treatment to competitive products, or
- limiting for any app whose revenues are primarily from advertising its ability to deliver, target, or measure the effectiveness of ads, or imposing fees or other charges related to its delivery of ads.[77]

In its 2012 Annual Report, Facebook warned that '[c]ertain competitors, in-   **18.55**
cluding Google, could use strong or dominant positions in one or more markets to gain competitive advantage against us in areas where we operate including: by integrating competing social networking platforms or features into products they control such as search engines, web browsers, or mobile device operating systems; by making acquisitions; or by making access to Facebook more difficult.'[78]

Facebook, given its apps' strong consumer appeal, has less to fear than smaller, lesser   **18.56**
known apps. To make it harder for consumers to access and use the smaller independent apps on their smartphones, the super-platform could:

- degrade the independent app's functionality by having it run slower than the operating system's app,[79]
- reduce or eliminate the independent app developer's ability to distribute its app by making it harder for consumers to find the app on its search engine or app store,[80]

---

[77] Facebook 2014 Annual Report, above note 15, p 11.

[78] Facebook 2012 Annual Report, above note 35, p 15.

[79] *See, eg,* Analysis of Proposed Consent Order to Aid Public Comment, In re Intel Corporation, FTC Docket No 9341, 4 August 2010, p 5, https://www.ftc.gov/sites/default/files/documents/cases/2010/08/100804intelanal_0.pdf (noting how Intel effectively slowed the performance of software written using Intel's compilers on computers with competing central processing units, and to the 'unknowing public, OEMs [original equipment manufacturers], and software vendors, the slower performance of non-Intel-based computers when running certain software applications was mistakenly attributed to the performance of non-Intel CPUs').

[80] This is the basis of the privacy app Disconnect's complaint filed against Google before the European Commission. Noah Swartz, 'Disconnect Files EU Anti-trust Complaint Against Google', Electronic Frontier Foundation, 3 June 2015, https://www.eff.org/deeplinks/2015/06/disconnect-files-eu-anti-trust-complaint-against-google. US smartphone users rely mostly on the app store to find apps.comScore, *The 2015 US Mobile App Report* (2015), p 19.

- limit a competing app's revenue stream by excluding the app from its online wallets, such as Apple Pay and Google Wallet, or
- give preferential treatment to its own products, by pre-loading its app on the smartphone, having it on the opening screen,[81] or integrating its own products into its other popular products, including its search engine and the operating system.

18.57 These concerns are real. One example is Bankrate Inc. Its website allows users to compare online the rates of over 300 financial products, including mortgages, credit cards, automobile loans, money market accounts, certificates of deposit, checking and ATM fees, home equity loans, and online banking fees. As the Internet's 'leading aggregator of financial rate information', Bankrate, according to its website, 'continually surveys approximately 4,800 financial institutions in all 50 states in order to provide clear, objective, and unbiased rates to consumers'.[82] During the fourth quarter of 2015, Google began testing a competing service called Compare Credit Cards. Google's search engine displayed its own service more prominently on credit card-related search results than Bankrate's service.[83] The fallout was significant. First, Google's actions 'adversely affected' Bankrate's 'Credit Cards segment growth and profitability'.[84] Second, Bankrate's stock price, after this news was released, declined 48 per cent in one day, a record drop for the 40-year old company.[85] Bankrate's stock plummeted even though Google earlier announced that it was terminating its Compare services, including Compare Credit Cards.[86] Investors were still jittery. Bankrate, along with many other companies, depends on Google's search engine to attract a significant portion of visitors to its website. As one analyst commented, 'Bankrate faces an uncertain future, in our opinion, as its ability to maintain low-cost traffic and consistent monetization appears threatened by changes over which it has little control'.[87]

18.58 The browser war between Microsoft and Netscape in the 1990s is another example. The DOJ challenged several actions Microsoft took in integrating its Internet Explorer browser into its Windows operating system. In technologically binding its browser to Windows, Microsoft, the district court found, both prevented original

---

[81] comScore, above note 80, pp 20, 55 (finding that 21% of US smartphone users have not changed their home screen, and app usage is 'reflexive, habitual behavior, where those occupying the best home screen real estate are used most frequently').

[82] Bankrate, 'About Bankrate', http://www.bankrate.com/coinfo/default.asp.

[83] Bankrate Inc, Form 8-K Pursuant to Section 13 or 15(d) of the Securities Exchange Act of 1934, filed 24 February 2016, p 4, http://phx.corporate-ir.net/phoenix.zhtml?c=61502&p=irol-sec&control_symbol=.

[84] Ibid.

[85] Kristen Scholer, 'Bankrate Is Hit by Anxiety on Google', *Wall Street Journal*, 26 February 2016, p C4. The company went public in 2011.

[86] Bankrate Form 8-K, above note 83, p 5.

[87] Scholer, above note 85, p C4.

equipment manufacturers from pre-installing other browsers and deterred consumers from using them.[88] The US Court of Appeals for the DC Circuit affirmed that Microsoft's commingling of its browser and operating system code violated section 2 of the Sherman Act.[89] So, too, the super-platform can abuse its dominant position by fusing its app with its operating system code, when it does not achieve any real integrative benefits, but helps maintain its data-advantage and monopoly by reducing users' likelihood of using competing apps.

Moreover, data-driven exclusionary conduct may unite some within the Chicago **18.59** and post-Chicago Schools. University of Chicago professor Dennis Carlton is a member of the Chicago School. Like others in the Chicago School, Carlton is generally sceptical about antitrust enforcement directed towards exclusionary conduct by a monopolist. Carlton, however, accepts that there is a legitimate role for antitrust in refusal to deal cases in certain situations.[90] Significantly, he has argued that antitrust enforcement is appropriate in dynamic industries (such as the computer industry) where network effects are present and where scale is especially important to the ability to compete. He argues that:

> in a dynamic model, the cost of being small initially can be magnified in later periods, especially with assumptions about network dependencies, importance of installed base, or scale economies. In those settings, strategic behavior designed to keep a rival small initially can yield later significant competitive advantage.[91]

Carlton finds these conditions satisfied (and enforcement appropriate) in *Lorain* **18.60** *Journal*, where the owner of a local newspaper, which was the major local advertising vehicle, responded to the entry of a local radio station by refusing to deal with customers who advertised on the radio.[92] Carlton notes that most commentators have viewed the case as suggesting that radio and newspapers are substitutes, but it is better to view them initially as complements for some advertisers—ways of reaching different demographic groups. However, over time, radio could grow into a substitute. So, Carlton suggests, the exclusionary conduct was 'designed to so limit the size of the radio station that it could not survive as a vigorous competitor later on'.[93]

Similarly, Carlton argues that the government's *Microsoft* cases were appropriate. **18.61** The first case involved de facto exclusive dealing by Microsoft, which required computer manufacturers to pay Microsoft a licence fee based not on how many

---

[88] *United States v Microsoft Corporation*, above note 12, p 64.

[89] Ibid, pp 66–7.

[90] Dennis W Carlton, 'A General Analysis of Exclusionary Conduct and Refusal to Deal—Why Aspen and Kodak are Misguided', NBER Working Paper No w8105, February 2001, http://ssrn.com/abstract=258504.

[91] Ibid, p 13.

[92] *Lorain Journal Co v United States*, 342 US 143, 72 S Ct 181 (1951).

[93] Carlton, above note 90, p 28.

computers they shipped with the Windows operating system but based on how many computers they shipped in total. The second case involved contracts with computer manufacturers that either required or created incentives for exclusivity in browsers. Carlton notes that these cases, similar to *Lorain Journal*, are properly viewed as limiting potential rivals to the operating system monopoly from attaining efficient distribution.[94]

18.62 The European Commission in 2015 opened a formal investigation involving Google's Android. Although Android is an open-source mobile operating system, which others can freely use and develop, Google controls the operating system through its licensing agreements. As the Commission stated, the 'majority of smartphone and tablet manufacturers...use the Android operating system in combination with a range of Google's proprietary applications and services. In order to obtain the right to install these applications and services on their Android devices, manufacturers need to enter into certain agreements with Google.'[95] The European Commission is investigating whether Google has

- 'illegally hindered the development and market access of rival mobile applications or services by requiring or incentivising smartphone and tablet manufacturers to exclusively pre-install Google's own applications or services';
- 'prevented smartphone and tablet manufacturers who wish to install Google's applications and services on some of their Android devices from developing and marketing modified and potentially competing versions of Android (so-called "Android forks") on other devices, thereby illegally hindering the development and market access of rival mobile operating systems and mobile applications or services'; and
- 'illegally hindered the development and market access of rival applications and services by tying or bundling certain Google applications and services distributed

---

[94] Ibid, pp 28–9.
[95] European Commission, 'Antitrust: Commission Opens Formal Investigation Against Google in Relation to Android Mobile Operating System', Press Release, 15 April 2015, http://europa.eu/rapid/press-release_MEMO-15-4782_en.htm. Others have stated that Google has more and more applications for its Android system, 'which are the lifeblood of any mobile operating system, under its closed source control'. Shane McGlaun, 'Google Seeks to Control Android by Making More Apps Closed Source', Slash Gear, 21 October 2013, http://www.slashgear.com/google-seeks-to-control-android-by-making-more-apps-closed-source-21302205/. In particular, the claim is that Google's 'real power in mobile comes from control of the Google apps—mainly Gmail, Maps, Google Now, Hangouts, YouTube, and the Play Store', which phone manufacturers must license from Google: 'It is at this point that you start picturing a scene out of The Godfather, because these apps aren't going to come without some requirements attached.' Ron Amadeo, 'Google's Iron Grip on Android: Controlling Open Source by Any Means Necessary: Android is Open—Except for All the Good Parts', *Ars Technica*, 20 October 2013, http://arstechnica.com/gadgets/2013/10/googles-iron-grip-on-android-controlling-open-source-by-any-means-necessary/3/. The complaint is that Google requires any licensee who wants Gmail and Maps, to also license 'Google Play Services, Google+, and whatever else Google feels like adding to the package'. Ibid.

on Android devices with other Google applications, services and/or application programming interfaces of Google'.[96]

Besides Android, the Commission is investigating several other Google business **18.63** practices:

(i) The use by Google without consent of original content from third-party web sites in its own specialized web search services.

(ii) Agreements that oblige third-party web sites ('publishers') to obtain all or most of their online search advertisements from Google.

(iii) Contractual restrictions on the transferability of online search advertising campaigns to rival search advertising platforms and the management of such campaigns across Google's AdWords and rival search advertising platforms.[97]

Moreover, the Commission in 2015 issued its statement of objections over Google degrading the quality of its search results by systematically favouring its own comparison shopping products in its general search results page.[98]

It bears noting that these allegations have not been proven in court. The **18.64** Commission's open investigations as of early 2016 have not reached statement of objections or formal action, and even the statement of objections are preliminary, with Google having the right to respond. Our point here is not Google's potential liability, but to illustrate the types of abuses by dominant firms that touch on Big Data. To adequately assess these claims, the competition authority and court must understand the competitive significance of the four 'V's—volume, variety, velocity, and value—of data, the data-driven network effects, and how these data-driven strategies may help companies attain and maintain their dominant position and leverage their power across markets.

G. An Object All Sublime, the Competition Authority Shall Achieve in Time—to Let the Punishment Fit the Crime

Lastly, competition authorities must respond swiftly to prevent data-opolies from **18.65** benefitting from their unfair data-driven practices. As we saw, data-driven network effects increase firms' incentives to resort to unfair tactics. As the benefits from illegality increase, so too must the magnitude and probability of punishment increase to deter the anticompetitive behaviour. Otherwise, monopolization pays.

---

[96] European Commission, 'Commission Opens Formal Investigation Against Google', above note 95.

[97] Ibid.

[98] European Commission, 'Fact Sheet: Commission Sends Statement of Objections to Google on Comparison Shopping Service', 15 April 2015, http://europa.eu/rapid/press-release_MEMO-15-4781_en.htm.

18.66 In the US, monopolization pays. The DOJ criminally prosecuted more persons in one year under the Migratory Bird Treaty Act (227 in 2012)[99] than it has civilly and criminally prosecuted monopolies over the past 35 years (13 since 1980).[100] Between 2005 and 2014, the DOJ opened only 19 monopolization investigations, and brought only one case (in 2011).[101] Thus a monopoly has more to fear about its wind turbine killing a golden eagle[102] than its executives killing off a competitor.

18.67 In the US, executives conceivably could go to jail for monopolization. Over the past 50 years, Congress has increased the maximum criminal fines and term of incarceration for Sherman Act violations. From a misdemeanour, the criminal penalties now stand as a felony with up to ten years' imprisonment and a fine up to USD 100 million for corporations and USD 1 million for individuals.[103] The Sherman Act does not delineate which conduct should be criminally or civilly prosecuted; this has been left to the DOJ's discretion. The DOJ, however, has not criminally prosecuted firms or individuals for violating section 2 since the 1970s.[104] Since the Reagan administration, the DOJ has criminally prosecuted only horizontal, per se illegal agreements among competitors, such as price-fixing, bid rigging, and customer and territorial allocations. Nor has the FTC brought many monopolization cases.[105]

18.68 The antitrust fines likely represent a fraction of the monopoly profits. This is especially so, when dominant firms can avoid antitrust liability for their abuses in jurisdictions like the US. Class action antitrust lawsuits, under the recent Supreme Court decisions, are harder to bring. If there is a problem with class action settlements in

---

[99] Migratory Bird Treaty Act of 1918, ch 128, 13 July 1918, 40 Stat 755, codified at 16 USC ss 703–12; Table D-2. US District Courts—Criminal Defendants Commenced, by Offense, During the 12-Month Periods Ending 31 March 2011 Through 2015, http://www.uscourts.gov/statistics/table/d-2/federal-judicial-caseload-statistics/2015/03/31.

[100] DOJ, *Antitrust Division, Workload Statistics: FY 1980–1989*, http://www.justice.gov/atr/division-operations; DOJ, *Antitrust Division, Workload Statistics: FY 1990–1999*, http://www.justice.gov/sites/default/files/atr/legacy/2009/06/09/246419.pdf; DOJ, *Antitrust Division, Workload Statistics: FY 2000–2009*, http://www.justice.gov/sites/default/files/atr/legacy/2012/04/04/281484.pdf; DOJ, *Antitrust Division, Workload Statistics: FY 2005–2014*, http://www.justice.gov/atr/antitrust-division-workload-statistics-fy-2005-2014.

[101] DOJ, *Workload Statistics: FY 2005–2014*, above note 100.

[102] DOJ, 'Utility Company Sentenced in Wyoming for Killing Protected Birds at Wind Projects', Press Release, 22 November 2013, http://www.justice.gov/opa/pr/utility-company-sentenced-wyoming-killing-protected-birds-wind-projects.

[103] 15 USC s 2.

[104] *See United States v Braniff Airways, Inc*, 453 F Supp 725 (US Dist Ct (WD Tex), 1978).

[105] A search of the FTC's Cases and Proceedings for *Single Firm Conduct* category identified two cases: *see* Advance Search options at: https://www.ftc.gov/enforcement/cases-proceedings. Intel, which was not listed, was another case. *In re Intel Corp*, FTC Matter No 061 0247, Docket No 9341, https://www.ftc.gov/enforcement/cases-proceedings/061-0247/intel-corporation-matter.

antitrust cases, the American Antitrust Institute found, 'it is that plaintiffs sometimes settle strong cases for too little, not weak cases for too much'.[106]

While running for president Barack Obama criticized the Bush administration for **18.69**
having 'what may be the weakest record of antitrust enforcement of any administration in the last half century'. [107] Obama noted that 'in seven years, the Bush Justice
Department has not brought a single monopolization case'.[108] Obama promised to
'reinvigorate antitrust enforcement' and 'step up review of merger activity.'[109] Now
with his second term coming to an end, the same criticism has been made about his
administration.[110]

Many tech firms' business models depend on collecting and monetizing consumer **18.70**
data. Several network effects can enable the company to become so firmly entrenched, so dominant in a given market, that it has both the ability and incentive
to squelch competition, including by mavericks who challenge that data-dependent
business model. When that happens, the incentive to innovate and take on that
data-opoly is diminished. Consumers, even though they continue to get many apps
and services for free, are nonetheless harmed, including the loss of technology that
advances their privacy interests.

Although the EU is more active in investigating abuse of dominance cases, this **18.71**
cannot be left to one jurisdiction. Monopolization pays today. The incentives to
abuse a dominant position, given the network effects, are even greater in data-
driven industries. So, too, are the opportunities, especially for data-opolies with the
nowcasting radar or controlling a critical platform, like smartphones. If the competition authorities ignore data-driven exclusionary and predatory conduct, then we
will likely see more industries dominated by a few firms. Thus another signpost of
progress is when the US and other jurisdictions investigate and swiftly prosecute
data-driven abuses.

---

[106] Albert A Foer (ed), *The Next Antitrust Agenda: The American Antitrust Institute's Transition Report on Competition Policy to the 44th President of the United States* (Lake Mary, FL: Vandeplas Publishing, 2008), p 234.

[107] Statement of Senator Barack Obama for the American Antitrust Institute, http://www.antitrustinstitute.org/files/aai-%20Presidential%20campaign%20-%20Obama%209-07_092720071759.pdf.

[108] Ibid.

[109] Ibid.

[110] Brent Kendall, 'Justice Department Doesn't Deliver on Promise to Attack Monopolies: Obama Administration Arrived Promising a Tougher Stance, but Few Antitrust Cases Have Been Pursued in U.S. and Enforcement Has Shifted to Europe', *Wall Street Journal*, 7 November 2015, http://www.wsj.com/articles/justice-department-doesnt-deliver-on-promise-to-attack-monopolies-1446892202.

19

UNDERSTANDING AND ASSESSING
DATA-DRIVEN EFFICIENCIES CLAIMS

19.01   We have mainly addressed the potential anticompetitive risks of data-driven mergers and data-opolies. Data-driven mergers, however, can yield significant procompetitive efficiencies, such as improving products, services, and internal business
processes. Nor is a dominant firm penalized for its growth or development, which
is the consequence of a 'superior product, business acumen, or historic accident'.[1] As
Big Data can be welfare enhancing, another signpost of progress is when competition officials account the myriad data-driven efficiencies.

19.02   No company, as of early 2016, has prevailed against a merger challenge by a US
competition authority on an efficiency defence.[2] Nonetheless the US and EU authorities do consider merger-specific efficiencies in deciding whether to challenge
a merger. In closing statements, for example, the US Department of Justice (DOJ)
highlighted the likely efficiencies from mergers in the highly concentrated telephone, satellite radio, and airline industries.[3]

19.03   As companies undertake data-driven business strategies, one might expect them to
raise data-driven efficiencies. The four 'V's of data and data-driven network effects

---

[1]   *United States v Grinnell Corp*, 384 US 563, 570–1, 86 S Ct 1698, 1703–4 (1966).

[2]   *FTC v Sysco Corp*, Case No 1:15-CV-00256 (APM), 2015 WL 3958568, p *56 (US Dist Ct
(D DC), 23 June 2015) ('The court is not aware of any case, and Defendants have cited none, where
the merging parties have successfully rebutted the government's prima facie case on the strength of
the efficiencies.').

[3]   US Department of Justice (DOJ), 'Statement by Assistant Attorney General Thomas O. Barnett
Regarding the Closing of the Investigation of AT&T's Acquisition of Bellsouth: Investigation
Concludes That Combination Would Not Reduce Competition', Press Release, 11 October 2006,
http://www.justice.gov/archive/atr/public/press_releases/2006/218904.pdf; DOJ, 'Statement of
the Department of Justice Antitrust Division on Its Decision to Close Its Investigation of XM
Satellite Radio Holdings Inc's Merger with Sirius Satellite Radio Inc: Evidence Does Not Establish
That Combination of Satellite Radio Providers Would Substantially Reduce Competition', Press
Release, 24 March 2008, http://www.justice.gov/archive/opa/pr/2008/March/08_at_226.
html; DOJ, 'Statement of the Department of Justice's Antitrust Division on Its Decision to Close
Its Investigation of the Merger of Delta Air Lines Inc and Northwest Airlines Corporation',
29 October 2008, http://www.justice.gov/archive/opa/pr/2008/October/08-at-963.html.

can be characterized as entry barriers or efficiencies. An enforcement agency may characterize the need to continually update a significant volume and variety of data as an entry barrier. The merging parties, on the other hand, may characterize their combining the volume and variety of their data, and increasing the velocity in processing the data, as a procompetitive efficiency, enabling them to deliver value to consumers, such as better quality products. We will evaluate several potential data-driven efficiencies, using the three criteria employed in the US and EU, namely whether the efficiencies benefit consumers, are merger-specific, and are verifiable.[4]

A. Efficiencies Benefit Consumers

The merging parties must demonstrate that their claimed efficiencies would benefit **19.04**
customers.[5] 'The relevant benchmark in assessing efficiency claims is that consumers will not be worse off as a result of the merger.'[6] Data-driven mergers may yield significant internal operational efficiencies. But the competition law 'does not excuse mergers that lessen competition or create monopolies simply because the merged entity can improve its operations'.[7] Customers must ultimately benefit for the efficiencies to count (at least in assessing the merger).

Nor can the data-driven efficiency be achieved by degrading non-price competi-   **19.05**
tion such as quality or privacy protection. Many online companies, like Facebook and Google, rely on advertising for nearly all their revenue. To track individuals, harvest their data, profile them, and target them with behavioural ads, they often do not elevate users' privacy interests. (Indeed, as we saw, some tech companies in their statements to investors view privacy-protecting technologies as a threat to their business.) In acquiring a company with a subscription-based model that offers greater privacy, they may claim as a data-driven efficiency that prices of the acquired product will decline post-merger. The emerging consensus is that privacy protection is a parameter of non-price quality competition. Thus the competition agency would likely reject this trade-off, where the merging parties would lower the price

---

[4] DOJ and Federal Trade Commission (FTC), *Horizontal Merger Guidelines*, 19 August 2010, s 10 ('US Horizontal Merger Guidelines'), http://www.ftc.gov/sites/default/files/attachments/merger-review/100819hmg.pdf; European Commission, *Guidelines on the Assessment of Horizontal Mergers under the Council Regulation on the Control of Concentrations Between Undertakings* [2004] OJ C 31/03, para 78 ('EC Horizontal Merger Guidelines'), http://eur-lex.europa.eu/legal-content/EN/TXT/?uri=celex:52004XC0205%2802%29.
[5] *Sysco*, above note 2, p *57; Case T-342/07 *Ryanair Holdings plc v Commission* [2010] ECR II-03457, para 387.
[6] EC Horizontal Merger Guidelines, above note 4, para 79.
[7] *Saint Alphonsus Med Ctr-Nampa Inc v St Luke's Health Sys, Ltd*, 778 F3d 775, 792 (US Ct of Apps (9th Cir), 2015); *see also* US Horizontal Merger Guidelines, above note 4, s 10 ('…Agencies are mindful that the antitrust laws give competition, not internal operational efficiency, primacy in protecting customers').

at the expense of privacy protection. Cognizable efficiencies 'do not arise from anticompetitive reductions in...service' and 'purported efficiency claims based on lower prices can be undermined if they rest on reductions in product quality or variety that customers value'.[8]

19.06 The European General Court in *Ryanair* rejected a similar trade-off. Ryanair, to put it charitably (for those who have never experienced their flights), is a no-frills airline. In seeking to acquire rival Aer Lingus, Ryanair cited as an efficiency the likely reductions in Aer Lingus's costs. But Ryanair failed to demonstrate that 'it could reduce Aer Lingus's costs without offsetting reductions in that undertaking's service quality'.[9] Thus the European Commission 'was entitled to call into question the verifiability of the efficiency claims in the light of the data provided by Ryanair on that point'.[10]

19.07 A tougher issue involves mergers in industries with data-driven network effects. The merger can tip the market in the parties' favour and thus create a monopoly. On the other hand, the merger could benefit consumers (for example, more apps could be developed for the platform). Generally the stronger the presumption of harm, given the increase in concentration and other evidence of anticompetitive harm, the greater the showing by the merging parties that the projected 'merger-specific' cost savings are substantial enough to overcome the presumption of harm.[11] If the data-driven merger may create a monopoly (or significantly help a dominant firm maintain its monopoly), efficiencies 'almost never justify a merger to monopoly or near-monopoly'.[12] If post-merger, the firm's market power falls short of a near-monopoly, the verifiable merger-specific efficiencies must be extraordinary.[13]

19.08 Economic evidence—for example, an analysis of how the merger lowers costs and showing why they would likely be passed on to customers—often plays a key role. But customer views on efficiencies, particularly by knowledgeable customers, can also influence the competition authorities. Customer support of the merger

---

[8] US Horizontal Merger Guidelines, above note 4, s 10.

[9] *Ryanair Holdings*, above note 5, para 414.

[10] Ibid.

[11] *Sysco*, above note 2, p *57; US Horizontal Merger Guidelines, above note 4, s 10 ('The greater the potential adverse competitive effect of a merger, the greater must be the cognizable efficiencies, and the more they must be passed through to customers, for the Agencies to conclude that the merger will not have an anticompetitive effect in the relevant market.').

[12] US Horizontal Merger Guidelines, above note 4, s 10; *see also* EC Horizontal Merger Guidelines, above note 4, para 84 ('It is highly unlikely that a merger leading to a market position approaching that of a monopoly, or leading to a similar level of market power, can be declared compatible with the common market on the ground that efficiency gains would be sufficient to counteract its potential anti-competitive effects.').

[13] *Saint Alphonsus*, above note 7 (because competition law 'seeks to avert monopolies, proof of "extraordinary efficiencies" is required to offset the anticompetitive concerns in highly concentrated markets'); *see also Ryanair Holdings*, above note 5, para 391.

and efficiencies reduces the likelihood of the agency challenging the merger, and increases the likelihood of the agency recognizing the merger-specific efficiency.

That was the case in the Microsoft/Yahoo! joint venture, which occurred, as we **19.09** saw in Chapter 12, in a highly concentrated industry with high entry barriers and several data-driven network effects. But market participants supported the transaction, the European Commission and DOJ found, based in part on the data-driven efficiency, namely how Microsoft's search algorithms, benefitting from the scale of data, could provide better quality search results.[14] Almost all the advertisers responding to the Commission's market investigation said that Microsoft 'did not have enough traffic volume to be an attractive alternative to Google'.[15] Moreover, because Microsoft and Yahoo! were at a significant disadvantage in scale of search queries (learning-by-doing network effect), they had less incentive to degrade the quality of their search results (in order to maximize advertising revenue).[16]

B. Efficiencies Must Be Merger-Specific

The merging parties must also prove that their efficiencies are merger-specific— **19.10** 'meaning they represent a type of cost saving that could not be achieved without the merger'.[17] The merging parties must demonstrate that 'there are no less anticompetitive, realistic and attainable alternatives of a non-concentrative nature (e.g. a licensing agreement, or a cooperative joint venture) or of a concentrative nature

---

[14] DOJ, Office of Public Affairs, 'Statement of the Department of Justice Antitrust Division on Its Decision to Close Its Investigation of the Internet Search and Paid Search Advertising Agreement Between Microsoft Corporation and Yahoo! Inc: Investigation Shows That Agreement Not Likely to Reduce Competition', 18 February 2010, http://www.justice.gov/opa/pr/statement-department-justice-antitrust-division-its-decision-close-its-investigation-internet (market participants 'believe[d] that combining the parties' technology would be likely to increase competition by creating a more viable competitive alternative to Google, the firm that now dominates these markets. Most customers view Google as posing the most significant competitive constraint on both Microsoft and Yahoo!, and the competitive focus of both Microsoft and Yahoo! is predominately on Google and not on each other.').

[15] *Microsoft/Yahoo! Search Business* (Case Comp/M.7217), Commission Decision C(2014) 7239 final, 18 February 2010, para 153, http://ec.europa.eu/competition/mergers/cases/decisions/M5727_20100218_20310_261202_EN.pdf.

[16] Maurice E Stucke and Ariel Ezrachi, 'When Competition Fails to Optimize Quality: A Look at Search Engines', 18 *Yale J L & Tech* (2016): p 70; *Microsoft/Yahoo! Search*, above note 15, para 219.

[17] *Sysco*, above note 2, p *57 (internal citation omitted); EC Horizontal Merger Guidelines, above note 4, para 85 ('Efficiencies are relevant to the competitive assessment when they are a direct consequence of the notified merger and cannot be achieved to a similar extent by less anticompetitive alternatives.'); *Ryanair Holdings*, above note 5, paras 387 and 427; US Horizontal Merger Guidelines, above note 4, s 10 (crediting 'only those efficiencies likely to be accomplished with the proposed merger and unlikely to be accomplished in the absence of either the proposed merger or another means having comparable anticompetitive effects').

(e.g. a concentrative joint venture, or a differently structured merger) than the notified merger which preserve the claimed efficiencies'.[18]

19.11 When the DOJ challenged Bazaarvoice's acquisition of PowerReviews, Bazaarvoice argued that the increase in the four 'V's of data was an efficiency. Bazaarvoice claimed that post-merger it 'now has access to a large amount of data and will be able to provide more value to its clients with additional and more powerful data analytics products, expand its social commerce marketing solutions focused on the retail channel for brands, and offer additional advertising and opportunities to engage with a wider audience for brands'.[19] Bazaarvoice said the acquisition, by expanding its number of clients, including retailers and brands, would increase the variety and volume of data it would obtain, which would improve its data analytics products and tools.[20]

19.12 Bazaarvoice, however, failed to show that the efficiencies were merger-specific. Bazaarvoice, the court noted, 'acknowledged that it could have shared data with PowerReviews absent the merger and, in the future, Bazaarvoice "fully expect[s]" to share data sets with other online software providers to expand analytic power'. [21]

19.13 It would seem then that the possibility of sharing data through licensing agreements would kill most data-driven efficiency claims. But the competition agencies 'do not insist upon a less restrictive alternative that is merely theoretical'.[22] Instead they only consider 'alternatives that are reasonably practical in the business situation faced by the merging parties having regard to established business practices in the industry concerned'.[23]

19.14 Thus to substantiate their data-driven efficiency, the merging parties must articulate why a licensing arrangement is not reasonably practical. This might be the case where the velocity of data is key, and the data's value would diminish by the time it is collected and shared. Or licensing the data might raise statutory or privacy issues. Or despite the best efforts of the drafters of the licensing agreement to align the contracting parties' incentives, a significant risk remains that one or both of the contracting parties would engage in strategic behaviour. Such was the case in the TomTom/Tele Atlas merger.

19.15 Tele Atlas, as we saw in Chapter 6, supplied navigable digital map data to portable navigation device makers, including TomTom. The merging parties characterized

---

[18] EC Horizontal Merger Guidelines, above note 4, para 85.
[19] *United States v Bazaarvoice*, Case No 3:13-cv-00133-WHO, 2014 WL 203966 (US Dist Ct (ND Cal), 8 January 2014), para 310.
[20] Ibid, para 315.
[21] Ibid.
[22] US Horizontal Merger Guidelines, above note 4, s 10.
[23] EC Horizontal Merger Guidelines, above note 4, para 85.

the four 'V's of data as a procompetitive efficiency, enabling them to produce 'better maps—faster'.[24] Specifically, they argued how their vertical merger would yield significant efficiencies 'due to the integration of TomTom's...data to improve Tele Atlas's map databases'.[25] TomTom gathered 'a very significant amount of feedback data from its large customer base through Map Share'.[26] Apparently users of TomTom's navigation devices would report to TomTom any errors in the maps. One can envision post-merger a positive feedback loop similar to Waze's community-sourced mapping data: users report errors in the maps to TomTom, which now owns the navigable digital map database and can quickly fix the mistakes, thereby improving its maps' quality, which attracts more users to TomTom's devices, whose feedback further improves the maps' quality and reduces TomTom's costs.

TomTom/Tele Atlas's data-driven efficiency, the European Commission found, **19.16** conceivably fell within the efficiencies that the Merger Guidelines recognized.[27] Moreover, the Commission agreed that 'end-customers would certainly benefit from the more frequent and comprehensive map database updates made possible by the merger'.[28]

The efficiency was also merger-specific. Some market participants disagreed: Tele **19.17** Atlas could contract with TomTom to secure the 'feedback data.'[29] The Commission was sceptical. There were no examples of such contracts in the marketplace.[30] Moreover, a licensing agreement, the Commission found, could not practically yield the same efficiencies due to the parties' concern over strategic behaviour:

> Although part of the efficiencies put forward by the parties could potentially be achieved through contract, both parties are unlikely to pursue investments of the same order of magnitude as the integrated company. Such investments are risky for the non-integrated company since they are very specific to the particular relationship and hence subject to a so-called hold-up problem. Such a situation arises when a party refrains from cooperating with another due to the concern that it would become captive of its partner, for instance, because of specific investments that are only valuable if used with this partner and therefore loses all bargaining power. In addition, the difficulty in specifying all the required investments upfront and the uncertainty about the future environment in which the parties will operate makes it impossible to provide full protection to a non-integrated company through a long-term contract.[31]

---

[24] *TomTom/Tele Atlas* (Case Comp/M.4854), Commission Decision C(2008) 1859 [2008] OJ C 237/53.
[25] Ibid.
[26] Ibid.
[27] Ibid.
[28] Ibid, p 54.
[29] Ibid, p 54 n 190.
[30] Ibid.
[31] Ibid, p 54 (internal footnote omitted).

19.18 Although TomTom and Tele Atlas persuaded the Commission that their data-driven efficiencies were merger-specific and likely to benefit customers, they struck out on the third condition: they failed to verify them. The Commission found the claimed efficiencies 'difficult to quantify' and the parties' estimates 'not particularly convincing'.[32]

C. Efficiencies Must Be Verifiable

19.19 As the TomTom/Tele Atlas merger shows, the efficiencies must be verifiable—'namely reasoned, quantified and supported by internal studies and documents if necessary'.[33] The 'more precise and convincing the efficiency claims are, the better the Commission can evaluate the claims'.[34] The agencies and courts are more likely to credit an efficiency documented as part of the internal valuation of the merger (rather than calculated after the fact to persuade the competition authority), including:

> internal documents that were used by the management to decide on the merger, statements from the management to the owners and financial markets about the expected efficiencies, historical examples of efficiencies and consumer benefit, and pre-merger external experts' studies on the type and size of efficiency gains, and on the extent to which consumers are likely to benefit.[35]

19.20 Bazaarvoice, for example, asserted that its acquisition brought 'together the very best technologies and capabilities from both companies with the goal of developing "a next-generation platform" for its customers'.[36] This efficiency, while potentially merger-specific, was never verified with evidence.[37]

D. Balancing Efficiency and Privacy

19.21 Data-driven efficiencies, at times, will not raise privacy concerns. Although our focus has been on personal data, Big Data encompasses technical data of the companies' internal production and distribution systems.[38] Companies will increasingly seek to create a smart manufacturing and distribution infrastructure, 'that lets operators make real-time use of "big data" flows from fully-instrumented plants in order to improve productivity, optimize supply chains, and improve energy, water,

---

[32] Ibid.
[33] *Ryanair Holdings*, above note 5, para 389; *see also Sysco*, above note 2, p *57.
[34] EC Horizontal Merger Guidelines, above note 4, para 86.
[35] Ibid, para 88.
[36] *Bazaarvoice*, above note 19, para 315.
[37] Ibid.
[38] Ericsson, *Data-Driven Efficiency*, http://www.ericsson.com/res/docs/2014/data-driven-efficiency.pdf.

and materials use'.[39] Big Data can be employed to monitor and optimize inventory levels, monitor machines for wear and tear of components, and reduce costs in the supply chain. These data-driven efficiencies involving internal manufacturing and distribution ordinarily will not raise privacy concerns.

But often Big Data involve consumers. Here too efficiencies can arise. As the Federal **19.22** Trade Commission (FTC) identified in announcing a 2014 workshop on Big Data, '[t]remendous benefits flow from the insights of big data, such as advances in medicine, education, and transportation, improved product offerings, more efficient manufacturing processes, and more effectively tailored advertisements'.[40]

The FTC identified how financial institutions, online and brick-and-mortar re- **19.23** tailers, lead generators, and service providers can use Big Data, not all of which are positive:

- 'To reward loyal customers with better customer service or shorter wait times.'
- 'To offer different prices or discounts to different consumers. For example, a financial institution may offer a consumer a discounted mortgage rate if that consumer has a checking, savings, credit card, and retirement account with a competitor.'
- 'To tailor advertising for financial products. For example, high-income consumers may receive offers for "gold level" credit cards and low-income consumers may receive offers for subprime credit cards.'
- 'To assess credit risks of particular populations. For example, some commentators have highlighted the use of unregulated "aggregate scoring models" that assess credit risks, not based on the credit characteristics of individual consumers, but on the aggregate credit characteristics of groups of consumers who shop at certain stores.'[41]

While the uses of Big Data can 'create efficiencies, lower costs, and improve the **19.24** ability of certain populations to find and access credit and other services', the FTC noted, at the same time, 'these practices may have an unfair impact on other populations, limiting their access to higher quality products, services, or content'.[42]

So if the relevant benchmark in assessing efficiency claims is that consumers will **19.25** not be worse off as a result of the merger, how will the agency tackle merger-specific

---

[39] The White House, 'President Obama to Announce New Efforts to Support Manufacturing Innovation, Encourage Insourcing', Press Release, 9 March 2012, https://www.whitehouse.gov/the-press-office/2012/03/09/president-obama-announce-new-efforts-support-manufacturing-innovation-en.

[40] FTC, 'Big Data: A Tool for Inclusion or Exclusion?', Conference Description, updated 2 November 2010, http://www.ftc.gov/news-events/events-calendar/2014/09/big-data-tool-inclusion-or-exclusion.

[41] Ibid.

[42] Ibid.

efficiencies that potentially benefits some customers (with 'gold-level' credit cards with perks) while harming others (with longer wait times, worse service, and onerous terms)? One likely outcome of Big Data is helping companies better price discriminate, where they charge different prices to different customers based on their estimate of how much the customer is willing to pay.[43] Competition authorities will need to understand these trade-offs of Big Data by not only verifying how some customers may be better off post-merger, but independently inquiring whether others would be worse off.

19.26 Besides price discrimination and behavioural exploitation, there is also at times a trade-off between efficiency (targeting customers with more relevant ads) and privacy (tracking people and compiling profiles on them). As Peter Swire noted,

> The topic of efficiencies shows an additional way that privacy harms can be logically included in antitrust analysis. To the extent proponents of the merger seek to justify the merger on efficiency grounds, such as personalization, then privacy harms to consumers should be considered as an offset to the claimed efficiencies. To give a simple numerical example, suppose that a merger analysis showed efficiencies of $10 million. If there are privacy harms estimated at $8 million, then the efficiencies that count should be no more than $2 million.[44]

19.27 One problem, however, is that privacy harms are often difficult to quantify. In assessing data-driven efficiencies, the EU and US competition agencies 'will not simply compare the magnitude of the cognizable efficiencies with the magnitude of the likely harm to competition absent the efficiencies'.[45] This suggests that if the merger lessens any important parameter of competition, then it should not matter whether the harm is quantifiable. The efficiencies must prevent *any* significant harm to consumers, including non-quantifiable privacy harms.

E. Challenges Ahead

19.28 Data-driven efficiencies claims, as the *Microsoft/Yahoo!*, *TomTom/Tele Atlas*, and *Bazaarvoice/PowerReviews* cases reflect, have received so far a mixed reception. The parties at times will use the scale of data as an efficiency, and the competition authorities must understand both the data-driven merger's competitive benefits and risks. At times, the merger may provide sufficient scale for smaller rivals to effectively compete. Thus, the competition agencies will want to know when data-driven

---

[43] For how Big Data can help companies approach perfect price discrimination and the welfare effects, *see* Ariel Ezrachi and Maurice E Stucke, *Virtual Competition: The Promise and Perils of the Algorithm-Driven Economy* (Cambridge, MA: Harvard University Press, forthcoming 2016).

[44] Peter P Swire, Professor, Moritz College of Law of the Ohio State University & Senior Fellow, Center for American Progress, Submitted Testimony to the Federal Trade Commission Behavioral Advertising Town Hall 3, 18 October 2007, p 7.

[45] US Horizontal Merger Guidelines, above note 4, s 10.

mergers are likelier to lead to market dominance or enhance consumers' welfare with better quality or innovative products and services.

As the competition authorities recognize, '[e]fficiencies are difficult to verify and quantify, in part because much of the information relating to efficiencies is uniquely in the possession of the merging firms.'[46] This is especially the case if the companies are much further along in assessing and calculating data-driven efficiencies. If the competition agency is unfamiliar with data-driven business strategies generally, it will not necessarily know whether the data-driven efficiencies are projected reasonably and in good faith. The burden of demonstrating efficiencies is on the companies, not the government. This is where it should be. The companies will almost always have better information (especially if efficiencies are real and not an afterthought) as well as strong incentives to make out a case if there is one to be made.

19.29

The Chicago School decried how earlier merger policy inhibited efficiencies. The recent economics literature on firm behaviour, while less developed than that on consumer behaviour, suggests that many large mergers do not yield significant efficiencies.[47] Thus even when the efficiencies are verifiable, the merger may turn out

19.30

---

[46] US Horizontal Merger Guidelines, above note 4, s 10.

[47] Kenneth M Davidson, *Reality Ignored: How Milton Friedman and Chicago Economics Undermined American Institutions and Endangered the Global Economy* (Seattle: CreateSpace Independent Publishing Platform, 2011), p 64; Ulrike Malmendier et al, *Winning by Losing: Evidence on the Long-Run Effects of Mergers*, NBER Working Paper 18024, April 2012, http://www.nber.org/papers/w18024 (collecting data on all US mergers with concurrent bids of at least two public potential acquirers from 1985 to 2009, comparing winners' and losers' performance prior and several years after the merger contest, and finding that post-merger, losing bidders significantly outperform winning bidders); George Alexandridis et al, 'How Have M&As Changed? Evidence from the Sixth Merger Wave', 18 *Eur J Fin* (2012): p 663; Klaus Gugler et al, 'Market Optimism and Merger Waves', 33 *Mgmt Decision Econ* (2012): pp 159, 171–2; Clayton M Christensen et al, 'The Big Idea: The New M&A Playbook', *Harv Bus Rev* (March 2011): pp 49, 49 (reporting that 'study after study puts the failure rate of mergers and acquisitions somewhere between 70 percent and 90 percent'); Spencer Weber Waller, 'Corporate Governance and Competition Policy', 18 *Geo Mason L Rev* (2011): pp 833, 873–9 (examining evidence from corporate finance that suggests that entire categories of mergers are 'more likely to destroy, rather than enhance, shareholder value'); Vicki Bogan and David Just, 'What Drives Merger Decision Making Behavior? Don't Seek, Don't Find, and Don't Change Your Mind', 72 *J Econ Behav & Org* (2009): pp 930, 930–1 (collecting some of the academic research showing that many mergers add no value or reduce shareholder value for the acquiring firm); Sara B Moeller et al, *Do Shareholders of Acquiring Firms Gain from Acquisitions?*, NBER Working Paper No 9523, February 2003, http://www.nber.org/papers/w9523 (in examining whether shareholders of acquiring firms gain when firms announce acquisitions of public firms, private firms, and subsidiaries, the study examined over 12,000 purchases between 1980 to 2001 for more than $1 million by public firms and found roughly that 'shareholders from small firms earn $8 billion from the acquisitions they made from 1980 to 2001, whereas the shareholders from large firms lose $226 billion'); James A Fanto, 'Braking the Merger Momentum: Reforming Corporate Law Governing Mega-Mergers', 49 *Buff L Rev* (2001): pp 249, 280 ('The systematic empirical evidence on past mergers and the available data on the mega-mergers, however, now supports the conclusion that a large majority of these transactions destroy shareholder value.'); Walter Adams and James W Brock, 'Antitrust and Efficiency: A Comment', 62 *NYU L Rev* (1987): pp 1116, 1117 n 8 (referencing earlier studies).

to be a bust. Competition agencies cannot presume, as some previously did, that the 'vast majority of mergers pose no harm to consumers, and many produce efficiencies that benefit consumers in the form of lower prices, higher quality goods or services, or investments in innovation'.[48] The agency must develop, through more post-merger reviews, a better understanding of when data-driven efficiencies will likely be realized. Moreover, at times the merging parties will discount any potential anticompetitive concerns by arguing that data is like sunshine, being both non-rivalrous and non-excludable. Other times, the parties will argue that their data-driven efficiencies are merger-specific, as the acquired firm's data is not otherwise publicly available. Thus the agencies must understand what data can be obtained outside the merger, the costs and time to amass the data, and viable alternatives for these categories of data.

19.31 What we can conclude is that data-driven efficiencies, which are recognized in the industry, cited by customers in support of the merger, and verified by the agencies, will more likely influence the agencies. It will be easier for the agency to understand how the data-driven efficiency benefits customers if they directly hear from the customers how the efficiency would significantly enhance the merging parties' competitive performance (such as Microsoft having access to a larger set of search queries would likely yield more relevant search results, particularly with rare, 'tail' queries), and how they would likely benefit in this more competitive environment. The customer effectively validates the efficiency and explains why it is merger-specific. In discussing how the efficiency would be passed on to them (rather than pocketed by the merging parties), the customer also undercuts a presumption of anticompetitive harm.

---

[48] FTC and DOJ, *Commentary on the Horizontal Merger Guidelines*, March 2006, p v, http://www.justice.gov/sites/default/files/atr/legacy/2006/04/27/215247.pdf.

20

NEED FOR RETROSPECTIVES
OF DATA-DRIVEN MERGERS

Competition authorities face the current dilemma. On the one hand, they have **20.01** not developed tools to intelligibly assess important non-price parameters of competition, such as quality, innovation, systemic risk, and greater instability to an industry's ecosystem. On the other hand, to be effective and credible advocates, they cannot ignore these important non-price parameters of competition. So how can the agencies develop tools to better assess data-driven mergers when they are still focusing on price (which is less relevant) instead of quality, choice, and privacy protection (which are more relevant)? Moreover, the post-merger reviews cast doubt on whether the agencies, with their current price-centric tools, are accurately predicting the competitive effects of many mergers in concentrated industries.

Where exactly does this leave us? Is competition law salvageable, or is it simply a **20.02** relic of the pre-digital economy? Or, perhaps paradoxically: is the less technocratic, more political, competition law of the US prevailing in the mid-20th century the right direction for current policymakers to travel?

The agencies cannot escape the current dilemma without first understanding how **20.03** lost they actually are. They need, besides a map, to know their current location. Thus another signpost of progress is when the competition authorities revisit significant data-driven mergers, such as Google/Waze and Facebook/WhatsApp, to assess whether the merger helped the firm attain or maintain their market power. The agency can test the extent to which its predictive tools are accurate. This tells them how far off they are in predicting mergers' competitive effects. Granted there may be unforeseen intervening events that no one anticipated. But the merger retrospectives will help the agencies assess how far off the mark they are. They may also recognize, from these retrospectives, that what is quantifiable is not necessarily what is important, and what is important should be captured by legal presumptions and standards. This chapter discusses several benefits of conducting merger retrospectives, including assessing the risk of false negatives under the current quantification paradigm.

A. Waiting for the Right Data-Driven Merger

20.04 At one antitrust conference on Big Data, a competition official was asked why his agency had not investigated (and challenged) more data-driven mergers. The competition official waved off the criticism: 'If the right case presents itself, we would be happy to dive in.' A year-and-a-half later, when asked the same question, another official from the same competition agency gave a similar response.

20.05 The officials' response assumes that their agency can identify the right case, because it currently has the right tools. If the agency is confident in assessing and predicting these mergers' likely competitive effects, it will likely disclaim any shortcomings in its current tools. It will also disclaim any need for merger retrospectives. The agency is confident that its current tools help it accurately predict most, if not all, mergers' competitive effects. Thus the agency will continue enforcing the competition laws the same way as it has in the past.

20.06 As we saw in Chapter 15, the post-merger reviews to date challenge this convention. One example is when the US Department of Justice (DOJ) predicted that Whirlpool's acquisition of Maytag, which reduced the number of major appliance manufacturers in the US from four to three, was unlikely to substantially lessen competition.[1] The DOJ predicted that 'any attempt to raise prices likely would be unsuccessful'.[2] Instead, consumers would benefit from the merger's estimated cost savings and other efficiencies. In reality, the DOJ predicted wrongly. Consumers ended up paying more (about 5 to 7 per cent more for Maytag dishwashers and about 17 per cent more for Whirlpool dryers) and had fewer choices post-merger.[3]

20.07 So why should we expect different results? If competition officials believe their agency has the right (price-centric) tools and is getting the right results, they will continue to wait for the 'right' data-driven merger to present itself. All the while, the agency will not consider (or ignore) the mergers' impact on harder-to-measure, but equally important, non-price parameters of competition, such as the level of privacy protection, other aspects of quality, innovation, and systemic risk. Our book addresses the significant risk of false negatives from the agencies' current review of data-driven mergers, including their focusing on what is readily measurable (such as the merger's short-term effects on pricing) rather than what is important.

---

[1] US Department of Justice (DOJ), 'Department of Justice Antitrust Division Statement on the Closing of Its Investigation of Whirlpool's Acquisition of Maytag', Press Release, 29 March 2006, http://www.justice.gov/archive/atr/public/press_releases/2006/215326.pdf.

[2] Ibid.

[3] Matthew Weinberg, Orley C Ashenfelter, and Daniel S Hosken, 'The Price Effects of a Large Merger of Manufacturers: A Case Study of Maytag-Whirlpool', NBER Working Paper No 17476, 21 April 2011, p 16, http:// ssrn.com/abstract=1857066.

B. Debiasing Through *Ex-Post* Merger Reviews

Belief perseverance is when one clings to a belief too tightly and for too long.[4]   **20.08**
Under this bias, individuals search for data that validates their opinion, and
are reluctant to search for evidence that contradicts their belief. When evidence contradicts their firmly held opinion, they often either discount it, or
misinterpret the evidence as actually supporting their hypothesis. Thus, belief
perseverance predicts that if people begin their antitrust careers believing in the
predictive power of their agency's merger guidelines, they may believe that
their intellectual journey has come to an end, even if compelling evidence to
the contrary has emerged.

So how does one debias? Consumers can make better decisions when they gain   **20.09**
experience, quickly receive feedback on their earlier errors, discover the biases and
heuristics in their earlier decisions, take steps to debias, and gain feedback on their
next decision. Key to this learning process is timely feedback on their decisions, the
assumptions they made, what they considered (or failed to consider), and whether,
and how, any of these errors impacted the overall decision.

Academics and, increasingly, competition officials recognize that post-merger   **20.10**
studies can inform the agencies on the validity of their methodological tools.[5]
Competition agencies often discuss in their closing memoranda their predictions
and assumptions underlying their conclusion that the merger is unlikely to substantially lessen competition. The closing memorandum consequently offers test-
able predictions (such as whether an entrant or big buyer would defeat the exercise
of market power or consumers would shift to other products or sellers in other
geographic areas). For companies identified as potential entrants in the original
merger review, one could assess whether (and why) these identified entrants did
not enter, and if they did enter, assess their impact and why they were effectual
or ineffectual.

---

[4] Nicholas Barberis and Richard H Thaler, 'A Survey of Behavioral Finance', in Richard H
Thaler (ed), *Advances in Behavioral Finance* (New York: Russell Sage Foundation, 2005), p 15.
[5] *See, eg*, Tomaso Duso and Peter Ormosi, 'Capacity Building Workshop on the Ex-Post Evaluation
of Competition Authorities' Enforcement Decisions: A Critical Discussion', Prepared for the OECD,
Directorate for Financial and Enterprise Affairs Competition Committee, Working Party No 2 on
Competition and Regulation, 26 October 2015, p 5, http://www.oecd.org/officialdocuments/
publicdisplaydocumentpdf/?cote=DAF/COMP/WP2%282015%298&doclanguage=en ('Our view
as academic experts who have been heavily involved in the ex post evaluation of competition policies
over the past decade is that these exercises should nowadays be seen as an integral part of the enfor-
cement of competition policy'); 'Roundtable Conference with Enforcement Officials', 12 *Antitrust
Source* (2013): pp 1, 23 (FTC Chair wanting her agency to conduct more merger retrospectives);
William E Kovacic, 'Rating the Competition Agencies: What Constitutes Good Performance?', 16
Geo Mason L Rev (2009): pp 903, 922.

20.11   The post-merger evaluations can help the agencies to understand not only whether their 'speculative exercise was successful, but also whether the instruments used to make this assessment were appropriate, precise, and effective'.[6]

20.12   The agencies, in re-examining past mergers, may find where, and the extent to which, they err in key aspects of their analysis (such as the likelihood of customers' perceiving small, but significant, non-transitory degradations in quality and switching to rivals). They may find that their tools do not capture key dynamics in certain industries. The merger retrospectives can help them better understand 'what specific economic market models are more adequate to represent specific industries'.[7]

20.13   One objection by the competition authority is the time and expense of such merger retrospectives. But these obstacles have diminished in recent years. Characteristic of its intellectual leadership, the Organisation for Economic Co-operation and Development (OECD) is developing a 'Reference Guide' for competition agencies to aid their *ex-post* evaluation of enforcement decisions. Its guide will build on 'the existing stock of knowledge developed in the past decades and has been intensively debated with the major competition authorities'.[8]

C. FTC's Retrospectives of Hospital Mergers

20.14   To illustrate the benefits of merger retrospectives, we will look at hospital mergers. After the DOJ and the Federal Trade Commission (FTC) lost in court a string of hospital merger challenges in the 1980s and early 1990s, the FTC undertook a hospital retrospective project, which the FTC Chair noted, 'played a crucial role in reinvigorating the agency's hospital merger enforcement efforts after a string of losses'.[9]

20.15   One reason for the litigation defeats was that the courts 'rejected the agencies' proposed geographic markets on the ground that a sufficient number of patients would respond to a price increase by traveling to other hospitals, sometimes over 100 miles away'.[10] The hospitals would argue that the relevant geographic market was broader than the government's definition. As the geographic market gets bigger, more hospitals are included in the relevant market, and the concentration levels and merging

---

[6] Duso and Ormosi, above note 5, p 5.

[7] Ibid.

[8] Ibid, p 6.

[9] Edith Ramirez, 'Retrospectives at the FTC: Promoting an Antitrust Agenda', Remarks at the American Bar Association (ABA) Retrospective Analysis of Agency Determinations in Merger Transactions Symposium, George Washington University Law School, Washington DC, 28 June 2013, p 2, https://www.ftc.gov/sites/default/files/documents/public_statements/retrospectives-ftc-promoting-antitrust-agenda/130628aba-antitrust.pdf.

[10] Ibid.

party's market shares decline. The hospitals generally relied on the Elzinga–Hogarty test, which is based on patient inflow and outflow data:

> Where there was a showing that some patients traveled long distances for care, the presumption was that many others would do the same in response to a SSNIP [small, but significant, non-transitory increase in price]. But the model overlooked that many of the consumers who traveled outside the market did so for services that were not available locally. The model also ignored that patients generally do not pay directly for health care services and have little incentive to switch in the face of a price increase.[11]

So in 2002, the FTC examined several completed hospital mergers to 'test whether its market assumptions were correct'.[12] The FTC studied the mergers' effects on price and quality of care and collected data from both hospitals and insurance companies. The FTC economists published four merger retrospectives, which 'showed that the methodology relied on by courts was flawed and failed to identify anticompetitive mergers'.[13] The studies found substantially higher prices post-merger,[14] and contrary to defendants' claims, quality of care did not necessarily improve with consolidation.[15] The merger retrospectives also demonstrated that 'hospital competition tends to be highly localized, with price effects even when a merger occurred in a city with many other hospitals'.[16]

20.16

One merger retrospective involved two nearby non-profit hospitals in California's Oakland-Alameda County region.[17] The state of California challenged this hospital merger under the federal antitrust laws.

20.17

The geographic market definition was crucial, namely where patients could practicably turn for acute hospital inpatient services. If the geographic market were defined broadly, then one would assume that the merged hospitals would face stiff competition from over 20 hospitals in the San Francisco and East Bay areas. The merging parties' hospitals were approximately two-and-a-half miles apart. In defending an Inner East Bay geographic market, California argued that many patients, because of traffic and loyalty considerations to their doctors, would not travel

20.18

---

[11] Ibid, p 3.

[12] Ibid.

[13] Ibid, p 4.

[14] Ibid, citing Steven Tenn, 'The Price Effects of Hospital Mergers: A Case Study of the Sutter-Summit Transaction', FTC Bureau of Economics, Working Paper No 293, November 2008, http://www.ftc.gov/be/workpapers/wp293.pdf; Michael G Vita and Seth Sacher, 'The Competitive Effects of Not-for-Profit Hospital Mergers: A Case Study', 49(1) *J Indus Econ* (2001): p 63.

[15] Ramirez, above note 9, p 4, citing David J Balan and Patrick S Romano, 'A Retrospective Analysis of the Clinical Quality Effects of the Acquisition of Highland Park Hospital by Evanston Northwestern Healthcare', FTC Bureau of Economics, Working Paper No 307, November 2010, http://www.ftc.gov/be/workpapers/wp307.pdf.

[16] Ramirez, above note 9, p 4.

[17] *California v Sutter Health Sys*, 130 F Supp 2d 1109, 1130 (US Dist Ct (ND Cal), 2001).

east through the Caldecott Tunnel and west across the Bay Bridge to these other hospitals. The plaintiff's economic expert showed that 85 per cent of all patients admitted to hospitals in the proposed Inner East Bay market resided in the Inner East Bay. Similarly, 85 per cent of patients who resided in the Inner East Bay were admitted to hospitals inside this area, while the remaining 15 per cent sought hospital treatment outside this area. The state argued that the 85 per cent Little In From Outside (LIFO) and Little Out From Inside (LOFI) results, along with its other evidence, were sufficient to prove geographic market.

20.19 The court disagreed. With conflicting economic expert testimony, the court unsurprisingly followed the approach by other courts. It relied on the Elzinga–Hogarty economic analysis for defining the relevant geographic market:

> [T]he first prong of the Elzinga-Hogarty test requires a determination of the merging hospitals' 'service area', that area from which they attract their patients. In the second step, two measurements are taken of the flow of patients into and out of the test market. The Little In From Outside ('LIFO') measurement calculates the percentage of patients who reside inside the test market that are admitted to those hospitals located within the test market. A LIFO of 100% would indicate that all hospital admittees who are residents of the test market are admitted to hospitals located within the test market. The Little Out From Inside ('LOFI') measurement calculates the percentage of the test market's hospitals' patients who reside in the test market. A LOFI of 100% would indicate that all hospital patients admitted to hospitals in the test market are residents of the test market. A LIFO and LOFI of 75% is considered a weak indication of the existence of a market and a LIFO and LOFI of 90% is considered a strong indication of a market.[18]

The court was wedded to the façade of exactitude of the LIFO and LOFI figures, holding that the state's 85 per cent results failed to meet 'the preferred 90% threshold' of LIFO and LOFI calculations that represent 'a strong showing that a market exists'.[19]

20.20 The court also believed that big buyers (namely the health insurance plans) had numerous ways to discipline the hospital's exercising market power. The health plan providers could keep hospital prices low by 'steering' patients to lower-cost hospitals (or other health care providers). Hospitals had high fixed costs in terms of the physical plant, equipment, and maintaining a highly skilled staff, and consequently would be sensitive to such declines in patient volume. So if the merging hospitals tried to increase prices for acute inpatient care, the health plans would steer enough patients to other hospitals to defeat the exercise of market power. Indeed, the president and CEO of the second-largest health plan in the East Bay downplayed the

---

[18] Ibid, pp 1120–1.
[19] Ibid, p 1123.

possibility of a price increase by the hospitals post-merger, in part due to the health plans' ability to steer patients to lower cost facilities.

The court expressed greater concern over false positives (than false negatives), fear- **20.21** ing that ' "judicial intervention in a competitive situation can itself upset the balance of market force, bringing about the very ills the antitrust laws were meant to prevent". This appears to have even more force in an industry, such as healthcare, experiencing significant and profound changes.'[20] Accordingly, the court permitted the merger to go through.

So what happened post-merger? The FTC used detailed claims data from three large **20.22** health insurers to compare the post-merger price change for the merging hospitals to a set of control group hospitals. Not only did prices increase post-merger, the FTC found, but the price increase was among the largest of any comparable hospital in California. The merged entity significantly raised prices for one of the merging hospitals, between 23.2 per cent and 50.4 per cent relative to the control group.[21]

The FTC used its hospital merger retrospectives to show 'how a merger can leave an **20.23** insurer—the direct payer for hospital services—with few alternatives to include in its network, increase the bargaining leverage of the combined hospital, and lead to higher prices'.[22] The agency's new approach, noted the FTC Chair, 'sparked a winning streak that now includes three successfully-litigated merger challenges and a growing tally of hospital deals abandoned after the FTC threatened a challenge'.[23]

D. The Benefits in Conducting Merger Retrospectives

Regularly undertaking merger retrospectives can yield many benefits. One benefit **20.24** is that the competition authority can evaluate its or the courts' assumptions and analytical tools. Granted the anticompetitive effects could be caused by unforeseen intervening events. Nonetheless, the agency and court typically assess mergers through their price-centric models, which rely on several assumptions, such as the likely reaction of rational, self-interested consumers with willpower to a SSNIP. The behavioural economic scholarship has drawn into question these assumptions of

---

[20] Ibid, p 1137, quoting *FTC v Tenet Health Care Corp*, 186 F3d 1045, 1055 (US Ct of Apps (8th Cir), 1999).

[21] The price increase at the other hospital was not statistically different from the control group for any of the insurers. Tenn, above note 14, p 20. One explanation for this asymmetry was 'that as a major provider of hospital services to commercial patients in the Oakland-Berkeley area, Alta Bates was a significant price constraint on Summit. However, Summit may have been less of a constraint on Alta Bates' price since Summit was a relatively minor provider of hospital services to commercial patients.' Ibid, p 22.

[22] Ramirez, above note 9, pp 4–5.

[23] Ibid, p 5.

rationality and willpower. Thus the merger retrospectives will reveal what happened to price and non-price competition and the extent to which actual marketplace behaviour comports with the predicted behaviour of rational agents with willpower.

20.25   As one report prepared for the OECD observed:

> …most of the existing studies look at the price effect of single competition policy decisions. There are many good reasons to focus on prices, as they are an important—and often (more) easily available—indicator of consumer welfare. Yet, other outcomes are also important and hence research and future evaluations should go beyond just looking at simple price effects. This includes several aspects among which:
>
> • Non-price effects such as the impact on quality, variety, innovation, entry/exit etc.
> • The identification of the broader effects of policy enforcement such as its overall welfare effects, its effect on productivity, its deterrence effects, the spill-over effects that some key decisions might have on different markets.
> • A clearer identification of type I errors—too much intervention—and type II errors—insufficient intervention.[24]

As the OECD report suggests, the merger retrospectives can take a broader view beyond the merger's price effects.

20.26   Second, merger retrospectives can reduce the risk of false negatives. The economic evidence, for example, shows that many US hospital markets have become increasingly concentrated.[25] As the US Medicare Payment Advisory Commission noted, '[o]ne key driver of higher prices in the United States is provider market power. Hospitals merge and physician groups consolidate to gain market power over insurers to negotiate higher payment rates.'[26] The economic evidence also shows that consumers were harmed as a result of the increased concentration from these hospital mergers.[27] Nonetheless, faced with their defeats in challenging hospital mergers, the

---

[24]   Duso and Ormosi, above note 5, p 17.

[25]   David M Cutler and Fiona Scott Morton, 'Hospitals, Market Share, and Consolidation', 310(18) *J Am Med Ass'n* (2013): pp 1964, 1966 (discussing high concentration in many hospital markets—nearly half of US hospital markets are highly concentrated, another third are moderately concentrated, one-sixth are unconcentrated, and '[n]o hospital markets are considered highly competitive').

[26]   Medicare Payment Advisory Commission, *Report to Congress: Medicare Payment Policy* (2014): p 28.

[27]   America's Health Insurance Plans (AHIP), 'Impact of Hospital Consolidation on Health Insurance Premiums', Data Brief, June 2015 (finding statistically significant positive correlations between health insurance premiums for coverage purchased on some federally-facilitated and state-based exchanges and the level of hospital consolidation, and how some studies suggest that by decreasing competition, hospital consolidation may also lead to lower quality of care); John B Kirkwood, 'Buyer Power and Healthcare Prices', *Washington Law Review* (forthcoming 2016), Seattle University School of Law Research Paper, 16 October 2015, http://ssrn.com/ab stract=2660553 (discussing how hospital mergers contribute to high levels of concentration and many retrospective studies have found that hospital mergers resulted in higher prices); Statement of Paul B Ginsburg, Norman Topping Chair in Medicine and Public Policy, Sol Price School of Public

---

FTC and DOJ could simply have accepted (or resigned themselves to) the courts' erroneous analysis for defining the relevant geographic market. As a result, the agencies would not have challenged hospital mergers where the LIFO and LOFI figures were below 90 per cent under the Elzinga–Hogarty economic test or where defendants could credibly claim that big buyers would steer patients to other hospitals. More anticompetitive hospital mergers would have occurred, with consumers and payers bearing the brunt.

Third, the empirical testing may improve the competition agencies' credibility **20.27** with the courts. Currently, each litigant retains its expert economists, often academics with little, if any, regular interaction or experience in the affected industry. Each party has its customers who favour or oppose the merger, and company documents that support the party's economic theory (or undermine the opponent's theory). The court wades through this conflicting evidence and ultimately decides which outcome is likelier under the rational choice theory, premised on rational profit-maximizers with willpower. Not surprisingly, the predicted outcome may be divorced from reality. Moreover, the US Supreme Court has reconsidered its decisions construing the Sherman Act when the theoretical underpinnings of its earlier decisions were called into question. This empirical testing may assist the courts in refining or reconsidering the theories underlying the competition laws.

Fourth, post-merger assessments can foster accountability. The staff at the com- **20.28** petition agencies, in our experience, are dedicated in enforcing the competition laws. But after devoting many days collecting data to evaluate a merger's likely anticompetitiveness, the staff may conclude that the data, when evaluated under the current price-centric analytical tools, is insufficient to reach any prediction. Even if the staff believe that the merger may substantially lessen competition or tend to create a monopoly, they may not recommend challenging the merger if proving it in court would be too difficult. Even when the staff amass sufficient customer testimony, business records, admissions, and other evidence to enjoin the transaction, the agency may ultimately not challenge the merger for various

Policy, Director of Public Policy, Schaeffer Center for Health Policy and Economics, University of Southern California, before the US Senate Committee on the Judiciary, Subcommittee on Antitrust, Competition Policy and Consumer Rights, Hearing on 'Examining Consolidation in the Health Insurance Industry and its Impact on Consumers', 22 September 2015, http://www.judiciary.senate.gov/imo/media/doc/09-22-15%20Ginsburg%20Testimony3.pdf ('Much of the research has focused on mergers among providers, especially hospitals, and clearly shows that hospital mergers have led to higher prices without measurable effects on quality.'); Laurence C Baker, Kate M Bundorf, and Daniel P Kessler, 'Vertical Integration: Hospital Ownership of Physician Practices is Associated with Higher Prices and Spending', 33(5) *Health Affairs* (2014): pp: 756–63; Martin Gaynor and Robert Town, 'The Impact of Hospital Consolidation—Update', The Synthesis Project, Policy Brief No 9, The Robert Wood Johnson Foundation, June 2012, http://www.rwjf.org/content/dam/farm/reports/issue_briefs/2012/rwjf73261.

reasons. One former Assistant Attorney General declined to bring many cases that the DOJ staff recommended because these cases did not make 'economic sense' or, in his opinion, were not in the public interest.[28] Even if the agency challenges the merger, the court, relying on faulty economic theories, may dismiss the action, thereby chilling future enforcement.

20.29   On the other hand, enforcement action may lead in some situations to undesirable outcomes. In determining an acceptable settlement, the agency must determine whether the divestiture of a particular brand, manufacturing plant, or other assets would remedy the perceived harms. Such divestitures may later prove to be inadequate.[29] Alternatively, the agency may require the merging parties to act or refrain from acting in such a manner that unintentionally leads to anticompetitive results. The settlement itself may be misguided as foreseeable dynamic forces indeed prevented the exercise of market power. By subjecting the agencies' actions to external review and criticism, the post-merger review would increase the accountability of those responsible for enforcing the competition laws.

20.30   Fifth, publicly disseminating the agency's post-merger findings increases transparency. This information will assist the competition community in determining where the agency's merger guidelines are or are not working, and enable other government agencies, foreign governments, and academics to further analyse and refine the economic theories. Rather than focusing on price in a competitive equilibrium, the agencies may instead incorporate important dynamic factors, such as competitive restraints that thwart innovators from entering and competing in that market. Public dissemination will also further one aim of the merger guidelines: assisting business communities in predicting which mergers the government is likely to investigate and challenge.

20.31   Sixth, such empirical testing may assist policymakers in other areas of the law. For example, if the lag in entry is attributable to the lack of data portability, policymakers can assess ways to lower consumers' switching costs and increase their control over their data. Merger retrospectives can highlight enforcement gaps, where competition, privacy, and consumer protection laws cannot redress a recurring consumer harm.

---

[28]   US General Accounting Office, *Report to the Chairman, US House of Representatives Committee on the Judiciary, Justice Department: Changes in Antitrust Enforcement Policies and Activities*, 29 October 1990, p 45, http://archive.gao.gov/d22t8/142779.pdf (quoting former Assistant Attorney General Douglas H Ginsburg).

[29]   *See, eg,* Brent Kendall and Peg Brickley, 'Albertsons to Buy Back 33 Stores It Sold as Part of Merger With Safeway: Judge Approves Purchase as Part of Haggen Holdings' Bankruptcy Process', *Wall Street Journal*, 24 November 2015, http://www.wsj.com/articles/albertsons-to-buy-back-33-stores-it-sold-as-part-of-merger-with-safeway-1448411193.

Finally, more merger retrospectives can help assess the risk and cost of false posi- **20.32** tives. The Chicago School decried how earlier merger policy inhibited efficien- cies. But the economic literature suggests that many large mergers do not yield significant efficiencies.[30] Post-merger review can empirically test this. The agencies would describe which, if any, of the merging parties' efficiencies they could verify post-merger, the magnitude of the efficiencies, and the extent to which consumers directly benefitted from the efficiencies. The agency can require any publicly held company that relies on an efficiency defence to report its claimed efficiencies in its public securities filings. If such disclosure would divulge a trade secret or other confidential, commercially sensitive information, then the company may disclose the information privately to the agency. For each year post-merger that the merging parties claim the efficiencies will be realized, the company would report the actual amount of efficiencies realized versus the projected amount. This should deter com- pany executives from inflating the claimed efficiencies and hold them accountable to the shareholders for pursuing a growth-by-acquisition strategy, while informing the agencies of those efficiencies for particular industries that are more likely to be cognizable and substantial.

The competition agencies are ideally suited for collecting this empirical data. **20.33** Although private parties in the US can challenge mergers under the Clayton Act, they rarely do. The competition agencies initially receive the merger filings. They largely spearhead the merger review. They can also bear the cost of such empirical testing.

By revisiting significant data-driven mergers, such as Google/Waze, and **20.34** Facebook/WhatsApp, to see whether the merger helped the company attain or maintain market power, the competition agency will better understand which data-driven mergers benefit or harm consumers. The competition authorities can develop the analytical tools to help them better screen and assess data- driven mergers.

In revisiting several of the mergers we examined in Chapter 6, the agencies can learn **20.35** whether the merger enabled the tech giant to entrench or further increase its market power. They can assess whether traditional network effects were stronger for text messaging than the Commission predicted in *Facebook/WhatsApp*. Did the merger lessen non-price competition, including changes in privacy policies post-merger? Did the expanded user base and data from WhatsApp or Waze provide a key com- petitive advantage? If so, did the merger significantly impede other potential text messaging or mapping apps from entering the market (aside from greater efficien- cies by Facebook and Google post-merger)?

---

[30] *See* Chapter 19 of this volume.

20.36 In undertaking more post-merger reviews, the agencies can learn which markets are more susceptible to data-driven and traditional network effects, which mergers are likelier to provide a data-advantage and market power, and to what extent firms can, post-merger, exercise market power by shrouding their quality degradations and diminished privacy protection. In undertaking these merger retrospectives and interviewing market participants, the competition agencies can appreciate any blind spots. Were there issues the competition officials should have considered? Were there questions they should have asked?

21

MORE COORDINATION AMONG COMPETITION, PRIVACY, AND CONSUMER PROTECTION OFFICIALS

As the data-driven economy expands, competition, privacy, and consumer protec- **21.01**
tion officials must coordinate to consider opportunities, synergies, and potential
inefficiencies in their laws to promote competition, individuals' privacy interests,
and ultimately well-being.

One myth is that market forces inevitably resolve any privacy issues. As Chapter 5 **21.02**
notes, market forces have not provided consumers the privacy protections they
desire. Indeed, as more data is collected on individuals, and with the rise of data
fusion, it will be even harder to strip data of personal identifiers.[1] Generally as the
volume and variety of data grow, 'the likelihood of being able to re-identify individuals (that is, re-associate their records with their names) grows substantially'.[2]
Privacy concerns will likely increase.

Privacy, consumer protection, and competition law, as we emphasize, are not **21.03**
coextensive. After all, there will continue to be defendants without any market
power who intrude upon the seclusion of others (such as the landlord who secretly

---

[1] Organisation for Economic Co-operation and Development (OECD), *Exploring the Economics
of Personal Data: A Survey of Methodologies for Measuring Monetary Value*, OECD Digital Economy
Papers, No 220, 22 April 2013, p 8, http://dx.doi.org/10.1787/5k486qtxldmq-en (noting how
'[d]istinguishing between personal and non-personal data is becoming increasingly difficult', that
'[o]nce any piece of data has been linked to a person's real identity, any association between this data
and a virtual identity breaks the anonymity of the latter' and that '[t]oday's techniques can often
enable data relating to search terms, websites visited, GPS positions, and IP address, to be linked
back to an identifiable individual') (internal citation omitted).

[2] Executive Office of the President, President's Council of Advisors on Science and Technology,
Report to the President, Big Data and Privacy: A Technological Perspective, May 2014, p xi ('PCAST
Report'), https://www.whitehouse.gov/sites/default/files/microsites/ostp/PCAST/pcast_big_
data_and_privacy_-_may_2014.pdf. For example, New York City publicly released anonymized
data of over 173 million taxi trips. Researchers 'quickly combined the data with known reference
points—addresses, for example—to pinpoint celebrities' cab trips and identify who frequented
local strip clubs'. Jia You, 'Hiding in plain sight', 347 *Science* (30 January 2015): p 500.

videotapes the tenants), give publicity to a matter concerning the private life of another, unreasonably place someone in a false light before the public, or appropriate someone's name or likeness. Privacy and consumer protection law also ensure that those without market power undertake sufficient precautions to prevent the inadvertent disclosure of sensitive personal data.

21.04 But rather than unrelated silos, privacy, consumer protection, and competition law, as we discussed, can intersect as well as inform each other. When the consumer protection laws are effectively enforced, users will more likely trust firms' privacy promises, which may help increase the incentives for firms to compete harder on privacy. With greater transparency and control, individuals will have greater reason to trust firms and divulge personal information.[3] In empowering consumers to easily select their privacy preferences, and choose providers that match their privacy preferences,[4] these privacy safeguards can lower consumers' search, transaction, and switching costs, and increase the incentive of companies to enter the market. The UK's privacy agency, the Information Commissioner's Office, for example, is exploring a privacy seal, which it hopes will help promote privacy as a brand differentiator.[5] Moreover, a more active, informed role by the competition agencies can foster an effective competitive process, where firms compete along this quality dimension in providing privacy safeguards. This in turn can reduce the need for some types of behavioural regulations by the privacy and consumer protection agencies.

21.05 To foster an effective competitive process, competition, privacy, and consumer protection officials will need to assess any enforcement and regulatory gaps, as well as issues that extend across the three bodies of law. This chapter identifies two initial areas for greater coordination: moving beyond the notice-and-consent paradigm and facilitating the preconditions to spur privacy competition.

A. Moving Beyond Notice-and-Consent

21.06 The consensus is that the current notice-and-consent regiment is inadequate to safeguard privacy.[6] Individuals are generally unaware who has access to their personal

---

[3] UK Competition and Markets Authority, *The Commercial Use of Consumer Data: Report on the CMA's Call for Information*, June 2015, para 4.153 ('CMA Report'), https://www.gov.uk/government/uploads/system/uploads/attachment_data/file/435817/The_commercial_use_of_consumer_data.pdf (72% of survey respondents 'agreed that they would be more willing to share their information if the recipient was clear how it would be used and if permission could subsequently be withdrawn').

[4] PCAST Report, above note 2, p xii ('A consumer might choose one of several "privacy protection profiles" offered by the intermediary, which in turn would vet apps against these profiles.').

[5] Information Commissioner's Office, 'Privacy Seals', https://ico.org.uk/for-organisations/improve-your-practices/privacy-seals/.

[6] *See, eg*, PCAST Report, above note 2, p xi (noting that 'the framework of notice and consent is...becoming unworkable as a useful foundation for policy') and p 38 ('As a useful policy tool,

information, what data is being used, how the data is being used, when the data is used, and the privacy implications of the data's use.[7]

Nor do companies envision all the ways that they will use the data.[8] Data fusion, **21.07** whereby companies seek to extract value from a variety of data, may yield potential uses that neither the company nor consumer envisioned when the data was originally collected.[9] Moreover, with machine-learning, computer algorithms may harvest databases for myriad uses, some of which the company may be unaware of.

---

notice and consent is defeated by exactly the positive benefits that big data enables: new, non-obvious, unexpectedly powerful uses of data. It is simply too complicated for the individual to make fine-grained choices for every new situation or app.'); CMA Report, above note 3, para 4.175 ('There appears to be widespread concern about the effectiveness of the current consent mechanisms available for consumers'); Viktor Mayer-Schönberger and Kenneth Cukier, *Big Data: A Revolution That Will Transform How We Live, Work, and Think* (London: John Murray, 2013), p 156 ('In the era of big data, the three core strategies long used to ensure privacy—individual notice and consent, opting out, and anonymization—have lost much of their effectiveness.').

[7] The Executive Office of the President, *Big Data: Seizing Opportunities, Preserving Values*, May 2014, p 51 ('White House Big Data Report'), https://www.whitehouse.gov/sites/default/files/docs/big_data_privacy_report_may_1_2014.pdf ('The average consumer is unlikely to be aware of the range of data being collected or held or even to know who holds it; will have few opportunities to engage over the scope or accuracy of data being held about them; and may have limited insight into how this information feeds into algorithms that make decisions about their consumer experience or market access.'); PCAST Report, above note 2, p 39 ('sources of data increasingly contain latent information about individuals, information that becomes known only if the holder expends analytic resources (beyond what may be economically feasible), or that may become knowable only in the future with the development of new data-mining algorithms. In such cases it is practically impossible for the data holder even to surface "all the data about an individual", much less delete those data on any specified schedule'); p 47 ('Cameras, sensors, and other observational or mobile technologies raise new privacy concerns. Individuals often do not knowingly consent to providing data. These devices naturally pull in data unrelated to their primary purpose. Their data collection is often invisible. Analysis technology (such as facial, scene, speech, and voice recognition technology) is improving rapidly. Mobile devices provide location information that might not be otherwise volunteered. The combination of data from those sources can yield privacy-threatening information unbeknownst to the affected individuals.'); p 38 ('Worse yet, if it is hidden in such a notice that the provider has the right to share personal data, the user normally does not get any notice from the next company, much less the opportunity to consent, even though use of the data may be different. Furthermore, if the provider changes its privacy notice for the worse, the user is typically not notified in a useful way.'); CMA Report, above note 3, para 4.6 ('widespread agreement in responses to [agency's fact-finding inquiry] that although most consumers know their data is being collected and could be used to target them with marketing, they are less aware of the various ways in which their data can be collected, or how else it might be used').

[8] Mayer-Schönberger and Cukier, above note 6, p 153 ('most innovative secondary uses haven't been imagined when the data is first collected').

[9] European Data Protection Supervisor (EDPS), *Privacy and Competitiveness in the Age of Big Data: The Interplay Between Data Protection, Competition Law, and Consumer Protection in the Digital Economy*, Preliminary Opinion, 26 March 2014, p 34 ('EDPS Preliminary Opinion'), https://secure.edps.europa.eu/EDPSWEB/webdav/shared/Documents/Consultation/Opinions/2014/14-03-26_competitition_law_big_data_EN.pdf ('If personal information is collected as a condition for using one particular service, and then processed by the same company for the purposes of another service, it is already difficult for users to predict what will be done with their data.'); PCAST Report, above note 2, p 21 ('Individually, each data source may have been designed for a specific, limited purpose. But when multiple sources are processed by techniques of modern

21.08 Some apps do not even publish a privacy policy.[10] Even for those apps with a privacy policy, very few clearly explain how they were collecting, using, and disclosing personal information.[11] Thus consumers have little inclination to read lengthy, detailed, and often opaque privacy notices (especially on smartphones).[12] One study calculated that it would take 'on average each internet user 244 hours per year to read the privacy policy belonging to each website they view, which is more than 50 per cent of the time that average user spends on the internet, and that these privacy policies 'typically contain statements about the future use of data which are concealed in legal small print or which require decoding due to vague, elastic terms like "improving customer experience".'[13] Another study of the privacy policies of Fortune 500 companies found that 'they were essentially incomprehensible for the majority of Internet users. Only one percent of the privacy policies were understandable for those with a high school education or less (like most teens and many consumers). Thirty per cent of the privacy policies required a post-graduate education to be fully understood.'[14]

21.09 Even if they read the privacy notices, consumers typically cannot negotiate better terms.[15] Consumers either accept the privacy terms or forego the service

---

statistical data mining, pattern recognition, and the combining of records from diverse sources by virtue of common identifying data, new meanings can be found.').

[10] EDPS Preliminary Opinion, above note 9, p 35 ('only 61% of most popular apps have a privacy policy').

[11] CMA Report, above note 3, para 4.32 (85% of studied apps failed to clearly explain).

[12] EDPS Preliminary Opinion, above note 9, p 35 (discussing difficulties of lengthy 'privacy policies'); PCAST Report, above note 2, p 38 ('In some fantasy world, users actually read these notices, understand their legal implications (consulting their attorneys if necessary), negotiate with other providers of similar services to get better privacy treatment, and only then click to indicate their consent. Reality is different.'); Public Citizen, *Mission Creep-y: Google Is Quietly Becoming One of the Nation's Most Powerful Political Forces While Expanding Its Information-Collection Empire*, November 2014, p 4, https://www.citizen.org/documents/Google-Political-Spending-Mission-Creepy.pdf (noting how '[m]ost Google users are likely aware that Google collects information about them, such as their Internet surfing practices. Few are likely aware of the extent or sophistication of the company's information-collection methods. Even privacy experts interviewed for this project said that they did not know the totality of information Google collects or how it uses it.'); Maureen K Ohlhausen and Alexander P Okuliar, 'Competition, Consumer Protection, and the Right [Approach] to Privacy', 80 *Antitrust LJ* (2015): pp 121, 148 ('Over time, it became apparent that notice and choice policies had weaknesses, potentially allowing companies to overwhelm consumers with lengthy policies filled with legalese.').

[13] EDPS Preliminary Opinion, above note 9, p 34.

[14] Concurring Statement of Commissioner Jon Leibowitz, *FTC Staff Report: Self-Regulatory Principles for Online Behavioral Advertising*, February 2009, 2009 WL 382264, p *2, https://www.ftc.gov/sites/default/files/documents/public_statements/concurring-statement-commissioner-jon-leibowitz-ftc-staff-report-self-regulatory-principles-online/p085400behavadleibowitz.pdf (citing Felicia Williams, *Internet Privacy Policies: A Composite Index for Measuring Compliance to the Fair Information Principles*, September 2006, p 17 and Table 2).

[15] EDPS Preliminary Opinion, above note 9, p 35 ('Customers have limited room, if any, to negotiate the terms and conditions of use, representing a "significant imbalance" between provider and user which could also trigger investigation into the legality of data processing. This calls into question the existence of a genuine choice under Article 7(a) of the Data Protection Directive and in

altogether. The imbalance of power between consumers and data users is a significant concern.[16] Mobile phone subscribers are effectively locked in, as they either accept the operating system's privacy policy (and critical updates) or forego using their smartphone.[17] As the President's Council of Advisors on Science and Technology concluded,

> The conceptual problem with notice and consent is that it fundamentally places the burden of privacy protection on the individual. Notice and consent creates a non-level playing field in the implicit privacy negotiation between provider and user. The provider offers a complex, take-it-or-leave-it set of terms, while the user, in practice, can allocate only a few seconds to evaluating the offer. This is a kind of market failure.[18]

Thus, simply increasing the transparency of privacy policies will not stimulate the **21.10** competitive forces necessary to promote quality and well-being. Transparency is a necessary, but not sufficient, condition for competition along this privacy parameter. Competition, privacy, and consumer protection officials must coordinate to ensure that the other preconditions for an effective competitive process are in place.

B. Several Preconditions to Spur Privacy Competition

The legal rights and protections over personal data have important competition **21.11** policy implications. For competition to deliver the privacy safeguards that individuals desire, several preconditions are necessary.

First, consumers must have a viable choice, aside from forgoing the technology or **21.12** service altogether. The European Data Protection Supervisor notes 'how the growth of a vibrant market for privacy-enhancing services can be encouraged by strengthening informed consumer choice'.[19] Choice will not arise if consumers are effectively

---

turn the validity of consent to processing of personal information. Where there is a limited number of operators or when one operator is dominant, the concept of consent becomes more and more illusory.'); PCAST Report, above note 2, p 38 ('One way to view the problem with notice and consent is that it creates a non-level playing field in the implicit privacy negotiation between provider and user. The provider offers a complex take-it-or-leave-it set of terms, backed by a lot of legal firepower, while the user, in practice, allocates only a few seconds of mental effort to evaluating the offer, since acceptance is needed to complete the transaction that was the user's purpose, and since the terms are typically difficult to comprehend quickly.').

[16] EDPS Preliminary Opinion, above note 9, p 8 (noting the 'market concentration involving a few overwhelmingly dominant players, and an ever greater imbalance between big companies on the one side, and SMEs and individual users on the other side').

[17] In contrast to iOS, Google's Android operating system 'presents permissions at the point of the download of an app as an all-inclusive "take it or leave it" list—that is, users are not able to select or deselect items on the list.' CMA Report, above note 3, para 4.150.

[18] PCAST Report, above note 2, p xii.

[19] EDPS Preliminary Opinion, above note 9, p 8.

locked-in. As the UK competition authority noted, '[m]ore flexible mechanisms for consumers to exercise choice and control could help address their concerns and enable them to make decisions according to their individual preferences.'[20] The competition authority suggested 'mechanisms that allow consumers to choose between accepting essential and non-essential cookies; and where possible, to have defaults that enable consumers to opt-in to sharing their data only if they want to'.[21] The Europeans' General Data Protection Regulation is also aiming to provide individuals with greater choice and control over their data.[22]

21.13   Second, for privacy competition to flourish, competition, privacy, and consumer protection officials must coordinate to promote an alternative to the advertising-dependent revenue model that dominates many online industries. Given that privacy trade-offs are so clearly a concern for most individuals, it is noteworthy that there are no viable alternatives to the Internet giants that provide free services, except those with a heavy cost to user privacy. While some may argue the market supplies adequate privacy protection, we have seen why that is not the case in many data-driven industries. Most significantly, the economic incentives run almost entirely in one direction—towards accumulating more personal data. As noted, online companies typically make money by utilizing data gleaned from their users to sell targeted behavioural ads; if the flow of user data slows down, so does the money. In other words, there is a competitive arms race, and the arms race is for more data.

21.14   In response, some have argued that online media offering privacy as a value to consumers have sprung up. However, these companies' market shares tend to be small. As we saw, Google had in 2014 over five billion daily searches while DuckDuckGo was in the low millions. From an economic standpoint, these privacy-enhancing services may be destined to remain niche players if, as appears likely, a 'dysfunctional equilibrium' has developed in which firms and consumers do not have aligned incentives on privacy protection.[23] A small firm will not simply break out of the

---

[20] CMA Report, above note 3, para 24.

[21] Ibid.

[22] The draft General Data Protection Regulation includes (i) 'a requirement for transparent and easily accessible privacy policies and to communicate information about processing of personal data in an intelligible form, using clear and plain language'; (ii) 'a right, with exceptions, not be subject to automated personal profiling (the creation of a "profile" in order to take decisions about a person or analyse or predict personal preferences, behaviours and attitudes)'; (iii) 'a right "to be forgotten", namely a right of individuals to request that organisations delete personal data relating to them (for example social media businesses)'; (iv) 'a right of data portability enabling individuals to obtain a copy of the data held about them in a reusable, electronic format'; (v) 'a requirement for data protection by design and by default (data controllers must implement appropriate technical and organisational measures and procedures to comply with the Regulation)'; and (vi) 'greater enforcement powers including substantial fines'. CMA Report, above note 3, box 5.2.

[23] Joseph Farrell, 'Can Privacy Be Just Another Good?', 10 *J on Telecomm & High Tech L* (2012): pp 256–9.

equilibrium by adopting more protective policies and clearer disclosures when its demand will not shift meaningfully and, as a result, it will mostly sacrifice revenue.

In contrast, a firm with market power may use information in ways that benefit it, **21.15** and not its customers. One measure of a firm's market power is the extent to which it can engage in behaviour 'without some benefit to consumers that offsets their reduced privacy and still retain users'.[24] Moreover, in dominating the ecosystem, the advertising-dependent revenue model can block innovative, more privacy friendly subscription-based models. Thus competition, privacy, and consumer protection officials can coordinate on ways to avoid (or reverse) a 'dysfunctional equilibrium', and promote alternative revenue models, where privacy need not be sacrificed.

Third, privacy competition can flourish when consumers have greater control over **21.16** their personal data. Competition, privacy, and consumer protection officials can coordinate in identifying ways to increase consumers' control over their data and data portability.

The law has not settled as to who owns the data.[25] As McKinsey and Company noted, **21.17**

> Laws are generally unclear on which constituency—from mobile operators, plat-form owners, application developers, and handset manufacturers, to actual users—owns the right to collect, aggregate, disseminate, and use personal location data for commercial purposes. Many commercial enterprises that state they will protect the privacy of these data have been able to use them relatively freely. But there are calls from citizens who want to know that their privacy and the security of their personal location data are protected and who believe that opt-in/opt-out agreements are un-clear. A framework that clearly describes the permissible and prohibited use of these data would be beneficial for all stakeholders.[26]

When individuals' legal rights over their data are unclear or limited, they must rely **21.18** on the data holder's beneficence to access and port their data. If they cannot easily port their data to alternative services that offer better privacy protection and value, then one competition-related problem is higher switching costs, which facilitates the exploitation of locked-in consumers. The European Data Protection Supervisor

---

[24] Howard A Shelanski, 'Information, Innovation, and Competition Policy for the Internet', 161 *U Pa L Rev* (2013): pp 1663, 1689.

[25] In *Remijas v Neiman Marcus Grp, LLC*, 794 F3d 688, 695 (US Ct of Apps (7th Cir), 2015), customers sued an upscale retailer, for inter alia, negligence in failing to prevent a data breach where their personal information was stolen. The customers alleged a 'concrete injury in the loss of their private information, which they characterize as an intangible commodity'. The Seventh Circuit denied standing on this ground. The plaintiffs assumed that the law recognizes such a property right, but offered no legal authority to support their claim.

[26] McKinsey Global Institute, *Big Data: The Next Frontier for Innovation, Competition, and Productivity*, June 2011, p 95, http://www.mckinsey.com/insights/business_technology/big_data_the_next_frontier_for_innovation; *see also* White House Big Data Report, above note 7, p 9 (noting that '[t]he technological trajectory... is clear: more and more data will be generated about individu-als and will persist under the control of others').

identified two ways greater data portability could release synergies between competition law and data protection law:

> First, it could prevent abuse of dominance, whether exclusionary or exploitative, and consumers being locked into certain services through the limitation of production, markets or technical development to the prejudice of consumers. It would emulate the benefits of number portability provided for in telecommunications law.

> Second, data portability could empower consumers to take advantage of value-added services from third parties while facilitating greater access to the market by competitors, for example through the use of product comparison sites or of companies offering energy advice based on smart metering data.[27]

21.19 One counterargument to data portability is the same as the one to interoperability (or other forced sharing): it reduces incentives to innovate. But here the argument for portability may be stronger, because there is a better claim that the personal data belongs to the consumer, not the company. Moreover, limited data portability can actually impede, rather than promote, welfare-enhancing innovation and create 'barriers for small firms that are seeking to give consumers greater control and visibility of their data'.[28] For example, what credit card, car insurance, or mobile phone service would best serve your particular needs? One way to find out is if a third-party website could readily access and analyse your usage data. With greater control over our personal data, we can allow third-party websites to discover the most suitable service based on our usage.[29] We may also entrust our data to third parties who can negotiate on our behalf. The computer science professor Pedro Domingos, for example, proposed creating a digital alter-ego: 'For a subscription fee, such a firm would record your every interaction with the digital world, build and maintain a 360-degree model of you, and use it to negotiate with other people's models.'[30]

21.20 Another buzzword involves personal data lockers, 'which allow users to contribute and edit the data they are willing to share with third parties in exchange for a

---

[27] EDPS Preliminary Opinion, above note 9, p 36 (footnotes omitted); *see also* PCAST Report, above note 2, at 41 ('Simply by vetting apps, the third-party organizations would automatically create a marketplace for the negotiation of community standards for privacy. To attract market share, providers (especially smaller ones) could seek to qualify their offerings in as many privacy-preference profiles, offered by as many different third parties, as they deem feasible. The Federal government (eg, through the National Institute of Standards and Technology) could encourage the development of standard, machine-readable interfaces for the communication of privacy implications and settings between providers and assessors.').

[28] CMA Report, above note 3, para 3.52.

[29] Ibid, para 2.109 (noting how website Gocompare.com 'launched an online comparison tool to enable customers of the UK's six largest current account providers to upload their statements and find out if they could switch to a current account that might better suit their personal banking history').

[30] Pedro Domingos, 'Get Ready for Your Digital Model: Algorithms Will Build Data-Driven Alter Egos for Us That Can Do Job Interviews, Shop for Cars and Go on Dates', *Wall Street Journal*, 12 November 2015, http://www.wsj.com/articles/get-ready-for-your-digital-model-1447351480?alg=y.

portion of the proceeds when their data is sold'.[31] As the Organisation for Economic Co-operation and Development (OECD) observed,

> These data lockers could potentially improve transparency about how data is collected, sold and used. Users may be willing to share even more personal data if they feel they have more control over how it is used and received a clear economic or social benefit for sharing. This is a new area and it is unclear if data lockers will emerge with viable business models but this is an area that should be followed.[32]

A fourth precondition for effective privacy competition is increasing the transparency of data's value. Increasing the portability of data can increase the demand of data agents, and also help individuals (and firms) appreciate the value of personal data. As consumers better understand how much their personal information is worth, they can demand more from the collectors. Data-driven companies will have to become more efficient. They can no longer collect and retain data with the hope of monetizing it eventually. As the UK competition authority observed, **21.21**

> ...without knowing the value of the data they are sharing and how much of their data is being used, consumers are unable to understand the price for the data-funded transactions they engage in. This may mean that firms have limited incentives to compete over the privacy protection they afford to consumer data, that is the minimum amount of data they need to collect to generate sufficient revenue to fund the service to consumers.[33]

Fifth, for privacy competition to flourish, competition agencies need to better understand the myriad forms of privacy degradation undertaken by firms unilaterally or collectively. In coordinating with privacy and consumer protection officials, competition officials could identify the causes of market power in these data-driven industries (including the role of data-driven network effects) and the myriad anti-competitive effects, including diminished privacy protections. By turning to privacy laws and the agencies that enforce them, competition officials can better assess degradations of privacy protections. As we saw, competition officials are more **21.22**

---

[31] OECD, *Exploring the Economics of Personal Data*, above note 1, p 34; CMA Report, above note 3, paras 2.106 and 2.107 (noting how these ' "personal data stores" may, for instance, charge companies a fee to access consumers' data', and how '[s]ome personal data services also aim to help consumers monetise their data, for instance by "renting" it to brands (eg Datacoup and Handshake), some of which also enable consumers to derive value directly from their information by sale or licensing'). Most people in a 2012 survey (85%) would prefer to hold their own personal information and exchange it for services when they choose, but there is also evidence that 'some consumers may find the prospect of managing their data daunting' and would prefer the government to prevent anyone misusing their data. Ibid, para 4.162.

[32] OECD, *Exploring the Economics of Personal Data*, above note 1, p 6 (noting how '[n]ew "data lockers" allow users to contribute and control data sharing with third parties in exchange for a portion of the proceeds from the use of their data' and how these 'data exchanges could provide new market-based estimates of monetary values, and potentially improve transparency about how data is collected, sold and used').

[33] CMA Report, above note 3, para 3.20.

comfortable inquiring over a SSNIP (a small, but significant, non-transitory increase in price) than an SSNDQ (a small, but significant, non-transitory decrease in quality). Privacy officials can help delineate the spectrum of privacy protections, and what an SSNDQ might entail for a particular industry.

21.23 Sixth, competition, privacy, and consumer protection officials can coordinate on legal issues of standing to ensure that illegal conduct does not escape punishment because the wrong plaintiff is before the court. For example, in the Belgian lottery and GDF Suez cases, the defendants abused their dominant position when they used the data collected as part of their regulated monopoly to compete in other markets. Conceivably, we have several different claims and groups of plaintiffs. The privacy authority might bring a claim if the monopoly impermissibly used the consumer data, but not necessarily a competition claim. Alternatively, if the defendant's use of the data was inconsistent with its privacy policy, the consumer protection agency could challenge the privacy policy as a false or misleading representation. Competitors and the competition agency could challenge the defendant's use of data as an abuse of its dominant position. The remedies would likely vary depending on the claim, and each agency by itself may be unable to provide effective relief (or generally deter future violations).

21.24 As a result, our last signpost of progress is when competition, privacy, and consumer protection officials coordinate to: (i) identify and understand the potential harms arising from a data-driven economy, including the harms that arise due to insufficient competition; (ii) update the analytical tools for free services to better assess how mergers and restraints can cause these harms; (iii) understand firms' current incentives (and disincentives) to compete on, and invest in, privacy-enhancing and enhanced technologies and services; (iv) provide the legal framework to foster new business models, which can offer consumers more choices between the advertising-dependent business models, where the product is the consumer, and subscription-dependent models; and (v) consider synergies (and potential inefficiencies) in the privacy, consumer protection, and competition legal frameworks to promote competition, consumers' privacy interests, and ultimately citizens' well-being.[34]

---

[34] OECD, *Data-Driven Innovation for Growth and Well-Being: Interim Synthesis Report*, October 2014, p 8, http://www.oecd.org/sti/inno/data-driven-innovation-interim-synthesis.pdf.

22

CONCLUSION

Competition law can play an integral role to ensure that we capture the benefits of **22.01** a data-driven economy while mitigating its associated risks.

One trap for policymakers is to assume that the privacy, consumer protection, and **22.02** competition policy concerns are so distinct that they should be left to their respective agencies. The sympathetic competition official, while nodding her head, might respond, 'But that is not a competition issue', and point the person down the street (or hall) to the privacy folks. At times she will be right. The US Supreme Court has praised the competition laws as 'the Magna Carta of free enterprise', and 'as important to the preservation of economic freedom and our free-enterprise system as the Bill of Rights is to the protection of our fundamental personal freedoms'.[1] Despite this broad mandate, one cannot assume that antitrust is a panacea for every privacy and consumer protection concern.

Likewise, the fact that privacy is a fundamental right in some jurisdictions does not **22.03** mean it is always relevant in competition policy.

But one cannot also assume that the privacy, consumer protection, and competi- **22.04** tion issues neatly fall into distinct compartments. The traditional belief is that we want firms to compete to provide the best mix of products and services. But if the critical resource in many multi-sided markets is data (not merely to target advertising, but also to optimize the products and services themselves), then the firms with a competitive advantage in the four 'V's of data are not merely in the best position to dominate their own sectors—they are also poised to take over adjacent fields. Even worse, to the extent such firms compile politically sensitive information about users, and mediate their experience of content, they are also powerful political actors. Competition authorities must take the lead in recognizing data's competitive importance and the implications of a few firms' unparalleled system of harvesting and monetizing their data trove. Speaking before the American

---

[1] *United States v Topco Associates, Inc*, 405 US 596, 610, 92 S Ct 1126, 1135 (1972).

Bar Association's antitrust bar, US Senator Al Franken discussed how privacy has become an antitrust issue:

> when companies become so dominant that they can violate their users' privacy without worrying about market pressure, all that's left is the incentive to get more and more information about you. That's a big problem if you care about privacy, and it's a problem that the antitrust community should be talking about.[2]

22.05 It made the news when smart televisions 'were reportedly "listening" to conversations, although the company involved was reported as saying that the aim had been to assist its voice recognition facility'.[3] The dominant advertising-dependent tech firms will power the Internet of Things. We will increasingly be surrounded by smart household utensils, smartwatches, self-driving cars, and voice-automated smartphones videoing, listening to, and tracking us. As the European Data Protection Supervisor observed, governments and companies are moving beyond 'data mining' to 'reality mining', which 'penetrates everyday experience, communication and even thought'.[4] It does not follow that perfecting methods to track our behaviour on- and offline, and harvesting more data about us represents progress. Nor will greater monitoring and data collection necessarily increase our well-being.

22.06 Few, until recently, have discussed the antitrust implications of data-driven mergers, network effects, and monopolistic behaviour. The costs and risks of ignoring or downplaying the issue are too great. The economics of data, as we have seen, favour market concentration and dominance. With the agglomeration of data through the Internet of Things, individuals will have even less privacy, control, and autonomy, and the private sphere will shrink. Individuals will continue to struggle with the imbalance of power that yields take-it-or-leave-it privacy notices that few people can afford to leave, if they wish to connect with friends and family. If the market power is left unchecked, the privacy harms will go straight to our democratic ideals of a loss of autonomy and freedom. The harms can reduce trust, and chill self-expression.

22.07 Wealth inequality is already at alarming levels in the US. One 2015 survey reflects Americans' diminished faith in capitalism: 55 per cent think the rich get richer and poor get poorer under capitalism; only 14 per cent believe that that the next generation will be richer, safer, and healthier than the last; and 65 per cent think most big

---

[2] Senator Al Franken, 'Remarks to the American Bar Association (Antitrust Section)', Speech, 29 March 2012, http://assets.sbnation.com/assets/1033745/franken_aba_antitrust_speech.pdf.

[3] UK Competition and Markets Authority, *The Commercial Use of Consumer Data: Report on the CMA's Call for Information*, June 2015, para 4.90, https://www.gov.uk/government/uploads/system/uploads/attachment_data/file/435817/The_commercial_use_of_consumer_data.pdf.

[4] European Data Protection Supervisor, 'Towards a New Digital Ethics: Data, Dignity and Technology', Opinion 4/2015, 11 September 2015, p 6, https://secure.edps.europa.eu/EDPSWEB/webdav/site/mySite/shared/Documents/Consultation/Opinions/2015/15-09-11_Data_Ethics_EN.pdf.

businesses have dodged taxes, bought favours, or polluted.[5] Anticompetitive data-driven mergers and monopolistic behaviour will exacerbate existing inequalities, as firms use individuals' data to better profile, target, and exploit them.

Over the past 20 years, the European competition authorities have been more active **22.08** in prosecuting monopolistic abuses than the United States. But, until recently, the Europeans did not believe that Big Data raised competition concerns. That is changing. Competition authorities in Europe are now beginning to make data, its uses, and its implications for competition law, a key focus.

In June 2014, policymakers, enforcers, and scholars discussed in Brussels the im- **22.09** plications of a data-driven economy on competition policy, consumer protection, and privacy law. The European Data Protection Supervisor hosted a workshop for 70 senior government officials (including from the US), academics, and lawyers over the intersection of these three areas. Among the themes were (i) the timeliness of these issues with the rise of Big Data and data-driven mergers, (ii) the importance of these issues, and (iii) the lack of research to date that has looked at the intersection of these three areas of law. Indeed, the preliminary report prepared by the European Data Protection Supervisor was the first to raise these issues. Its workshop helped spark the debate and this book.

In October 2014, the European Union's newly minted antitrust chief, Margrethe **22.10** Vestager, dubbed personal data as the 'new currency of the Internet', and vowed to focus on how its large-scale collection entrenches the strength of big tech companies. The *New York Times* reported that Vestager 'told lawmakers at the European Parliament... that Google was "a business with a huge, huge, huge market share", and she signalled that she would look more deeply into whether amassing data was a factor entrenching the strength of digital companies like Google'.[6] And some national competition agencies in Europe are engaged on this issue.

But other competition officials are less engaged, less willing to consider the impli- **22.11** cations of data-driven mergers and abuses by dominant firms, far less concerned over false negatives than false positives, less prepared to assess privacy competition, less willing to conduct post-merger reviews, and far more (over)confident in their getting the right results with their current price-centric tools when evaluating one side of multi-sided platforms. They cannot justify ignoring or downplaying Big Data. They cannot continue granting early termination for significant data-driven mergers (over the concerns of citizen groups). They cannot ignore the complaints

---

[5] Tim Montgomerie, 'A Fading Faith in Capitalism', *Wall Street Journal*, 7–8 November 2015, p C3.

[6] James Kanter, 'Antitrust Nominee in Europe Promises Scrutiny of Big Tech Companies', *New York Times* Bits blog, 3 October 2014, http://bits.blogs.nytimes.com/2014/10/03/antitrust-nominee-in-europe-promises-eye-on-big-tech-companies/.

about the abuses of dominant tech firms. And they cannot travel around the world pontificating about false positives, while criticizing those competition authorities that are considering the implications of Big Data (and investigating complaints of monopolistic abuses).

22.12 We cannot afford a widening enforcement and policy gap among jurisdictions. Like data itself, data-related enforcement issues do not stop at the border. Such a gap leaves our enforcers ill-equipped to identify and address the anticompetitive risks and privacy harms from data-driven mergers and abuses by dominant firms, subjects companies to inconsistent enforcement, and leaves consumers and start-ups vulnerable.

22.13 Consequently, no major competition authority can afford to lag further behind, characterizing their inactivity as evidence of prudence. For if the competition agencies are indifferent, eventually, Americans, like the Europeans, will ask their elected officials:

> What are you, the people we have elected, doing to protect the freedom of... citizens and assert the fundamental rights of the analogue world in this digital age? If you don't succeed, who will? Who decides what rules we are to abide by? Who should protect the law?[7]

---

[7] Sigmar Gabriel, 'Political Consequences of the Google Debate', *Frankfurter Allgemeine Feuilleton*, 20 May 2014, p 3, http://www.faz.net/aktuell/feuilleton/debatten/the-digital-debate/sigmar-gabriel-consequences-of-the-google-debate-12948701-p3.html.

INDEX